Using

from conversation to canon

Au

The English Language: past, present and future *course team*

The Open University
Sally Baker (liaison librarian)
Pam Berry (compositor)
Helen Boyce (course manager)
Martin Brazier (cover designer)
David Calderwood (assistant project controller)
Joan Carty (liaison librarian)
Christine Considine (editor/editorial co-ordinator)
Anne Diack (BBC producer)
Sue Glover (editor)
Sharon Goodman (author/book co-ordinator)
David Graddol (author/book co-ordinator)
Martin Kenward (assistant project controller)
Julie Laing (BBC production assistant)
Avis Lexton (secretary)
Rob Lyon (designer)
Paul Manners (BBC producer)
Gill Marshall (editor)
Janet Maybin (author/book co-ordinator)
Barbara Mayor (author and course manager)
Neil Mercer (author/book co-ordinator)
Ray Munns (cartographer/graphic artist)
Kay Pole (developmental testing co-ordinator)
Pam Powter (course secretary)
Cathy Rosario (editor)
Lynne Slocombe (editor)
Gill Smith (editor)
Joan Swann (course team chair)
Nikki Tolcher (main compositor)
Iva Williams (BBC production assistant)

External assessor
Professor Peter Trudgill, University of Lausanne

Assessors for this book
Professor Ron Carter, University of Nottingham
Professor Jennifer Coates, Roehampton Institute, London

Developmental testers and critical readers
Kim Beckley
Nigel Blake
Susan Gander
Gilberto Giron
Anthea Fraser Gupta
Lindsay Hewitt
Diana Honeybone
Karen Hovey
Mike Hughes

The four volumes of the series form part of the second level Open University course U210 *The English Language: past, present and future*. If you wish to study this or any other Open University course, details can be obtained from the Central Enquiry Service, PO Box 200, The Open University, Milton Keynes MK7 6YZ.

For availability of the video and audiocassette materials, contact Open University Educational Enterprises Ltd (OUEE), 12 Cofferidge Close, Stony Stratford, Milton Keynes MK11 1BY.

Using English

from conversation to canon

Edited by
Janet Maybin and Neil Mercer

The Open University

ROUTLEDGE

LONDON AND NEW YORK

First published 1996
by Routledge
11 New Fetter Lane
London EC4P 4EE

Simultaneously published in the USA and Canada
by Routledge
a division of Routledge, Chapman and Hall, Inc.
29 West 35th Street, New York, NY 10001

Published in association with The Open University

Copyright © The Open University

Edited, designed and typeset by The Open University

Printed in Great Britain by Bath Press Colourbooks, Glasgow

A catalogue record for this book is available from the British Library

Library of Congress Cataloguing-in-Publication Data applied for

ISBN 0 415 13120 0 (paper)
ISBN 0 415 13119 7 (hardbound)

Book editors

Janet Maybin is a lecturer in the Centre for Language and Communications at the Open University School of Education. Trained as a social anthropologist, she is particularly interested in the role of culture in language and learning. She is editor of *Language and Literacy in Social Practice*, and co-editor of *Language, Literacy and Learning in Educational Practice* and *Researching Language and Literacy in Social Context*, all published in 1993 by Multilingual Matters.

Neil Mercer is Reader and Director of the Centre for Language and Communications at the Open University School of Education. He is a psychologist with special interests in language use and the process of teaching and learning. He is co-author, with Derek Edwards, of *Common Knowledge: the development of understanding in the classroom* (Methuen/Routledge, 1987) and author of *The Guided Construction of Knowledge: talk amongst teachers and learners* (Multilingual Matters, 1995).

Other original contributors

Mike Baynham works at the University of Technology, Sydney, where he is Director of the Centre for Language and Literacy. His book, *Literacy Practices* was published by Longman in 1995. His current research interests include the role of language in adult numeracy teaching and learning, and specific aspects of academic writing across different disciplines.

Anima Chakraverty is a senior lecturer in English at Isabella Thobeum College, Lucknow. Her areas of interest are applied linguistics, teaching of literature and ELT.

Guy Cook is Reader in Education and head of English for Speakers of Other Languages at the London University Institute of Education. His research interests include applied linguistics and language teaching, discourse analysis, literature theory and teaching, and language and biology. His publications include *Discourse* (Open University Press, 1989), *The Discourse of Advertising* (Routledge, 1992), *Discourse and Literature* (Open University Press, 1994) and (with B. Seidlhofer) *Principle and Practice in Applied Linguistics* (Open University Press, 1995).

Rib Davies is Artistic Director of the Living Archive Project in Milton Keynes as well as being a freelance playwright and scriptwriter for stage, community theatre, radio and television. He has developed a number of scripts from verbatim extracts of tape-recorded interviews.

Lizbeth Goodman is a lecturer in literature (theatre studies/gender studies specialist) at the Open University. She has published widely on the subject of theatre as a platform for communication and cultural exchange, and she directs and produces comedy. Her book *Contemporary Feminist Theatres* was published by Routledge in 1993, and she is editor of *Literature and Gender* (Routledge, 1996) and co-editor of *Shakespeare, Aphra Behn and the Canon* (Routledge, 1996).

Lesley Jeffries is a senior lecturer in English language at the University of Huddersfield. She works on the stylistics of both literary and nonliterary texts. In particular, she is interested in the language of contemporary poetry and the discourse of the body. She is author of *The Language of Twentieth Century Poetry* (Macmillan, 1993).

Catherine Kell is a lecturer and researcher in the Department of Adult Education, University of Cape Town. She has worked as an adult literacy teacher and trainer and is now involved in the evaluation of adult literacy programmes. She is interested in the relationship between ethnographic research on communicative practices and policy formation in adult basic education.

Jo Longman was a project officer in the Centre for Language and Communications of the Open University School of Education, and has since worked on community education projects in India. Her research has been on functional literacy and the discourse of interviews. She has a particular interest in applied research in vocational training and guidance.

Peter Medway teaches in linguistics and applied language studies at Carleton University, Ottawa. Formerly a high school English teacher in Britain and lecturer in education at the University of Leeds, he conducts research on written and spoken language in professional contexts and particularly in architecture. He is co-editor with Aviva Freedman of two recent books, *Learning and Teaching Genre* (Boynton Cook, 1994) and *Genre and the New Rhetoric* (Taylor & Francis Ltd, 1994).

Jane Miller is Reader in Education at the University of London Institute of Education, where she teaches in the English department. She is author of *Many Voices: bilingualism, culture and education* (Routledge, 1983) and of *Seductions: studies in reading and culture* (Virago, 1990). Her most recent book, *School for Women* (Virago, 1996), considers the effects on schooling of women's predominance as teachers.

Julu Sen is a senior lecturer in English at the Central Institute of English and Foreign Languages, Hyderabad. Her areas of interest are distance education, teacher development, testing language and literature, action research and stylistic analysis of oral communication.

Rahul Sharma is a senior lecturer in English in DAV college, Amritsar. His areas of interest are curricular studies and the development of materials for English teaching.

John Thompson is a lecturer in the Centre for Journalism Studies, Cardiff University, Wales. He is co-author, with Ann Thompson, of *Shakespeare: meaning and metaphor* (Harvester, 1987), and co-editor (with Manuel Alvarado) of *The Media Reader* (British Film Institute, 1990) and (with Antony Easthope) of *Contemporary Poetry Meets Modern Theory* (Harvester, 1991). He maintains an ongoing interest in questions of film and television performance.

Margaret Wetherell is a senior lecturer in the Social Sciences Faculty at the Open University. Her main research interest lies in the development of discourse theory and method in social psychology. She is co-author (with Jonathan Potter) of *Discourse and Social Psychology* (Sage, 1987) and *Mapping the Language of Racism* (Harvester Wheatsheaf, 1992).

Robin Wooffitt is a lecturer in sociology at the University of Surrey. He is interested in language and social identity and in the analysis of factual accounts. His publications include *Telling Tales of the Unexpected: the social organization of factual discourse* (Harvester Wheatsheaf, 1992), and (with Sue Widdicombe) the *Language of Youth Subcultures: social identity in action* (Harvester Wheatsheaf, 1995).

Simeon Yates is a lecturer in the Social Sciences Faculty at the Open University. He has written on social and linguistic aspects of computer-mediated communications. Currently he is researching the effects of new communication technologies in the production of TV news.

CONTENTS

INTRODUCTION

Janet Maybin and Neil Mercer

English has achieved a special, distinctive place in the communicative and cultural life of people throughout the world. Like some other world languages – Spanish and Cantonese, for example – it is a language spoken by many millions of native speakers. But there is probably no other language in the world today which is used by so many non–native speakers for so many social purposes, in work and play, in art and in science. This book examines some of this contemporary diversity. The chapters deal with uses of both spoken and written English across a wide range of settings, and for a variety of purposes. Their complementary effect, we believe, is to show not only how the English language can be used in such various ways, but also how the language itself is shaped by being adapted to different ends, and to suit particular social settings and cultural practices. The earlier chapters (Chapters 1–4) focus on the use of English within various kinds of interpersonal communication – casual conversations, letters, public speeches. The later chapters (Chapters 5–8) look at the artistic and creative products of English speakers and writers, and discuss the kinds of cultural achievement these represent.

The book deals with variation in English in a number of different ways. Some of the chapters refer to variation in English in terms of accents and dialects, and other social and regional forms. Thus Chapter 5 deals with the ways different varieties of English (such as regional accents and dialects) are represented in novels, plays and poetry. A second kind of variation is that between spoken and written forms of English. Chapter 2, in particular, considers the nature and significance of new forms of text which blur the distinction between speech and writing that has traditionally been upheld in language studies. Also considered throughout the book is the kind of diversity in English that is associated with the pursuit of particular human aims and goals – the kind of variation described by terms like 'jargon', 'genre' and 'discourse'. Chapters 1 (Everyday talk), 2 (Literacy practices in English) and 3 (English at work) include many illustrations of how English is adapted to serve particular purposes and to conform to the conventions of particular kinds of cultural event. Chapters 5 (What makes English into art?), 6 (Language play in English), 7 (An English canon?) and 8 (A tongue, for sighing) look at the varieties of English used in artistic contexts.

We have tried to capture the dynamic nature of English, as a language which is constantly changing through its use. This is most explicitly dealt with in Chapter 7, where notions of quality in literary English are shown to be much less stable than is sometimes claimed. Other chapters also show how conventional ways of using English change over time, and how such changes are related to the emergence of new cultural practices and social purposes.

To be meaningful, language needs a context. Making sense of what is said and written depends on listeners or readers using more information than is provided by the words they hear or see. Several of the chapters show how joint understanding by speakers/writers and listeners/readers is achieved. The concept of context is defined by Janet Maybin in Chapter 1 and is an important theme throughout the book. For example, in Chapter 3 Neil Mercer discusses some ways in which the common experience and purposes of particular kinds of work have generated

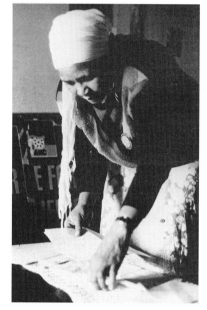

From conversation to canon

distinctive varieties of English, while Guy Cook in Chapter 6 shows that various 'playful' uses of English depend on cultural, contextual factors for their effectiveness. In Chapter 4 one of Robin Wooffitt's messages is that in order to understand how effective English political rhetoric is achieved we need to look not just at a speaker's words but also at the ways language is used to manage the relationship between speaker and audience. Mike Baynham and Janet Maybin's treatment of English literacy in Chapter 2 likewise stresses the ways in which written communication is embedded in social practices and the cultural knowledge of communications. And in Chapter 8 Jane Miller looks at how the cultural and linguistic context within which authors are writing affects the ways in which they relate to and use English.

We use the concept of identity in the book to focus on the relationship between speakers and the language, and on how using English shapes relationships between speakers. At its most cryptic, our view is that whenever someone uses English, they represent themselves (knowingly or otherwise) as a certain kind of person to whoever they are communicating with. Issues of gender, class and nationality are obviously relevant here. For instance, many of the examples in Chapter 1 are of people representing themselves in the spoken, casual conversations of everyday life, while Chapter 3 shows how important the use of specific varieties of English can be for people's identities as workers. In a rather different way, Chapters 7 and 8 show that national identities can be immensely influential in shaping people's perceptions of what constitutes high-quality literary English.

In addition to the themes described above, the book draws on a range of theoretical ideas in the study of language in use; Michael Halliday's functional approach and Mikhail Bakhtin's dialogical perspective are particularly important. The chapters also demonstrate how a variety of analytic methods can be used effectively for understanding the use of English in its social context. For example, the methods of conversation analysis are an important resource for the author of Chapter 4, while Chapters 5 and 6 draw on methods associated more with descriptive linguistics. And while Chapters 1–4 are clearly social-scientific in their approach, the later chapters are more within the traditions of literary studies.

We have tried to ensure that all chapters are accessible to readers from different linguistic and cultural backgrounds. We have selected examples of research and other evidence from different contexts, perspectives and experiences of English. In particular, the readings that accompany each chapter are wide-ranging, representing ideas and research from Australia, Britain, Canada, the Caribbean, India, Kenya, New Zealand, Nigeria, Singapore, South Africa and the USA. These readings include accounts of research, reviews of certain topics, arguments for or against certain positions; some are extracts from existing books or articles, others have been specially commissioned for this book. They are presented not as definitive statements on an issue, but as texts that are open to critical evaluation – as of course are the main chapter texts themselves.

The book is designed for readers who have an interest in English, but who do not necessarily have any detailed knowledge of linguistics or other forms of language study. It can be read independently but it is also the second in a series of four books (listed on the back cover) designed for an Open University undergraduate course: U210 *The English Language: past, present and future*. We occasionally refer interested readers to these books, as well as *Describing Language* (Graddol et al., 1994), for further discussion of topics touched on here.

Features of each chapter include:

- *activities*: these provide guidance on the readings or suggestions for tasks to stimulate further understanding or analysis of the material;
- *boxed text*: boxes contain illustrative material or definitions or alternative viewpoints;
- *marginal notes*: these usually refer the reader to further discussion in other parts of the book, or to other books in the series, or to *Describing Language*; where necessary, they are also added to explain conventions used in the text;
- *key terms*: key terms in each chapter are set in bold type at the point where they are explained; the terms also appear in bold in the index so that they are easy to find in the chapters.

A note on transcribing spoken English

Those with an interest in spoken English face the question of how to represent speech in writing. This can be a problem particularly when transcribing conversations, which differ in several ways from written texts. Some analysts use normal written conventions (standard punctuation and spelling, etc.), so that the text looks like a play script. Others use special layouts (such as columns for different speakers); transcription conventions that represent pauses, stress and pitch raising, as well as the hesitations, fillers and overlaps that are characteristic of most spoken dialogue; and occasionally devices that allow them to show accompanying nonverbal information.

Conventions are selected not simply to provide greater accuracy but to allow the researcher to focus on some features at the expense of others.

When quoting from other research in this book we have kept close to the transcription conventions adopted in the original, so that readers will see something of the range of possible conventions and their different purposes.

1 EVERYDAY TALK

Janet Maybin

1.1 INTRODUCTION

> Conversation is without doubt the foundation stone of the social world –
> human beings learn to talk *in* it, find a mate *with* it, are socialized *through*
> it, rise in social hierarchy as a result *of* it, and, it is suggested, may even
> develop mental illness *because* of it.
>
> (Beattie, 1983, p. 2)

What kind of knowledge do you need in order to be able to have a conversation in
English? And how do people actually use conversation to get things done, pursue
relationships and negotiate various kinds of knowledge? In this chapter I explore
the various kinds of linguistic and cultural knowledge that people bring to English
conversations and the ways in which these are used in dialogues.

English has tended to be described by linguists in terms of its linguistic
structure – its phonology, grammar and so on. By definition the structure of
English is an intrinsic part of the language. But it is well short of the whole story,
when we consider how English is used on a day-to-day basis. While people use the
structural resources of English to express ideas, they are also simultaneously using
language to express and pursue relationships. The linguist Halliday (1978)
suggests that language has a dual function; it communicates **ideational meaning**,
in terms of the information and ideas expressed, and it also communicates
interpersonal meaning, expressing the degree of friendliness, or status difference, between speakers. In addition, language takes meanings from the context
in which it is used, and in spoken language in particular the distinctions between
language and context, and language and culture, begin to blur.

Some linguists define 'conversation' in the strict sense as informal talk
between equals, but, like Geoffrey Beattie in the quotation above, in this chapter I
use the term more loosely and will draw on a wide range of examples from
different contexts to try to give some sense of the diversity of ways in which English
is used today in everyday talk. Chapters later in the book look at the more
specialized role of talk in specific institutional contexts such as the workplace or
political speech making.

1.2 THE STRUCTURE AND FUNCTION OF CONVERSATION

Linguists have tended to view informal conversation as rather disorderly, pointing
out its inexplicit use of language, random subject matter, general lack of planning
and high proportion of 'errors'. When we look closely at actual examples of talk,
however, we find that what is said draws meaning from a vast amount that is left
unsaid because of the way language is embedded in social activities and relationships. Language alone does not make meaning: it is used to invoke a whole range
of shared knowledge and experience between speakers, from aspects of a joint

physical activity, to past conversations together, to shared cultural values. Thus, the very aspects of talk that might be seen as incoherent are in fact an important part of the way talk is used to bind people together and to enable them to negotiate shared understandings about the world. In order to understand the structure of talk, therefore, we need to look at its function in specific contexts.

Inexplicitness

Activity 1.1   How informal talk works *(Allow about 15 minutes)*

Here are three examples of informal talk. How far do you agree with those who would consider such language use is inexplicit, with many errors and a general lack of planning? What might be the function of the talk in each case?

1   In a university in the south of England, Julie has come to her tutor's office to receive comments on an assignment.

[*Knocks on door*]

Tutor	come in
Julie	hallo
Tutor	hallo (.) have a seat (.) better this time
Julie	yeh (.) tired (.) I'm (—) dead now (.) I can't wake up I'm thinking of going back to bed (.) ohh God (.)
Tutor	first to ar first to arrive (.) that's a (.) I wonder if anybody else a I always get a ⌈bit worried
Julie	⌊somebody after me
Tutor	yes I know that there's somebody, there's somebody all day

Transcription conventions

- (.) means a brief pause
- (—) represents inaudible speech
- deep brackets [indicate overlapping speech

(Adapted from Cheepen and Monaghan, 1990, p. 199)

2   Two adolescent boys chatting informally in Northern Ireland.

R	Did you see the match last night?
T	Aye
R	It was great wasn't it
T	It must have been one of the best matches I have seen
R	Ya see the goal Hoddle scored (.) fuck me that was brilliant
T	Aye he seemed to hang in the air as he hit it

(Adapted from Wilson, 1989, p. 27)

3   Two young women in a Singapore department store.

[*A is trying on a pair of shoes*]

B	Can fit or not? Not bad what? Cheap what? Can buy lah!

[*B tries on a pair*]

A	Eh, can fit your leg
B	The leg down there a bit uncomfortable [*looks at some other shoes*]. This one don't have less, ah? I don't want to buy
A	We walk down lah
B	Can also

(Adapted from Platt et al., 1984, p. 160)

Comment

Let's look first at the talk between Julie and her tutor in the first extract. Informal talk is of course largely unplanned because it arises spontaneously out of fluid and changing everyday activities and relationships. Talk in this example certainly contains inexplicit references (for example, *better this time* and *somebody after me*), as well as unplanned and overlapping utterances which look nothing like whole grammatical sentences. These would count as 'errors' in written English, but they are a completely normal part of the spoken language. One of the key points about talk is that it is **dialogic**. In other words, people constantly refer implicitly to what previous speakers have said, anticipate what they might say next and assume a large amount of shared experience. The tutor's *better this time* is perfectly comprehensible to Julie, who seizes the opportunity to let her tutor know she still isn't feeling too good. Similarly, Julie's *somebody after me* is immediately understood by the tutor to mean another student who has booked the next time slot, and we can use our knowledge of the context to interpret the tutor's rather enigmatic *yes I know that there's somebody, there's somebody all day* as referring to his own busy tutorial timetable.

What about the function of the talk? This is the beginning of what may be a rather stressful session for Julie, and after the exchange of greetings the tutor is probably showing he remembers Julie's previous health problems as a way of putting her at ease. One function of this kind of 'small talk' before getting down to business is to bind people together (what the anthropologist Malinowski (1923) calls **phatic communion**) and establish an interactional framework for the encounter. Here the tutor, as the higher status speaker, is the one who asks the personal questions and leads the conversation.

The second extract, from Northern Ireland, is clearly an exchange between equals, enthusiastic in a shared interest and comfortable in using expletives with each other. T immediately knows which *match* R is referring to and, although their utterances seem more 'complete' than Julie's and her tutor's, this conversation is also highly cooperative. The boys collaboratively recall the game and its high point, following up and building on each other's utterances. Interestingly, the point here is not to give T any new information since he also has seen the match; rather it seems to be about two friends bringing together their individual experiences into one shared evaluation of the game as *great, brilliant, one of the best matches I have seen.*

The third extract illustrates the highly elliptical nature of talk around an activity, in this case buying shoes. Because speakers here can assume a closely shared physical context, language can be very implicit, and still perfectly comprehensible and appropriate. They also share knowledge of a particular variety of English. These young women are speaking colloquial Singaporean English, where *what?* means 'you really must agree with me', *feet* and *legs* are used interchangeably (as in Chinese), *don't have less* means 'doesn't have any discount' and *can also* is a polite way of expressing agreement. Colloquial Singaporean English, or **Singlish**, is usually spoken in informal contexts, and in the example above its use reflects the intimacy and informality of the relationship between the two friends. Like the speakers in the other examples, these young women will switch to a more formal variety of English in other contexts. Differences between the Singaporean women's use of language in formal and informal contexts is particularly obvious because it involves a change of dialect, but speakers in the other two examples above will also use different vocabulary and grammatical constructions in a more formal situation (imagine Julie giving a seminar presentation, or the boys speaking to their headteacher).

Closings, face and politeness

In extract 1 we saw speakers establishing an interactional relationship at the beginning of a conversation, and the other two examples showed people in mid encounter jointly reconstructing an experience and talking around an activity. How do we close a conversation and withdraw from the relationship it involves? In the next example P and C are English women in their thirties who became friends because they both had children at the same school. P has been spending the afternoon at C's house.

P	I must go (.) taking up your time (.) have a nice day tomorrow
C	oh thanks and thanks again for the things (.) this is lovely (.) cyclamen isn't it(.) cyclamen
P	yeh (.) cyclamen (.) I think it is
C	's gorgeous (.) have a lovely time
P	all this evening to look forward to (.) oh *[squeak]*
C	enjoy it
P	I will
C	have a lovely time and thanks again
P	thanks (.) bye
C	bye
P	bye

Transcription convention

- (.) means a brief pause

(Adapted from Cheepen and Monaghan, 1990, p. 41)

In terms of language structure, conversation endings are usually highly repetitive: people repeat their own and each other's utterances, and sometimes refer back to topics from earlier in the conversation (*all this evening to look forward to*) which necessitates a quick sidetrack of conversational turns before the speakers can continue with the closing and reach their final exchange of goodbyes. This repetition is part of the emphasis on solidarity at the closing point of an encounter. Before parting, speakers express positive evaluations of their time together, using phrases such as *thanks again*. It is important for them to guard against any possible loss of face or apparent rejection, and the person initiating the closing often cites an external reason for needing to go or effaces her or himself in some way (e.g. *taking up your time*). There may well also be reference (though not in this example) to a future meeting.

The American sociologist Erving Goffman (1967) calls this kind of verbal consideration and 'stroking' **face work**, and stresses its importance in maintaining the persona and status of speakers throughout interaction. Loss of face for any speaker disrupts the conversation and may need to be repaired, for instance by the rephrasing of a comment, or an apology. Thinking back to the examples in Activity 1.1, one aspect of the boys' talk about the match is their mutually positive face work as they agree and amplify each other's evaluations. And Julie's remark about feeling tired may be a pre-emptive face-saving move, in case her performance at the tutorial doesn't come up to scratch. Face work is related to the status of the speakers, both inside the encounter and in terms of their more permanent status – their socio-economic class, gender and so on. The aspects of status most relevant to the goal of an encounter (e.g. teacher–student in Julie's case) tend to be given most attention in the talk.

Politeness

- *Face needs*

  Building on Goffman's work, the British linguists Penelope Brown and Stephen Levinson (1987) define politeness in terms of positive and negative face needs. **Positive face** needs relate to the desire to be liked and admired, and are supplied through greetings, compliments and other direct expressions of approval. **Negative face** needs relate to the desire not to be imposed on, and are fulfilled by accompanying requests with apologies, hedging expressions (like *kind of* or *I think maybe*) and using other indirect forms to avoid a **face threatening act**: for example, saying *there seems to have been a bit of an accident in here* rather than *how the hell could you have been so stupid!* Generally speaking, we try to satisfy the face needs of others, while protecting our own. Brown and Levinson suggest that particular cultures may stress one kind of politeness more than others; for instance, they see Britain as a 'negative politeness' culture.

- *Relationship constraints*

  Politeness involves using appropriate terms of address, and appropriate degrees of directness and formality, according to a person's relationship with you in terms of **social distance/solidarity** and **relative status**. For example, *Eat up your lunch, dear!* might be an appropriate command to a child, or even to an intimate friend, but not to one's boss at work, and possibly not to one's grandmother, depending on the formality of status relationships within the family. Generally speaking, people in a lower status position pay more attention to face needs than those in a higher status position, and women use more polite forms than men.

- *Social and cultural context*

  Being linguistically polite also involves sensitivity to the formality of the occasion and to sociolinguistic rules about behaviour: how to accept or refuse an invitation, the appropriate language practices around giving and receiving hospitality, greetings formulae, terms of address, taboo terms and so on. These conventions vary in different English-speaking communities, as do the values governing the way formality, social distance and status are expressed.

So far, the examples we have looked at show people assuming an amount of shared knowledge, and communicating easily and amicably. It can of course happen that people are mistaken in their assumptions, and misunderstanding may lead to an embarrassing loss of face for at least one of the speakers. Again, a remark may be misinterpreted in conversation and speakers have to backtrack, or change the topic, in order to get the conversation running smoothly again. But in general people are remarkably adept at interpreting the inexplicit references, the subtle nuances and the unspoken implications which abound in conversation, so that accounts of experience become essentially collaborative affairs.

Turn taking

Within this collaborative process, the turn taking which is taken so much for granted is in fact accomplished through the complex management of a range of linguistic and social cues and signals. Like the previous examples, the next extract involves a negotiation, but a less amicable one.

Activity 1.2 *(Allow about 10 minutes)*

Look at the conversation below between a mother (Anna) and her teenage daughter (Jess) about the thorny subject of money. Notice the face work which is going on. Even in this quite tense situation, how do they manage the turn taking so smoothly?

	Anna	How much is it going to cost you tomorrow?
	Jess	Tomorrow? A couple of pounds. Nicola said just take a fiver and you probably won't have to use it all
	Anna	Well you'll have to find it
5	Jess	Yes well what am I going to spend tonight?
	Anna	I can't afford for you to go to the pub, and I'm not going to
	Jess	Yeah well I'll give you the money back once I've spoken
		⌈ to Dad
	Anna	⌊ I don't *want* you to spend this much money on sitting in a pub
10		drinking
	Jess	Well drinking ⌈ (—)
	Anna	⌊ Fifteen pounds you've spent already and you'll
		spend another ⌈ five pounds
	Jess	⌊ I haven't spent fifteen pounds mum. OK just
15		give me a pound then
	Anna	What for?
	Jess	[*Exasperated sigh*] God, you don't listen at all!

Transcription conventions

- (—) represents inaudible speech
- deep brackets [indicate overlapping speech

You may have noticed Anna's face-threatening comments in lines 9–10 and 12–13, and Jess's face-protecting vagueness about the amount of money she needs in lines 2–3 and her use of *Yes well*, to signal acceptance of Anna's point and soften the force of her own.

Linguistic knowledge about turn taking in English has been strongly influenced by the work of Sacks, Schegloff and Jefferson (1974), American sociologists with a particular interest in the management of everyday encounters. They suggest that English speakers conform to basic turn-taking rules which mean that only one person speaks at a time, and instances of overlap (e.g. lines 8–9 and 13–14 above) are quickly repaired. People have shared knowledge about the kinds of 'script' used in particular kinds of speech event (e.g. parent–teenager argument), so the content of some turns can be roughly predicted. Sacks and his colleagues, however, are particularly interested in the way people use their intuitive knowledge of the structure of English in managing turn taking. A considerable amount of conversation, they suggest, is based on **adjacency pairs**, where particular kinds of utterance and response tend to occur together. For instance, one of the obvious ways in which Anna and Jess allocate turns is through the use of question and answer. Other adjacency pairs in English include greeting–greeting, invitation–acceptance/rejection, complaint–denial, request–accedence/denial.

In addition to knowledge about adjacency pairs, speakers unconsciously use their grammatical knowledge of English and respond at the end rather than in the middle of a grammatical unit. Such units range from sentences: (*I can't afford for you to go to the pub, and I'm not going to*) to single words (*Tomorrow?*) At the end of each unit is what Sacks et al. call a **transition relevance place**, which is where the speaker may pause for a response, or other speakers come in, sometimes slightly overlapping the previous speaker (e.g. lines 9 and 14 above). Breaking in before a transition relevance point, as Anna does in line 12, counts as an **interruption**.

The Sacks, Schegloff and Jefferson model has provided an important base-line for the study of how conversations are managed, and for the development of the research tradition known as **conversation analysis**, which focuses on the structure and management of interactions, highlighting the predictable patterns of turn taking, conversational openings and closings, and how topics are developed. This approach has, however, also been criticized for not giving much attention to how conversation management is affected by:

- the relative status of the participants, which may not be directly referred to but still influences the management of turns;

- the cultural knowledge required to recognize what counts as an invitation, request and so on, particularly when these are expressed indirectly (e.g. *what am I going to spend tonight?*);

- intonation and body language – the use of voice pitch and rhythm, eye contact, gesture and posture. These are all important both for conversation management and for the communication of meaning and feelings.

For further details of work on turn taking, and a full account of the use of intonation and body language in conversation, see *Describing Language* (Graddol et al., 1994).

Let's try to draw together the main points about the structure and functions of conversation covered in this section.

- *Structure*

    If we apply criteria from written English, the language used in everyday talk can seem hesitant, ambiguous and full of half-finished sentences and interruptions. It may include local varieties of grammar and vocabulary which would not be acceptable in formal written texts. In spontaneous everyday interactions, however, this kind of language use is perfectly appropriate; an utterance makes sense in relation to its cultural and social context. Elliptical structures, which assume a considerable amount of shared knowledge and experience between speakers, also signal solidarity and intimacy.

    We have seen how there are predictable structures in conversation around turn taking, and openings and closings (most of the examples we have looked at are from the British and American contexts and there may be different conventions in other cultures).

- *Function*

    The examples above show the close intertwining of the ideational and the interpersonal functions of language. For example, we have seen that talk used to convey information about health is also managing a tutor–student relationship, and chat about a football match is simultaneously consolidating a friendship. There is constant feedback between these two functions; relationships constrain the content of what is said, but what is said can also build or change a relationship. The meanings communicated in a particular conversation depend partly on the actual words used, but they are also shaped by the negotiation of relationships between the participants, and by other aspects of the social and cultural context.

I consider this issue of context in the next section.

1.3   CONTEXT AND MEANING

I have already touched on the importance of context in using and interpreting language appropriately: the British college tutorial context which determines the roles in the Julie extract, the physical activities involved in trying on shoes in the Singapore department store conversation, and the importance of cultural conventions in the expression of politeness. In a broad sense, **context** can include the following (overlapping) elements, all of which will influence the use and interpretation of particular words and phrases:

* the physical surroundings;
* the relationship between speakers;
* their past shared experience, and current conversational goals;
* the social events of which the conversation is a part;
* broader cultural values and expectations.

In addition, language also creates its own context, even as it is being used, in two different ways. First, the meaning of a word or utterance is shaped by other words or utterances which have gone before, e.g. when Julie says *somebody after me* we know that *somebody* means another student, because of the tutor's preceding comment. This remark by the tutor contextualizes Julie's use of the term *somebody*. Secondly, words evoke nuances and associations from our experience of their use in other contexts; think of how your interpretation of the term *brilliant* in Activity 1.1 extract 3 reflects your experience of its use on other occasions. In addition to their dictionary meaning, words gather a collection of contextual associations which reflect the history of their use within the language.

Anthropologists have demonstrated that in order to use and interpret language we draw on a considerable amount of cultural as well as linguistic knowledge (e.g. see the 'Politeness' box in section 1.2). Within any single community there will also be a range of ways of speaking: different uses of language associated with legal, educational and religious institutions, with particular relationships and with particular social events. In order to understand the function and meaning of any conversational exchange, we need to know the values and expectations about language held by those speakers in that particular cultural context.

Bearing all this in mind, let's look at one particular practice in English, to see what kinds of factors influence the use and interpretation of language.

Terms of address

In some languages the relationship between speakers is encoded grammatically; for example, the *tu/vous* distinction between informal and formal 'you' in French, the choice of high or low Javanese in Java depending on whom you are addressing, and in Japanese the addition of particular morphemes or 'word bits' to the terms you are using to signify respect to the listener. In English, however, relationships between speakers are not so immediately obvious. One has to look across a whole conversation to gather clues from the way language is used to see how particular relationships are being marked, negotiated or contested. However, one way in which relationships are quite explicitly marked in English is in the terms people use to address each other – whether one is 'on first name terms', for instance.

Activity 1.3   *(Allow about 10 minutes)*

Jot down all the names or terms that people use to address you. What are the reasons for people calling you one name rather than another? And would it be appropriate for you to address them in a similar manner?

Comment

My own list for this activity includes variations on my first and last names, together with *Miss, Ms* or *Mrs*, nicknames, *mum, mother, aunty, madam* (in shops), *love* and the local variant *me duck* (in markets), *miss* (in schools), and various terms of endearment and abuse. Some of these names are kinship terms (with some variation between more and less formal versions); while *miss* used by children in schools signals a particular work role (like *doctor* or *your honour*). Honorific terms, like *madam*, mark not just formal respect, but also certain genteel politeness conventions – hence the difference between the ways I am addressed in smart department stores and in the local market. A male colleague who carried out this activity commented on the large number of terms there are in Britain for men addressing each other (e.g. *mate, guv, chum, captain, squire*) and how some of these are used by lower status men to mock and subvert the status differential between themselves and the higher status men they are addressing, as in *Sorry, squire, no can do!*

In addition to identifying a large number of different terms, you may have found that the same term can mean rather different things in different relationships; for instance, a woman may be addressed as *love* (though she may not always use the same term back) by her mother, her husband, an older male colleague and the local butcher.

By way of illustration, consider the options used to address Lo Wing Yu listed below.

Lo Wing Yu, aged 21, Singapore

Terms of address	*Explanation*
Debbie	Although this name is not included on my birth certificate, it was given to me at the age of three. Most of my friends, except my primary school classmates, know me by that name. I'm also known as Debbie in my various workplaces.
Deb	Reserved only for my best friend of seven years. An indication of our 'closeness'.
Wing Yu	Used by almost all my primary school classmates. At that time, all teachers called me that because I was registered in school with that name. Anyway, it wasn't that 'fashionable' to have English names then.
Wing Yu (pronounced in Cantonese)	Used by my family members, except my elder sister.

Yingyu (hanyu pinyin name i.e. Mandarin pronunciation)	Used mostly by my Mandarin teachers in school and a seamstress whom I always go to.
Lo Wing Yu	My full name is occasionally used when I am either at some government departments such as the Immigration Department, at the hospital/clinic, or somewhere where strangers happen to be holding my IC [identification card] or some information about me.
Ah Mui (pronounced in Cantonese, meaning 'little sister')	Used by my family members, especially my elder sister. Also used by my friends to disturb me because they find that term of address very funny (if they happen to hear that being used to address me, e.g. when they call and my family members call for 'Ah Mui' to answer the phone).
Xiao mei mei ('little girl/sister' in Mandarin)	Used by older guys who are trying to be funny, or older women who think that I am actually very, very young.
Jie Jie ('older sister' in Mandarin)	Used by children, or parents of little children whom I meet at the clinic. I hardly ever use this term to address strangers. If it is someone I know, I might call her by her name followed by Jie Jie.
Aunty	Used by children, or parents of little children whom I meet at the clinic where I am working. I may use the same form of address for female adults who are very obviously older than me.
Xiao jie ('Miss' in Mandarin)	Mostly used by strangers or patients in the clinic where I work part time. I would use the same term for Chinese strangers who are female and young.
Miss	Usually used by strangers. I would use the same term to address other female strangers who do not look that old.
Miss Lo	Usually used in a more formal context e.g. during the job interview which I went for during my vacation. Also used by shop assistants or waiters/waitresses if I happen to use my credit card.
Ma'am	Used by counter staff at fast-food restaurants. Also used more in formal contexts when people/strangers are trying to be polite.
Sweetheart/honey	Used by some of my closer friends for fun. Sometimes used by myself to them as well.
Woman	Usually used by closer girl friends. Sometimes used by myself to them.
Girl	Often used by strangers older than me who are trying to catch my attention, or ask me to do something.

So are there sociolinguistic rules that tell us who has the right to use which terms to whom? **Terms of address** are a part of politeness, and will depend on:

- difference in status between the speakers, for example in relation to age, gender, class, work-role (hence the asymmetrical use of many terms);

- social distance between speakers: how well they know each other;

- formality of situation: some contexts mark particular roles, for instance *miss* in school, and *your honour* in court; also, you would probably not wish to embarrass a dear one by using a special private nickname in a more public formal situation;

- the cultural context: notice, for instance, the variety of personal names from different languages used for Lo Wing Yu above. In Singapore, older family members tend to be addressed by a kinship term rather than by a personal name, and the word *aunty* is frequently used as a friendly term of respect for an older woman.

But although terms of address are sensitive to status, social distance and context, they also have a particular force of their own which can mark, construct or change some aspect of a relationship. Notice the way Lo Wing Yu feels positioned by certain people calling her *little sister.* There was also the lower status male's ironic use of *squire* mentioned above, or, again in Britain, people have commented on estate agents' alacrity in adopting rather informal terms of address for their clients, presumably to try to establish a close, trusting relationship as rapidly as possible. Conversely, an irate parent who addresses their child as *James* rather than *Jamie* symbolically increases the social distance between them as part of the reprimand.

As the famous example in the box below shows, terms of address are powerful ways of expressing and asserting relationships. We have already seen how in some communities speakers have access to terms from a number of languages, and there may be a particular reason why a term from one of these is used rather than another. For example, Indian English speakers often use Indian language kinship terms to signal that they want to invoke Indian conventions, rather than those associated with British culture (Pandharipande, 1992). In Indian languages kinship terms, as in Singapore, are extended beyond biological relations. So, for instance, an Indian English speaker may address a listener who is not a blood relative as *didi* or *di* (elder sister), to indicate a particular relationship of respect and affection; someone addressed as *didi* then has the right to behave as if she

---

In the 1960s, a black man was stopped and questioned on a public street in America:

> 'What's your name, boy?' the policeman asked …
> 'Dr Poussaint. I'm a physician …'
> 'What's your first name, boy? …'
> 'Alvin.'

The policeman manages to insult Dr Poussaint three times in this short exchange: once by his initial use of the term 'boy' which denies adult status on the grounds of race, secondly because he ignores the doctor's stated preference for how he should be addressed, and thirdly by repeating the denigrating term 'boy' even when he knows the doctor's name. Dr Poussaint's own experience of the encounter was 'profound humiliation' – 'For the moment, my manhood had been ripped from me' (Ervin-Tripp, 1969, pp. 93 and 98).

were the speaker's elder sister, advising them, or interrupting their speech. Indian English speakers may also address a wider range of people as *aunty* and *uncle* than British English speakers. This extension of English kinship terms is common in many of the new Englishes (e.g. Hawaiian English, Singaporean English, Nigerian English), reflecting the greater social importance of kinship for these speakers in comparison with most British speakers.

If there are interesting variations in the use of terms of address across different English-speaking cultures, there are also significant changes over time within any single cultural context (see box below). Look back at your notes for Activity 1.3. How do you think these might compare with answers from your parents or grandparents for the same activity?

> From a 1922 American book, *Etiquette* by Emily Post
>
> 'It is also effrontery for a younger person to call an older by her or his first name …
> Only a very underbred, thick-skinned person would attempt it.'
>
> (Cited in Ervin-Tripp, 1969, p. 29)

1.4 COMMUNICATIVE STRATEGIES AND CONVERSATION STYLE

In its broadest definition, **style** refers to a combination of features relating to meaning and management of conversation: prosody (rhythm and intonation), overlapping, repetition, use of laughter, tolerance of noise and silence, and ways of using anecdotes, asking questions, linking topics and expressing particular emotions (Tannen, 1984). At the individual level we all may be said to have our own particular style of talking – the way we use stories, for instance, or how much personal information we tend to reveal, or how we express politeness. Aspects of our style can probably be traced to where we have come from, our class, our age and our gender. In this section I look at three approaches to studying style: Deborah Tannen's influential study of the differences within a group of friends in America, Diana Eades' work with Aboriginal Australians and the body of research around the notion of a 'women's style'.

A more detailed discussion of phonological and grammatical aspects of speaking style is included in Chapter 8 of the first book in this series, *English: history, diversity and change* (Graddol et al. (eds), 1996).

How do conversational styles vary?

There can be a remarkable diversity of styles within one social group, as Tannen showed when she analysed the conversation of five friends and herself during a Thanksgiving dinner party. These friends came from different geographical backgrounds: two were Californian men, three (two men and Tannen) were New Yorkers, and there was one English woman. Tannen was intrigued by the striking difference between the New Yorkers and the rest when she asked them afterwards how much they had enjoyed the conversation during the meal. Whereas the New Yorkers remembered it as lively and satisfying, the others had found it 'all over the place and frenetic', and had felt bulldozed and marginalized.

When Tannen calculated the amount each person said during the meal, she found that the three New Yorkers had indeed dominated the event, talking twice as much as the other three. But it was not just the amount of talk that was different. The New Yorkers seemed to share what Tannen calls a 'New York Jewish high-involvement' style, with a preference for personal topics, rapid enthusiastic speech which often overlaps with other people's, 'machine gun questions' and a considerable amount of joking and storytelling. This created problems for the others. For instance, one of the Californian men commented 'I'm amazed at how you guys talk over each other, saying the same thing at the same time. When I have a conversation there are pauses.' And the other Californian man felt intimidated by the way the woman and two men from New York kept firing rapid personal questions at him like *How do you know that?*, *How did you feel?*, and interrupting what he was saying. The New Yorkers thought they were expressing interest and enthusiasm and couldn't understand why he clammed up. There were also stylistic differences in the way people told stories; the New Yorkers all laughed at each others' stories but couldn't understand the English woman's because she seemed to use a more 'dead-pan' style, without any changes in intonation to signal when the punchline was coming.

In contrasting the New Yorkers' conversational style with those of the others, Tannen highlights the following differences:

- expectations about what it is appropriate to talk about, for example whether topics should be 'personal';
- how turn taking is managed, for instance whether pauses and silence are tolerated, and whether interruptions are meant to encourage or stop the other speaker;
- the degree of directness in questions and whether these are perceived as supportive or off-putting;
- use of intonation and voice quality (to signal enthusiasm, the punchline of a story, and so on);
- willingness to enter ironic routines or story rounds, and expectations about what constitutes a joke or story worth telling.

Tannen emphasizes that she is analysing talk on one particular occasion and that the members of the dinner party group may well behave differently in other contexts. The English woman, for instance, might well talk more and tell more successful stories with friends in London.

We might query how far the features Tannen identified as 'New York Jewish high-involvement conversation style' arose from the fact that the three New Yorkers were the most intimate friends at the dinner party and shared a considerable amount of personal history. It could be that one reason why they told stories and interrupted frequently was because they felt more relaxed and at home than the other guests, and could count on long shared experience with each other. Interestingly, however, some of the differences in communication strategies that Tannen identifies between her friends are also highlighted in studies of different cultural groups and in studies of how men and women talk differently. In the next two subsections, questioning strategies, ways of seeking and expressing personal information, and the role of pauses and silence crop up again as important aspects of communication style that can have quite far-reaching effects if they are not used in the same way by people trying to talk to each other.

Aboriginal English

Diana Eades, an Australian linguist, has studied the 'ways of speaking' of Aboriginal English speakers and the effects these have on their experience of communicating with white Australians. She suggests that Aboriginal ways of using English are closely related to their lifestyle and culture, and to their beliefs about how people should relate to each other.

Activity 1.4   *(Reading A)*

Read the extract from 'Communicative strategies in Aboriginal English' by Diana Eades (Reading A). Try to keep a mental note of the features of Aboriginal communicative style she identifies. What kinds of misunderstanding arise between speakers of Aboriginal English and white Australians?

Comment

Eades suggests that the lack of personal privacy in the Aboriginal lifestyle is balanced by an indirect verbal style. Aboriginal people are reluctant to express personal opinions, supply information or account for actions directly. Indirectness is often achieved through what she calls the 'multifunctional' nature of utterances. Whether a question is also a request, for instance, can be negotiated between the speakers concerned. Responses to the directness of white interactions often include 'gratuitous concurrence' (agreeing with whatever they say), which can cause misunderstanding whenever direct questions are used in legal, medical and educational settings.

Is there a 'women's style'?

If one way of identifying significant aspects of style is to compare different cultural groups, another is to compare different genders. Research in this area has tended to be carried out among middle-class, white British or American women, but, as we shall see, ideas developed in this area are beginning to be applied to other contexts and cultures.

Activity 1.5   Gender voices   *(Allow about 10 minutes)*

Spend a few moments noting down your personal experience of any differences between men's and women's talk – the way they interact, their choice of words and phrases, the topics they like to discuss. Why might these differences exist? My comments follow.

Research shows that in mixed company women usually talk less than men (contrary to popular belief), and that in most situations they are less competitive, more cooperative and work harder to make things run smoothly; for instance, encouraging others to talk and using more face-saving politeness strategies. One explanation for this is that women are brought up to occupy a less powerful position in society, and to display deference towards men, which they do through being more hesitant and indirect. Robin Lakoff (1975) suggests that women use more tag questions (e.g. *isn't it? don't you think?*) more indirect polite forms (e.g. *could you possibly?*) more intensifiers (e.g. *really*); and what she sees as generally weaker vocabulary (e.g. words like *lovely* and *Oh dear*).

Lakoff's observations are largely intuitive and anecdotal, but they raised interesting questions, and her point about women's deference is borne out in linguists' later studies which show how men tend to dominate the topics and the management of mixed gender conversation, interrupting more and giving less feedback and support.

An alternative explanation is that men and women speak differently, not because of an asymmetrical power relationship between them, but because they are socialized into different gender subcultures as children through play. For instance Goodwin (1990), who studied Afro-American children playing in the street, found that while boys played in groups with hierarchies and those higher up issued clear directives like *Gimme the pliers*, the girls organized in more cooperative groups and made more indirect suggestions, such as *Let's do it this way*. Boys' arguments, which challenged the group hierarchy, were sorted out straight away through direct competition and verbal confrontation, while girls who organized friendship around inclusion and exclusion tended to have protracted discussions about other girls in their absence. Here then might be the seeds of an indirect, collaborative speech style for women, with an interest in topics concerning people's motives and feelings, and a more direct competitive style for men, with a focus on the physical world.

Further, some researchers have argued that through their socialization into different subcultures, men and women attach different kinds of meaning to specific speech behaviours which can lead to significant misunderstandings between the sexes. For instance, women may use many more minimal responses (e.g. *mhm, yeh*) because for them these mean 'Carry on. I'm listening' while for men minimal responses carry the rather stronger meaning of 'I agree with you' (Maltz and Borker, 1982).

Most researchers into women's language would now acknowledge the importance (and the limitations) of both the 'dominance' and the 'difference' theories. In addition there has been a growing interest in the importance of context, and in cross-cultural studies. One study of courtroom language showed that high-status expert female witnesses did not use Lakoff's 'female' style features, while lower status male witnesses did (O'Barr and Atkins, 1980). In a different context, Beattie (1983) found in his university tutorials that female students interrupted just as much as the men and suggested that in this instance the most important motivation was to capture the floor and impress the tutor. Gender differences, then, may be differently expressed in different contexts. In Reading B Janet Holmes explores both the form and the function of how men and women give and receive compliments across a number of English-speaking communities.

❖   ❖   ❖   ❖   ❖

Activity 1.6   *(Reading B)*

Read 'The role of compliments in female–male interaction' by Janet Holmes (Reading B). How consistent are her findings with the points about women's speech style discussed above? How does what she has to say about giving compliments relate to your own experience? Notice how Holmes combines the two dimensions of cross-gender, and cross-cultural, comparison.

Comment

Holmes suggests that compliments express solidarity. She found that they were used most frequently by women to other women, who also used more intensifiers in their compliments, and terms like *lovely* and *nice*. The fact that women give and receive many more compliments than men is consistent with other research that suggests women's linguistic behaviour is affiliative and facilitative, rather than competitive or control oriented. Although compliments in English have a simple predictable linguistic structure, Holmes shows that knowing how to use them requires sophisticated sociolinguistic knowledge. In situations where speakers have different cultural expectations about complimenting behaviour, their different patterns of cross-sex use may increase the possibility for miscommunication and offence.

So far we have been mainly comparing men's and women's styles in cross-gender talk. What happens when women are talking together on their own, without men? In a rather different kind of study from Holmes's quantitative corpus work (i.e. the analysis of a large number of spoken or written texts by computer), Jennifer Coates has made a detailed small-scale qualitative study of informal talk among female middle-class friends in England. She found that instead of the 'one person talks at a time' rule (Sacks et al., 1974), conversations between these women were structured around the collaborative production of utterances and the joint sharing of the conversational floor. In this context, interruptions are not competitive, but cooperative. In the next example K is wondering if her neighbour can see her, because she happened to see him undress in his living room.

1	K	and I thought my God
2	C	yeah
3	K	if I can see him
4	C	he can see you
5	K	and I don't always just get undressed in my living room
6	C	(laugh)
7	K	you know I mean OK I'm sure he's not
8	C	peeping
9	K	peeping or anything
10	C	but he
11	K	but it just
12	C	you accidentally saw him
13	K	that's right
14	C	oh I don't blame you I think it needs screening trees round it

(Coates, 1993, p. 181)

K and C collaborate to produce utterances (7–8 *he's not/ peeping*; 3–4 *if I can see him/ he can see you*) and share in the search for appropriate words (10–11 *but he/ but it just*). Turns are thus jointly produced, and Coates suggests the floor can also be shared by those adding back-channel support (*yes, mhm, yeah*), like D, B and A in the next example:

Transcription conventions

- deep brackets [
  indicate overlapping
  speech

- = = indicates no
  discernible gap
  between utterances

C	I mean in order to accept that idea you're
C	having to ⌐ completely
E	mhm completely review your ⌐ view of your
D	yes
C	change ⌐ your view of your husband=
E	husband ⌐ = =that's right
B	=yes
A	yeah mhm

(Coates, 1993, p. 182)

Coates found that the women in these groups did not stop talking when they were overlapped, nor did they seem to find the overlaps intrusive. Rather, overlaps were part of the solidarity, like the collaborative production of utterances ('duet-ting') and the cooperative sharing of the floor. Coates suggests that these prac-tices are an important part of accomplishing female friendship, although she also notes that they may be related to the intimacy of the setting, the relative equality of status between the speakers and the kinds of topic discussed. (Think back to Anna and Jess's argument which is also talk between women in an intimate setting but does not involve the collaborative floor-sharing of Coates's women; and to the different attitudes towards interruptions among Tannen's group of mixed friends, which seem to be based on culture rather than gender.) There is as yet little research on all-male intimate talk among equals, and it would be interesting to see if this, like women's talk, is structured differently from their behaviour in cross-gender interactions.

To summarize, researchers have suggested that there is a particular women's speaking style in English which involves more hesitations, indirectness, qualifiers, polite forms and tag questions. Some researchers relate this to women's inferior social position and claim that men dominate cross-gender talk through their control of the topic, interruptions and lack of supportive feedback. Other researchers describe women's use of English as not weak, but different; such differences have been related to boys' and girls' socialization in different gender subcultures. While both the dominance and difference arguments provide useful explanations for certain language behaviour patterns, recent research studies show how style, function and meaning vary across different contexts, and suggest that there may be more complex reasons underlying the patterns of women's (and men's) language use.

1.5   STORIES, ACCOUNTS AND IDENTITY

One aspect of style that we mentioned in the discussion above is people's use of storytelling. If you remember, Tannen saw the New Yorkers as sharing a particular style, and Eades (Reading A) described how Aboriginal people may respond in-directly to questions, using a narrative. In fact, a large amount of informal talk in English seems to take the form of narrative. Bruner suggests that conversational story-telling is the major way in which we account for our actions and the events we experience and that 'our sensitivity to narrative provides the major link between our own sense of self and our sense of others in the social world around us' (Bruner, 1986, p. 69). So how do narratives and accounts construct the world in particular ways and develop our own sense of identity?

Storytelling and voices

Stories told in conversations can range from the briefest of anecdotes to long, detailed accounts of experiences or incidents and from the mundane to the extraordinary. An important element of every story is the way in which narrators convey (or try out) their own evaluation of the events and people involved. This evaluation is the point of the story – why the narrator has chosen to tell it – and it also conveys social and moral values which are an important part of the narrator's personal identity.

Activity 1.7   The estate agent story   (Allow about 15 minutes)

We pick up the following narrative after an American man announced to a friend that he had just pulled off an excellent deal on a house purchase. The friend asked 'How come?' and the man explained that the house he wanted belonged to an elderly sick widow, who had moved into a nursing home and had been trying to sell her house for some time. Snyder was the estate agent.

What kinds of evaluative comment is the narrator making, either directly or indirectly, of the events and people involved?

> … when I went to see it, the guy says to me, says, 'We got a bid for thirty-three – thirty-four,' says, 'If you bid thirty-five,' he says, 'You'll get it.' I said, 'Okay, let me think it over.' And I went home and called up my wife's cousin who's a realtor. Well, his partner knows Snyder very well, so he called him up. The bid was for twenty-seven, five! So I figured they could do the same thing I was going to do … So he calls me the next day and I told my wife exactly what to say. So he gets on the phone and so my wife says, 'Look, we're not talking land, we're talking house. The house isn't worth it and it needs a lot of work.' You know, and we made up a lot of things … So she says, 'Yes, we have to lay down new floors, the rugs are no good (the rugs happen to be in good shape), we have to- -there's too much shrubbery, we have to tear out some of the shrubs.' (The shrubbery around the house is magnificent if it's done right, if it's done right.) So really we made up everything. So he says to my wife, he says, 'Well, what would you bid?'. So she says, 'It's stupid for me to talk,' she says … 'Why should I even talk to you? It ain't gonna be anywheres near.' So he says to her, he says, 'Well,' he says, 'the person at thirty-four backed out.' So she says, 'Oh, yeah?' He says, 'Yeah,' he says, 'What would you bid?' So she says, 'Twenty-eight.' He says, 'Oh,' he says, 'No, that she'll never go for.' So she says, 'Okay, that's my bid, Mr Smith. You want it, fine; you don't, fine.' Got a call that afternoon. It was accepted!'
>
> She finally went – we settle at November 18th. And I got to sell my house now – three weeks now.

(Adapted from Wolfson, 1982, pp. 25-7)

My comments are in the following text.

Some of the ways in which storytellers convey particular evaluations of the events they are relating are not visible in the transcription – for instance their use of prosody, sound effects, facial expressions and gestures. But there are two important ways of communicating evaluation which are clearly present in the example above.

- Narrators step outside the story at particular points to bring in important additional information, or to justify their actions. For instance, the narrator here tells us that, in spite of what his wife claims on the phone to the estate agent, the house and garden are actually in very good condition: *The rugs happen to be in good shape* and *The shrubbery around the house is magnificent*. He makes sure that the listener appreciates the cleverness of the trick by explaining *So really we made up everything*, and guards against his strategy being condemned as dishonest by his remark near the beginning of the story, *So I figured they could do the same thing I was going to do*.

- Many conversational narratives use reported speech, particularly when it gets to the key part of the action. But we hardly ever report someone else's exact words when we are relating an incident or anecdote; we paraphrase and reframe them to make a specific point and to show ourselves in a particular kind of light (Volosinov, 1973; Tannen, 1989). One can sense the narrator's triumphalism behind the confident, no-nonsense voice he has constructed for his wife, and the clear evaluation of his actions as 'pulling off a great deal' rather than, for instance, 'how we cheated a sick elderly widow'.

Evaluation strategies are tied in with the structure of conversational stories, as Labov demonstrated in his influential US research.

The structure of conversational narrative using Labov's 1972 categories

- *Abstract: what is the story about?* (*I've just pulled off a really good deal.*)

- *Orientation: who, when, what, where?* (*She's a widow, she put the house up originally during the winter …*) This section is often more grammatically complicated than when the action gets going, because the teller wants to sketch out what was happening before, or alongside, the main narrative events.

- *Complicating action: then what happened?* This is the main action part of the story, the account of significant events, with switches in and out of the present tense; it often includes plenty of reported speech.

- *Evaluation: so what?* In order to make sure the listener gets the point of the story, the narrator may step outside the story at particular points to bring in additional important information (*the rugs happen to be in good shape*), to make evaluative points (*So I figured they could do the same thing I was going to do*), or to use sound effects and gestures.

- *Result: what finally happened?* (*It was accepted!*) This resolves the story, and often again emphasizes the point of telling it.

- *Coda* (*And I got to sell my house now.*) An additional remark or observation usually bridges the gap between story time and real time, bringing the teller and listener back to the present.

In conversation, stories are often told collaboratively. Notice in the next example how eleven-year-old Karlie provides an evaluation right at the beginning for her friend Nicole's story, which they told together. I had just asked Nicole who else lived at her house and Karlie mentioned that Nicole's sister Terri had recently had a baby.

Janet	So does your sister live quite near you?
Nicole	She lives with us
Karlie	Cause ⌈she's only quite young
Nicole	⌊She's young, she's sixteen
Janet	Ah right ·
Karlie	She did the best thing about it though, didn't she, Nicole?
Nicole	She didn't tell a soul, no one, that she was pregnant
Karlie	Until she was due, when she got into hospital, then she told them
Nicole	On Saturday night she had pains in her stomach and come the following Sunday my mum was at work and my sister come to the pub and my Aunt Ella was in it and my sister went in there and said 'I've got pains in my stomach' so my Aunty Ella went and got my mum, and took her to hospital, and my mum asked her if she was due on and she said 'No, I've just come off' and when they got her to hospital they said 'Take her to maternity!' My mum was crying!
Janet	Your mum didn't realise she was pregnant?
Nicole	No, and my mum slept with her when she was ill!
Karlie	My dad said she did (.) Terri did the best thing about it (.) her sister's Terri
Nicole	Or if she did tell, as she's so young, she weren't allowed to have him

(Maybin, 1993, pp. 142–3)

Transcription conventions

- (.) means a brief pause
- deep brackets [indicate overlapping speech

This story is actually introduced by Karlie's evaluation *She did the best thing about it*, before Nicole and Karlie together give the abstract of the story: *She didn't tell a soul, no one, that she was pregnant – Until she … got into hospital, then she told them*. Nicole provides additional information which emphasizes the extraordinary nature of the story in her comment *and my mum slept with her when she was ill* (i.e. 'and still didn't notice that she was pregnant').

Interestingly, although Karlie's initial evaluation is presented as her own, later in the conversation we learn that it is in fact her father's: *My dad said she did – Terri did the best thing about it*. Karlie seems initially to have taken on her father's voice, and presented his judgement of Terri's actions as if it were her own. Bakhtin (1981) suggests that this direct taking on of other people's voices (in addition to reporting them) is a common feature of all spoken language, that we are forever using words and phrases from other people's mouths. He argues that whenever we take on a voice, we also take on an evaluative stance (as Karlie obviously does here). In fact, our taking on of voices and their attitudes is part of 'the ideological becoming of a human being' (Bakhtin, 1982, p. 341).

Codeswitching

Speakers who have a number of dialects of English in their language repertoire, or who speak English and other languages, may switch between their language varieties (termed **codeswitching**) to create voices for different characters in their conversational stories.

The following example, from research carried out in London by Mark Sebba, shows Andrew (A), a fifteen-year-old of Jamaican parentage, in conversation with Barry (B), a friend aged sixteen with parents from Barbados and the southern USA. Andrew switches between London English, a London variety of creole based

Further discussion of codeswitching and identity is included in Chapter 8 of the first book in this series, *English: history, diversity and change* (Graddol et al. (eds), 1996) and in Chapter 2 of the third book in the series, *Learning English: development and diversity* (Mercer and Swann (eds), 1996).

on Jamaican Creole and spoken by black people born in Britain within families originally from the West Indies, and Standard English with a near Received Pronunication accent, to create different personae in the story he is telling Barry.

1   A   yeah man, I was on the till on Saturday (.) and this this black man *come* in (.) and you know our shop, right, they u:m give refund on Lucozade bottles

    B   m:

5   A   a black man *come in an' im b(h)u::y* a bottle (.) of *Lucozade* while 'e was in the shop ⌈*an'*

    B   ,   ⌊free p- e's e got free pee [3p] off is it?

    A   yeah

    B   small ones or big ones?

10 A   big ones and 'e drank the bottle in fron% of us an then ask(d) for the money back (see man) *'me want me money now'*

    B   ⌈heheh

    A   ⌊he goes (pnk) (I'm on) the till guy hhh (I jus) I jus' look round at 'im I said well you can't 'ave it (.) I said I 'ave

15   to open the till (w) wait till the next customer comes (.) *'now! open it now and give me the money'* I said I can't (.) the man *just thump 'is fist down* an' (screw up dis for me) (s no man) the manager just comes would you leave the shop before I call the security: hh the man *jus' take the bottle an' fling it at me* an (I)

20   jus' catch it at the (ground)

(Sebba, 1993, pp. 119–20)

Sebba comments:

> Andrew's own reported speech, like most of his narration, is in London English. The customer's is mostly in Creole, cf. lines 11 and 16, where the boundaries of the Creole stretches correspond with quotation marks. However, there are other Creole stretches of talk in this narrative, especially lines 5, 17 and 19. (Note that 'thump' [tomp] and 'fling' are characteristically Creole words.) These Creole stretches are just those parts of the narrative where the customer himself and his actions are described: *come in an' 'im b(h)u::y, just thump 'is fist down, jus' take the bottle an' fling it at me,* all of which have 'the man' as subject.
>
> Although the correspondence between the use of Creole and the description of the customer's action is not perfect, what the narrator seems to be doing is creating a persona for his character 'the difficult customer' by linking him to Creole. The impersonation of the shop manager at lines 19–20, done in a near-RP 'posh' voice, is an even clearer evocation of a persona, but this time using maximally Standard style.
>
> (Sebba, 1993, p. 120)

Like the house buyer and Nicole and Karlie in the earlier examples, Andrew uses animated voices not just to replay an event, but to convey a particular evaluation of his own and the customer's actions. Andrew's representation of his own courageous stand, and of the customer's unreasonable and violent behaviour, is accomplished almost entirely through the ways he reports the voices.

Codeswitching in conversation is also tied up with the transmission of complex messages about identity and allegiance. One unusual study illustrating this is

Roger Hewitt's account of white working-class teenagers in south London who on certain occasions switch to using London Jamaican Creole. Many black adolescents, particularly boys, speak more Jamaican Creole than they did when they were younger, and it has come to represent a prestigious symbol of group solidarity and resistance within black youth culture. Hewitt found that white users also increased their use of Jamaican Creole in adolescence. In the following example both boys are using a strong Jamaican pronunciation, except for the white boy's substitution of the cockney *f* for the Jamaican Creole *t* in *fink*.

White boy	Oh, Royston, ya goin' football on Saturday?
Black boy	Mi na go football! Who for?
White boy	Check some gyal later.
Black boy	Na. Mi na wan check gyal now.
White boy	Rassclaht! Fink ya bent.

(Hewitt, 1986, p. 94)

For white boys, creole signifies toughness, street credibility and adolescent solidarity, but because of the black adolescents' scepticism, they have to negotiate carefully the way they use it within established friendships. In taking on the voices of their black friends, Hewitt suggests, the white adolescents cut through the barrier between the local black and white communities, to establish a solidarity based on age rather than race.

Conflicting identities?

In their negotiation of friendship and identity, the white teenagers in Hewitt's study have somehow to manoeuvre between the values and beliefs around adolescent solidarity, and prevailing racism in the local and broader community. Part of what we are doing through talk, then, is the exploring and taking on of social beliefs and values, which become part of how we view the world and who we are.

The identities invoked by speakers are associated with different **interpretative repertoires** (Potter and Wetherell, 1987); that is, different collections of ways of accounting for events, tied to particular uses of language and images. Potter and Wetherell, who are social psychologists, suggest that in our everyday talk we are constantly drawing on a variety of different interpretative repertoires, in order to account for our behaviour and present ourselves to others. For instance, we might use ideas around the notion of a 'good parent' to explain why we need to leave work early one day, but employ a 'good professional' repertoire to account for not being able to attend a function at our child's school on another occasion. Potter and Wetherell suggest that our use of different interpretative repertoires is tied up with our efforts to try to negotiate the conflicting ideological messages around us.

In the next reading Margaret Wetherell explores some of the conflicting messages about fatness which confront teenage girls in Britain, and shows how they try to resolve these in relation to their own emerging identity.

Activity 1.8   *(Reading C)*

Read 'Fear of fat: interpretative repertoires and ideological dilemmas' by Margaret Wetherell (Reading C). Note the four different repertoires she identifies in the ways the teenagers talk about fatness. Why does she see the way they resolve the apparent contradictions between these as an ideological trap? Why would it be difficult to sustain a 'defiantly fat' position?

Comment

Wetherell suggests that the apparent inconsistency in the way the girls talk about fatness is a normal feature of everyday talk, where people constantly shift between interpretative repertoires and the subject positions they entail. The redefinition of the cultural value attached to thinness in the west (fatness is after all considered beautiful and desirable in some other parts of the world) as a natural, healthy, biological imperative means that the girls see fatness as a personal failure, and believe that they can only 'be their own person' if they are thin. Thus ideologies make particular values appear 'natural' and are internalized as part of individual identity. Being 'defiantly fat' is a possible position within the individualistic repertoire, but would be continually undermined by the other three repertoires on which the girls are drawing.

❖   ❖   ❖   ❖   ❖

1.6   CONCLUSION

Talk is a central part of most of our lives; through it we carry out activities, negotiate relationships, try to construct understandings about the world around us and develop our own sense of identity. In this chapter we have looked at the structure of informal talk, both at the level of language, where we discussed reasons for its frequent inexplicitness and apparent incoherence, and at the level of conversational management, where there are predictable structures around openings, closings and turn taking. Particular language practices within conversation also have predictable structures – for instance, storytelling, or paying compliments. But we found that structure is closely tied up with both the ideational and interpersonal functions of language. As well as conveying and negotiating ideas, talk is used to pursue social relationships; through it intimacy and status are negotiated, and people position themselves, and are positioned, in various ways. Face work and politeness are enormously important, but are expressed differently in English across different cultural settings.

We have seen how people and groups may vary in conversational style, but that these differences are also cross-cut by social and contextual factors. Not only do people speak differently according to the context, but the forms they use may have different significance and meaning depending on where and when they are used, for example, whether interruptions have a competitive or collaborative function. Practices to do with questioning, the disclosure of personal information and the use of silence vary across cultures, gender and even individuals, depending on the context of the talk and the relationships involved.

An important aspect of relating experience is negotiating how this should be evaluated, and the way we convey or try out evaluations in stories and accounts is an important part of developing our own beliefs and values about the world. There also exist, in any community, patterned ways of using language to represent and talk about experience which encode particular evaluations and positions. We inevitably invoke these, as part of our cultural linguistic repertoires and through the voices we take on and reproduce. The English language provides a variety of resources for pursuing individual purposes, but it also shapes those purposes, and ourselves, even as we use it.

Reading A
COMMUNICATIVE STRATEGIES IN ABORIGINAL ENGLISH

Diana Eades

Sociocultural context of Aboriginal English

Varieties of Aboriginal English are spoken as the first language of Aboriginal people living in most areas of Australia, primarily in urban and rural parts of 'settled' Australia (as opposed to remote Australia). The majority of speakers of Aboriginal English are of mixed descent, and many are undeniably biculturally competent, increasingly participating in mainstream Australian institutions, such as education and employment.

Irrespective of the language spoken, Aboriginal people throughout Australia today belong to overlapping kin-based networks sharing social life, responsibilities and rights, and a common history, culture, experience of racism and ethnic consciousness. Social relations are characterised by on-going family commitments within groups, and the highest priority is placed on the maintenance and development of these commitments (rather than, for example, on financial security, employment, or individual fulfilment). Moreover, Aboriginal social life is very public. In towns and cities the openness of traditional Aboriginal camp life has been replaced by the openness of frequently overcrowded housing and vehicles. Much of the business of day-to-day living occurs in open outside areas, for example, in parks and other public places, on the main streets of towns, and on verandahs of houses. Because people have on-going commitments to a wide network of kin (far beyond the nuclear family) virtually every aspect of their lives is shared in some way with a number of relatives.

While Aboriginal societies place a high priority on constantly maintaining and developing social relations, there is also provision for considerable personal privacy. This personal privacy is ensured not in terms of physical privacy as it is, for example, in mainstream Australian society, where walls, an indoor lifestyle and a strong prohibition on directly observing many of the actions of others, are all essential factors in the maintenance of personal privacy. It is through their indirect style of verbal interaction that Aboriginal people experience much personal privacy, as is shown below.

Indirectness in Aboriginal English

Seeking information

While questions are frequently used in Aboriginal English in certain contexts and functions, there are constraints on their use which protect individual privacy ... Direct questions are ... used to elicit orientation information, for example in a typical greeting such as 'Where you been?' Frequently, however, the orientation question takes the form of a statement uttered with rising intonation, e.g. 'You been to town?' Rather than asking directly, the speaker presents known or supposed information for confirmation or denial.

This strategy of seeking information by presenting information is also seen clearly in the ways in which English is used by Aboriginal speakers to seek substantial information, such as important personal details, a full account of an

event, or the explanation of some event or situation. In these situations questions are not used, but the person seeking information contributes some of their own knowledge on the topic, followed often by silence. This strategy serves as an invitation (or hint) for another participant to impart information on this topic. There is no obligation on the knowledgeable person to respond, and, further, it is rare for silences to be negatively valued in Aboriginal conversations. Important aspects of substantial information seeking are the two-way exchange of information, the positive, non-awkward use of silence, and the often considerable time delays (frequently of several days) between the initiation of substantial information seeking and the imparting of such information.

Making and refusing requests

Aboriginal people rarely make direct requests. A question frequently serves to make an indirect request, as well as to seek orientation information. For example, a typical Aboriginal way of asking for a ride is to ask a car owner a question, such as 'You going to town?' or 'What time are you leaving?' Such questions can be interpreted as information seeking of a kind common in Aboriginal conversations, but they can also be interpreted as a request for a ride, depending on the relationship between speakers. Even if speakers understand questions such as these as requests for a ride, the ambiguity enables a person to refuse a request in a similar indirect fashion, for example, 'Might be later', 'Not sure'. In this way Aboriginal people can negotiate requests and refusals without directly exposing their motives (see Eades, 1988).

Seeking and giving reasons

Research with Aboriginal speakers of English in south-east Queensland reveals that the questioning of a person's motives or reasons for action is always carried out indirectly through the use of multifunctional linguistic forms (Eades, 1983).

Thus, for example, an orientation question such as 'You went to town yesterday?' would be used to seek information concerning a person's movements, but this answer might also provide evidence of the reasons behind some of their actions. The use of multifunctional forms makes the requests for reasons indirect and ambiguous, and it gives people considerable privacy; they are never confronted with an inescapable request for a reason (e.g. 'Why didn't you visit us yesterday?').

Just as the seeking of reasons relies on the use of multifunctional forms, so too does the expression of reason. There is frequently no unambiguous linguistic marker of reasons (cf. Standard Australian English *because, in order to, so*). Speakers rely on the non-linguistic context for their interpretation of a statement as a reason. Specifically, it is shared experiences and knowledge which provide the evidence that a multifunctional statement is intended as a reason ...

Expressing opinions

A number of studies of Aboriginal communicative strategies provide evidence that it is important for Aboriginal people to present opinions cautiously and with a degree of circumspection. Von Sturmer first discussed the use of disclaimers as a strategy of 'not presenting oneself too forcefully and not linking oneself too closely with one's own ideas'. Examples of such disclaimers are 'might be I right or wrong' (Von Sturmer, 1981, p. 29), and 'this is just what I think' (Eades, 1988) ... Many Aboriginal people in south-east Queensland do not express a firm or biased opinion, even if they hold one. A common strategy involves general discussions on a topic, while speakers gauge each other's views gradually, before a definite presentation. When speakers realise a difference between their views and those of others, they tend to understate their own views. This style of gradually and indirectly expressing an opinion is a significant factor in cross-cultural miscommunication, and will be discussed below.

Also relevant here is the widespread Aboriginal notion of 'shame', which is a combination of shyness and embarrassment occurring in 'situations where a person has been singled out for any purpose, scolding or praise or simply attention, where he/she loses the security and anonymity provided by the group' (Kaldor and Malcolm, 1979, p. 429).

Aboriginal communicative strategies in cross-cultural communication

Aboriginal people have developed a number of ways of accommodating the directions of non-Aboriginal interactions but some of these ways of accommodating can actually lead to further misunderstanding. For instance, one way in which they respond to the much more direct communication style of white speakers is through the use of '**gratuitous concurrence**' (Liberman, 1981; 1982; 1985), where Aboriginal speakers say 'yes' not necessarily to signal agreement with a statement or proposition, but to facilitate the on-going interaction, or to hasten its conclusion. Occasionally, Aboriginal people switch to a vociferous, confrontational style which they perceive as appropriate to interactions with Whites. In some situations the Aboriginal participants are, in fact, more direct and confrontational than the White participants.

Aboriginal speakers' use of gratuitous concurrence has serious implications for all cross-cultural situations in Australia where direct questioning is used, in particular in police interviews, law courts, employment interviews, medical consultations, classrooms at all levels, and government consultations. Differences in degrees of directness lead to misunderstandings in many settings. In meetings, for example, Aboriginal people are often offended and feel dominated by the White participants, who express forceful opinions, often in direct opposition to those expressed by a previous speaker. On the other hand, White people often mistakenly assume Aboriginal agreement with a particular viewpoint after listening to the initial statements of an Aboriginal speaker, and not allowing time for the expression of a different opinion. If asked directly whether they agree with a particular issue Aboriginal speakers may frequently respond with the 'yes' of gratuitous concurrence. The indirect and roundabout Aboriginal style requires a non-linear meeting organisation and a much longer time span than is typical of White meetings, before participants can express important contradictory viewpoints. Thus, in meetings of Aboriginal organisations, for example, the lengthy discussion of issues often causes non-Aboriginal participants to become frustrated with the seeming lack of organisation and inability to make decisions.

My current research with Queensland Aboriginal students at University and College indicates that the bicultural competence of many, but not all, of these students includes the ability to participate successfully in the mainstream strategies of information seeking, which are so central to the western education system. For some Aboriginal students, however, the direct interrogative style used in tutorials is quite unsuccessful in involving them in discussion, and in assessing the extent of their knowledge of a topic. These students are often uncomfortable and annoyed about views expressed by non-Aboriginal students, and the forceful manner of their expression, but are unable to respond in the same manner. Without the Aboriginal students' feedback, non-Aboriginal students continue in the direct expression of opinions upsetting to Aboriginal students, who in their turn become more resentful of the non-Aboriginal students.

Such situations of miscommunication, potentially disastrous in a cross-cultural setting, are being constructively approached by discussions between Aboriginal students, fellow students and staff (some of whom are Aboriginal and some of whom are non-Aboriginal, with some bicultural competence). The resulting processes of in-group discussion and analysis, and particularly the support and responsibility assumed by the successfully bicultural Aboriginal students, is an important factor in the on-going positive resolution of such challenges.

References

EADES, D.M. (1983) 'English as an Aboriginal Language in South-east Queensland', PhD thesis, University of Queensland.

EADES, D.M. (1988) 'They don't speak an Aboriginal language, or do they?' in KEEN, I. (ed.) *Being Black: Aboriginal cultural continuity in settled Australia*, Canberra, Aboriginal Studies Press.

KALDOR, S. and MALCOLM, I.G. (1979) 'The language of the school and the language of the Western Australian Aboriginal school child – implications for education' in BERNDT, R.M. and BERNDT, C.H. (eds) *Aborigines of the West: their past and their present*, Nedlands, University of Western Australia Press, pp. 407–37.

LIBERMAN, K. (1981) 'Understanding Aborigines in Australian courts of law', *Human Organization*, vol. 40, no. 3, pp. 247–54.

LIBERMAN, K. (1982) 'Intercultural communication in Central Australia', *Working Papers in Sociolinguistics* no. 104, Austin, Texas, South West Educational Development Laboratory.

LIBERMAN, K. (1985) *Understanding Interaction in Central Australia: an ethnomethodological study of Australian Aboriginal people*, Boston, Mass., Routledge and Kegan Paul.

VON STURMER, J. (1981) 'Talking with Aborigines', *Australian Institute of Aboriginal Studies Newsletter* 15.

Source: Adapted from Eades 1991, pp. 84–93

Reading B
THE ROLE OF COMPLIMENTS IN FEMALE–MALE INTERACTION

Janet Holmes

Compliments are positive speech acts which are used to express friendship and increase rapport between people, as the following example illustrates.

Context	Two good friends, meeting in the lift at their workplace.
Complimenter	Hi, how are you. You're looking just terrific.
Recipient	Thanks. I'm pretty good. How are things with you?

A range of studies, involving American, British, Polish, and New Zealand speakers, have demonstrated that compliments are used more frequently by women than by men, and that women are complimented more often than men (Nessa Wolfson, 1983; Janet Holmes, 1988; Barbara Lewandowska-Tomaszczyk, 1989; Robert Herbert, 1990.)

My own analysis of New Zealand patterns was based on a corpus of 484 compliments collected by students using an ethnographic approach (Holmes, 1988). In this corpus of compliments between mainly middle-class Pakeha [European origin] New Zealanders, women gave and received significantly more compliments than did men.

Women gave two-thirds of all the compliments recorded and received three-quarters of them. Women in fact complimented each other twice as often as men complimented them. Compliments between males were much less frequent, and even taking account of females' compliments to males, men received considerably fewer compliments than women. Research in other places confirms these patterns, though the differences between women and men are not always so dramatic (Herbert, 1990).

In general, then, complimenting appears to be a speech act used much more by women than by men. This is consistent with extensive research which suggests that women's linguistic behaviour can be broadly characterised as affiliative, facilitative and co-operative, rather than competitive or control oriented, concerned with 'connection' rather than status (Philip Smith, 1985; Holmes, 1990; Deborah Tannen, 1991). If compliments are considered expressions of rapport and solidarity, the finding that women give more compliments than men illustrates the same pattern.

Topics of compliments

Mostly compliments refer to just a few broad topics: appearance (especially clothes and hair), a good performance which is the result of skill or effort, possessions (especially new ones), and some aspect of personality or friendliness (Joan Manes, 1983; Holmes, 1986; Herbert, 1990). In the New Zealand data the first two topics accounted for 81.2 per cent of the data.

Women tend to receive most compliments on their appearance, and they compliment each other most often on aspects of their appearance. Over half of all the compliments women received in the New Zealand data related to aspects of their appearance, and 61 per cent of all the compliments between women related to appearance, compared to only 36 per cent of the compliments between males.

New Zealand men do receive compliments on their appearance (40 per cent of all compliments they receive). It is interesting to note, however, that the vast majority of these (88 per cent) were given by women. According to Wolfson (1983), the American pattern is different. Though men rarely compliment each other on appearance in either community, the appearance of American men seems not to be an appropriate topic of compliments from men or from women. Wolfson comments that only when the male is much younger than the female does this occur at all, and in general she says 'there seems to be a rather strong if not categorical constraint against the giving of appearance-related compliments to higher-status males, especially in work-related settings' (1983, p. 93). A further interesting feature of the New Zealand data was a distinct male preference for complimenting other men on their possessions rather than women on theirs.

Vocabulary and grammatical patterns

Compliments are remarkably formulaic speech acts. Most use a very small number of lexical items and a very narrow range of syntactic patterns (Wolfson, 1984; Holmes, 1986; Herbert, 1990). A small range of adjectives, for instance, is used to convey the positive semantic message in up to 80 per cent of compliments. In Wolfson's American data 'two-thirds of all adjectival compliments in the corpus made use of only five adjectives: *nice, good, beautiful, pretty* and *great*' (1984, p. 236). In the New Zealand data, the five most frequently occurring adjectives were *nice, good, beautiful, lovely* and *wonderful*. Most of the non-adjectival compliments also depended upon a very few semantically positive verbs (*like, love, enjoy* and *admire*) with *like* and *love* alone accounting for 86 per cent of the American and 80 per cent of the New Zealand data.

The syntactic patterns used in compliments are also drawn from a remarkably narrow range. Four syntactic patterns accounted for 86 per cent of the 686 compliments in Wolfson's American corpus, for example, and 78 per cent of the New Zealand corpus. While many of the syntactic patterns used in compliments seem to be pretty equally distributed between women and men, there are some patterns which differ, as Table 1 illustrates for the New Zealand data.

Women used the rhetorical pattern *what (a) (ADJ) NP!* (e.g. *what lovely children! what a beautiful coat!*) more often than men, while men used the minimal pattern *(INT) ADJ (NP)* (e.g. *great shoes; nice car*) more often than women. [These abbreviations are explained overleaf.] The former is a syntactically marked formula, involving exclamatory word order and intonation; the latter by contrast reduces the syntactic pattern to its minimum elements. Whereas a rhetorical pattern such as pattern 4 can be regarded as emphasising the addressee- or interaction-oriented characteristics of compliments, the minimal pattern represented by formula 5 could be regarded as attenuating or hedging on this function. It is

Table 1   Syntactic patterns of compliments according to speaker sex

Syntactic formula		Female No.	%	Male No.	%
1a	NP BE (INT) ADJ	121 ⎫	42	51 ⎫	40
b	BE LOOKing	19 ⎬		13 ⎬	
	e.g. *That coat is really great*				
	You're looking terrific				
2	I(INT) LIKE NP				
	e.g. *I simply love that skirt*	59	18	21	13
3a	PRO BE a (INT) ADJ NP				
	e.g. *That's a very nice coat*				
or		38	11	25	16
b	PRO BE (INT) (a) ADJ NP				
	e.g. *That's really great juice*				
4	What (a) (ADJ) NP!				
	e.g. *What lovely children!*	26	8	2	1
5	(INT) ADJ (NP)				
	e.g. *Really cool ear-rings*	17	5	19	12
6	Isn't NP ADJ!				
	e.g. *Isn't this food wonderful!*	5	2	1	1
Total		285	86	132	82

NP = noun phrase
BE = the verb *be*
INT = intensifier
ADJ = adjective
PRO = pronoun

interesting to note that there are no examples of pattern 4 in male–male interactions, providing further support for the association of this pattern with female complimenting behaviour.

In another study of American English, Herbert (1990, p. 206) found that only women used the stronger form *I love X* (compared to *I like X*) and that they used it most often to other women. And in students' written reviews of each other's work, Donna Johnson and Duane Roen (1992) noted that women used significantly more intensifiers (such as *really, very, particularly*) than men did, and that they intensified their compliments most when writing to other women.

Cross-cultural differences in complimenting behaviour

... Paying compliments and responding to them appropriately is an aspect of learning English which can be troublesome for those from different cultural backgrounds. Indonesians in the United States, for instance, comment on the very high frequency of compliments between Americans (Wolfson, 1981). Malaysian students in New Zealand are similarly surprised at how often New Zealanders pay each other compliments, while for their part New Zealanders tend to feel Americans pay far too many compliments and, judging by their own norms, assume that American compliments are often insincere. South Africans apparently respond similarly to American complimenting norms (Herbert, 1986; Herbert and Straight, 1989).

The patterns of cross-sex complimenting behaviour described above obviously compound the potential for miscommunication and offence. Women from cultures where compliments are rare, experience them as embarrassing. They often respond inappropriately to compliments from native speakers of English by disagreeing or rejecting them. On the other hand, they may not offer enough compliments, by the standard of native speakers, especially to their English-speaking women friends. Conversely, men from different cultures may embarrass their English-speaking male friends by the frequency of their compliments.

Wolfson (1983, p. 90) suggests that in America the safest compliments to offer to strangers relate to 'possessions (e.g. *That's a beautiful car*)' or to 'some aspect of performance intended to be publicly observed (*I really enjoyed your talk yesterday*)'. This advice appears to be particularly useful when complimenting male addressees. But it would not be appropriate in some Polynesian cultures, as the following example illustrates.

Context	Pakeha New Zealand woman to Samoan friend whom she was visiting.
Complimenter	What an unusual necklace. It's beautiful.
Recipient	Please take it.

The complimenter was very embarrassed at being offered as a gift the object she had admired. This was perfectly predictable, however, to anyone familiar with Samoan cultural norms with respect to complimenting behaviour.

The exchange in this example occurred in New Zealand where there is a relatively large Samoan population. When sociopragmatic norms differ, cross-cultural misunderstandings involving compliments are perfectly possible between ethnic groups within one country. There is abundant anecdotal evidence, for instance, of embarrassment experienced by Maori people in New Zealand by what they perceive as compliments from Pakeha people which go 'over the top'. The relative strength of what Geoffrey Leech (1983, p. 132) calls the Modesty Maxim may differ quite markedly between groups.

As illustrated in this paper, most compliments are formulaic: they draw on a very restricted range of vocabulary and a small number of grammatical patterns. The linguistic features of compliments are easy to acquire. Learning how to use compliments appropriately is not so easy, however. Each speech community has norms of use involving the relative frequency of compliments, the kinds of topics which may be the focus of a compliment and the contexts in which compliments are appropriate, mandatory or perhaps even proscribed. These norms interact with the gender of speakers and addressees, so that knowing who to compliment, how, and when is a sophisticated aspect of sociolinguistic competence. *You look wonderful tonight!* may be a welcome compliment from your partner, but your boss may just find it embarrassing.

References

HERBERT, R.K. and STRAIGHT, H.S. (1989) 'Compliment rejection vs compliment avoidance', *Language and Communication*, 9, pp. 35–47.

HERBERT, R.K. (1986) 'Say "thank you" – or something', *American Speech*, vol. 61, pp. 76–88

HERBERT, R.K. (1990) 'Sex-based differences in compliment behaviour', *Language in Society*, vol. 19, pp. 201–24.

HOLMES, J. (1986) 'Compliments and compliment responses in New Zealand English', *Anthropological Linguistics*, vol. 28, no. 4, pp. 485–508.

HOLMES, J. (1988) 'Paying compliments: a sex-preferential positive politeness strategy' *Journal of Pragmatics*, vol. 12, no. 3, pp. 445–65.

HOLMES, J. (1990) 'Politeness strategies in New Zealand women's speech' in BELL, A. and HOLMES, J. (eds) *New Zealand Ways of Speaking English*, Clevedon, Avon, Multilingual Matters.

JOHNSON, D.M. and ROEN, D.H. (1992) 'Complimenting and involvement in peers reviews: gender variation', *Language in Society*, vol. 21, no. 1, pp. 27–56.

LEECH, G. (1983) *Principles of Pragmatics*, London, Longman.

LEWANDOWSKA-TOMASZCZYK, B. (1989) 'Praising and complimenting' in OLESKY, W. (ed.) *Contrastive Pragmatics*, Amsterdam, John Benjamins.

MANES, J. (1983) 'Compliments: a mirror of cultural values' in WOLFSON, N. and JUDD, E. (eds) *Sociolinguistics and Second Language Acquisition*, Rowley, Mass., Newbury House.

SMITH, P. (1985) *Language, the Sexes and Society*, Oxford, Blackwell.

TANNEN, D. (1991) *You Just Don't Understand*, London, Virago.

WOLFSON, N. (1981) 'Compliments in cross-cultural perspective', *TESOL Quarterly*, vol. 15, no. 2, pp. 117–24.

WOLFSON, N. (1983) 'An empirically based analysis of complimenting in American English' in WOLFSON, N. and JUDD, E. (eds) *Sociolinguistics and Second Language Acquisition*, Rowley, Mass., Newbury House.

WOLFSON, N. (1984) 'Pretty is as pretty does', *Applied Linguistics*, vol. 5, no. 3, pp. 236–44.

Source: Holmes, 1994, pp. 39–43

Reading C
FEAR OF FAT: INTERPRETATIVE REPERTOIRES AND IDEOLOGICAL DILEMMAS

Margaret Wetherell

I examine here the connections between people's accounts of themselves in everyday talk, and broader social and cultural beliefs and values. These connections are not straightforward. When trying to make sense of a social or political issue, people move between different ideological perspectives and this variability is closely tied to the ways in which personal identity is constructed.

The everyday talk I consider comes from a study of young British women discussing eating, dieting and body image (White and Wetherell, 1988). This study involved in-depth interviews with a small sample of twelve- and seventeen-year-old girls. Our aim was to look for patterns in representations and arguments *across* the interviews, in the way these white, mostly middle-class, young women interpreted their eating habits, their social situation and their own and others' actions.

Interpretative repertoires

Transcription convention

• (.) means a brief pause

Extract 1

C   I remember reading, it was in *Woman* or something, about this woman who lost so much weight and she was absolutely massive and she went down to about nine stone and I sat there and thought – 'You cow – oooh'.

Extract 2

E   I just eat everything. I feel terrible about it afterwards. There's these em Food Direct places that have opened. You just go around with a bag and I spend an absolute fortune in them. It's just recently – it's an absolutely terrible thing to do. I feel guilty afterwards, but I can't do anything about it. No will power.

Extract 3

A   It's just society – that the media says you have to wear these figure hugging things so you've got to be really thin.

Interviewer   What do you think about that? Does it work do you think?

A   It probably does with some people.

B   I don't really (.) well it would work maybe but people would sort of look at it and it (.) wouldn't really go in.

A   I don't think people really look at adverts so much.

Interviewer   You don't think they do?

A   Not in a magazine – no.

B   They don't really bother so much about them. I would never think about the advert. It just doesn't get through to me.

A   No it wouldn't bother me. It would just wash over my head.

When reading interview transcripts like these, two features generally become clear. First, people's accounts of events, of their motives, and the reasons for their actions are flexible and shift from context to context. People are inconsistent; they set up one version of events and then, as the communication situation changes, this version alters. Secondly, however, this variation often occurs between relatively internally consistent, bounded discursive themes. It is these themes which we call *interpretative repertoires* (Potter and Wetherell, 1987; Wetherell and Potter, 1988). As we read the transcripts from these young women, we were impressed by a regular line of argument which occurred many times across the interviews and can been seen in Extract 3 above. The young women are talking with the interviewer about social pressures found in the media and elsewhere for women to be thin and beautiful. They are dismissive of these pressures. Participant A describes this as *just* society and notes how these images *wash over my head*.

The girls are stressing the desirability of being seen as an individual separate from society. Indeed the devalued subject position in this context was to admit to being influenced by others. In these parts of the interviews the young women were

at pains to distance themselves from the identity of 'fashion victim'. An interpretative repertoire is a discursive theme like this which often works through
distinctive tropes (*it's just ... the media*), which sets up contained subject positions
or voices sometimes in opposition to each other (strong individual versus fashion
victim), and which develops recognizable and bounded links of arguments
(claims and statements).

I also stated that people's accounts are variable and inconsistent – that people
move between interpretative repertoires. To illustrate this point, take a look at
Extract 1. This extract also indicates a discursive theme evident across the
interviews. Here C is expressing admiration and envy of women who lose weight
(*You cow – oooh*). In this context, to be thin is enviable, to be fat is problematic. The
desire to become thin is taken as obvious and reasonable and this assumption
fuels the logic of the anecdote. This type of discourse which attributes positive
characteristics to being thin and negative traits to being fat presents an alternative
interpretative repertoire, an alternative way of making sense, to the 'just the
media' repertoire noted above.

We now have two possible versions for formulating a sense of identity. The
young women interviewed could set up an account which endorsed and displayed
their credentials as individuals, as people who are not swayed by social influences,
or they could speak about themselves and others in ways which endorsed the value
of thinness and the problem of fat. Most of those interviewed did both; they
moved in and out of these repertoires at different points in the interviews. Here,
for example, is another extract from the interview with C and D, where they are
discussing a caption from an article in a slimming magazine:

Extract 4

Interviewer	This caption here says, 'The day I can wear my bikini with pride will be the happiest day of my life'.
C	That is sooo stupid.
Interviewer	Why?
C	Because if they want to wear a flipping bikini why can't they just wear it?
D	And say – oh to hell with everybody else.

The response from C at this point is to criticize the desires of the woman in the
article. In Extract 1, however, C was immersed in a different logic, one where the
value of thinness and the problem caused by fatness was obvious.

In drawing attention to the variability in C's talk as she moves from one
account to another, I am not wanting to suggest that C should be taken to task for
this inconsistency. This movement between versions as people talk and communicate is typical of everyday talk. Shortly, I want to argue that the discovery of such
variability is crucial for understanding the way ideological positions are commonly expressed in everyday talk. First, I want briefly to introduce two other
interpretative repertoires evident in the transcripts from this study.

A further type of talk or repertoire can be seen in Extract 2 above. The subject
position here is the weak and wicked woman who gives into temptation. E is
confessing to behaviour she presents as *terrible*. The morality is driven by a logic
which suggests that bodies and their illicit desires should be disciplined. To fail to
do so is to take up a negative subject position as a 'sinner'.

The final major theme or repertoire in the young women's talk is based on
the importance of the 'natural self' and 'natural behaviour'. A key element here
is the image of a pattern of eating regulated by natural appetite so that, ideally,

one eats and wants to eat only the amount that the body actually requires. Implicit, too, is a notion of equilibrium or balance so that appetite should adjust to maintain this balance. Some of this reasoning can be seen below.

Extract 5

F   I don't get hungry. That's the point you see. I've eaten
        so much the other days that, em, there's an excess
        amount – whatever. Because most people do eat too
        much anyway. We don't need as much food as we do eat,
        so I find that when I'm eating and I'm not particularly
        hungry I think no – no way – I'm just going to stop
        eating for a while. (.) I've actually got quite a small
        appetite so I can't eat much.

Related to this 'natural' repertoire is the argument that people should diet only for legitimate health reasons, not for illegitimate desires to be thin. The young women interviewed were particularly likely to describe their own dieting in these terms. They dieted not for fashion but because, they said, it was healthier to be thinner. We can see here how the 'needs' of the body have been redefined once more – these needs (for less food than we think we require) are to be listened to rather than struggled against. Now the body tells us what we should do.

What I have tried to show is some of the range of ways in which young women make sense of eating, dieting, fatness and thinness. As we have seen, their accounts privilege some subject positions – being your own woman, being thin, being guided by 'natural' appetites, being a moral self with will power. A dialogue is set up with other possible subject positions which are disavowed, undercut, or the subject of confession – being a person who is influenced by others' opinions, who gives into temptation, being guided by 'unnatural' appetites, failing to control one's body, being fat. I argued that the snippets analysed above and much of the rest of the interview material could be fitted into four, recognizably different, broad interpretative repertoires – an individualistic repertoire (*just society*), a 'personological' repertoire concerning fatness and thinness (*you cow – oooh*), a confessional repertoire (*it's an absolutely terrible thing to do*) and a repertoire of the natural body (*we don't need as much food as we do eat*).

Ideological dilemmas

So far I have paid close attention to the text, identifying interpretative repertoires and their associated subject positions. Now I want to consider some of the implications for the analysis of ideology and everyday talk (Billig et al., 1988). The term ideology suggests that interpretative repertoires have a broader social significance. It is not a random matter that young women have come to talk about their bodies and the process of eating in certain ways. There is some connection between this talk and the general position of women in society (see Bordo, 1990; Chernin, 1983; Lawrence, 1987; Orbach, 1978).

As I suggested earlier, discourse is not consistent and coherent but variable, made up of a patchwork of heterogeneous resources. One very obvious ideological dilemma for young women is set up between the subject position of the thin women in the 'personological' repertoire of fatness and thinness (see Extract 1 – *you cow – oooh*), and the subject position of the strong individual against society in the individualistic repertoire. These two identities can be seen as being in debate and disputation. The dilemma is this – if you view the issue of body shape and eating through the repertoire of individualism then it becomes a betrayal of individual autonomy and a sign of weakness to give in to social pressure. How can you account, then, for wanting to be thin?

For our group of young women the dilemma presented by this clash of repertoires tended to be resolved, when it emerged in the interviews, through the repertoire of natural bodily processes, or the image of 'natural' appetites. It is healthy living, rather than fashion, which comes to dictate thinness. The young women typically would say that they wanted to be thin not because they were swayed by the media but because it was natural and healthy to be so.

Recourse to this method of explaining emerged most noticeably in relation to talk about dieting. Most of those interviewed were extremely reluctant to describe their often severe regimes of restraint as diets. Indeed, to admit to dieting can also imply taking up the subject position of a fat self as well as the position of being concerned with what the world thinks. Thus, typically, one young woman said:

Extract 6

H   Well I sort of stopped eating but I, I wouldn't call it a
               diet, it's just 'Oh my God I think I've been eating too
               much lately – I'm going to stop'.

Participants frequently described restraint as motivated by a 'natural' process of regaining balance. They are not dieting because of social pressure but because of a totally personal decision that one is eating more than is naturally good and healthy to eat. With the 'natural' repertoire the dilemma can be solved in quite a skilful way. Stringent measures are taken to match the ideal, but these measures don't indicate the sway of the media, or that you are a fat self who needs to diet; you remain an autonomous individual with an independent character.

The 'solution', of course, is one which is common now in women's magazines, which similarly emphasize 'health' over cosmetic justifications. From a feminist perspective, however, this resolution has been gained at the expense of mystifying social processes, turning cultural imperatives into natural and biological ones. In this discourse thinness does not become a social or cultural imperative but is represented as an obvious value in itself, an unquestioned standard which is difficult and dangerous to think about, criticize or deconstruct because to do so contradicts a dominant repertoire in which the subject is constituted as free agent in control of her life, contrasted with others who are victims of mere social pressure.

A similar type of dilemma sustains the confessional repertoire evident in Extract 2. It is an excellent thing to be thin and it is an excellent thing to be autonomous. How, then, can one make sense of failure defined in this talk as overeating or being fat? Typically the young women blamed themselves as 'weak and wicked women'. Failure was presented as a failure of will, of personality. Hence the admissions of guilt. Fat becomes constituted as a personal attribute, for which one is accountable, not a social judgement.

There seem to be three main effects of this combination of repertoires which from a feminist perspective could be seen as dangerous for young women. First, eating and dieting are desocialized and naturalized. Secondly, the issue is pathologized into narratives of character weakness and sinfulness; and, finally, women's resistance or struggle against oppressive practices is undercut and subverted as they attempt to be 'their own women'.

In working through the logic of the young women's talk about this topic, I have tried to develop a critique and to show why this combination of repertoires can be described as ideological; why, that is, this discourse entrenches young women in disadvantageous cycles. It is important to stress, finally, that in criticizing this logic I am not criticizing the young women, or implying they should know better. I am suggesting that the pathology lies in the collective social resources available for making sense. Those we interviewed struggled as best they could to construct some positive options and identities, most notably through the 'individualistic repertoire'. The irony is that this struggle to maximize the autonomy of the individual against society and to resist social pressure also seemed to entangle them more deeply in the ideological knots I have tried to identify.

Acknowledgement

The interviews described in this reading were conducted by Shuna White.

References

BILLIG, M., CONDOR, S., EDWARDS, D., GANE, M., MIDDLETON, D. and RADLEY, A. (1988) *Ideological Dilemmas: a social psychology of everyday thinking*, London, Sage.

BORDO, S. (1990) 'Reading the slender body' in JACOBUS, M., KELLER, E.F. and SHUTTLEWORTH, S. (eds) *Body/Politics: women and the discourse of science*, New York, Routledge.

CHERNIN, K. (1983) *Womansize: the tyranny of slenderness*, London, Women's Press.

LAWRENCE, M. (ed.) (1987) *Fed up and Hungry: women, oppression and food*, London, Women's Press.

ORBACH, S. (1978) *Fat is a Feminist Issue*, London, Hamlyn.

POTTER, J. and WETHERELL, M. (1987) *Discourse and Social Psychology*, London, Sage.

WETHERELL, M. and POTTER, J. (1988) 'Discourse analysis and the identification of interpretative repertoires' in ANTAKI, C. (ed.) *Analysing Everyday Explanation*, London, Sage.

WHITE, S. and WETHERELL, M. (1988) 'Fear of Fat: young women talking about eating and dieting', paper presented at the BPS Social Psychology Section Annual Conference, University of Kent.

This reading was specially commissioned for this book.

2 LITERACY PRACTICES IN ENGLISH

Mike Baynham and Janet Maybin

2.1 INTRODUCTION

Chapter 1 focused on spoken English in everyday situations. In this chapter we turn to written English, and its use across a variety of social and cultural contexts. Written English of course includes a wide range of texts, from the literature canon and the laws of the land, down to street signs and scribbled messages to friends. We start by examining the linguistic differences between written and spoken English and then go on to show that the ways English is used in different kinds of text, and the ways we read these texts, are strongly influenced by social factors. The writer's purposes, the relationship between writer and reader, and the social conventions and practices surrounding the text all shape our use and interpretation of language. In this chapter we use examples of different kinds of reading and writing from monolingual and multilingual settings to show what people do with literacy in English, and also what they make of what they do.

2.2 SPEECH AND WRITING

There are certain immediately obvious differences between speech and writing. Spoken language often includes hesitations, self-corrections and interruptions, and part of the meaning is conveyed through intonation and gestures. Written English is organized along certain standard conventions concerning spelling, punctuation, and the organization of the text into sentences and paragraphs. But apart from these features, is there something about our use of English vocabulary and grammar in writing which is somehow different from speech?

Activity 2.1   *(Allow about 5 minutes)*

Which of the two extracts below would you say was more likely originally to have been spoken, and which written? Why?

1   It probably means if you invest in something to do with trains, it means that you'll have to leave your money there and you probably won't be able to get your money back for quite a long time.

2   Investment placed in a rail facility implies a long-term commitment.

(My comments are in the text that follows.)

Some features of spoken English are usually lost in transcription. Nevertheless, although it is possible to imagine some contexts where (1) is written and (2) spoken, it is much more likely that you decided the longer, more informal sounding first extract was originally spoken and the more concise, formal second extract was written.

What are the precise linguistic differences between the two pieces of language in Activity 2.1 which make them so obviously 'speech' and 'writing'? Some suggestions follow.

Vocabulary

Because of the different ways in which spoken and written language is produced (we can take hours to compose a formal piece of writing, drafting and redrafting, finding the most concise terms and editing out repetitions), it has been suggested that written texts contain a wider vocabulary than spoken language and more polysyllabic words – such as *investment, facility* and *commitment* in extract 2. All three of these words are lexical borrowings: they come from Latin and do not belong to the basic Anglo-Saxon word stock. Spoken English has a higher proportion of Anglo-Saxon words, and more repetition of individual words (notice the repetition of *you, probably* and *money* in extract 1).

Lexical density

Linguists have found that spoken English tends to have many more words which knit the text together (called **grammatical items**) in proportion to words which carry content (**lexical items**).

Because words change their meaning and function in different contexts, the distinction between grammatical and lexical items is not always clear-cut. Generally speaking, however, grammatical items in English maintain the relationships between the lexical items and keep the text together. They include:

- articles – *a, an, the*
- pronouns – *he, she, you, them*
- most prepositions – *in, beside*
- conjunctions – *and, because, while*
- some classes of adverbs – *usually, often*
- certain auxiliary verbs – *have, was* (as in *have left, was going*, etc.)

Grammatical items belong to a closed system in the language in the sense that we do not invent new prepositions or conjunctions. They are part of the grammatical system we use to make meaning. Lexical items, on the other hand, are an open system of nouns, verbs, adjectives and so on, which can be added to in response to new ideas and new technology (Halliday, 1985). In extract 1 the lexical terms are *means, invest, trains, leave, money, get, long, time* (eight items), and there are 30 grammatical items. In extract 2, however, there are seven lexical items (*investment, placed, rail, facility, implies, long-term, commitment*) and only three grammatical ones (*in, a* and *a*). Because the proportion of lexical to grammatical items is usually higher in written texts, they are said to have a higher lexical density.

Nominalization

If you compare extracts 1 and 2, you'll see that the verb *invest* in extract 1 has been replaced by a related noun *investment* in extract 2. This business of replacing a process by a thing has been termed **nominalization**, and is said to be particularly characteristic of formal written texts. Halliday (1987) comments that spoken language tells a story in verbs, while written language tells it in nouns. Nominalizations make a text more lexically dense.

Written texts may be more precise in terms of choice of vocabulary, but the use of nominalizations often means that information about processes, about who did what to whom, is lost. For example, in a clause from a formal written text such as 'The reinstatement of the chairman was not well received' we do not know who reinstated the chairman or why, or how he came to lose his chair in the first place. The passive tense, in this case *was not well received*, is also used much more commonly in written than in spoken English, and similarly conceals who is the agent (the person or people who are unhappy about the reinstatement).

Grammatical intricacy

Written English is often thought of as more complex than the spoken language; for instance, writing frequently contains (embedded) subordinate clauses (e.g. 'The letter *which had been delivered the previous week* was subsequently lost'). However, Halliday (1987) points out that although spoken language may appear simpler, in fact there are often complex grammatical relationships between clauses. Compare extract 2, which consists of a single main clause, with the string of short clauses in extract 1:

(a) It probably means

(b) if you invest in something to do with trains

(c) it means

(d) that you'll have to leave your money there

(e) and you probably won't be able to get your money back for quite a long time

The spoken extract seems to show the effects of planning 'on the hoof'. The speaker begins *It probably means*, then reformulates *if you invest* ... From here to the end of the utterance there is a matrix clause *it means* with two types of dependent clause:

*   (b) is a conditional dependent clause;
*   (d) and (e) both function like a direct object of *it means*.

Modality

One final contrast you may have noticed between the two texts is that even though they are dealing with the same topic, the first seems more personal, informal and subjective. For instance, the speaker's relationship to the listener is expressed more explicitly (through the use of *you*), and there are expressions of vagueness (*something to do with, probably means*), and modal auxiliary verbs (*have to, won't be able to*). **Modal forms** express the speaker's attitudes, towards him or herself, listeners or subject matter (Fowler and Kress, 1979), and are much more common in spoken English, with its direct, face-to-face interactional purposes, than in the more 'distant' medium of formal writing.

The topic of modality is also dealt with in the first book in this series, *English: history, diversity and change* (Graddol et al. (eds), 1996).

Activity 2.2   *(Allow about 15 minutes)*

The following sentence comes from an article by a student in his school magazine, reviewing the activities of the student dance company over the previous year. What features of the text make it much more likely to have been written than spoken?

> The Dance Company's performances showed a deep understanding and respect for their work which was executed with the utmost professionalism and focus.

(*Stantonbury Campus News*, issue 12, summer 1995)

(We would analyse the lexical items in this text as *Dance, Company, performances, showed, deep, understanding, respect, work, executed, professionalism, focus.*)

2.3   TEXT AND CONTEXT

As we explained at the beginning of the last section, there is an enormous range of different ways in which English is used in writing, and the linguistic differences discussed above come from contrasting somewhat idealized, 'typical' examples of informal speech with formal writing. In fact, distinctions between the two kinds of language use are not always so clear. When we start to look at a range of texts we find that many examples of writing contain a mix of 'oral' and 'literate' features, depending on the formality of the writing, the relationship between the writer and reader, and how ephemeral or permanent the text is intended to be. In order to understand the meaning and significance of any text in English we need to look beyond the words on the page, to consider the purposes of the readers and writers involved, and the social and cultural aspects of their literacy activity.

Let's look now at another text which raises these issues directly.

Activity 2.3   *(Allow about 10 minutes)*

Figure 2.1 is an extract from a letter written by an Indian father to his daughter in England. In what ways does it conform to the features of written English discussed above? What additional kinds of information might you need in order to understand the full meaning of the letter?

In Figure 2.1 the underlined item in Sanskrit in the middle of the top of the page is *Om Sri Ram*, which means 'In God's name'. Blessings in Kannada (the state language of the south Indian state of Karnataka) for each member of the family then follow: 'May you live long, may you live like a king' for males, and 'May you live long, may you be prosperous' for females. The last two lines in Kannada read: 'To all of you, abundant good wishes. We expect by the grace of God that both you and we are well, and now let me commence the letter.'

The English part of this letter (starting with *Well*) uses fairly simple repeated verbal structures with a lexical density somewhere between that of extracts 1 and 2 in Activity 2.1 (38 lexical items and 47 grammatical ones). The phrases *eagerly awaiting, latest photos* and *erect posture* all suggest the formality of writing, but the numerous references to people and feelings are closer to the subjective involvement of oral communication. The blessings at the beginning seem much more formal, and this reflects the generally more formal style in which letters in Kannada are written. Notice how the *Well* at the beginning of the English section signals not just a switch in language, but also a switch to the chattier, more informal conversational style of personal letters in English.

Apart from the additional family information we need to have in order to understand the references to particular individuals in this letter, we also need to

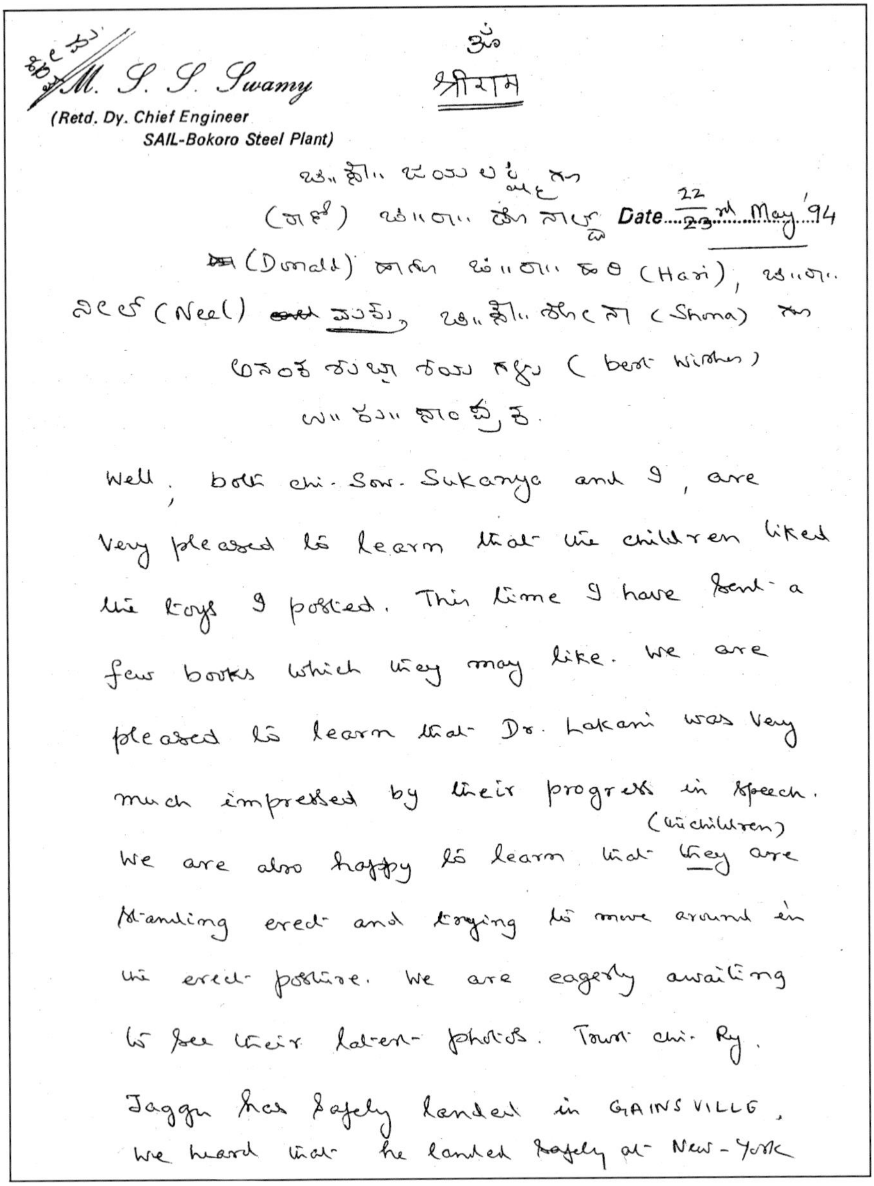

M. S. S. Swamy
(Retd. Dy. Chief Engineer
SAIL-Bokoro Steel Plant)

श्रीराम

Date 22nd May '94

(Donald) ... (Hari), ...

(Neel) ... (Shona) ...

(best wishes)

Well, both chi. Sow. Sukanya and I, are very pleased to learn that the children liked the toys I posted. This time I have sent a few books which they may like. We are pleased to learn that Dr. Lakani was very much impressed by their progress in speech. (the children)
We are also happy to learn that they are standing erect and trying to move around in the erect posture. We are eagerly awaiting to see their latest photos. Town chi. Ry.

Jaggu has safely landed in GAINSVILLE, we heard that he landed safely at New-York

Figure 2.1   First page of a letter from M.S.S. Swami to his daughter Jayalakshmi

(We are grateful to G.D. Jayalakshmi for permission to reproduce this letter.)

know something about letter-writing conventions in Kannada in order to understand the significance of the phrases written in this language. For instance, someone receiving a letter in Kannada always looks first at the top left-hand corner to check for the word 'safe' (as shown in the margin), which indicates that the letter does not contain news of a death. If the corner is empty, then the reader knows to expect bad news. The blessings and greetings at the beginning of Jaya's letter are those usually given by a higher status person to a lower status one (e.g. a father to a daughter), and are set out appropriately for everyone in the family depending on whether they are male (in this case, Donald and his sons Neel and

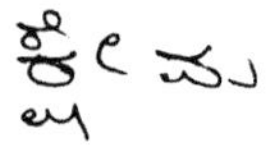

= safe in Kannada

Hari) or female (Jaya and her daughter Shona). This is a standard formula for the openings of letters in Kannada, but it has a special significance in Jaya's case.

Jaya is a fluent Kannada speaker, but because her family moved to northern India when she was still a child, she was taught to read and write Hindi and English, rather than Kannada, at school. When she left home to go to university in Hyderabad, Jaya was keen to strengthen her original language roots and asked her father to teach her some written Kannada through the letters he wrote to her. He decided that the opening formulaic phrases might be a useful place to start. Although Jaya has never become fully literate in Kannada, her father has continued to write to her in this way. Some years after leaving university, Jaya married a Scotsman and settled in England. Her father's use of the Kannada phrases now has an added importance in reminding his daughter of their shared cultural background and of her own efforts while at university to reaffirm both this background and her relationship with her father through letter writing.

Here we have a fairly informal personal letter (with some formal features) passing between close family members with much shared knowledge and history. In order to read and understand the letter we do not just need to be literate in English and Kannada, we also need to know about the social conventions of letter writing in these two languages, and how Jaya and her father use and adapt these conventions to pursue individual purposes to do with their own identity and relationships.

To understand any text in English we need to know something about its context (for instance, whether it is a personal letter received in the post, part of a business correspondence, a newspaper article, a work from a literature syllabus, a legal treaty) and about the conventional practices which people usually follow in engaging with such texts. Some texts, particularly those from a genre with which we are not familiar, may require a conscious struggle not just to decode the words, but also to try to understand unfamiliar ground rules. When presented with a clause in a legal agreement, for example, or a complex assignment set by a tutor, our response needs to be conventionally presented to comply with legal or educational ground rules respectively. At the other extreme, we read and interact with numerous texts as part of our daily life without being particularly conscious of all the knowledge about social and cultural practices which we are using in the process. Think, for instance, about the different texts you encounter on your regular route to work, school or shopping.

Activity 2.4   *(Allow about 10 minutes)*

There are further photographs of street texts in the colour section of this book.

The photographs in Figure 2.2 were taken in streets in Singapore, India and Britain. What are the main purposes of each photographed text (for example, to persuade, to entertain, to inform)? Which texts carry the greatest authority, and are some more legitimate than others? How far does the writing medium and the context of each text influence your answers?

In order to investigate further the idea of the street as a textscape, you might like to extend this activity: note down the written texts that are found in the public space of your local shopping area. What media are they written in (type-set/neon/handwritten)? What languages and language varieties do they represent? Is there any attempt to regulate explicitly what counts as legitimate text? Are there examples of slogans and graffiti and other 'illegitimate' texts?

Singapore

Lancaster

Singapore

Singapore (English, Tamil and Chinese)

Bangalore

Bangalore (English and Kannada). The Kannada phrases translate (top to bottom) as: 'with love', 'we will build' and 'this world'

Lancaster

Figure 2.2   Street texts from Singapore, Bangalore (India) and Lancaster (Britain)

2.4   READING AND WRITING PRACTICES IN ENGLISH

Think about your own uses of reading and writing in English and other languages. You are reading now. Are you sitting comfortably? Where are you reading? Are you alone in a room, in a library, on a bus, in a doctor's waiting room? How are you reading? Are you reading for study, marking the margin of the page, underlining with highlighter, writing notes as you read? What other kinds of reading have you done during the day? Think also of your own various different uses of writing, at home and at work. Is there a division of labour within your family in terms of the different writing tasks which need to be done? Do you ever write collaboratively with others, or on their behalf?

Activity 2.5   *(Allow about 15 minutes)*

Look through the Mass Observation Archive extract below and note the different uses of writing described by the speaker. How do these compare with your own?

In the extract a correspondent for the archive is talking about writing. The Mass Observation Archive at the University of Sussex runs a research project in Britain which asks numbers of 'ordinary' people to write in regularly about their everyday activities and about their thoughts concerning key national issues and events of the day. The aim is to document unofficial everyday experience, which is not necessarily recorded in history books. Mass Observation began to collect information during the 1930s and the archive has been sending out regular 'directives' (giving topics for writing) to people all over Britain since 1981. In the extract the researcher (D) is interviewing a regular current correspondent (W).

D   How do you find the time to write for the Mass Ob[servation] project?

W   [*Laughs*] Well at the moment I do it – when it [the directive] arrives I read through it and I think about it at odd moments you know like waiting for the train or on the train going up to work and sort of scribble bits down on bits of paper here there and everywhere and then when I've got the time, which might not be for – nearly 'til the next directive is due, I sit down and write it all out. So – one day, yeah. [*Laughs*]

D   And do you write it in this room, or in another room in the house?

W   No I'm usually sitting in the chair and there's probably football or something on the telly that I don't want to watch so I write it then. [*Laughs*]

D   Do people mind you sitting there writing away –

W   Oh no they're quite used to it now – I usually do my books [household accounts] in the chair, the finances and a crossword or something, you know – I'm not usually sitting watching television, I'm usually doing something else as well …

D   Do you – do most of the kind of writing and things in the house, I mean like the books that you talked about, or correspondences and –

W   Yeah, writing letters, everything, yeah … I don't very often now but I used to write letters to the newspaper and belong to other groups, or – and – yes I read all the mail that comes in and answer the letters and everything … other people are just not comfortable with writing – I know my dad never was – my mum always wrote the letters. If he did sit down to write a letter he was asking how to spell every other word, and she said to him 'It's laziness with you.' And he said, 'I can't write and think at the same time.' [*Laughter*] And my husband leaves it to me to write all the letters – he'll sign them but he leaves it to me to write the letters. And again it's laziness because he can do it …

D   – And I also remember from reading your literacy diary that at work you seem to do a lot of reading and writing with other people.

W   Yes, formulating training notes – so with each group, with each – might only be one person – but with each section I would be writing and writing and writing – is this what we want, is this what you're saying we're getting, to make sure … if I have a meeting like I'm having a meeting with you now, then I would go and write it up afterwards and say do you agree this is what the meeting was about, before I then started to incorporate it into testing or procedures or so on. And then they could come back and say, well no I didn't quite agree to that point, or they come back and say yes, but you missed out that I agreed to more than that, and you've left out this – so that it's to-ing and fro-ing the whole time.

(Interview transcript 2 November 1992, Mass Observation Archive Project (W632))

Was it clear to you even before she mentioned her husband that the correspondent in the extract was a woman? If so, why? Are there gender differences in the literary practices within your own household?

It is common practice in many British households for the women to do most of the letter writing to relatives, remembering birthdays within the family network and so on. People also have distinctive patterns for organizing communication between members of the household and for organizing the many texts which come into the house. For example: both of us, in addition to using a diary to communicate with ourselves and organize our work life, use a family calendar on the wall at home to note down important family appointments and dates.

Activity 2.6 *(Allow about 10 minutes)*

A recent Australian newspaper article facetiously pointed to the role of the fridge door in household communication. The list below shows what I (Mike Baynham) found on my fridge door this morning. (Some items were stuck on to the door and some were attached by magnets.)

- a recipe for bread;
- details of a local vet;
- a picture of a stegosaurus with the word 'stegosaurus';
- details of a local estate agent and calendar;
- details of a removal company;
- a Christmas greeting with a collage of photographs from friends in Scotland;
- a child's party invitation;
- a child's plastic magnetized alphabet, jumbled on the fridge, with one word 'pad' spelled out;
- an advertisement for an antibiotic medicine recommended for respiratory infections.

Figure 2.3
Everyday literacy practices involve
a wide range of texts, purposes
and interactions with others

I had no idea before I did this exercise of the range of texts I would find. All were in English. Is the fridge a focus for written material in your household? If not, where would written material typically be gathered? One of the people who read this chapter in draft form remarked that in houses where she had lived 30 years ago, letters, bills and so on were kept behind a clock in the middle of the mantelpiece. If you are reading this book at home, put it down and check where you gather current texts in your house. What might this collection of texts (on a noticeboard, behind the clock, or whatever) tell a stranger about the typical social activities of your household members?

These kinds of text and the various different reading and writing activities you are regularly involved in, reflect the different '**literacy domains**' within your life – for example, home, workplace, school, shops, bureaucracies, the street. These different domains are associated with different kinds of text and practices, and sometimes in multilingual communities with different languages. Domains are of course not totally discrete and in fact literacy activities in English and other languages may cross the boundaries: a child brings her English-language schoolwork home to a house where Panjabi is the primary means of communication; a letter from a government department in Standard English is read at the kitchen table and discussed in a nonstandard variety; a personal letter is written in a mix of Kannada and English during a tea break at work.

Activity 2.7 *(Reading A)*

Read 'Multiliteracy practices and values: an ethnographic account of a Panjabi family in Britain' by Mukul Saxena (Reading A). This is an extract from a more extensive ethnographic study of literacy carried out by Mukul Saxena in Southall, London.

Note the range of purposes of the different members of this family in reading and writing texts in various languages as they move through the day, and the social nature of many of the literacy events.

What differences do you notice between the use of English by different family members in their literacy practices? In what ways are these associated with different literacy domains?

It may be useful to draw up a grid like the one below:

Family member	Text	Language	Reading/writing purpose	Other people involved

Comment

You will probably have found that the grandmother and mother read and write mainly in Hindi or Panjabi, while the grandfather pursues his cultural and political interests through reading and writing in Urdu, Panjabi, Hindi and English. The father's employment, his involvement in the management of the temple and his interest in national and international news all involve reading and writing in English (as well as other languages). Notice too how he acts as a **literacy mediator** in translating the note in English from his son's school into Panjabi for his wife. The young son is the family member most consistently involved in English literacy, through his attendance at school, but he is also exposed to, and familiar with, practices in other languages. School and the workplace are literacy domains where English is dominant; Hindi is the main language for literacy practices at the temple; and at home there is a mixture of Panjabi (family letter), Hindi (novel, magazine) and English (child's book, newspaper).

Reading A shows how people's literacy practices are tied up with social and work activities, and are used in maintaining and developing their social networks. Family and social networks can also provide support for people who have particular difficulties with literacy, as was found in a study of people's writing practices in Lancaster, in the north of England:

> Sometimes there was support for people who identified problems. Often it was within the family. Neil, Paul, and Bob all mentioned getting help from their partners. Mark took writing problems to his sister, while Duncan relied on his parents. Liz got help from her husband and her daughter as well as from a friend who worked 40 miles away. Sometimes particular people were chosen for help; Julie's mother would approach an uncle 'because he worked in an office' – one of several examples where work skills extend into the home. When Sally got married, she found that there were many everyday tasks she could not deal with, and she turned to her mother to help her learn the new writing tasks.

(Barton and Padmore, 1991, p. 69)

In multilingual communities, relatives or friends may perform a particularly important role in helping people to deal with bureaucratic literacy in English. In a study of the communicative practices of urban adolescents in Philadelphia, Amy Shuman describes the ways that Puerto Rican teenagers, bilingual in English and Spanish, are drawn upon to accomplish literacy purposes within their families:

> Many of the Puerto Rican girls took responsibility in their families and community for reading English and translating texts into spoken Spanish. They filled in forms for medical or governmental offices ...
>
> Particularly in their roles as interpreters, the Puerto Rican adolescents performed specialised tasks that were not duplicated by other members of the family. Ordinarily, teenage girls would not be involved in family business of this kind, and their participation as translators sometimes disrupted the social conventions for appropriate age behaviour. All of the teenage girls, black, white, and Puerto Rican, had responsibilities at home, but such assignments did not conflict, as did Puerto Rican translating tasks, with either one's social role in the family or attendance at school. Girls who stayed home to help when a parent was sick tended to be those who preferred not to go to school. The Puerto Rican girls whose skills were needed as translators were most often the best students who otherwise did not miss school and who saw their assistance with translation as a necessary choice between family and school responsibilities.

(Shuman, 1993, p. 259)

Activity 2.8 *(Allow about 15 minutes)*

Can you think of any occasions when you have made use of someone else as a
mediator to accomplish a literacy purpose, in English or another language?
Conversely, have there been occasions when you have been enlisted by someone
else to accomplish a literacy purpose for them? Here are two rather different
examples adapted from Baynham (1995).

The first involves making use of someone else to accomplish a literacy
purpose. When I (Mike Baynham) worked as an adult education worker in
London in the 1970s and 1980s, I frequently needed to have publicity information
about courses translated into different community languages. My friend
Mohammed F., who had been educated in Qur'ānic school, wrote a beautiful
Maghribi Arabic script and I would occasionally visit him to ask him to translate a
publicity leaflet into Arabic. Conversely, I would often receive a message at work
asking me to drop round to see Mohammed as he had a form that needed filling in
in English. Both Mohammed and I were serving as mediators of literacy for each
other in different languages and for different purposes.

The second example involves being made use of to accomplish a literacy
purpose. I am watching children's television with my eldest son (aged four) in the
early morning. We are tuned to a commercial channel and at regular intervals
there are details of competitions with lavish prizes, which involve writing to a PO
Box address in Brisbane. My son becomes very excited about one particular
competition and insists that I copy down the PO Box address so that we can do the
competition. Here I am being enlisted to accomplish a literacy purpose by a four-
year-old, who is not yet able to copy down the address himself, yet who is clearly
knowledgeable about how to go about entering for the competition.

The use of mediators is just one aspect of the social activity which often occurs
around reading or writing a specific text. When Shirley Brice Heath studied the
language practices of people living in Trackton, a black working-class community
in North Carolina, USA, she found that 'when something is read in Trackton, it
almost always provokes narratives, jokes, sidetracking talk and active negotiation
of the meaning of written texts among the listeners' (Brice Heath, 1983, p. 196).
For instance, she describes the way that the evening newspaper is read:

> The evening newspaper is read on the front porch for most months of the
> year. The obituaries on the back page are usually read first, followed by
> employment listings, advertisements for grocery and department store
> sales, and captions beneath pictures and headlines. An obituary is read
> for some trace of acquaintance with either the deceased, his relatives,
> place of birth, church, or school; active discussion follows about who the
> individual was and who he might have known. Circulars or letters to
> individuals regarding the neighborhood center and its recreational or
> medical services are read aloud and their meanings jointly negotiated by
> those who have had experience with such activities or know about the
> forms to be filled out to be eligible for such services. Neighbors share
> stories of what they did or what happened to them in similar circum-
> stances.
>
> (Brice Heath, 1983, p. 196)

Brice Heath describes how Lillie Mae, a Trackton resident, receives an official
letter about a children's day-care project and how neighbours are drawn into a

Plate 1   Las Vegas, USA (Chapter 2)

*Plate 2
Chinese and English in
Singapore (Chapter 2)*

Plate 3
Street sign in Pennsylvania, USA
(Chapter 2)

Plate 4   Nepali and English in Kathmandu, Nepal (Chapter 2)

Plate 5
Kannada and English in
Bangalore, India (Chapter 2)

Plate 6   Chinese and English in Singapore (Chapter 2)

THE DING DONG SONG

Here's an old Chinese number that was popular in the fifties, dedicated to my dear mother, who, incidentally, kindly consented to sing on the track. Thanks to her, I was introduced to Rebecca Pan, Asia's songbird. This song is a bit of a family affair, with my brother Wah going, "What is this thing called love?"

I hear that bell go ding dong
Deep down inside my heart.

Each time you say, "Kiss me"
Then I know it's time for Ding Dong to start
Each time you say, "Hug me", Ding Dong, Ding Dong.
Each time you say, "Love me", Ding Dong, Ding Dong
I hope I won't wait too long
You hear my bell go Ding Dong
You hear my bell go Ding Dong

MUSTAPHA

This song figures vaguely somewhere in my childhood. I've ressurrected it — with new lyrics — as a tribute to my favourite Saturday afternoon pastime — Tamil movies! (P.S. This also features my fave Tamil Actress — Jacintha!)

CHORUS.

Cherie je t'aime, cherie jet t'adore
My darling I love you a lot more than you know
Cherie je t'aime, cherie je t'adore,
My darling I love you a lot more than you know.
Oh Mustapha, Oh mustapha
Yen Kathalan my Mr. mustapha
Sayang, sayang, na chew sher wo ai ni
Will you, will you fall in love with me.

Oh your lovely eyes, I feel I know them well.
Let me look into them and fall right under their spell.
Oh, my sweetness what a beauty
You are such a pretty cutie
I can't tell you, tutti frutti,
All the things you're doing to me.

(Repeat chorus)

Honey, honey, sugar's not as sweet
Oh, my papadam, you're good enough to eat.
Mama, mama, you are such a tease,
Oh, my harm cheen pang, can
I give you a squeeze?

(Repeat chorus)

Putumayam, I am asking, please
Won't you come and give your Mustapha a kiss?
Onde-onde, can I quench your thirst?
But to take a sip, you have to catch me first!

LITTLE WHITE BOAT

A Chinese nursery rhyme with an endearing melody. Something I've always wanted to redo.

Sailing in my little white boat
Far as I can be
Drifting in my little white boat
Set my spirit free.
Take me deep inside my dream
over seas of blue
To your magic place
Where I can be with you.

I AM BABA

A "soundtrack" based on my recollections of Peranakan songs, sung to me by my granny when I was a child. Folksongs featured: Lenggang kangkong, Chan Mali Chan, Trek Tek Tek, Suah Suih Kemuning. As a true Singaporean, you ought to know the words!

Plate 7
The Singapore songwriter and performer Dick Lee, with lyrics in Singlish (Chapter 6)

Plate 8
Hindi and English on film
poster in Kathmandu, Nepal
(Chapters 2 and 6)

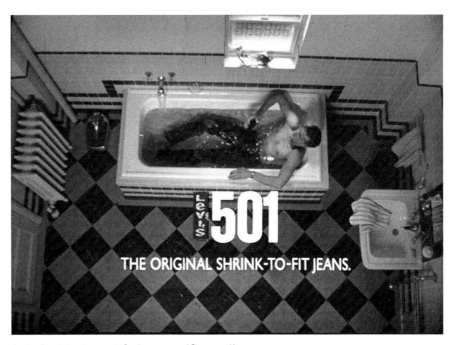

Plate 9   Advertisement for Levi jeans (Chapter 6)

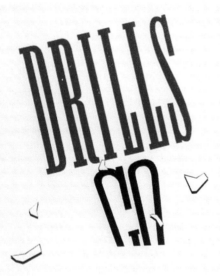

LAMBS G⊛

Plate 10
Advertisement for P&O Ferries
(Chapter 6)

VIRAGO MODERN CLASSICS

Dorothy Richardson

PILGRIMAGE 1

Plate 11   *The first volume of Dorothy Richardson's thirteen-volume experimental novel written between 1913 and 1938 (Chapter 8)*

Street typist, Bangalore, India

When asked about his work, the street typist says that he types for 'all sorts of people', including those who are quite well off but might not have a typewriter at home. Almost all the typing he does is for communication with government departments or the courts, including legal documents such as contracts. Some people may bring a handwritten document that he retypes; others may speak English but are not literate in English and will dictate a letter; others may be literate, but not in English, so he will translate from Kannada; he may also compose a letter for those who aren't sure how to do this. He charges 4–5 rupees per page, irrespective of the nature of the task: those who need most help are also the poorest. He makes 100 rupees a day (a modest but sufficient daily wage). He also has a photocopier and employs a man to operate it. He says that many street typists are graduates and some have higher degrees. They need to be fairly well educated as they give advice; they don't just type.

(We are grateful to Donald Mackinnon for this photograph and information.)

discussion that lasts nearly an hour, exchanging their knowledge of such projects and discussing the pros and cons. Reading leads naturally to narrative and the pooling of experience. 'Lillie Mae, reading aloud, decoded the written text, but her friends and neighbors interpreted the text's meaning through their own experiences' (Heath, 1983, p. 197).

Heath's work shows that even quite small local communities have distinctive ways of using and interacting with texts. These practices change from one generation to the next; think of the differences between the grandfather's, father's and son's experiences in Reading A.

The next reading focuses on a community that is experiencing particularly dramatic political, economic and social change. It examines how the associated changes in literacy practices are having an impact on people's lives.

❖   ❖   ❖   ❖   ❖

Activity 2.9   *(Reading B)*

Read 'Changing literacy practices in a South African informal settlement' by Catherine Kell (Reading B). In what ways are the changes in literacy practices in Site 5 affecting Winnie's role within the community?

Comment

The subject of this case study, Winnie, is living through the period of rapid change brought about by the ending of apartheid in South Africa. At the beginning of the case study we see the powerful role that she plays within her community as a problem solver, a political activist, working in three languages – Xhosa, English and Afrikaans – within the horizontal communication networks (i.e. between people and groups of equal status) in the local struggle against apartheid. At the end of the case study, it seems that the pace of political and social change has shifted the communication practices to such an extent that Winnie and other women like her have become disempowered within the fast-developing new networks of bureaucratic communication, and the new **discourse** of reconstruction. (Kell uses the term 'discourse' to refer to particular patterns of language use tied to social practice and ideological positions.)

2.5   DIVERSITY AND CHANGE

We have seen how reading and writing in English are not just abstract language skills, but are always an intrinsic part of particular social activities and practices. **Literacy practices** are tied up with individual identity, personal relationships, community membership, religious practices and political manoeuvring. In both monolingual and multilingual settings, literacy in English is often associated with education and power. Specific reading and writing practices are imbued with values, explicit and implicit, so that acquiring skill in new practices is not just a question of language proficiency, but of taking on different values and, sometimes, different identities.

Just as social groups and institutions shift over time, so do literacy practices. Specific technological developments, for example printing in the fifteenth century and computers in the twentieth, have spawned numerous new varieties of texts and practices.

Let us take as an example the way texts and practices have changed in the British legal profession.

The significance of the invention of printing in relation to the history of English is explored in the first book in this series, *English: history, diversity and change* (Graddol et al. (eds), 1996).

Activity 2.10   *(Allow about 10 minutes)*

Look at the two letters in Figures 2.4 and 2.5, each written from one solicitor to another about the sale and purchase of property. What differences are there in the two texts and what clues do they give us about changes in practices?

Comment

You were probably immediately struck by the different overall appearances of the two letters. The long copy hand 1803 letter with only the seal imprint to identify the solicitor's office looks very different from the short 1995 version, printed on paper letterheaded with all kinds of information, from lists of the firm's members and of the locations of its various branches, to the authorizations from the Law Society and the Legal Aid Board. In addition, the initials and figures used for 'Our ref' at the top right-hand side of the 1995 version not only identify the individual solicitor and secretary who produced the letter, but also give the client number, which can be used by members of that law firm to access a whole range of information held on the firm's computer.

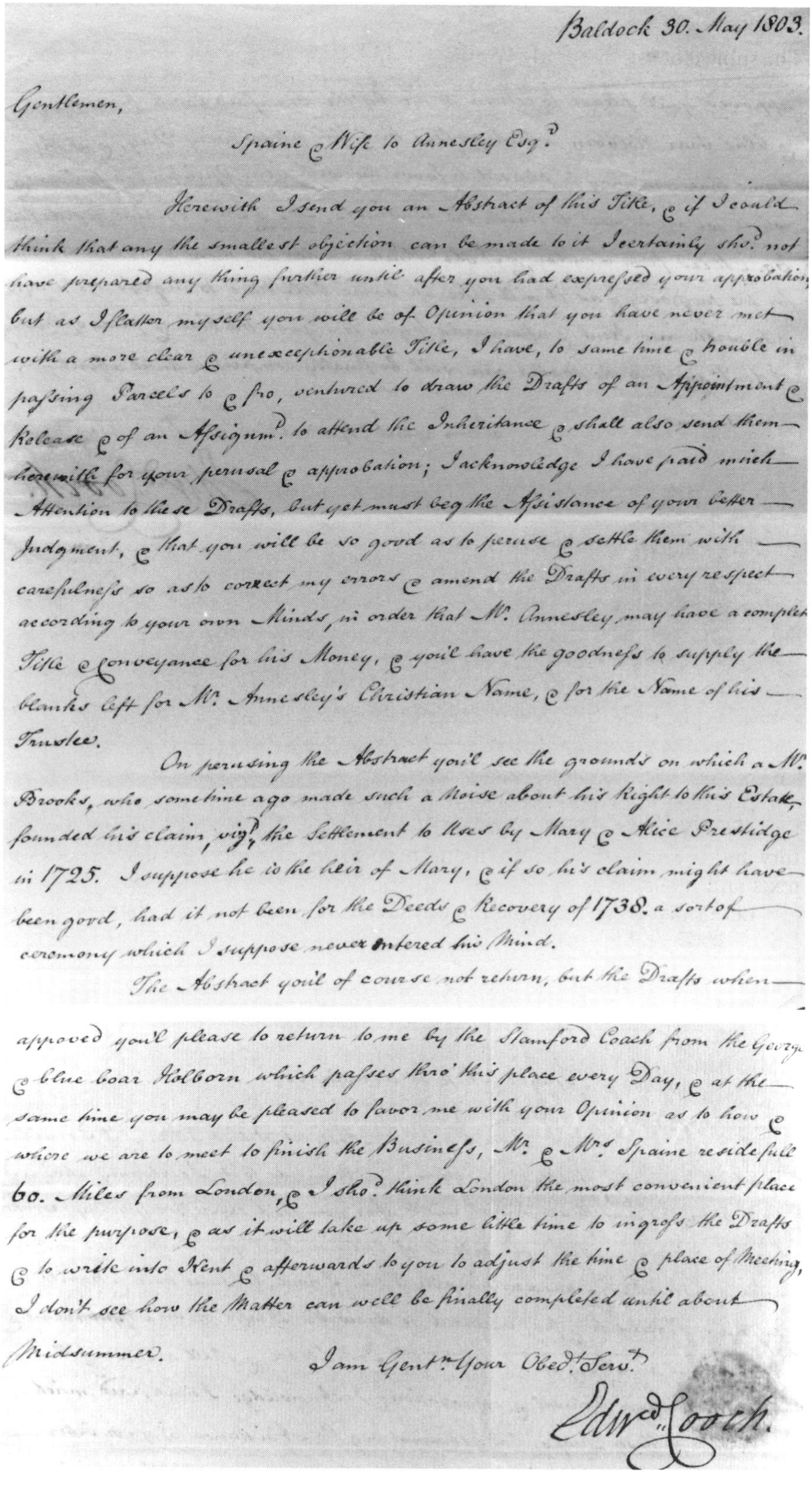

Baldock 30. May 1803.

Gentlemen,

Spaine & Wife to Annesley Esq.r

Herewith I send you an Abstract of this Title, & if I could think that any the smallest objection can be made to it I certainly sho.d not have prepared any thing further until after you had expressed your approbation; but as I flatter myself you will be of Opinion that you have never met with a more clear & unexceptionable Title, I have, to save time & trouble in passing Parcels to & fro, ventured to draw the Drafts of an Appointment & Release & of an Assignm.t to attend the Inheritance & shall also send them herewith for your perusal & approbation; I acknowledge I have paid much Attention to these Drafts, but yet must beg the Assistance of your better Judgment, & that you will be so good as to peruse & settle them with carefulness so as to correct my errors & amend the Drafts in every respect according to your own Minds, in order that M.r Annesley may have a complete Title & Conveyance for his Money, & you'l have the goodness to supply the blanks left for M.r Annesley's Christian Name, & for the Name of his Trustee.

On perusing the Abstract you'l see the grounds on which a M.r Brooks, who sometime ago made such a Noise about his Right to this Estate, founded his claim, viz.t the Settlement to Uses by Mary & Alice Prestidge in 1725. I suppose he is the heir of Mary, & if so his claim might have been good, had it not been for the Deeds & Recovery of 1738. a sort of ceremony which I suppose never entered his Mind.

The Abstract you'l of course not return, but the Drafts when approved you'l please to return to me by the Stamford Coach from the George & blue boar Holborn which passes thro' this place every Day, & at the same time you may be pleased to favor me with your Opinion as to how & where we are to meet to finish the Business, M.r & M.rs Spaine reside full 60. Miles from London, & I sho.d think London the most convenient place for the purpose, & as it will take up some little time to ingross the Drafts & to write into Kent & afterwards to you to adjust the time & place of Meeting, I don't see how the Matter can well be finally completed until about Midsummer.

I am Gent.n Your Obed.t Serv.t

Edw.d Cooch.

Figure 2.4 Letter written 30 May 1803 from Edward Cooch, Baldock, concerning the conveyance of property from Spaine to Annesley. (This letter has been reduced to approximately half of its original size.)

PARTNERS	M.A. Hughes*	J. Lloyd-Jones LL.B	J.E. Clarke BA
M.J. Linnell*	J.P. Sutton BA	C.P.G. Gregan LL.B	C.A. Plews BA
A.E.R. Beesley MA*	A.M. Cowell LL.B	A.G. Hopgood BA	S. Jackson LL.B
M.N.E. Ess LL.B*	S.N. Potter MA	C. Oster MA	E.M.F. Temple MA
J.C.W. Burrough	P.F. Quigley LL.B	ASSOCIATES	CONSULTANT
J.S. Deech MA D.PHIL	J.P.T. Irwin-Singer MA	J.M. Stansfield LL.B	Peter Butler MP

Linnells
SOLICITORS

60 High Street, Newport Pagnell,
Milton Keynes, Bucks MK16 8AQ

Telephone (01908) 613545

Fax (01908) 210654 DX 90905 Newport Pagnell

Messrs. Wenfields
DX 41090 Milton Keynes

OUR REF: NH.AT.RK.Clarke.30751-1-4
YOUR REF: 09.SP.Lapinott

21st May 1995

Dear Sirs,

Re: 6, Browns Lane
   Mr & Mrs Clarke to Mr Lapinott

We enclose herewith Epitome of Title, draft Contract in duplicate, fixtures and fittings form and Replies to Pre-Contract Enquiries. Kindly supply details of your client's full name and address to be inserted into the Contract.

We look forward to receiving one part of the Contract as soon as possible together with an indication of when your client would be ready to exchange. We wish to complete by 24th June 1995 at the latest as our clients have a dependent purchase which is part of a chain.

Yours faithfully,

Linnells

Linnells

BICESTER   HEADINGTON   KIDLINGTON   CENTRAL MILTON KEYNES   NEWPORT PAGNELL   OXFORD   WALLINGFORD

LEGAL AID FRANCHISE

* Notary Public   This firm is regulated by the Law Society in the conduct of investment business.   A QUALITY SERVICE
Approved by The Legal Aid Board

Figure 2.5
Letter written 21 May 1995 from Linnells, Newport Pagnell, concerning the conveyance of property from Clarke to Lapinott. (This letter has been reduced to approximately half of its original size.)

At a more detailed level, there are differences between the two versions in orthography, letter-writing conventions and grammatical style.

Orthography

- In the 1803 letter capital letters are used for most nouns.

- Different forms of abbreviation (e.g. *you'l*, *sho.^d*) were used in 1803.

- The form of the ampersand *&* and the long *s* (see margin) where a word contains two consecutive *s*'s (e.g. *expre∫sed*) are no longer used in contemporary English.

c = ampersand
∫ = long *s*

Letter-writing conventions

- Abbreviations and ampersands were acceptable and are used in the 1803 version.
- There are different ways of opening and closing the letters.
- The 1803 letter has a more personal tone and uses *I* as opposed to the more impersonal *we* of the 1995 letter.

Grammatical style

- The more tentative, negotiating tone of the 1803 letter comes from its greater use of modal verbs; for example *could* and *should*, and hedging expressions such as *you will be so good, you'l have the goodnefs.*
- Although the earlier letter does include nominalizations (e.g. *perusal, approbation, assistance*), it is less lexically dense than the 1995 version, with its high concentration of legal vocabulary and phrases (*Epitome of Title, draft Contract, fixtures and fittings form, Replies to Pre-Contract Enquiries, exchange, complete, dependent purchase which is part of a chain*).

The differences we have identified between the two letters in Activity 2.10 show how a particular **genre** of text, in this case solicitors' letters, develops and changes over time. The genre of a text is determined by its medium (e.g. spoken, written, visual), the way it uses English (e.g. vocabulary and grammatical forms, text presentation), type of content, and the relationship between writer and reader. Particular genres emerge as the result of institutional needs and practices, and they change alongside them. The first letter comes from a small family law firm which has longstanding personal relationships with its clients, and the second is part of a much faster moving, streamlined transaction by a company dealing at a distance with large numbers of clients every day. The telephone and fax machine, together with more rapid mail services, have largely replaced face-to-face meetings such as the one being arranged in the 1803 letter, and business can now be conducted in a much swifter and more impersonal manner.

The 1803 letter is longer because of its more personal, long-winded tone, but it also has to be longer because the business of proving ownership of a property was more complex and more open to dispute in the nineteenth century. Since the 1925 Land Registration Act, British documentation is more exhaustive and easily obtainable; in the few instances where properties have not yet been registered, photocopies of all existing deeds are supplied to the buyer (the 'Epitome of Title'), replacing the abstracted and handcopied summaries necessary in the 1800s (the 'Abstract of this Title').

Thus, although these letters both come from a series of correspondence between solicitors about buying and selling property, the contrasts between them reflect changing practices in business and law, and changes in technology, between the early nineteenth and the late twentieth centuries. There are therefore both technological and social reasons behind the changes in genre between the first and second solicitors' letters.

Genres encode social relations (compare, for instance, the way English is used in the personal letter written by Jaya's father with the business letter from Linnells – see Figures 2.1 and 2.5), and they also position the writer and the reader as, for instance, friend, colleague, client, supplicant (think of the different kinds of positioning of people in the texts produced in Site 5 in Reading B; for example, the memo asking for permanent homes and the Development Forum minute).

It has been claimed that certain genres serve the needs of some people more than others. For instance, the language of insurance policies, tenancy agreements, contracts and legal forms in Britain has been criticized for being too complex for ordinary citizens to understand. One response to this issue comes from the 'Plain English' movement. Although it has been argued by the legal profession that the intricacies of the law require very precise specialized language to ensure accuracy, a number of Plain English groups have been campaigning over the last 20 years for a change in the way language is used in documents and literature produced by government departments and public services. The Plain English campaigners want written public information to be expressed in shorter sentences, using active rather than passive verb forms, without unnecessary jargon or 'gobbledegook'. Campaigners are also concerned about the way text is laid out on the page – making the best use of type sizes and faces, space and colour, and effective subheadings and lists (Plain English Campaign, 1992; Cutts, 1995). Notice how in the examples in the box below Martin Cutts advocates changes in sentence length, vocabulary and grammatical organization in rewriting legal clauses. In particular the relationship between noun phrases and verb phrases is much clearer in the revised versions.

Plain English groups produce guidance notes and courses to help departments and organizations make documents more clearly comprehensible to the intended user. The call for 'Plain English' in Britain and other parts of the English-speaking world echoes similar campaigns in other European countries. In 1995 consumer groups from across Europe succeeded in obtaining a new EU Directive which requires that all consumer contracts should be in 'plain, intelligible language … Where there is doubt about the meaning of a term, the interpretation most favourable to the consumer shall prevail' (quoted in Cutts, 1995, p. 48).

Plain English

As a Plain English campaigner, Martin Cutts has rewritten the United Kingdom Timeshare Act, which regulates agreements for people buying rights in a property so they can use it for holidays for one or two weeks a year (some timeshare sellers have been criticized for not giving customers proper information about their property). Here are examples of how he has rewritten two clauses:

Original

The offeree's giving, within the time allowed under this section, notice of cancellation of the agreement to the offeror at a time when the agreement has been entered into shall have the effect of cancelling the agreement.

Revision

An agreement is cancelled if the customer gives the seller notice of cancellation within the time this section allows.

Original

This Act shall have effect in relation to any timeshare agreement or timeshare credit agreement notwithstanding any agreement or notice.

Revision

No agreement or notice can prevent this Act from applying.

(Cutts, 1995, p. 46)

We have looked at some examples of how changes in literacy practices, technological development and social organization are all closely interconnected. The literacy practices of particular workplaces may be quite distinctive and throw up learning issues for those new to these settings, while changes in work practices may dramatically alter current language and literacy practices. The introduction of new technology, or an innovation such as just-in-time stock delivery, may involve a wide range of workers using the computer keyboard for activities like reordering stock.

In Reading C, Simeon Yates talks about the language practices in English associated with a new form of technology: computer-mediated communication (CMC).

Activity 2.11 *(Reading C)*

Read 'Computer-mediated English: sociolinguistic aspects of computer-mediated communication' by Simeon Yates (Reading C). Is CMC producing a new kind of literacy in English? If so, what is it like?

Comment

CMC appears to be reworking in a particularly interesting way the distinctions between speech and writing which we discussed at the beginning of this chapter. It is similar to writing in its vocabulary range, but close to speech in terms of its pronoun usage. And it differs from both in its greater use of modals, which Yates in Reading C sees as reflecting its use for academic discussions of knowledge. It seems as if CMC is providing a medium where criteria such as ephemeral/permanent, formal/informal and on paper/through the air, which have been regarded as typical features of the spoken/written distinction, have different kinds of meaning and significance. Yates is suggesting that new literacy practices will emerge within this new medium. He has discussed elsewhere (Yates, 1993) the different kinds of genre he sees developing in the university environment where he works, such as the genre of discussion between academics, or the genre of communications between tutors and their students. The genres emerging in the broader use of the international Internet have not yet been documented in any kind of detail.

2.6   LITERACY AND IDENTITY

In this chapter we have discussed a wide range of texts, from street hoardings to legal documents, and a wide range of literacy practices, from submitting a poem for publication in a Panjabi newspaper, to committee minute taking, to computer e-mail. Literacy practices are the observable activities in which reading and writing play a part, but they also depend on the meanings people attach to what they do: the values, attitudes and ideologies that are interwoven with literacy activities.

Many researchers into literacy have been very concerned with what literacy practices can tell us about people's interpretation of notions such as 'self' and 'personhood' both within and across cultures (Street, 1993; Besnier, 1993). Others have been concerned with how literacy practices in particular domains, for example the teaching/learning of academic writing, allow people to construct a range of possible writer identities for themselves (Ivanič, 1993). In this section we consider briefly how values, attitudes and ideologies shape literacy practices in English.

I (Mike Baynham) remember several years ago noticing the following graffiti on the climbing frame of a north London playground:

SHARON IS ILLITERATE

What do those three words tell us about the social values connected with literacy in a society like Britain? Perhaps the first thing is that 'illiterate' counts as a term of abuse. The kind of social knowledge that the reader brings to the message draws on the emotive force of powerful values, attitudes and ideologies ('literacy good, illiteracy bad') which shape what we read in the newspapers and debates about educational standards. Literacy itself as a social construct is a powerful sorter and categorizer of persons into those who can and those who can't. We saw in the South African case study (Reading B) how Winnie's son taunts her for her inability to read and write, mimicking the discourse of school with its levels and categories of achievement:

He [the younger son] laugh now, he say 'Mama, are you Sub A?'

These powerful values, attitudes and ideologies attached to literacy, often expressed as moral imperatives, are clearly a significant feature in the social landscape of most countries in the contemporary world. The linkage between literacy/illiteracy is one we ignore at our peril, since it makes up part of the discursive framework within which literacy is conceptualized and discussed.

Activity 2.12   *(Allow about 10 minutes)*

What metaphors and models of literacy do you find in the following quotations from the media in various different English-speaking countries?

1   Like a germ that learns to enjoy penicillin, illiteracy consumes all the armies sent to fight it. No matter what we do about it – and we do a good deal, contrary to complaints from the literacy lobby – the condition persists. Depending on how you count them, adult illiterates make up anywhere from a tenth to a fifth of the Canadian population.

    (*Financial Times of Canada*, 4 July 1988, quoted in Barton, 1994, p. 10)

2   Literacy: A Shameful Problem for Every Seventh Australian? Illiteracy is a bigger problem in Australia than most of us probably realise. Some say up to two million people – 14 percent of our population – are afflicted …

    (Australian *Women's Weekly*, 24 September 1977, pp. 16–17, quoted in Hodgens, 1994, p. 17)

3   TV Tutors to Battle Illiteracy

    (Sydney *Morning Herald*, 3 December 1976, p. 3, quoted in Hodgens, 1994, p. 17)

4   Employers had noticed a steady decline in reading, writing and basic arithmetic standards over the past four years, the organisation's secretary, Mr I.C. Spicer, said yesterday.

    (*The Australian*, 3 March 1975, p. 3, quoted in Hodgens, 1994, pp. 18–9)

5   NSW [New South Wales] schools are turning out a growing number of
     irresponsible and often illiterate citizens. But the students are not to blame,
     according to Professor Harry Messel ... 'Changes' had wrecked the system
     and students were encouraged to do whatever they liked, Prof Messel said.

     (*Daily Telegraph* (Australia), 22 May 1978, p. 5, quoted in Hodgens, 1994,
     p. 22)

2.7   CONCLUSION

In this chapter we started out by looking at differences between speech and
writing in English at the level of text, but moved on to show that engaging with any
kind of text involves far more than decoding the symbols on the page (or screen,
or wall). Texts are written and read in particular contexts and this influences both
their form and their meaning. Because texts are used to achieve social purposes
they are written with particular aims in mind, and these also shape their form and
structure.

   We have looked at how literacy practices in English vary across different social
and cultural contexts and across monolingual and multilingual settings. We have
also looked at how the characteristics of specific genres of texts change over time,
alongside changes in social organization and technology. Literacy practices in
English are always imbued with social values, and are also an important aspect of
the development and expression of people's personal and social identity.

Reading A
MULTILITERACY PRACTICES AND VALUES: AN ETHNOGRAPHIC ACCOUNT OF A PANJABI FAMILY IN BRITAIN

Mukul Saxena

The literacy practices in the Panjabi community in Southall, west London, have changed enormously since the first group of Panjabi men came to Britain in the 1950s. The third generation Panjabis are now living and growing up in a much more varied and complex situation of multilingual literacies than the first and second generation Panjabis ever did.

In the first part of this [reading] I present a case study of a Panjabi Hindu family in Southall ... It will provide examples of how they make use of different literacies in their daily lives and, hopefully, throw some light on the literacy repertoire and literacy practices of the Panjabi Hindu community and the larger Panjabi community in Southall. We shall see, in this section, how individuals in this community are exposed to different print media; how they make literacy choices for different purposes; and how they value different literacies in their repertoire.

This family consists of a 4-year-old boy, his parents and grandparents. I chose this family because its members are fairly representative of the Panjabi Hindu community in Southall. They are brought up and have lived in different cultural and linguistic environments in India, East Africa and Britain. They are of different age groups and sex; they have had their education in different political, religious

Panjabi is normally written in Gurmukhi script and associated with Sikhs.

ਨਸਲੀ ਭੇਦਭਾਵ ਦੇ ਵਿਰੁੱਧ ਸਾਲ
ਦੀ ਪਾਲਿਸੀ ਦਾ ਵਿਸਥਾਰ

Hindi is normally written in Devanagari script and associated with Hindus.

नस्ली भेदभाव के विरुद्ध वर्ष
की नीति के बारे में बयान

Urdu is normally written in Perso-Arabic script and associated with Muslims.

نسلی منافرت کے خلاف سال - پالیسی کا بیان

All three languages can be written in all three scripts. Everyday spoken Hindi and Urdu are very similar, especially in their grammatical structures. However, in certain contexts, users of these languages try to bring in the words of Sanskrit or Perso-Arabic origin in their speech and writing to show their allegiance to Hindus or Muslims.

Figure 1 Script choices and religious identities

and cultural climates; and they have different attitudes towards different languages and orthographies.

This is one of the families in Southall with whom I have spent most time. Over the course of five years, I stayed with them on many occasions and observed their literacy practices. Initially, my visits to and stays with this family were a matter of hospitality extended to a student from their country of origin having the same linguistic background. However, over the period, the acquaintance gradually grew into a close relationship. As I was accepted and treated as a member of the family, I could participate in their day-to-day activities. This relationship also provided me with the freedom of questioning and discussing their actions and views, even though they were fully aware of my study and its purpose.

The literacy events presented below all took place but did not necessarily happen in one single day. In order to give the account more cohesion they are presented as if they occurred in a single day.

Grandfather

(*Educated in the Panjab in pre-liberated India [i.e. before 1947]; migrated to East Africa before coming to England.*)

He takes bus No. 74 signposted in English 'Greenford' to go to the Community Club for the elderly people. There he reads a local newspaper in Urdu about the South Asians in Britain, Southall's local news, and political news from India and Pakistan. He picks up a national newspaper in English, skims through it to get general news about British and international affairs.

He then walks down a few blocks to a publishing house which publishes a fortnightly newspaper to promote Panjabi nationalism in terms of its secular political ideology and Panjabi culture. He exchanges greetings with the editor in Panjabi and shows him a poem he has written in Panjabi/Gurmukhi in praise of Panjab rivers. The editor considers it for publication.

On the way home, he goes to a book store which specialises in print media (newspaper, magazine, children's and literary books, novels, etc.) from India, Pakistan and Britain in various South Asian scripts. He buys a Hindi film magazine from India for his daughter-in-law. He also notices advertising posters in English in the street.

At home, when his grandson comes back from school, he reads him a nursery book written in English.

Grandmother

(*Brought up in East Africa with little formal education; learnt Hindi at home.*)

She waits for a bus, at the bus stop, to go to a Hindu temple. She does not read English. One of the buses that go to the temple is No. 36. When buses other than No. 36 come, she checks with the drivers (bus drivers in Southall are mostly Panjabi) if the buses go in the direction of the temple. None does. No. 36 arrives with the Hayes sign written in English. Though she does not read English, she recognises the shape of the word, because she sees it often. She also recognises the driver and the adverts on the bus. She boards the bus without feeling a need to check it with the driver. She compensates for her lack of knowledge of written English by relying on her memory of certain objects, events, people, etc., and assistance from other people.

On entering the temple, she reads a notice in Hindi about the weekend's events at the temple. Inside the main hall, after offering prayers to each of the Hindu gods, she asks the priest about the date of a particular festival. The priest then checks a yearly magazine from the Panjab, written in Perso-Arabic script, about the Hindu religious calendar.

Note: one would expect a Hindu calendar to be written in Devanagari script, rather than in Perso-Arabic script. But the people of [the] priest's generation, ... who were educated in the pre-partition period in India, still refer to magazines and other journals written in Perso-Arabic.

Later, with other women and some elderly men, she listens to a Hindu religious book read out in Hindi by the priest. Then she goes upstairs where there is a Hindu cultural centre and a library. She reads a Hindi newspaper from India there, and borrows a religious book in Hindi.

On the way home, she notices shop names displayed in bilingual signs in Panjabi-English, Hindi-English or Urdu-English. She goes into a *sari* (an Indian woman's dress) shop. The shop has an English-Hindi bilingual sign outside. The shop owner is the president of the Hindi temple.

Note: as I found out in interviews with shop owners, different linguistic signs represented their interest more in terms of their ideological stance and less of their commercial need.

Father

(*Born in East Africa, but brought up and educated in England from an early age.*)

In the morning, he reads an English newspaper for national and international news before leaving for work. At work, he supervises about 250 workers of South Asian origin in a factory. As and when required, he also mediates, as an interpreter, between the workers and the factory bosses. He also has the responsibility of making available bilingual materials published by social service agencies on safety, workers' legal rights, medical benefits, etc. in the factory.

After work, in the evening, he goes to a Hindu temple where he is a member of the temple executive committee. With other committee members, he prepares a draft letter in English about the annual general meeting to be sent out to the registered members of the temple. It was agreed that when the temple has enough funds, the committee will send English-Hindi bilingual letters and notices to its members, as one of the roles of the temple is to promote Hindi. At the moment, the temple has only an English typewriter. The committee members also prepare some hand-written notices in Hindi for the temple notice board regarding the agenda of the annual general meeting.

On the way home, he notices some new Sikh nationalistic and communal slogans on street walls written in Panjabi. He discusses these slogans with his family when he comes home. At home, his mother reads to him from a weekly Hindi newspaper published locally about some local news and some news from the Panjab. This newspaper also has a few articles on Indian Hindi films written in English which he reads himself.

Mother

(*Born, brought up and educated in the Panjab during and after reorganisation period of the Panjab in India [1966] before coming to England for marriage.*)

In the morning, she takes her son to a nearby nursery. She brings back a note in English from the teacher about some activity which the child and the parents have contributed to. She shows it to her husband in the evening. He reads it and explains it to her in Panjabi.

After finishing the household chores, she gets a little time to read a few pages from a Hindi novel. Later, with her mother-in-law, she writes a letter to a relative in Delhi. They discuss and write the contents of the letter in Panjabi-Hindi mixed code using Devanagari script. She also writes a letter in Panjabi-Gurmukhi to a friend in the Panjab.

In the evening, before putting her son to sleep, she tells him a story in Panjabi.

Son

(*Born in Southall.*)

In the morning as he enters the school, he sees bilingual signs. He can distinguish between Gurmukhi, Devanagari and Roman scripts. In the classroom, he is exposed only to the Roman script for teaching and learning purposes.

At home in the afternoon, his grandmother sends him with a small shopping list in Hindi/Devanagari to a corner shop next door. The shopkeeper records the goods sold to the boy in Hindi/Devanagari in his ledger.

During the day, the boy observes his parents and grandparents using different literacies for different purposes.

Dinner time

One of the topics discussed during and after dinner is why the child should learn Hindi or Panjabi. The grandfather wants his grandson to learn Panjabi in the Gurmukhi script when he goes to school, but not in the Sikh temple. He thinks this way his grandson can learn Panjabi and retain Panjabi culture. He favours Panjabi because it is also the official language of the Panjab state. However, grandmother, mother and father think that the child should learn Hindi/Devanagari. Grandmother and father take more of a religious stance whereas mother takes the nationalistic/secular stance. Grandmother and father think that it is important to learn Hindi to retain Hindu culture and religion; whereas mother thinks that the child should learn Hindi because it is the national language of India. A further argument put forward in favour of Hindi related to the interpersonal communicative functions of literacy: grandmother, mother and father argue in favour of Hindi by saying that with the knowledge of the Hindi script the child will be able to correspond with the relatives both in Delhi and the Panjab, whereas the knowledge of written Panjabi would restrict him only to the Panjab. Grandfather is outvoted, and it is decided that the child would go to the Hindi voluntary classes held in the Hindu temple initially and later would also opt for Hindi in school.

Source: Saxena, 1994, pp. 195–200

Reading B
CHANGING LITERACY PRACTICES IN A SOUTH AFRICAN INFORMAL SETTLEMENT

Catherine Kell

In this reading 'Winnie' is the real name of Winnie Tsotso. All other names are pseudonyms.

I am sitting in Winnie's wood and iron shack. The relentless wind is blowing, whipping up the sand in the informal settlement and sending it back inside the houses through holes in the iron and plastic roofs. In the darkened room, I am talking with Winnie, and while we talk, a stream of people come in and out of the house, asking for things. It is difficult for me to understand what they say as all the conversation is in Xhosa, but Winnie goes to the cupboard and takes out a tin, riffling through some papers in it, while the person watches. I notice that the tin contains numerous documents. 'No,' she says, 'your identity document has not yet arrived' … 'Is this your clinic card?' … 'Here is your ANC [African National Congress] membership card.' Winnie, who speaks fluent English, Xhosa and Afrikaans (and knows a little Sotho, Tswana and Zulu), plays the role of unappointed and unpaid community advice worker. Yet she does this largely without literate skills, and is in the local night school class for those who cannot read and write, classified as a 'beginner'.

The establishment of Site 5

Winnie, a 48-year-old black woman, presides over a household of ten people, including her partner, his son, her three daughters, one grandchild, a neighbour's daughter who had been abused, a disabled friend and a white tramp whom she has taken in. The house is a rambling corrugated iron, wood and plastic shack in an informal settlement outside Cape Town in South Africa, where I was researching literacy in the months prior to the first national democratic elections (April 1994). The informal settlement of about 3,500 people, simply called Site 5, was established in 1993, after decades of struggle by its residents for the right to live and own land in what was proclaimed a white area of the Cape Peninsula.

The residents, who are black Xhosa speakers, were originally mainly employed on the white local farms. As the farms gave way to suburbs in the 1970s and 1980s, many residents started to live in the bush, working as domestic workers or gardeners in the surrounding white homes. The authorities harassed them, repeatedly breaking down their shelters and forcing them to move elsewhere. In 1987 the minority government sent the police in to break up small squatter settlements in the area. The houses were broken down with bulldozers, people's possessions were loaded into trucks and tents were put up for them in a black township 40 km away.

Some local leaders were thrown up during these years of struggle, especially a group of women which included Winnie. These women, with assistance from anti-apartheid organizations, took the residents' case to the South African Supreme Court in 1988 and won the right to stay in the area. As apartheid started to collapse, the local Member of Parliament said that 'it is time we stopped talking about these people, and started talking with them'. In 1989 the government announced that land would be found for the squatters, and the search for a suitable site began.

Four years later, the site had been chosen and cleared, plots demarcated, streets put in and a tap and toilet per household site installed. People built their shacks quickly, with whatever materials came to hand. A slightly larger shack served as a church, and there was a temporary clinic and public pre-school. A few residents sold basic commodities (candles, soap, mealie meal and Coca Cola) from the front rooms of their shacks. At the time of my research, the chunk of land granted to the squatters still had a raw, barren quality about it, although there were small gardens and patches of mealies (corn used to make flour and porridge). The new roads and streetlights sat uneasily on swathes of sand, and all around the settlement the bush had been pressed back to create dense boundaries that clearly demarcated Site 5. Surrounding the raw patch I could see white suburban homes, with large gardens, many with swimming pools. The cleared land spoke of haste, urgency, newness – but the little shacks that sat on the land spoke of age, reuse and poverty.

During the 1970s and early 1980s the squatters did not really have a voice or any audience outside their own groupings. In the mid 1980s a number of anti-apartheid non-governmental organizations (NGOs) started to support the squatters and some sort of public voice began to be heard. Reporters came from the Cape Town newspapers and sometimes reported direct speech from the squatters. One of the NGOs produced and distributed press statements, fact sheets and pamphlets. During the legal proceedings documents were produced by the lawyers and groups acting in consultation with the squatters. All of these texts were in English, and couched in the oppositional, anti-apartheid language of the NGOs involved.

Figure 1   Site 5
The handwritten sign pinned
to the post outside Primrose's
house (in a mixture of English,
Afrikaans and Xhosa) lists the
different kinds of women's
dresses which she makes
and sells

Sometimes the NGOs brought the squatters together with other groupings facing
similar problems. At these meetings and workshops there was no reliance on text:
problems were talked out, expressed through narrative, drama and song.
Together the NGOs and the squatters planned collective action such as marches
or sit-ins. Sometimes memoranda were drawn up together. At times the squatters'
own voices were represented, but these were mediated by the NGO activists, as in
this extract from a memorandum written by the squatters with NGO help, and
sent to the Cape Provincial Administration in 1988. The memo asks for the right
to permanent homes and freedom from harassment:

> We write to you as elected representatives of the above communities. All
> of us are people who have moved from bush to bush for many years
> searching for a permanent place to stay … What we want are houses we
> can afford, near our places of work. We see houses being built around us,
> but they are for people who already have houses. They are not for people
> like ourselves. Although some of us are grey we have never had a key to
> our own home …

In the late 1980s and early 1990s, horizontal communication between the squatters
remained oral, in Xhosa and face to face. Vertical communication, however, between
the squatters and more dominant groups with power and resources, was increasingly
taking written form, in English, through the mediation of the NGO staff.

In the new South Africa there will be big changes for places like Site 5. Civic
Associations (developed from the old squatter committees) have been legiti-
mated and in theory will negotiate on an equal footing with local authorities; the
role of the NGOs is diminished and the informal settlement will be formally
incorporated into structures of local government. As incorporation gets under-

way, however, something of this separation between horizontal oral communication in Xhosa, and vertical written communication in English, seems to be living on and becoming stabilized in the different institutions being formed to organize the process of incorporation. Throughout their history of resistance, the squatters have never gained access to the means of delivering their words themselves beyond their community. For this, English schooled literacy and the means of distributing it are becoming increasingly necessary.

Literacy in Site 5

While I was researching in Site 5 I found remarkably few signs of public literacy; there was very little print – no street signs, adverts or brochures to be seen. Now and then a political poster was put up, or a small photocopied sign advertising Aids Day. Some residents made their own signs advertising services or goods (see Figure 1). In most houses, the walls were papered with recent English newspapers, but no one whom I met in Site 5 ever bought a newspaper to read.

I have listed in the Appendix all the texts that I found in the settlement. For example, in Winnie's house a pile of eight books and pamphlets in English sits under a table. It includes one women's romance, one booklet of recipes called *Food for the Soul* and two booklets on health issues and ANC matters. All of these are in English. The children's books are discards from households where Winnie had worked as a domestic worker and I noticed children looking at them once or twice. The white tramp and Winnie's teenage daughter had read the thriller and the romance and discussed them. In one cupboard Winnie kept her tin of documents, ANC membership book and invoice book for her soup kitchen. At one point she brought out a box of papers from the ANC: agendas, resolutions and minutes (mainly in English, with a few items in Xhosa) (see Figure 2). On another occasion a group of ANC members was sitting in her lounge working on ANC posters advertising a local meeting. These were the only texts I saw in her house, and this was by far the highest number I saw in any house in Site 5.

Figure 2   Winnie

Winnie's fluency in the three main languages of the Cape region has enabled her to develop something of a cosmopolitan identity, and until recently an important political role for herself in the community. For instance, she is one of the longest standing key members of the squatter committee which is now the official Civic Association (CA). She is also a member of the health committee and the pre-school committee in Site 5, and of the Catholic Welfare and Development Committee (CWDC). Over a period of ten consecutive days when I visited her house, I calculated that she attended eleven meetings or functions.

Despite her own lack of literacy skills, Winnie's role in these meetings involves dealing with a variety of literacy practices. For instance, one night she told me she had to attend a commemoration meeting for an ANC marshal who had died in a fire in a nearby squatter area. I was later told that Winnie gave a speech in Xhosa and that photocopied sheets were given out with the words of *Nkosi Sikelel'iAfrika* (the national anthem) on them. I asked her about the photocopies, and she said that one day two senior ANC people came to Site 5 and were upset that people didn't know the words of the national anthem. 'So we took a copy to the ANC office and made other copies to give to the people.'

On another occasion Winnie told me that she was worried because the pre-school teachers had come to her demanding an extra month's money (as it was close to Christmas time and they had not had a bonus). 'But I know that it was not written on that what do you call it?' (conditions of employment). Winnie is constantly involved in literacy practices such as these, initiating and organizing them, yet she sees herself as 'illiterate'.

New South Africa, new literacy practices?

But things are changing for Winnie, and others like her. As Site 5 becomes more established and integrated into the surrounding infrastructure, new demands are being made of the leadership. Various bodies are involved in development in Site 5; in some ways they draw on old traditions, in others they bring in new discourses. Gradually, the oppositional anti-apartheid discourse of the NGOs is being replaced by new discourses of reconstruction and development. There is a contrast between the CA, with its roots in the early years of local struggle, and the newer and powerful Development Forum (DF), which was set up to co-ordinate development efforts in Site 5. The CA meets after dark, in the shack attached to the primary school. Proceedings are entirely in Xhosa, and I never saw anyone from outside Site 5 attending them. In contrast, the DF meetings are held in the primary school building in the afternoon and the proceedings are all in English, with minutes and agendas. It is attended by representatives from welfare agencies and NGOs, and by interested individuals from the surrounding white areas, as well as by representatives from the CA.

One incident at a DF meeting which sticks in my mind seems to bring into focus the conflict between the old and new discourses in Site 5. Mrs Brown, a local white woman who owns a building company with her husband, had organized donations to construct the new primary school for Site 5 and had managed to procure fencing and roll-on lawn. She reported that the school committee wanted the men of Site 5 to spend a Saturday putting these in place, and asked if this could be discussed at the next CA meeting. The DF minutes (taken by the white ex-mayoress of a neighbouring suburb) duly noted:

> 4. Education: Community to assist with erecting fencing for school, school committee to progress. Need for liaison between school and civic committee stressed.

The clause structure and verb forms here are typical of English committee minute writing, but they are difficult for someone who is unfamiliar with such literacy practices to understand. In fact the minute did not seem to me to reflect the proceedings at the meeting, since the community had not yet agreed to assist and the CA representatives present at the meeting did not make any contribution at all to the discussion about the grass and fencing.

Three months later the fencing had still not been put up and the schoolchildren themselves had laid the lawn. It was reported that the men were not prepared to do the fencing unless they were paid. They needed to sit at the Four-Way Stop (a large crossroads near Site 5, where men wait to be offered casual work) on a Saturday morning, to try to pick up a day's gardening work in the white suburbs.

At the next DF meeting, Mrs Brown asked exasperatedly why the men couldn't do the work. For a few minutes there was an electrifying silence. Miriam, the pre-school co-ordinator in Site 5, then explained:

> The men are angry that they should contribute to the school, when the community has been deprived of education and facilities for so long. They feel the DET [government department] should be taking over the school and providing these things.

Winnie added: 'And also the people are angry that they have to pay a lot of money to use the school for meetings.'

The discourse of reconstruction and development with its underlying assumption that 'we must all work together for the betterment of Site 5' is reflected in the DF minute, but for most of the Site 5 members the dominant discourses are still those of opposition and survival. The primary school, welcome as it is for the children, charges a high rental when its rooms are used by local groups; and as one young community leader explained to me, 'The community feels that this whole school has just been dictated to them.'

Winnie, who occupied such a key community role during the years of struggle, only made three brief contributions during the three DF meetings we attended together. I wondered why she contributed so little, especially as she is fluent in spoken English. When I considered her history, and scrutinized the DF proceedings more carefully, the reasons for her lack of involvement became clearer to me.

Winnie gained her confidence and her fluency in the situations of horizontal communication that I referred to earlier, in workshops among squatters, ANC gatherings and Civic Association meetings. Communication was largely in Xhosa, and there was little reliance on text. Events such as these were dominated by discourses of opposition and survival, with an ethos of collective participation. In these contexts, Winnie could draw on her great strengths in horizontal communication – her facial expressions, body postures and gestures, and her reliance on prosodic devices and narrative. In the DF, however, in the politics of the 'new South Africa', the oppositional discourse is disallowed in the cause of reconstruction. In the context of the rapid formalization of Site 5, its incorporation into mainstream governance, its dependence on outside agencies for resources and the urgency of the reconstruction, vertical communication (that which takes place between squatters and dominant groupings) has rapidly become more regular and important. The DF is saturated with committee and other bureaucratic literacy practices in English. Contacts to obtain resources from outside the area are made in written English, with the DF acting as mediator.

Winnie is all too aware of the growing importance of being able to read and write in English. She explained how she wanted to get a job as a community worker in Site 5 so she could be paid for all the work she currently does informally.

The fact that she is seen as 'illiterate' has excluded her from such a post. She has started attending the Site 5 night school every night where, as is common policy in South Africa, she has to learn to read and write in Xhosa before being allowed to start learning literacy in English.

Adults at the night school learning English work exclusively from photocopied materials produced by an ESL (English as a Second Language) and Literacy Organization in Cape Town. Learners are taught basic comprehension skills, such as identifying the topic of a text and understanding relationships between paragraphs. I never saw any materials being brought in to the classes which were not part of the pre-planned curriculum: not one text, or even one written word from the context of the learners' lives entered the classroom. This can be contrasted with an experience I had with Winnie at home: when I went through an invoice for her soup kitchen with her, I found that she could actually read quite a few of the words on it.

What became clear to me was that a very particular type of schooled literacy was being promoted in the night school, which did not mesh with the existing literacy practices in the community, or with any of the learners' more specific reasons for wanting to attend the school.

I was disturbed by the way that powerful women like Winnie were being somehow positioned in the night school as deficient and incompetent. Winnie says that previously her children didn't know that she was unable to read or write. Now they do:

> He [the younger son] laugh now, he say 'Mama, are you Sub A [reception class]?' Sometimes I'm sitting here and write my things and he say 'Ooooh, look my mother, she's Sub A! Come, come and look.' If he roep [calls] his friends, I just close my door.

Conclusion

Unfortunately, the thrust towards modernization in South Africa means that literacy (including English) is being seen as a commodity which must be delivered for the purposes of human resources development, rather than as a critical social practice in which power relations are deeply implicated. But so much is possible in the new political conditions in South Africa. Before 1994 there were two official languages, English and Afrikaans. Now there are eleven official languages, including Xhosa. This may start to make a small difference in places like Site 5, as long as development workers and literacy activists are aware of the particular relationships between languages, literacies and power in the South African context. If they are, they could swing the balance of power back towards the local community and seriously address its historical disadvantage. A simple insistence on the principle of translation in meetings, or the occasional taking of minutes in Xhosa, could make a big difference. Literacy provision which draws on current support networks and existing social practices could strengthen learners' positions rather than undermine them, and the great strengths that were developed during the years of liberation struggle, such as empowerment, participation and democratic decision making, could be affirmed.

Appendix

List of texts encountered in Site 5

I would like to stress that this is a list of every single text I encountered in Site 5. It is not a selection of them. I did not manage to obtain a picture of literacy practices and associated texts in the domains of shopping, post offices or travelling, as my research was limited to what happened inside Site 5. Of my informants, some went outside Site 5 every day, and some only went out once a fortnight.

Apart from Winnie, two other informants were Primrose and Miriam. Primrose is a middle-aged woman who works as a domestic worker in the white suburbs and sews dresses to sell at home. She is the treasurer of the pre-school committee and a member of the ANC Women's League. Miriam is in her late twenties. She works for a welfare agency and is involved in setting up pre-schools in the area. Her husband is 'illiterate'. They run a shop in Site 5 and are doing very well financially. All the people mentioned here by name are Xhosa speakers.

1   Texts encountered within households and families
   - newspaper wallpaper
   - 1 newspaper, not for reading (in Khumbula's house)
   - 1 women's magazine (in a teacher's house)
   - letters, mainly personal
   - wall calendars (in three houses)
   - Bibles (in every house)
   - Xhosa/English dictionary (in Mxolisi's house)
   - photograph album (Paulina's, without words)
   - books and journals (only evident in Winnie's and Primrose's houses):

      in Winnie's house:
      Food for the Soul (recipe book)
      1 Enid Blyton book
      3 women's romances, in English
      1 spy thriller
      1 children's annual
      2 *Reader's Digests*
      1 Hamlyn's True Adventures

      in Primrose's house:
      1 Afrikaans/English dictionary
      1 Paddington bear story
      1 book of fairy tales
      1 1986 diary
      1 English/Xhosa grammar book
      2 books of fables in Xhosa: *Amabalana Neentsomi* and *Isitiye*
      1 car maintenance brochure
   - pamphlets (only evident in Winnie's house):

      boxes full of ANC brochures
      box full of health-related pamphlets

2   Texts encountered within the development domain, all in English
   - personal diaries
   - CA, DF and Joint Working Group minutes
   - banners at CA launch with the words 'People's Development for Empowerment' and 'Local government for all'
   - building plans:

      temporary clinic
      informal market area

- constitution of National Nutrition and Population Development Programme
- attendance registers
- memorandum about office for CA

3   Bureaucratic: health and welfare
- financial contributions to Burial Societies were mentioned, but receipts were not given
- in Winnie's house:

    identity documents and application forms
    old age pension cards
    clinic cards
    baby cards
    list of names of residents who had contributed financially to funeral expenses of resident in neighbouring squatter area
    plans for CWDC building to be erected in Site 5 (talked about)
- texts generated by the clinic:

    scabies pamphlet, in English
    booklet and pamphlet on Aids, in English and Xhosa
    recipe sheet from margarine company, in English
    posters advertising Health Day and Aids Day

4   Work and business (in Site 5)
- Small Business Development Corporation workbook for setting up a small business, in English
- list of names in sewing group and record of sales
- Primrose's handwritten advertisements for bus rides and dressmaking
- in Miriam's house:

    ledgers
    invoices
    bills etc.

5   Religion
- Bibles
- adverts for visiting evangelists
- envelopes with money for funeral expenses

6   Politics
- in Winnie's house, in English, Xhosa and Afrikaans:

    ANC membership cards
    ANC broadsheets
    ANC pamphlets
    ANC membership lists
    ANC resolutions, minutes and agendas
    ANC posters
- in environment, mainly in English:

    ANC posters
    people wearing ANC T-shirts

7   Schooling and education
   - invitation to school launch
   - programme of Launch Day events
   - bursary application forms
   - conditions of employment for pre-school teachers (talked about)
   - cheques to be signed for pre-school expenses (talked about)

This list only covers texts outside the classroom. Obviously there were many texts inside the school, but only one child encountered during the research was doing homework in the house.

8   Personal upliftment or pleasure

No such texts were encountered, although some were talked about. Novels are listed under item 1 above.

9   Sport and recreation
   - Netball club minutes, in English

10   Night school
   - curriculum materials, all from the English and Literacy Organization
   - 4 children's books from the Breakthrough to Literacy scheme for children learning to read and write
   - stories written by 3 learners
   - graduation and attendance certificates

This reading was specially commissioned for this book. (Catherine Kell's research in Site 5 is more fully documented in her thesis (Kell, 1994).)

Reading C
COMPUTER-MEDIATED ENGLISH: SOCIOLINGUISTIC ASPECTS OF COMPUTER-MEDIATED COMMUNICATION

Simeon Yates

Introduction

Modern society has brought numerous new media into many areas of our daily lives; television and the telephone are but two obvious examples. These media have in one form or another drawn upon already existing practices, but they have also generated new forms of linguistic practice as human beings seek to make sense of the new opportunities available. This paper is concerned with another new medium, that of computer-mediated communication (CMC) and its effects on the use of the English language. CMC is a medium which exists at the intersection of many interesting issues and technological developments.

Computer-mediated communication: the medium

CMC is a form of computer-based interaction, mostly using typed electronic text as its base, conducted across local and wide-area networks. Indeed anyone with access to the Internet, the world's computer network, can interact with anyone else on that system.

Types of CMC system

CMC comes in a number of forms, which are explored below and can best be described as any human communications system based on the use of networked computers which utilizes the computer as both the transmission and the reception system. The number of possible media in which the message can be transmitted and received is now expanding far beyond the simple text-based systems which emerged with large-scale computer networks in the early 1970s.

CMC systems come in two principal forms: synchronous and asynchronous CMC. Synchronous CMC can be considered equivalent to other synchronous communications systems (e.g. the telephone or face-to-face interaction), in that all the communicating parties need to be present at the same time, whether this is true physical presence or the tele-presence of the telephone and CMC. Synchronous text-based CMC messages often consist of short one-line utterances typed into the system. These are either received as small texts which flash up on a participant's screen, or form part of the growing interactive text visible to both parties.

CMC example 1: synchronous CMC interaction

```
VAX/VMS Phone Facility 8-JUL-1993%

------------------------------------------------------
VAX3::SJ_YATES
Hi there, did you get my note about the conference?
Yeah, it came yesterday.
Did you think that it would be a good idea to attend?
Not sure, we might have to shift the focus a bit.
That's fine with me.
------------------------------------------------------
VAX::JT_SMITH
Hi there, did you get my note about the conference?
Yeah, it came yesterday.
Did you think that it would be a good idea to attend?
Not sure, we might have to shift the focus a bit.
That's fine with me.
------------------------------------------------------
```

Asynchronous CMC, on the other hand, does not require the co-presence of the participants, in the same way that written interaction by post does not require the co-presence of the correspondents. Asynchronous CMC is of course far faster than the postal mail system (known by network users as 'snail-mail'), taking no more than a few minutes to deliver a message to a user on the other side of the globe. One obvious advantage of asynchronous CMC is the way in which it allows the participants to react in their own time, especially as they may be in different time zones across the globe. Text-based asynchronous CMC messages are often longer than those sent in synchronous CMC and may be more substantive in content.

Asynchronous CMC itself comes in two main forms. The difference here concerns the individual or group nature of the communication. The classic form of individual asynchronous CMC is that of electronic mail (e-mail). The analogy to written postal mail is deliberate, as all users of contemporary computer networks have an electronic mail address to which CMC messages may be sent. My present address is:

s.j.yates@open.ac.uk

This address details the individual user (s.j.yates), the university where the user is (open), the wide-area network the university is situated on (ac [the UK's Joint Academic Network – JANET]), and finally the country in which this network exists (uk). This address allows a message sent by one user to navigate its way from network to network until it reaches its destination, where it waits for the recipient to read it, using his or her electronic mail software.

CMC can also be conducted by groups of users, which can number thousands. Some systems (e.g. the UNIX UseNet) are open to anyone on the Internet. Group discussions can be conducted using e-mail through the co-ordinated sending of messages to many users at once. The interactions are described as 'e-mail lists', as any message sent to the 'list' is forwarded to all those users on the 'list'. This method of interaction is of course automated. The automated systems are known as 'list-servers' and the interactions as 'list-serve' discussions.

Other dedicated group asynchronous CMC systems are available. These usually take the form of computer conferencing. Computer conferencing systems and listservers are similar in their functioning except that computer conferencing systems hold the messages of the interaction in an indexed database. It is possible to re-examine the history of the communication and follow the chains of interaction within it. The Open University uses a computer conferencing system (CoSy) as a teaching medium on a number of courses.

Lingua franca of the Internet

CMC example 2: an e-mail message on the Linguist list

```
Date: Fri, 21 Jan 1994 14:12-EST
From: Marion.Kee@A.NL.CS.CMU.EDU
Subject: Re: 5.71 Lingua franca on the Internet
```

I do hope I'm not out of line in observing this, but it's begging to be commented upon. Celso Alvarez-Caccamo, in Linguist Issue #5.71, remarks:

>I quite honestly don't feel I'm now writing >in "English", not even in "bad English": I'm >writing in "Computer".

While I believe I understand his point, to me the designator "Computer" refers to a specialized sub language of English, one in which I have been competent for nearly ten years. Given this overlap of terminology, this claim seems quite humorous when juxtaposed with the portion of his text immediately preceding it:

>Within [the Internet's] linear territory, >discussants discursively manage locally->bound hegemonic or subaltern positions…

Certainly, nothing in "Computer" has prepared me to understand this! I have to switch to "Linguist", where I find that perhaps I require further competency in the sub-sub language "Sociolinguist". (I would agree, by the way, that it isn't "English".)

CMC is not only interesting as a new medium. Its role in globalization is also of concern, and considerable debate has developed around both global CMC and its main language, namely English. A discussion on the Linguist international electronic mail list, a part of which is quoted above, made clear that the problems of intercultural communication that CMC generates are the direct consequence of its reliance upon the de facto standard of English as the main language of communication. CMC is not the only medium to have become reliant upon English as a default standard; another example is satellite television. The reasons for the use of English as a default standard for international communication via new media is of course the product of such economic, social and political factors whereby the USA, the UK and Europe have been the centre of both the technological and the social development of their use. This paper is not concerned with the numerous problems for non-English-speaking nations and peoples that such an imbalance creates, but rather with some of the effects which this role and the medium itself are having upon the English language.

Computer-mediated communication: the issues

CMC, speech and writing

From the above examples one might immediately conclude that CMC is a written medium. Such a conclusion, however, makes a large number of assumptions about what it means to engage in the practice of writing. Though these examples are clearly printed upon the written page and consist of typed letters, it may never have been an intention of their producers to create a printed text. CMC is part of a family of computer-based communications technologies that use the electronic text as their basis, and the above examples of CMC form part of ongoing and dynamic interactions. The implications of CMC for communication in general go well beyond the issues discussed in this paper, which covers just one of the computer media that rely upon the electronic text. (For an interesting discussion of the effects of the electronic text, see Poster, 1990.)

Many researchers investigating CMC have attempted to explore it as a mode of communication by comparing it to either speech or writing, or both of these media. Many of these studies have attempted to meld models of spoken interaction to those of CMC. One analysis of educational interactions between teenage students around the globe has attempted to map the classroom discourse structure of *initiation* from the teacher, *response* from the pupil and subsequent *follow-up* by the teacher (IRF) on to their CMC discourse (Levin et al., 1990). Not surprisingly, given the asynchronous nature of CMC, very few of these IRF structures were found. Often an initiation from a teacher might trigger four or five responses, which might lead to one generic follow-up message from the teacher or to a number of different follow-up messages, which themselves generate more responses from the students. Unlike the classroom IRF structure where teachers account for nearly two-thirds of communication, the CMC interaction was dominated more by student than by teacher comments. Such an example makes clear that one cannot easily transfer a model of spoken interaction structure to another medium.

In order to explore CMC as a mode of communication I conducted a corpus-based study of CMC, speech and writing. A **corpus-based study** requires the analysis of a large number of sample texts and utterances from a number of different sources in order to make clear specific linguistic features. It allows the researcher to explore real rather than theoretically constructed linguistic data. In order to examine how CMC was either similar to or different from spoken and written English, I compared three language corpora: one of speech (some 500,000 words), one of writing (some 1 million words) and one of CMC (some 2 million words) across a number of theoretical factors. (The corpora used in this analysis were the London-Lund corpora of spoken UK English and the Lancaster/Oslo Bergen corpus of written UK English. The CMC corpus was constructed from interactions taking place on the Open University's CoSy conferencing system and is fully documented in Yates, 1993a, 1993b.)

If one considers the *production* differences between speech and writing, one of the most important differences is the time available to the speaker or writer. Chafe and Danielewicz (1987) argue that the vocabulary of spoken language is more limited, because speakers do not have the time to sift through possible choices; instead, they tend to use the first words that occur to them.

A measure of the vocabulary used in a text is the **type/token ratio**. This measures the number of different words (the types) against the total number of words (the tokens) in a given passage. In a hypothetical text of 100 words, each of which was the word 'dog', the type/token ratio would be 1 to 100, or 1 per cent. In a text of 100 words, all of which were different, the type/token ratio would be 100 to 100, or 100 per cent. Of course almost all texts of more than a few words will contain some repetition and some difference. Type/token ratios can therefore give us a measure of the range of vocabulary used. The three corpora in this study were analysed for their type/token ratios. As might have been expected, there was a lower ratio, and therefore a smaller range of vocabulary, in speech compared with writing (see Table 1). CMC was found to have a type/token ration that was very similar to writing but none the less statistically significantly different.

Table 1   Vocabulary use in CMC, speech and writing

Corpus	CMC	Writing	Speech
Mean type/token ratio	59%	62%	40%

Such a result could imply that CMC is actually a written medium, but vocabulary range is only one difference between speech and writing. Another difference is the use of pronouns. In formal written English we seldom make direct reference to ourselves, while in speech we are constantly referring to ourselves and those directly around us. Such differences in pronoun usage reflect not just pragmatic production differences but specific social practices. For instance, in western culture the first and second personal pronouns 'I' and 'you' are not usually considered appropriate in formal writing in newspapers, textbooks or scientific articles.

If we count the number of first- and second-person pronouns per 1,000 words for each of the three corpora, we find that CMC is closer to speech than it is to writing (see Table 2).

Table 2   Pronoun use in CMC, speech and writing

Corpus	CMC	Writing	Speech
Mean pronouns per 1,000 words	50	20	67

This is only part of the story. If the use of first- and second-person pronouns is measured as a percentage of total pronoun use, we find that this accounts for 64 per cent of all pronoun use for CMC, compared with 58 per cent for speech and 27 per cent for writing. CMC is therefore similar to speech in its use of direct personal references, but very different in terms of more general personal references. Such a result implies that CMC discourse is highly concerned with those directly involved in the communication and makes little direct reference to people and objects beyond the immediate context of the communication.

The reference to self and other is not the only area where CMC differs from speech and writing. Another lies in the use of modalities. Modalities within a text indicate the relationship between the speaker and the objects spoken about, or the speaker's perception of the relationship between the subjects of an utterance. For instance, if a speaker says something emphatically, we know we are being asked to believe it is true. If on the other hand he or she uses a hedge (such as 'it might be' or 'you could perhaps'), then we know the speaker is being more tentative about the knowledge or opinions being presented (Hodge and Kress, 1988, p. 121). Many of these emphatics and hedges are created through the use of a class of words called modal auxiliaries. English modal auxiliaries include such words as *can, could, would* and *shall.* Table 3 makes clear that modal auxiliary use (measured as modal auxiliaries per 1,000 words) is far higher in CMC than in either speech or writing. Such a result indicates that definitions of knowledge are more likely to be under discussion within CMC (at least in the academic contexts from which my data comes) than in spoken or written discourse.

Table 3   Modal use in CMC, speech and writing

Corpus	CMC	Writing	Speech
Mean modals per 1,000 words	18	13	14

These three basic results indicate that CMC has specific similarities and specific differences compared with speech and writing. First, CMC has a similar vocabulary range to writing, as indicated by the type/token results. Secondly, there are similarities between the subjective or interpersonal references in CMC and in those of speech, as indicated by the pronoun usage result. Lastly, CMC is dissimilar to both speech and writing in terms of its representation of knowledge, as indicated by the modal auxiliary results. Such findings are of course very general, and there are varieties in language use within CMC, depending on the purposes of the communication.

Computer-mediated communication: flaming

If CMC represents a new mode of communication that reflects aspects of both spoken and written language, what social consequences does this entail? One area of CMC practice that has come in for considerable scrutiny is that of '**flaming**'. This can be defined as a variety of behaviours, ranging from impolite statements, through swearing, to the use of positive exclamations both in general and as expressed towards others (Kiesler et al., 1984). In their overview of the literature on flaming, Lea et al. (1992, p. 90) describe it as 'the hostile expression of strong emotions and feelings'. Flaming is often seen as one of the main problems or drawbacks associated with the use of CMC systems. There are many arguments and debates as to whether or not this is the case, and it may in fact be that extreme forms of flaming, such as profanity, are quite rare occurrences, though highly visible to a large number of people. This mix of points brings us to the important issue of why such matters as socio-emotional content or flaming have become important areas of study. Lea et al. (1992, p. 90) consider this, arguing that such studies have challenged the view that CMC is a 'cool' medium where information is paramount and social factors minimized.

In a statistical analysis of a set of CMC messages Rice and Love (1987) found that nearly 30 per cent of the total message content was socio-emotional, while Lea et al. (1992) point out that the socio-emotional content in CMC is only remarkable in the context of beliefs about the 'cool' role of written texts. Such outbursts on the telephone, or in face-to-face interaction, would not appear so remarkable (or visible).

It is not so much that CMC as a medium produces the phenomenon of flaming but rather that users and managers of CMC systems expecting to see 'traditional' written texts are challenged by the dynamic, interactive and interpersonal forms that CMC takes. This challenge is at variance not just with their expectations of 'good' written behaviour but also with their control over literate communication. This causes such 'bad' literate behaviour to be defined as problematic; for instance, to be described as 'flaming', with all the implications of heat, fire and danger that the word evokes. Zuboff's (1988) classic study of the impact of information technology on a US corporation made clear how issues such as flaming and the interpersonal use of CMC challenged the systems by which managers had previously controlled the visible literate communication within the company. Indeed, such conflicts can sometimes lead to the removal or transformation of CMC systems.

Conclusion

As a new communications medium with similarities to both written and spoken language, CMC often challenges users' assumptions about the socially defined differences and boundaries between written and spoken English. CMC requires new forms of communicative practice which differ from those normally associated with oral and literate behaviour. As such, CMC provides useful insights and contrasts to structures, practices and cultural ideas which have often been assumed to be fixed or obvious. But CMC in its present basic electronic text form may prove to have been just a brief window on such issues. As computer networks and computers themselves become ever more powerful, CMC itself is changing. For those users with the requisite resources it is possible today to send voice messages, moving colour images, music, or any form of digitized data across the global computer network. This is the world of the multimedia 'document', where many different modes of communication become bound up and combined within a single text. As Halliday (1987) suggests, what counts as 'literacy' has to change, as our reading and writing practices change in response to ever more compex and dynamic developments in communication technology.

References

CHAFE, W. and DANIELEWICZ, J. (1987) 'Properties of spoken and written language' in HOROWITZ, R. and SAMUELS, S.J. (eds), *Comprehending Oral and Written Language*, Orlando, Flor., Academic Press.

BAYNHAM, M. (1995) *Literacy Practices*, Harlow, Longman.

HALLIDAY, M.A.K. (1987) 'Spoken and written modes of meaning' in HOROWITZ, R. and SAMUELS, S.J. (eds) *Comprehending Oral and Written Language*, Orlando, Flor., Academic Press.

HODGE, R. and KRESS, G. (1988) *Social Semiotics*, Cambridge, Polity.

KIESLER, S., SIEGEL, J. and McGUIRE, T. (1984) 'Social psychological aspects of computer-mediated communication', *American Psychologist*, vol. 39, pp. 1123–34.

LEA, M., O'SHEA, T., FUNG, P. and SPEARS, R. (1992) '"Flaming" in computer-mediated communication: observations, explanations, implications' in LEA, M. (ed.), *Contexts of Computer-Mediated Communication*, Hemel Hempstead, Harvester Wheatsheaf.

LEVIN, J.A., KIM, H. and RIEL, M.M. (1990) 'Building electronic communities – success and failure in computer networking', *Instructional Science*, vol. 19, no. 2, pp. 145–69.

POSTER, M. (1990) *The Mode of Information*, Cambridge, Polity.

RICE, E.R. and LOVE, G. (1987) 'Electronic emotion: socioemotional content in a computer mediated network', *Communication Research*, vol. 32, pp. 1492–512.

YATES, S.J. (1993a), 'Speech, writing and computer conferencing: an analysis.' in MASON, R.D. (ed), *Computer Conferencing: the last word?*, Beach Holme, Victoria.

YATES, S.J. (1993b) 'The textuality of computer-mediated communication: speech, writing and genre in CMC discourse', PhD thesis, The Open University.

ZUBOFF, S. (1988) *In the Age of the Smart Machine: the future of work and power*, Oxford, Heinemann.

This reading was specially commissioned for this book.

 ENGLISH AT WORK

Neil Mercer

3.1 INTRODUCTION

This chapter looks at how English, spoken and written, is used as a language for work. In all of the cases I discuss, at least one of the people involved is self-evidently doing what millions of people the world over do every day – using English to get a job done. I have limited myself to interactions involving only a few people, because the language used by professional writers, broadcasters and the like (who by the nature of their work are communicating with mass audiences) is dealt with in other parts of this book and in other books in this series.

A tool for the job

The Russian psychologist L.S. Vygotsky (1978, p. 26) describes language as the most important 'cultural tool' that humans possess. The idea of language as a tool is useful, because it focuses attention on the purposes and effects of using a language, and helps us see that the contrast between 'doing things' and 'just talking' is a dubious one. People achieve things through talk as much as through physical action.

To understand the ways English is used at work we need to look at how occupational or professional interests are represented in the dynamic structure and content of the language. That is, we must see how English is used to get work done, and how the language itself is adapted to serve as a suitable tool for different kinds of work.

The structure of language events

Activity 3.1   A business negotiation   *(Allow about 5 minutes)*
Read the following extract from a real conversation. What kind of business is being done?

Speaker A

We'd like to get some state business.

Do you control Mr Gordon?

How do you and I develop a relationship?

I can give you $2,000 now, with a 50–50 split of the commission.

Speaker B

I will have to work out something, Joe, where you could visit with the trustees.

He'll go along with a lot of the things I recommend.

I have a public relations firm ... and I do business other than what I'm doing here.

Keep talking.

I deal only with you. There's $4,000 a month possible in this.

Here's $2,000. Let's shake hands on it. Do we have a deal?

We'll deal on a case by case basis. Can you handle X Insurance Company politics?

We have a deal.

There's 50 people I can send you. I have contacts in Boston.

(Adapted from Shuy, 1993, p. 24)

The conversation in Activity 3.1, as you may have guessed, shows two people involved in negotiating a bribe. It comes from the research of a sociolinguist, Roger Shuy (1993), and is a conversation between an undercover agent for the American law enforcement agency the Federal Bureau of Investigation (FBI), Joe Hauser (Speaker A, who secretly recorded the talk), and a trade union official (Speaker B) who was a target of the FBI's enquiries. Roger Shuy has studied many such secretly recorded, clandestine conversations, and has offered the following analysis of the structure of an archetypal 'bribe' transaction:

Phases	Speaker A	Speaker B
Problem	We'd like to get some state business.	
		I will have to work out something, Joe, where you could visit with the trustees.
	Do you control Mr Gordon?	
		He'll go along with a lot of the things I recommend.
	How do you and I develop a relationship?	
		I have a public relations firm … and I do business other than what I'm doing here.
Proposal	I can give you $2,000 now, with a 50–50 split of the commission.	
		Keep talking.
	I deal only with you. There's $4,000 a month possible in this.	
		We'll deal on a case by case basis. Can you handle X Insurance Company politics?
Completion	Here's $2,000. Let's shake hands on it. Do we have a deal?	
		We have a deal.
Extension		There's 50 people I can send you. I have contacts in Boston.

(Adapted from Shuy, 1993, p. 24)

Shuy claims that this 'phase' model can usefully be applied to all the tape-recorded data that he has seen presented by the FBI in bribery cases. Entry into each of the phases depends on the successful completion of the previous one. After some initial greetings (which might be considered to constitute a preliminary phase in themselves), a *problem* is presented by the first party. This usually amounts to a request for help. During this phase, the first party usually also checks on the other's authority and capacity to deliver. The next phase is the *proposal*, in which rewards are discussed and promises made. If things are going well, this phase may be used to build some kind of intimacy, with common acquaintances being mentioned, anecdotes told and so on. The final part of the negotiation is marked by entry into the *completion* phase, classically symbolized by the handshake and expressions like 'We have a deal.' There may then follow an *extension* phase, with future possibilities being introduced.

Shuy's method of analysis is intended as a practical one, and its use has influenced the course of some court cases and retrospectively cast doubt on the validity of the verdicts of others. For example, in a number of US bribery cases involving politicians and other public servants it has been claimed by the state prosecution that the fact a public servant has even engaged in a conversation with a would-be briber is sufficient to show that they are corrupt. Shuy suggests that juries are often persuaded by this line of argument, because people generally assume that two people talking together in reasonable tones, without explicit disagreement, must have shared values and purposes. Those accused of corruption are then convicted on the basis of what he calls 'conversational contamination'. Shuy also comments that many American trial judges are unwilling to admit a linguist as an expert witness in court because they claim that any normal person can understand a conversation when they hear it, and that to analyse talk in depth is to impose false levels of meaning on 'common-sense' understandings. However, he shows that a more careful analysis of events may reveal that the attempted bribery did not follow the model pattern, that the accused person did not collude in the construction of a model event, and that the crucial stage of completion (in which 'the deal' is made) may never have materialized. An example is the following extract from a recorded conversation between a US politician (Williams) accused of corruption and an FBI agent (Farhart) masquerading as an Arab sheikh seeking residence in the United States. In earlier conversation Williams has agreed to advise the sheikh on how he might best present his case to immigration, but with no suggestion of impropriety:

> Farhart   I will, for your help, uh, assistance, I would like to give you … some money for, permanent residence.
>
> Williams   No. No. No. No, when I work in that kind of activity, it is purely a public, not uh, No, within my position, when I deal with law and legislation, it's not within … (*telephone rings, interrupting*). My only interest is to see this come together.

(Shuy, 1993, p. 32)

As Shuy comments, on this occasion a proposal for a bribe may have been made, but it was clearly rejected. However, his analysis did not save Senator Williams, who was convicted and imprisoned on this and similar tape evidence (none of which, Shuy suggests, was any more convincing about the senator's guilt than the example above).

Talk in its work setting

I have spent some time on Shuy's forensic analysis of tape recordings because it raises some interesting points about the use of the English language as a tool of work:

- doing a certain kind of work is likely to involve the creation of distinctive patterns and content of discourse in the English language;

- the distinctive features of these language events may not be apparent to the participants, or even to a casual observer who listens to a recording of the event, but they can be revealed by an analysis which is based on an under-standing of how the English language operates as a system and how it is used, in practice, in particular social contexts;

- the analysis of such non-obvious features of English in use can have practical applications.

Bribery may be an unusual form of work, but in this respect – that it is accom-plished through certain distinctive ways of using the English language – it has something in common with a great many perfectly legitimate kinds of profes-sional and commercial activity. Sometimes the distinctive, work-related features of the language are most obviously those of vocabulary: the 'jargon' or technical language of a trade or other occupation. (I deal with such technical language later in this chapter.) But sometimes, as in the case of bribery, the work-related quality of language may be more distinctively represented in the structure of an interaction, rather than the fact that technical English words are used. Shuy's analysis also demonstrates how language is used to construct and maintain 'working relationships', social bonds and commitments between people which develop through doing a certain kind of work and which may be closely bound up with the nature of the work itself.

Two types of language event

At this stage I would like to distinguish between two kinds of social event in which English can be used as a 'working language'. First, there are *events in which the people involved are members of the same, or a closely related, occupation, trade or profession.* Secondly, there are *events in which a working person is, as part of his or her job, dealing with a member of the public.* Do not think of this as a hard and fast distinction, but as a rough one which can be useful for understanding the nature of some kinds of 'working Englishes'. In the next part of this chapter I deal with the first type of event and then later I consider professional–public types of interaction.

3.2   ENGLISH AMONG CO-WORKERS

In research on the use of English and other languages at work there has been a tendency to focus on occupations in which language *constitutes* the work to a great extent; one product of the work of lawyers and journalists, for example, is spoken or written language. It may be less obvious that language also plays an important role in 'getting the job done' for other kinds of occupation, such as manual, constructional ones and those which rely heavily on types of representation besides language (such as the plans and blueprints of engineers and architects).

Figure 3.1   Talk is an important 'tool of the trade' for the construction industry

Activity 3.2   *(Reading A)*

Read 'Constructing the virtual building: language on a building site' by Peter Medway (Reading A). As you read, pay particular attention to Medway's use of the concepts of ideational function, interpersonal function and intertextuality.

Comment

You can see from Medway's research that the business of constructing a building is achieved to a great extent through language. It is not simply a matter of an architect drawing up plans and then handing them to the builder who converts them into three-dimensional reality. The whole process is one of explanation, interpretation and negotiation as the architect attempts to construct a 'virtual building' in advance of the real one, through conversations with builders and others involved. Medway uses Halliday's concept of the ideational function of language to explain this. These conversations, in different settings such as an office or a building site, may vary in structure and style (he notes how 'the building site is a macho environment where [bad] language may be a way of declaring masculinity'). But he also points to the intertextuality of the discourse – the ways that various conversations, at different times and involving different sets of partners, are woven 'into a single multi-stranded web of discourse' which 'knits the diverse participants together into a discourse community'. Medway refers to Halliday's concept of the interpersonal function of language for establishing and monitoring relations in such a community. I will return to the concept of discourse community a little later in the chapter.

Chapter 1 discusses the interpersonal and ideational functions of talk in more detail.

Englishes for trading

In some parts of the world, English has for many years been used as a trading language, a **lingua franca** between people who have different mother tongues (the term 'lingua franca' reflects the fact that French has been used in the same way). In being adapted to this use, a lingua franca may evolve into a new language variety with a simplified grammar and limited vocabulary. Elements of the grammar of one or more of the local mother tongues may be incorporated into the new variety, which is then technically called a **pidgin**. Pidgins sometimes eventually become the main language of some communities, rather than a specialized kind of 'work talk'. If this process results in children learning the pidgin as a mother tongue, the new language technically becomes a **creole**. A good example of a work language which has expanded in this way is the Tok Pisin (talk pidgin) of Papua New Guinea. According to the sociolinguist Suzanne Romaine (1990), it was born in the colonial era. It was used first as a means of communication between the indigenous population and their European colonizers but then became the most important lingua franca for Papua New Guineans, who have around 750 indigenous languages between them. The example below is an extract from a radio interview broadcast in 1972. The speaker is a student, and the written version of what he says represents a conventional, 'standardized' form of spelling. Romaine provides both a 'word-by-word' translation into Standard English (in the second column) and a more thorough, meaningful translation (in the third column).

Mi salim eplikeson bilong mi na skul bod i konsiderim na bihain ekseptim me na mi go long skul long fama.	Me send application belong me and school board consider and behind accept me and me go to school of farmer.	I sent my application to the school board and then they considered and accepted me and I'm going to agricultural school.

(From Healey, 1975, cited in Romaine, 1990, p. 197)

Once a pidgin is established, the redefined meanings of some English words (e.g. *bihain = behind* as an adverb for creating past tenses) will become common knowledge to all involved, and pose no problem to the mutual understanding required for trade.

However, even when business partners have established some variety of English as a common language, difficulties of comprehension may arise for other reasons. Helen Marriott (1995) has carried out research on what she calls 'intercultural business negotiations' – transactions which involve people from significantly different cultural backgrounds. Some of her data come from video-recorded talk, all in English even though the conversation was held in Japan, between a Japanese businessman and an Australian cheese manufacturer. Here is an extract from their conversation.

Transcription conventions

- J = Japanese speaker
- A = Australian speaker
- [indicates simultaneous speech
- (.) indicates a pause

J   And eh what your object to eh visit to me, is that eh introduce for eh this

A   We'd like to sell to Japan

J   sell to Japan

A   yeh

J   uh huh

A   or make it in Japan.

J   mm ah here yes

A   Either way, whichever is the best.

J   mm

A   Maybe make it here for um six months and eh if it's acceptable

J   ah six, six months

A   well we could send some samples from ⌐Australia
J   └in Melbourne uh huh
A   and just test the market (.) if it's good we could then make it in Japan
J   uh huh (.) uh huh
A   with a joint venture.

(Marriott, 1995, pp. 260–1)

Marriott found that there were significant differences between the two men's behaviour in the interaction. The Japanese man often sought clarifications, and periodically offered summaries of information discussed. That is, he used strategies to check that there was shared understanding of matters being negotiated. After the recording Marriott interviewed the two men to gain their views of how the transactions had gone. Both felt that the other had not talked in the ways they would have expected, given their business role. So, for example, the Japanese commented 'in Japan maybe the salesman speak more, more explanation about the eh his company's and the condition of the trading' (Marriott, 1995, p. 263). The Australian, on the other hand, felt that the brevity and noncommittal nature of the Japanese man's reactions to his comments (as in the extract above) left him feeling 'that I don't really know what he's going to do. It finished a little bit unconcluded' (p. 262). Overall, then, the two men constructed rather different understandings of events from the conversation; and the Australian was left feeling much more dissatisfied with the encounter than his Japanese partner.

Although the Japanese speaker was very ready to admit to inadequacies in his English, Marriott suggests that this was not a major cause of misunderstanding. Instead she suggests that the different expectations held and interpretations made about the conversation by the two reflected other, less obvious differences in their cultural backgrounds and experiences. To some extent, this may be a matter of Japanese and Australian people having different habitual conversational styles – ways of expressing intent, interest and so on, through words and gestures which vary considerably across societies. But Marriott emphasizes that explaining misunderstandings in terms of cultural experiences does not mean simply making generalized comparisons between Japanese and Australian ways of talking. In the international business world of today other cultural factors besides national origin might be important for shaping speakers' ways of 'talking business' in English, and for shaping their interpretation of events. The Japanese man worked in a large, international organization: he had much more experience of intercultural business negotiations than the Australian; he had dealt a lot with foreign business people in Japan and had made several work trips abroad. The Australian, on the other hand, worked for his own small firm, had travelled little, and his previous work had not engaged him in these kinds of negotiation. In other words, the Japanese businessman was probably more familiar with the discursive practices of international trading, and so may have had a clearer and more confident set of expectations about the 'ground rules' for carrying on such a business conversation, and for predicting its structure and outcomes.

Trade through written English

English of a specialized and limited kind is still commonly used in the pursuit of certain international trades in the world today. An interesting example provided by the linguists Cremer and Willes (1991, 1994) comes from Macau, an island in south-east Asia. Macau is a former Portuguese colony, and the Portuguese language is still used in many business transactions there. The garment industry – producing items like jeans, blouses, children's garments – is organized, controlled and documented by written language at every stage; in these processes, however, the predominant language is English, even though it is the native language of none of the participants in the trading process.

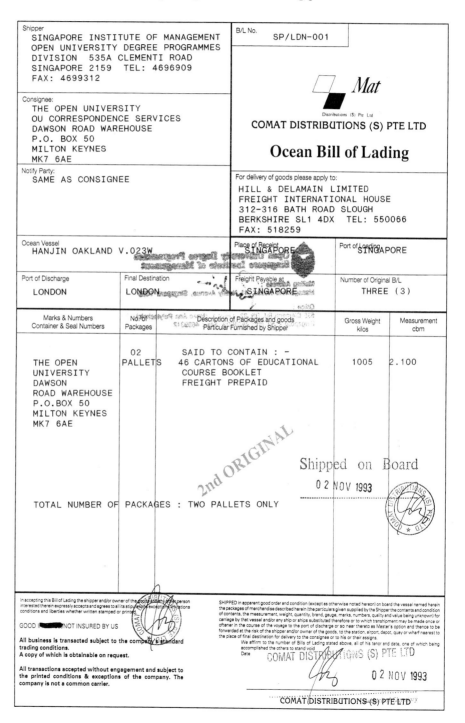

Figure 3.2 English as an international trade language: 'bill of lading' accompanying a shipment of goods from Singapore to the UK

In Macau an important form of trade is the manufacture and export of textiles to the United States, the European Union and (to a lesser extent) Japan. The continued success of this trade depends in part on the ability of traders to secure international orders and to deliver them efficiently (which involves dealing with complex sets of international import–export regulations). Cremer and Willes point out that even though English is in daily use as a working language in Macau (and other parts of south-east Asia), its use is confined to specific domains:

> Most of those who use English in this daily traffic would not claim to know the language well, and are uneasy where they correspond with counterparts in North America. They are altogether more confident in interaction with agents in Sweden (say) or Spain, where both parties to the correspondence handle the only available medium of communication with some difficulty and, even if they recognise each other's errors, disregard rather than tolerate them.
>
> (Cremer and Willes, 1994, p. 7)

For many people in Macau's textile trade 'the question is not how much English can be learnt and how well, but rather how little English can be made to serve their purposes?' (Cremer and Willes, 1991, p. 2).

Cremer and Willes describe how the success of this specialized and restricted use of English depends upon two main factors. First, English is used in a very limited, related set of contexts. Business is essentially to do with five stages of a process: ordering, manufacture, inspection, shipment and payment. Any document in English can be easily related to well-established rules and procedures for each of these stages. Secondly, the language itself is of a reduced, specialized and highly context-specific kind. Cremer and Willes therefore suggest that although it is essentially a written variety, the English of the Macau garment trade has something in common with the original oral trading languages called pidgins discussed earlier. (They note that it has more or less replaced such pidgins, based on Portuguese and English, which were used in Macau in the past.)

English as the special language of work

Compared to many languages in the world English is unusual in that it is, for so many people, a language which is not their 'mother tongue' but which they have to use at work. Look, for example, at the box below. It contains information about language use on the premises of a firm in central southern India called Wipro Fluid Power. Wipro makes hydraulic equipment. The vast majority of its workforce speak the regional language, Kannada, as a mother tongue, but it is the official policy of the company that English should be used for some of the most important internal communications. This policy reflects the company's recognition of the common use of English between Indians who speak different regional languages. It also wishes to expand its international trading activities, and sees the development of working English among its workforce as a positive step in this direction. In daily practice the use of the two languages will not be as neatly segregated as might appear from the box. For example, managers may have to explain an employment contract (written in English) to an employee in Kannada.

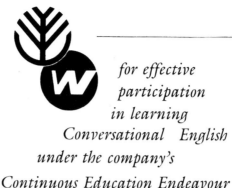

Certificate of Merit
awarded to

_____

for effective
participation
in learning
Conversational   English
under the company's
Continuous Education Endeavour

Wipro Fluid Power

Figure 3.3
Certificate of
competence in
English

Wipro Fluid Power, Bangalore, India

On the company premises English is used for …

*   writing notices, permanent signs, instructions for operating machinery, employees' contracts, job specifications and records of work completed

*   informal talk among management, formal public communications, training courses.

On the company premises Kannada is used for …

*   informal speech among production workers

*   informal communications between managers and production workers.

(Information supplied by Anil Kumar, Wipro Fluid Power, Bangalore)

If for some people English is a language associated with the more official or formal aspects of working life, then for those people the choice of English in any particular conversation may have a special social significance.

❖   ❖   ❖   ❖   ❖

Activity 3.3   Switching languages   *(Allow about 5 minutes)*

The transcript in the box below is an extract of a conversation recorded in an office in the USA, presented and discussed by the sociolinguist Joshua Fishman (1971). The conversationalists are a manager of a commercial enterprise (male, called 'boss' in the transcript) and his (female) secretary. Both are Hispanic Americans whose main language of home and personal life is Spanish. The transcript begins part way through their conversation, when the 'boss' is talking about the social habits of some people in the local community.

You will see that the speakers switch from Spanish into English. Both are fluent conversationalists in Spanish and English, and on the face of it their switch from one language to the other might seem quite unnecessary. However, Fishman suggests that the 'codeswitch' from Spanish to English on this occasion carries a subtle, social-psychological meaning. What do you think might be the meaning of this switch? (An English translation of the Spanish is given in the third column.)

Boss	embargo, cuando tienen que ir a la iglesia, o la misa para pedirle ...	then, when they have to go to church or to mass, to ask ...
Secretary	(laughter)	
Boss	A Dós entonces no van.	God then they don't go.
Secretary	Sí, entonces no van.	Yes, then they don't go.
Boss	Pero, así es la vida, caramba.	But that's life, you know.
	Do you think that you could get this letter out today?	
Secretary	Oh yes, I'll have it this afternoon for you.	
Boss	OK, good, fine then.	
(Fishman, 1971, pp. 238–9)		

Comment

Fishman suggests that the switch signals a move back from local community matters to business matters and the English language of work. The relationship between the conversationalists shifts dimensions, from that of two people who share membership of a Hispanic community and culture, into the working relationship of a 'boss' and 'secretary' which is firmly embedded in the dominant Anglo-American culture.

Status and gender at work

Fishman's Spanish–English conversation in Activity 3.3 also illustrates something else about the use of English at work, besides the influence of the work culture on speakers' choice of language. It illustrates how status differences between co-workers are commonly acted out in their conversations. The switch from English to Spanish is determined by the boss, so that his higher status in the office is acted out in his control over the choice of language.

Of course, the 'boss' and 'secretary' are also male and female, respectively. In Chapter 1 Janet Maybin reviews research on conversations between women and men which suggested that men tend to exert most overt influence over the choice of topics, to interrupt female partners and generally to dominate interaction. They may also tend to control codeswitching to or from English in bilingual conversations, though I am not aware of any research which has specifically looked at this. One methodological problem in conducting such research would be to determine the separate effects of *job status* and *gender* on who exerts most control over a conversation and the ways people contribute to it.

Some research has tried to distinguish the relative effects of job-related status and gender on speakers' control of conversations (though with monolingual English speakers). For example, Nicola Woods (1988) tape recorded nine three-person conversations involving women and men colleagues in a British office. Her method was based on Sacks et al.'s (1974) analysis of 'turn taking' in conversations, which is discussed in Chapter 1. Woods decided to measure the relative extent to which speakers (female or male, high or low status) took substantial turns at speaking. She called this 'floor apportionment'. She also observed how the various speakers gained the floor, such as by interrupting or carrying on speaking beyond the end of what is called a 'transition relevance place' (TRP) – a point in the conversation where a speaker can be considered to have reached the meaningful end of what she or he is saying. Woods's method of distinguishing the effects of job status and gender, and her main results, are summarized in the box below.

Talking shop: sex and status as determinants of floor apportionment in a work setting

By sampling interactions in a work setting which included both sexes in the roles of 'boss' and 'subordinate', the present study was able to [examine] the variables of gender and occupational status and their relative influence on patterns of floor apportionment.

…

Results showed that when the two power bases of gender and occupational status are at work, then the former – gender – tends to exert the greatest influence on floor apportionment. Essentially, while the power base of occupational status did influence the way that both men and women organized conversation (generally, speakers in high occupational status spent more time holding the floor than their subordinates …), nevertheless even when women held high-status occupational positions male subordinates still organized the interaction in a way that allowed them to dominate the floor: for instance, by interrupting more often, speaking through more TRPs and giving less assent to women participants.

(Woods, 1988, pp. 141, 149)

Woods's research suggests that gender can be a very significant factor in shaping the conversations that take place at work – more powerful, she suggests, than job status. As she readily admits elsewhere in her article, however, hers is a small-scale study that cannot be used to draw sweeping conclusions.

There is now an established line of research on gender and the language of women in their workplaces (see, for example, West, 1990; Coates, 1994). However, the participation of women in English at work seems only slowly to be becoming acknowledged in the teaching of international 'business English'. For example, in a widely used textbook and video, *English for Business Purposes* (Esnol et al., 1985), the scenarios that students are asked to consider show only males in the major relevant roles: women make brief appearances as a receptionist, secretary and the wife of a main character (who departs with a gift of flowers, saying 'Well, I'd better put these in water', when the men get down to business).

Jobs and jargons

Even people who speak English as their first language will often use a specialized variety of it, at least in terms of vocabulary when they are at work.

Activity 3.4   House talk *(Allow about 15 minutes)*

Read the telephone conversation transcribed below and consider the following questions.

- What kinds of job (in general terms) do you think that the speakers do?
- Are they strangers, or do they work in the same business?
- How many jargon words do they use that are not part of your vocabulary for your own working life?
- Do you feel confident that you understand what they are talking about?
- Is it likely to be problematic, for the effective purposes of this working conversation, that the speakers use jargon?

Caller	Is Ellen there? It's Bill.
Switchboard operator	I'll put you through.
Ellen	Hello, Bill.
Bill	Oh, hi. Just a quick, um, query. Umm. You know, uh, with the CNS job.
Ellen	Yeah.
Bill	Umm, you know we were talking about the, the range which it's possible, the salary range?
Ellen	Yeah.
Bill	The two scales just join on, do they, end on?
	[Or ...
Ellen	[Yeah.
Bill	... you know the discretionary range?
Ellen	Yeah, well ...
Bill	[*Interrupting*] Is that an overlap?
Ellen	Um. Strictly speaking it isn't.
Bill	Oh right.
Ellen	But we had someone appointed to the PTA ...
Bill	[Yeah.
Ellen	[who was earning above the top of the scale [where
Bill	[Yeah
Ellen	... she came from.
Bill	Yeah.
Ellen	And that was a short-term post and she was allowed to be appointed ...
Bill	[Aah.
Ellen	[to a discretionary point, so that might be an option.

Transcription conventions

- [indicates simultaneous speech
- ... indicates continuous speech
- punctuation has been inserted to make the transcription easier to read

You may have guessed that this was a conversation between two people who work in the same business; they are in fact a manager (Bill) and an administrator (Ellen) in the same university. Their work often brings them into contact, and this is one reason why they can begin the conversation with few preliminaries or extended explanations. They both know the nature of each other's jobs, and in their conversation can build easily on the common knowledge of their shared workplace and of past conversations they have had on related topics (hence the use of expressions like *you know we were talking about* and *you know the discretionary range*). They are continuing an earlier discussion of the point on a salary range at which an appointment could be made to a post in the university. The most obvious jargon words are the acronyms (CNS and PTA – Centre for Nursing Studies and Professional Training Area), which, because they are not real English words at all, would be completely incomprehensible to outsiders. Three-letter acronyms (TLAs) have become a common feature of 1990s business English. The phrase *discretionary range* is made up of two English words with established meanings, but the meaning for the speakers in this conversation depends on some very specific, shared knowledge about the financial working practices of British universities. Because the speakers' past experience has prepared them well for this conversation, the jargon used is certainly no problem. It is one normal feature of the English language being used efficiently as a specialized tool of work.

Of course, the use of jargon (the word itself seems to have entered English from French) often does create problems. Its use by professionals when communicating with a 'lay' person can result in noncomprehension and frustration (or at the very least irritation) on the lay person's part. In discussing many 'uses and abuses' of jargon, however, Walter Nash (1993) points out that jargon words and phrases often become incorporated into the mainstream of English language use. Some examples commonly heard in Britain are *IQ* (from psychology), *programmed* (from information technology/mass media) and more recently *power dressing* (to refer to someone trying to create an impressive work image through their clothes, a term taken from the fashion industry). A rather different kind of extension of the use of jargon English is where technical words are taken up as 'loan words' or 'borrowings' by speakers of other languages operating in specific areas of work. According to the Moscow-based journalist David Hearst (1994) 'business Russian' has incorporated such words as *lizing* (leasing), *bankrotia* (bankruptcy), *fond* (fund) and *privatizatsionny* (the meaning of which I leave you to guess).

Communities of discourse

In Chapter 1 Janet Maybin makes two important points about the language of 'everyday conversations' and the knowledge that speakers need to have in order to take part in them. First, *the meanings of words are shaped by the contexts in which they are used*; and secondly, the communicative success of almost all conversations depends heavily on speakers and listeners having some *shared cultural knowledge and understanding*. These points are very relevant to understanding how English is used as a working language, especially if we also make use of the concept of a **discourse community**. This concept has mainly been developed by the linguist John Swales. As Swales (1990) explains, the basic idea is that there are types of 'community' in which people do not necessarily live close together or even ever see each other face to face. ('**Discourse**' here means the ways in which language, spoken or written, is used in the social practices of such a community.) Yet they use spoken or written language, among themselves, to pursue some common goals in ways that distinguish them from other groups.

The concept of discourse community is helpful for analysing English at work, because it helps us relate the nature of specialized varieties of English to the shared experience and common interests of the groups of people who use them.

Swales (1990) suggests that to qualify as 'communities of discourse' groups need not only a technical discourse but also common interests and goals. Even so, specific discourse communities may be hard to define. For example, although 'Joe' in Reading A is a member of the professional community of architects, the reading shows that he is also a member of a wider 'construction industry' community of discourse, in which some technical language, interests and goals are also shared.

Activity 3.5   *(Allow about 5 minutes)*

Think back through your own life experience. Have any of your activities involved membership of a group that used a distinctive variety of English with specialized genres and vocabulary? If so, try to list up to five vocabulary items that would not have been easily understood by people outside the group.

Emotive aspects of professional discourses

Many written working Englishes are, by intention, unemotional and 'dry' in their content and style. The processes of reporting scientific experiments, surveying buildings and conducting financial transactions are meant to be guided by rationality, rather than emotion, and this is reflected in the usual absence of references to the personal feelings of those doing the work. In such formal writing, the 'agency' of the writer is often rendered invisible by the use of passive forms of verbs (so *a survey was carried out* rather than *I carried out a survey*) and this too emphasizes the supposedly detached and impersonal nature of the process being described. However, the dry and impersonal style of such working Englishes should not blind us to the fact that the use of professional discourses can be important for creating and maintaining the professional and personal identities and relationships of those involved. Moreover, not all working Englishes are formal, and emotions may need to be expressed at work as well as outside it (recall Medway's explanation in Reading A of the use of swear words by an architect on site). There are many ways of acting out one's identity as a member of a working discourse community through language.

In some professional communities the emotional involvement and impact of members' engagement with their professional lives may be enacted through the use of a professional slang – a kind of informal in-group talk whose function is perhaps more interpersonal than ideational. A sinister example of such slang which came to public attention in the 1970s was that used by American soldiers in action in the Far East. They were observed to describe Indo-Chinese people as *geeks* and *slants*, and to talk about *wasting* or *losing* them rather than killing them. A plausible explanation for the use of this slang is that it enabled soldiers to ignore the humanity of the victims of war and to talk in their own discourse community in ways which avoided or redefined the moral significance of their activities. The chilling phrase *ethnic cleansing*, which appears to have entered English in the early

1990s as a translation from Serbo-Croat, may have been intended to perform a similar function.

Some insights into the ways in which professional slang is used to represent emotional involvement, and to express identities, are provided by the linguist Kathleen Odean's study of the talk of stockbrokers on New York's Wall Street (see Activity 3.6).

Activity 3.6   *(Reading B)*

Read Kathleen Odean's 'Bear hugs and Bo Dereks on Wall Street' (Reading B) and consider the following questions.

- What does Odean suggest are some of the social and emotive functions of the Wall Street slang?
- How do the themes of *dominance, sexuality* and *dirt* appear in the slang (and how does Odean explain their appearance)?
- On the basis of earlier discussions of gender issues (in this chapter and in Chapter 1), how well does the style and content of the slang reflect the fact that an increasing number of American stockbrokers are women? What effects might its use have on women entering that workplace?

Designing a discourse

The specialized English of Macau traders and the slang of stockbrokers are very different kinds of 'in-house' professional discourse, but both have developed to fulfil communicative needs of people working in a specialized field of work. Most professional discourses have not been self-consciously designed for their purpose, but have evolved through the processes of natural selection and conventionalization within the range of ways of using language that people have employed over the years.

In some other areas of working life, however, the demands of unusual working circumstances on communicative needs have required people to become quite inventive in their use of English. One example from the late nineteenth/early twentieth century was demonstrated to me by my grandmother, who used to work in the cotton mills of Lancashire. Because of the very high noise level in the mills, the women workers could only communicate at a distance across their looms by speaking with exaggerated mouth movements which allowed a 'listener' to lipread what the speaker had said. This style of speech, known locally as *mee-mawing* (Figure 3.4), came to be used by women in Lancashire in other areas of life (e.g. when speaking across from one garden to the next), and its stylistic effects are still apparent in the speech styles of older women in Lancashire.

More recently, different special communicative needs have led to the careful design of other kinds of specialized varieties or genres of English. In situations where speakers cannot see each other, and have to rely on imperfect telecommunication channels to do their work, operational varieties of English have been devised to cope. Good examples are the English used internationally by air traffic controllers (known as ATC), and Seaspeak, a similar variety used by mariners. A recent development is Policespeak, which has emerged from a project set up by the Kent police force in south-east England. The aim was to develop a form of

Figure 3.4   Lancashire mee-mawing developed in noisy work environments such as this

English for use in telephone communications between police officers (e.g. between someone in a police car and another officer in the police station). There were apparently two main reasons for setting up this project. First, it was realized that some of the ways in which police officers talked to each other by radio-phone was leading to confusions and misunderstandings. A Kent officer involved in the project told me that 17 per cent of 'failed transmissions' (i.e. telephone communications in which one or other party was seriously misled or left in doubt about a message) were attributed to the lack of clarity of the first words spoken in each conversational turn. An example is what the police spokesman described as the 'ive' problem. Following a style similar to the English of military communications, officers tended to say *Affirmative* and *Negative* rather than *Yes* and *No* when talking to each other on the phone. However, words tend to get clipped in the rapid switch between speaker/listeners in radio-telephone communications, with the result that both responses were often simply heard as *ive*. The second reason for Policespeak was the new Channel Tunnel, opened in 1994, between France and England. This led to the need for more effective communications between French and English police officers in the regions close to the tunnel entrances (Kent and Calais), few of whom were fluent in each other's language. One way it was hoped to achieve this was by setting up an agreed vocabulary of specialized terms used in police reporting, with words being chosen from French and English that were most likely to be comprehensible to speakers of either language.

Owing, it seems, to the initiative being made by the Kent police rather than those in Calais, this lexicon was largely English based. Thus it included the opening key word *Calling*, the response *Hello/Allo*, specific terms for describing the type and appearance of road vehicles, and the simple replacement of the *ive* words with *Yes* and *No*.

Speaking the same discourse

At the beginning of this chapter I suggested that we can usefully make a distinction, even if not a very firm one, between two general kinds of work-related language events. These are:

- Language events in which only 'professionals' are involved (i.e. involving people who may well both be members of the same community of discourse);

- Language events involving both professional and 'lay' persons (in which both participants are not likely to be members of the community of discourse for the work involved).

So far, I have dealt mainly with the ways in which English is used as a working language within certain communities of discourse. In the next section I concentrate on the ways in which English language is used by 'professionals' as they deal with 'clients', 'customers' or other members of the public.

3.3   WORKING WITH THE PUBLIC

One obvious but nevertheless critical aspect of many communications between 'professionals' and 'lay' people is the extent to which the professional is willing and able to talk about relevant topics in a way that is clear to the uninitiated outsider. The issue here is not simply a matter of professionals remembering to avoid the use of jargon. For example, there is the well-known phenomenon of 'blinding with science' whereby a professional tries to maintain control and exert power over a lay person by deliberately not making allowances for lack of understanding, thus representing themselves as experts and the gatekeepers to powerful knowledge. Of course, some professionals may, out of force of habit or because of the technical nature of their activities, find it very hard to speak of their work in any language other than that of their discourse community.

In section 3.2 I referred to Marriott's (1995) research on 'intercultural' communications. Similarly the lack of common knowledge and understanding between a professional and a client may not be confined to technical matters, but may be related to other differences in the cultural and linguistic experiences of the people involved. Roberts and Sayers (1988) have directly addressed this issue by recording and analysing job interviews and other similar interactions involving white, British English-speaking interviewers and interviewees who were immigrants to Britain (mainly from the Indian subcontinent) and for whom English was a second language. Their research was aimed at providing good equal opportunities training for interviewers who dealt with people of varied ethnic and linguistic backgrounds. Like Marriott, they found that problems sometimes arose because the speakers did not have the same shared understanding of the ground rules for carrying out this specialized kind of conversation. They also considered how an interviewee's lack of fluency in English affected the process and outcomes of the interview. You can read about some of the results of their analysis in the box below. (Note that supplementary benefit used to be a form of welfare assistance available in Britain, and that a supplementary benefits officer was a civil servant responsible for deciding people's eligibility for this.)

Keeping the gate: how judgements are made in interethnic encounters

In ... cases where interviewers have recognized second language difficulties as playing a role within the interview, there is a tendency to use the language factor as a reason for not clarifying misunderstandings. They assume that any of the candidate's talk which they did not understand was therefore meaningless, i.e. not meaningful for the candidate. Instead of clarifying such utterances, interviewers choose to ignore them. In this way they often fail to grasp where key points for the candidate are occurring, and the whole interaction starts to go wrong. As a case in point, see [the] example [below]. Here, an unemployed Bangladeshi worker was afraid that the amount of money he had managed to save was near the limit for supplementary benefit [eligibility]. He was persuaded to ask a supplementary benefits officer on one of our training courses [about this]. It was a risky thing to ask and he put the question indirectly by first stating how he was unemployed and living as best he could on little money but still managing to save small amounts.

Example

Int	What's your enquiry please, Mr. A?
Mr A.	Enquiry?
Int	What's your enquiry? What's your problem?
Mr A.	Me? Not problem, you know. Yes. Me, after three years, been three years, you know, unemployed.
Int	Three years unemployed, yes.
Mr A.	Unemployed, no money, you know.
Int	Not enough money
→ Mr A.	Yes, if I saving next time any money, you know, ten pound, five pound, I keeping bank and building society.
Int	Yeah, I see. What sort of money do you have coming in at the moment?

The interviewer then goes on to ask a long series of questions to check whether Mr A. is getting all the benefit he might be entitled to, and Mr A. is never given the opportunity to ask his question about savings. The interviewer was quite happy at the end of the interview that Mr A. had come to check that he was receiving the correct benefit and was very surprised when we (the trainers) told him of Mr A.'s intended question. The key part of Mr A.'s introduction (marked → on the transcript above) where he begins to mention savings is also the place where the surface structure of his English deviates most from standard. It is also the only part of Mr A.'s introduction where the interviewer does not repeat back what Mr A. said. The interviewer had failed to understand the surface structure (here syntax and prosody) of what Mr A. said, and consequently disregarded its content and did not seek to clarify it. The interviewer confirmed this for us afterwards on viewing the video recording of this interview.

(Roberts and Sayers, 1988, pp. 130–1)

Roberts and Sayers suggest that problems of understanding in interviews are as likely to be caused by the ways that interviewers react to an interviewee's lack of fluency in English, as by the lack of fluency itself. They also refer to the greater control that an interviewer usually has over the content and structure of the talk, so that interviewers can choose to ignore or pursue topics in ways that interviewees would not dare. Issues of power and control can also be important for understanding the structure and outcomes of any language event (as I suggested in relation to the bilingual conversation between a boss and a secretary in Activity 3.3). I consider these issues in more detail in the next section.

Power and control in professional–client relationships

The following is a transcription of a telephone conversation I had a few months before writing this chapter. I had answered the phone at home, at about 8.30 in the evening. I reached the phone too late to switch off the answerphone, which is why the conversation was recorded.

Me	Hello [telephone number].
Caller	Hello. [*Conversation is then halted by the recorded message on my answerphone.*]
Me	Sorry about that, I didn't reach it in time.
Caller	Mr Mercer?
Me	Yes.
Caller	I'm speaking from Holmes Insurance, we sent you a letter recently, did you get it?
Me	Uh, um, I'm not sure, uh …
Caller	We wrote to offer you a free consultation, with no obligations, on your personal finances. We are completely independent financial advisers, who can offer a wide range of insurance and investment tailor-made for our clients. Could we call and discuss this with you?
Me	Uhhh, no, no thanks, I think that we have, we don't need anything like that right now. If your letter turns up I'll read it. So thanks, cheerio. [*Hangs up quickly*]

In the past year or so, I have been plagued by what seems like an excessive amount of telephone selling (though I have no real standards of comparison). This rather informal evidence encourages me to believe that the call transcribed above was fairly typical in that it had the following characteristics.

1   As with all incoming telephone calls, I was the first speaker. Once I had spoken, the caller addressed me formally by my (assumed) title and last name, in an enquiring manner that begged confirmation.

2   Once I had confirmed my identity, the caller talked quickly and fluently in a 'sing-song' way that suggested either reading or performing a rehearsed script.

3   All the caller's turns ended with a question addressed to me. That is, having imparted some information, the caller then *elicited* information and a conversational turn from me.

4   I terminated the call.

On the recording I initially sound hesitant and confused, while the caller sounds relatively confident and 'in command'. Yet I terminated the call, because ultimately I have control. An unsolicited salesperson has no right to my time and in such encounters I can choose to have the last word. On the part of telephone sales staff, one of the earliest stages of their training must be developing a familiarity with the 'scripts' of their trade, with the intention that they can confidently and effectively deliver the message and interest their potential customers in their product. The risk of this strategy, however, is that hearing a script that is obviously prepared and rehearsed may alienate a potential client or customer, because they feel they are being set at a disadvantage, having to think and talk spontaneously without the benefit of such preparation. Early recipients of telephone sales calls, say back in the 1960s, were probably caught even more off balance, because such conversations then were novel events. They would not have had past experience to help them categorize the event and predict how it would unfold.

In a telephone sales encounter control of the conversation may shift, at various times, between the participants. In some other kinds of encounter, the relative status and authority of the participants may be such that control remains much more consistently in one person's hands. One common and much researched kind of language event is the interaction between a doctor and a patient. Think of one particular kind of medical consultation, where a patient returns to the doctor for the results of an earlier diagnostic test. On the basis of casual reflection on our experience of such events, we may think of such consultations invariably having the following structure (after some initial exchange of greetings):

1 Patient (or patient's representative, such as a parent) asks what has been found out.

2 Doctor tells the patient.

In fact, research (such as that by Maynard, 1992) shows that events rarely follow this pattern. Patients rarely begin encounters with doctors with direct requests for information. Perhaps out of deference to the perceived status and authority of the medical profession, patients usually allow the doctor to organize and control the encounter. And doctors do not necessarily provide diagnoses in a straightforward, informative way.

Consider the following discussion between a doctor (Dr) and the mother (Mo) of a child who has been found to have severe learning difficulties. It is a simplified version of a transcription presented by Maynard. (This is not an initial consultation, but a discussion following identification and investigation of the child's problem by the doctor.)

Dr   What do you see as – as his difficulty?

Mo   Mainly his uhm: the fact that he doesn't understand everything. And also the fact that his speech is very hard to understand what he's saying lots ⌐of time.

Dr   └right.

Dr   Do you have any ideas <u>why</u> it is? Are you: d ⌐o you?

Mo   └No.

Dr   Okay I, you know I think we <u>basically</u> in some ways agree with you insofar as we think that Dan's <u>main</u> problem, you know, does involve you know <u>lang</u>uage.

Mo   Mm hmm.

Dr   You know both, his being able to under<u>stand</u> you know what is said to him, and also certainly also to be able to ex<u>press</u>, you know his uh his thoughts, hh uhm, hhh in general his development.

(Adapted from Maynard, 1992, pp. 337–8)

Transcription conventions
- [indicates simultaneous speech
- words spoken emphatically are underlined

Maynard suggests that a model of this encounter would consist of three turns, as follows (he uses the US English 'clinician' to refer to any consulting doctor):

1   clinician's opinion-query, or perspective-display invitation;

2   recipient's reply or assessment;

3   clinician's report and assessment.

(Maynard, 1992, p. 333)

He suggests that this model represents a generic conversational strategy (used by other 'experts' as well as doctors) for giving one's own assessment of a situation in a cautious manner, by initially soliciting the viewpoint of another interested party. The strategy is useful because it offers the doctor the possibility of *exploring* the patient's own understanding of the condition, *confirming* the patient's own perspective (which may well draw on earlier conversations with the doctor) and then *reformulating* the patient's explanation of events. The analysis of professional–client language has been an active area of research in recent years, and some research of this kind is described in the Reading C by Jo Longman.

Activity 3.7   *(Reading C)*

Read 'Professionals and clients: form-filling and the control of talk' by Jo Longman (Reading C).

Notice how Longman discusses the processes of:

1   *Filtering*, whereby a professional selectively responds to what a lay person says according to its perceived relevance to their work (note the links here with the research of Roberts and Sayers (1988), presented earlier in this section);

2   *Reformulation*, whereby a professional paraphrases and recasts the contributions of lay participants so that their content and style is in accord with the professional's conception of appropriate style and context. (And note here, too, the link with Maynard's (1992) research on doctors and patients, discussed above.)

It is interesting to consider how well the practices of filtering and 'reformulating' the language of lay people can be justified in different professional settings where a written account of events is generated by a professional person. It might seem, at first consideration, that any distortion of what has actually been said must be wrong, so that for example police officers who transform statements from suspects' spoken words into their own might well be considered to be fabricating evidence. However, although in most English-speaking countries formal interviews with suspects are tape recorded and transcribed, police officers who are taking statements from witnesses and others at the scenes of crimes are not commonly required literally to *transcribe* what they are told. Rather, they are expected to use what the suspects said to prepare on their behalf a written statement. It can therefore be argued that a necessary part of a police officer's job is to use their professional understanding of the needs of the law court (and of the discourses of the legal community) to 'distil' the most relevant information provided by the suspects and present it in a suitable form.

In the case of the counsellors studied by Longman (see Reading C) a similar but perhaps even stronger justification for acts of filtering and reformulation can be made, because (as she explains) an explicit part of the role of counsellor is to act as a kind of public relations agent for clients, helping them to present themselves in the best possible light to trainers and potential employers through the 'Personal Training Plan' form. One could argue that the counsellors would be failing in their responsibilities to their clients if they did *not* filter and reformulate clients' statements in preparing the forms. The acts of filtering and reformulation can therefore carry quite different moral implications in relationships between lay people and professionals, according to the situation and the job being done.

Some interesting and perfectly justifiable acts of reformulation and filtering are carried out in the legal profession in the preparation of 'last will and testament' documents, contracts and other legal statements by lawyers on behalf of their clients. Part of the professional responsibility of a lawyer in preparing a will is to render the wishes and intentions of a client, perhaps expressed in partial and unsystematic ways by the client in an interview with the lawyer, into the supposedly precise and unambiguous written English discourse of the legal community. For example, in English law the lawyer's own financial relationship with the client on the client's eventual death can be represented as follows (as it is in my own will):

> Any Trustee (other than my spouse) being a solicitor or any other person engaged in a profession, business or trade may charge and be paid all professional or business and trade charges transacted or done by him and for the time expended (or by any employee or partner) in connection with these trusts including any acts which a Trustee not being in any profession, business or trade could have done personally.

In Britain, the training of solicitors and other professional will writers includes specific direction on the use of English punctuation. A basic rule is that except in the listing of items, commas are to be avoided (see the example above), as they can encourage alternative interpretations.

Activity 3.8   Reading the will   *(Allow 10 minutes)*

Could the choice between the following statements affect the interpretation of a last will and testament?

* Those friends named below, and my brothers and sisters who have so obviously helped me achieve success, shall each receive the sum of £10,000.
* Those friends named below and my brothers and sisters, who have so obviously helped me achieve success, shall each receive the sum of £10,000.

Comment

As you probably concluded, the statements can be interpreted differently. The first might in effect exclude any brother or sister who had not obviously helped the deceased achieve success (of course, with such use of commas neither statement would be considered good practice in legal English). An error of reformulation on the part of the lawyer which resulted in a will being ambiguous in its execution (as one might say in the discourse of the legal community!) could have serious legal, financial and personal consequences.

3.4   CONCLUSION

One of the main points made in this chapter is that, as a 'tool' for many occupations, the English language takes on a range of distinctive forms. We can see the specialized nature of spoken and written 'working Englishes' in characteristic textual structures, syntax and vocabulary. We can also see that language used at work performs not only the ideational function of representing ideas, events, etc. but also the interpersonal function of developing and maintaining working relationships.

The concept of a discourse community is useful for understanding the ways that English is used in communications between professionals in a trade or other occupation. The discourses of professional communities may have characteristics which reflect the professional aims and goals, the social settings in which communication takes place, and the specialized nature of the knowledge shared by members. The ways English is used as a discourse of work can also be seen to embody social, emotive aspects of workers' identities and relationships, as well as the more obvious needs of effective information exchange. As in the rest of life, work-related language events embody issues of power, control and accountability. Understanding the use of English at work must include a consideration of these and other social and cultural factors.

Reading A
CONSTRUCTING THE VIRTUAL BUILDING: LANGUAGE ON A BUILDING SITE

Peter Medway

Building a building is a physical process, a process of moving matter into new arrangements, so why should language come into it? Common sense and experience suggest a reason must be the need to coordinate the efforts of a sometimes large and shifting group of participants. Division of labour creates a need for language. People need to be told what to do, and to tell each other what they are doing, need to do and are about to do. And if the building process is not straightforward there is a need, too, for consultation and deliberation as well as instruction and information; people need to work out solutions together, and that implies using language. Sometimes the language is spoken, face to face or over the phone, and sometimes written, on paper or in electronic media.

So what exactly gets done in language, and how does the English language work to coordinate action? Evidence from recordings I made of a construction job in Ottawa, Canada, will provide some answers. On the one hand, talk and writing during construction are highly task-oriented; there is a pressing physical job to be accomplished, through content-laden, reference-heavy communications about hard facts and problematic situations (what Halliday (1985) calls the **ideational** function of language). However, the participants are also always building, maintaining and enacting relationships, adjusting their utterances and texts to express those interpersonal recognitions of status, authority, expertise, dependence and the like on which the smooth running of the job depends (which Halliday calls the **interpersonal** function).

The ideational aspect of language works mainly by encoding two sorts of reference, to entities (including things, people and abstract ideas) and to processes, relations and actions. These referential needs are realized in English roughly through noun phrases on the one hand and verb phrases on the other. As we would expect, the needs of particular contexts, such as a building site, require a repertoire of specific encodings for the things and processes of that world. Talking about walls, floors and wiring is different from talking about psychological traumas or international trade flows. At the most obvious level a vast number of architectural and building entities and processes will need to be nameable, as well as the size, extension, location and material properties of the elements of the building. There will be references to the way elements relate in space or to the way they are joined, separated and grouped.

We know that drawings fulfil many of the communicative needs of architects and builders, often much better than language could. (Try describing a complicated run of ductwork in words.) But some vital things only language can do. An example: an architect (let us call him Joe) was working on a building which was to have a roof skin of stretched fabric. Because the technique of installation was tricky, Joe wanted the subcontractor to do a mock-up section before proceeding to the main operation.

What Joe said to the subcontractor was, 'I want to see the connection between this and that.' *Speaking*, in the sense of performing speech acts such as requesting, asserting, ordering, promising, denying and proposing, is precisely what drawings cannot do.

Consider now a continuous exchange of utterances. At one point in his tour of the site, inspecting progress and being alerted to problems, Joe was led by Harry, the consultant responsible for heating and ventilation, to a spot on the third floor. A third member of the party was the site supervisor, Luc.

Harry had earlier phoned to tell Joe that the heating and ventilation duct-work had proved bulkier than anticipated, so that the planned space to accommo-date it, between the ceiling (not yet installed) and the concrete slab above, would now be inadequate. Here is how the transaction opens.

Transcription conventions

* <> indicates an inaudible word
* <...> indicates a short string of inaudible words (building sites are noisy places)

1   Joe   OK, next.
            [*He looks up towards the underside of the concrete slab. Harry walks a couple of steps, pointing upwards. Joe and Luc accompany him.*]

2   Harry   <...>, right? <> the ductwork coming down that way is supposed to <>

Harry's sentence probably finished with something like *is supposed to go through there*. Two forms of symbolic communication are in evidence: language and gesture. (It is easy to forget that pointing is a sign which has meaning only because of convention.) Here, as in a great deal of the communication in building construction, gesture works symbiotically with language, giving meaning to words; *coming down that way* has meaning because it is accompanied by a pointing movement. Language is here doing one of the things it can do best – refer to absent entities. (No ductwork has yet been installed.) The verbal resources by which this is done include the technical term *ductwork*, the verb phrases *coming down* and the second one that was inaudible, and, very importantly, those English resources used to specify and elaborate the verb phrase. The choice of *is supposed to* here gives the location, extension and direction of the ductwork the status of a reality that does not but should exist.

To Joe the solution seems immediately obvious: just lower the ceiling. In fact, Harry has already proposed this:

3   Joe   Well as you were saying yesterday on the phone, Harry that if [*9-second pause*] if we lower this part by three inches [Harry: yes] that will be fine, right?

4   Harry   This should be fine, [?because] the ductwork can be penetrating through there OK <>

5   Joe   Because this is at twenty-six hundred and this is twenty-seven seventy-five.

6   Harry   That's right.

(The dimensions are ceiling heights in millimetres.) So far, then, we have noted the simultaneous operation of two semiotic systems, and the key role taken by the array of resources for giving specificity to the verb phrase. Despite the shortness of the extract, there are two more important points to be made. First, what the transcript does not show, but the video recording does, is a crucial shift in reference and the introduction of a third semiotic system. What Joe was doing during that nine-second gap in his first utterance was spreading out on a waist-high pile of drywall sheets the roll of large drawings he had been carrying. From that point, his and Harry's 'deictic' references – to *this* and *that, here* and *there* – are not to the actual building but to its graphical representation. In fact, the entities for which the dimensions 2,600 mm and 2,775 mm are given are levels for a ceiling which does not exist. That raises the interesting question of what these deictic expressions refer to. Since the reference is neither to the actual building nor, presumably, to the piece of paper, it must be to the *planned* building.

In contexts where things are made or done and in which planning is a distinct operation, separate from execution and performed by different people, what is communicated to those who will realize the plan is a *representation* of the desired state of affairs. Like all representations, it is constructed with a system of signs – verbal and graphical signs in the present instance. What the participants talk about, though, is not the representation but the thing represented, even if that thing has no material reality. We might say that it has a *virtual* reality, and that Joe and Harry are talking about the *virtual* building. Similarly, since there is no ceiling, there is no question of anything in the actual building being lowered; the *lowering* will be to the *virtual* ceiling (it will be achieved simply by substituting one figure for another in the height indication on the drawing). The builders will lower nothing. They will just install the ceiling, but at a lower level than originally specified.

The remaining point is about **intertextuality** (the way in which one piece of discourse implicitly or explicitly refers to another, often deriving part of its meaning from that reference). Joe makes a specific intertextual link through the clause *as you were saying yesterday on the phone, Harry.* Then *if we lower this part by three inches* is either a near-exact quotation or conveys the semantic content (i.e. the meaning) of part of yesterday's phone conversation. Thus the same semantic material, and possibly even the same verbal material (I can't say which because I don't have a recording of the phone conversation) is here getting recycled. And it may well be that Harry's initial noun phrase, *the ductwork*, is intertextual, too – the article *the* indicating a topic that has already been referred to. Intertextuality is of central importance in workplace discourse. It ties all the separate written and spoken communications into a single multi-stranded web of discourse (a *text* is a textile, something woven) and in the process knits the diverse participants together into a discourse community.

A bit later Joe says:

19   Joe   So let me look at the elevations [elevation drawings], I'll just study this whole area all over, I'll have to study this area over, because I know the lights, I mean my concern is A501. [*12-second silence*]

Something is nagging at Joe. His preoccupation is revealed by the way his discourse fails to move decisively forward. What is gnawing at his consciousness is revealed by that unexpected new verbal item, *the elevations*, that must have seemed to the other participants to have come inexplicably from nowhere. The elevation drawings, such as drawing no. A501, are different from the 'reflected ceiling plan' they have been looking at in that they show vertical features such as walls. In the twelve-second silence Joe turns up the drawing in question. Then he says:

Fucking lights. [*5-second silence*]

He stands up straight and looks at Harry.

It's right in front of the fucking window. [*3-second silence*] Yes, see the back here all, you see the back here? I think this is why this is set at twenty-seven fifty in the back so maybe we should just lower this portion.

To explain. *Lights* means glazing or windows. Elevation drawing no. A501 reveals an internal wall, the upper portion of which is glazed (i.e. a clerestory); it was some vague recollection of this that caused Joe to keep nagging at the problem, testing his partners' conversational patience to the limit. Lowering the ceiling would bring it below the top of this glass – clearly an unacceptable situation; hence Joe's frustration. That, Joe surmises, was why the ceiling level had originally been set (by him, but many months earlier) relatively high (2,750 mm) in that area.

Joe's swearing obviously serves an expressive need, but it has other dimensions. (Language rarely does only one thing.) First, the building site is a macho environment where language may be a way of declaring masculinity, an expectation with which even visiting male professionals may feel it useful to conform for the sake of 'street credibility'. But it may also have been Harry's presence that provoked the vehemence of the outburst, since it was Harry who originally supplied the incorrect ductwork dimensions which caused Joe to set the ceiling level where he did. At a subtext level of interpersonal meaning the expletive may be directed to some degree *at* Harry. Joe would never allow himself to respond with even semi-overt irritation to a mistake made by Luc, on whose cooperativeness he depends, showing constant concern to keep him sweet.

This contretemps shows incidentally how real was the virtual building, of which one element was the clerestory. Forgotten over many months, this had now re-emerged to block the straightforward action that had been contemplated.

The issue of the ceiling receives its final verbal expression, after much discussion between Joe and his boss in the office, in a written document called a site instruction, sent by the architect to the site supervisor:

> Lower ceiling @ corridor 327 as per attached sketch SK 26–01 and revise to acoustical lay-in tile as shown.

Like much of the spoken discourse, this written text works as much by intertextual reference as by overtly expressed meaning. The immediate participants, Luc, Harry and Joe's boss in the office, *recognize* in the words the same solution they have talked about. For Luc, for instance, the instruction is no instruction because he had already agreed he was going to lower the ceiling; the only question was about dimensions.

But there are other potential readers, a second audience waiting hypothetically in some unspecified future, shadowy at present but to be taken with great seriousness when or if they materialize. The management of the firm of contractors, the client's accountant, even some tribunal judge, could use the paper to allocate responsibilities and costs; Joe's *signature* confirms that the change was at the architect's orders. (The written act we learn to accomplish first, writing our name, remains the one with the most momentous possible consequences for our lives; think of cheques and confessions.) For this audience the text has to work differently, depending not on the conversations it reawakens but by the meaning of the words in themselves; functioning not as an awaited message (*Go ahead, Luc*) but as a device set to go off later, away from the context of its production and immediate reception.

The builders build a building with steel and concrete. Joe, with words and drawings, creates two other structures, one ideational, one interpersonal: a virtual building and a social network, a web of intertwined understandings, agreements and consents. Without both in place and constantly maintained, no building would happen; and both depend critically on language.

Acknowledgements

My thanks are due to the architectural firm and the individual architects who allowed me to study their work. They must remain anonymous: all names in the paper are pseudonyms. The research was carried out with the assistance of Stephen Fai as part of the study 'The relationships between writing in the university and writing in the workplace' funded by Strategic Grant 884–94–0030 from the Social Sciences and Humanities Research Council of Canada, with additional support from Carleton University Office of Graduate Studies and Research. I gratefully acknowledge also the assistance I have received in analysing the data from my colleague Dr Lynne Young.

References

HALLIDAY, M. (1985) *An Introduction to Functional Grammar,* London, Edward Arnold.

This reading was specially commissioned for this book.

Reading B
BEAR HUGS AND BO DEREKS ON WALL STREET

Kathleen Odean

When the stock market crashed on 19 October 1987, before the day was out Wall Streeters had started calling it *Black Monday.* The next day, another frantic one for investors, immediately became *Terrible Tuesday.* In the months that followed, exchange officials sought methods to prevent the market from plummeting again. Wall Streeters soon dubbed the proposed measure *circuit breakers,* a term for the electrical device that temporarily shuts off power in the case of an overload.

Like many occupational groups, brokers and traders have an extensive body of slang, known mainly to those on the Street. As I found when collecting Wall Street slang over several years, the oral nature of the stock market makes it a fertile ground for coining slang words and phrases that describe its people, places, and products.

Despite its widespread use in the financial markets, Wall Street slang has been largely overlooked by students of language, who may have assumed that all business language is dull and bureaucratic. Yet the stock market has a long and rich tradition of creating snappy words and apt images. The *OED* gives citations for *bear* in 1709 and *bull* in 1714 as stock market terms; the slang lexicon has been expanding ever since, in England and the United States.

While slang experts have neglected the stock market, they have given disproportionate attention to the language of the military and of criminals, including prison slang. All three groups share several characteristics: they are made up primarily of men who spend a lot of time together in close quarters and whose lives fluctuate between boredom and great tension – during busy markets or crashes, during war, and during prison riots or criminal acts. Fluctuating conditions are unusually conducive to slang inventions, but the world of Wall Street, which encompasses investment businesses throughout the country, invents it constantly because Wall Streeters talk so much in their work. Traders shout and chat on exchange floors all day, while brokers spend their time on telephones trying to make sales. The spoken word clinches agreements, for the proverb 'My word is my bond' is taken seriously in this milieu. Any newcomer who renegs on an oral promise will be shunned by fellow traders.

In the same spirit, brokers take, buy, and sell orders from their customers on the telephone and execute them before any paperwork is mailed out. A customer who places an order but later denies it because the stock price has dropped will have to find a new brokerage firm, if possible.

While traders work *on the floor,* as the exchanges are called, brokers work *upstairs,* the term for brokerage offices. There, novice brokers sit in an open space dubbed the *bullpen* and make cold calls to find new customers, a practice known as *dialing and smiling* or *dialing for dollars. Big producers,* brokers who bring in large commissions, occupy individual offices with several telephones.

Because establishing a congenial atmosphere is essential in telephone sales, brokers like to open their conversations with jokes, anecdotes, and colorful slang terms, including nicknames: 'Want to buy some Bo Dereks? or some James Bonds?' *James Bonds* are bonds that will mature in the year 2007, and *Bo Dereks,* which were issued when the movie '10' starring Bo Derek was in the theaters, are bonds that will mature in 2010.

Brokers who serve retail customers often chat first about what's happening on the Street, bringing up nicknames for prominent Wall Street figures such as *Icahn the Terrible* for Carl Icahn, *Irv the Liquidator* for Irwin Jacobs, or *Dr Gloom* for Henry Kaufman. Hearing the slang makes the customer feel more 'in the know,' more like a true Wall Streeter, a feeling investors relish. At the same time, the esoteric language serves to mystify and impress customers and other outsiders, who would like to be closer to this realm of money.

Within the expanse of Wall Street exist many subgroups with their own specialized language, such as the traders on the exchange floors who create dozens of nicknames for stocks, many of which the brokers upstairs don't know. These nicknames not only serve to identify members of the group but occasionally form part of an elaborate practical joke reminiscent of a college fraternity hazing. Before computers replaced chalkboards on exchange floors, a new trader would receive an order from the brokerage he worked for to buy a hundred shares of Transatlantic Bridge (or Third Avenue Railroad or Coney Island Sand), although no such stock existed, whereupon his fellow traders would gather around a specialist, one of the exchange members who buy and sell stocks, bidding on Transatlantic Bridge. The specialist would ignore the novice's attempts to bid, and meanwhile the stock price would climb steadily. Finally, when the price had gone way up, the specialist would sell some to the new broker. But as he walked away, the broker would hear the price drop dozens of points – and be convinced that he had failed miserably on one of his first trades.

Many of the nicknames are derived from the stock symbols that appear on the electronic ticker tape and computer screens. Thus, North-west Airlines' stock symbol NWA becomes *Nawa,* and DMP for Dome Petroleum becomes *Dump.* Traders turn GHO for General Homes into *Ghost;* HUM for Humana into *Hummer,* and MDR for McDermott into *Murder.* They call Dayton Hudson (DH) *Deadhead* and General Instrument (GRL) *Gorilla.*

A trader will approach a specialist and ask for a stock price by saying 'How's your *Dynamite?'* for General Dynamic stock or 'How's your *Organ?'* for Wurlitzer. Nicknames function as shorthand when they can be said more quickly or clearly than stock symbols, most of which consist of three letters. Speed matters during brisk trading, since the more transactions a trader makes the better. But because mistakes are costly, distinct names are prized over brief ones. Nicknames are also easier to remember than symbols, an important feature for the floor's *two-dollar brokers*, who trade in many stocks and must remember them all.

Besides stock symbols, a corporation's products or the corporate name may provide the basis for nicknames. Kellogg's nickname is *Cornflakes*, Ralston Purina's is *Dog Chow*, and Wrigley's is *Gum*. Traders call stock in Lucky Stores *Unlucky* and stock in Chesebrough-Pond *Cheeseburgers*.

Market inhabitants have been coining nicknames for over a hundred years. In a list compiled in 1895, A. J. Wilson gives eighty 'Slang, or Corrupted Names' from the London Exchange. *Marbles* stood for Marbella Iron Ore Shares and *Imps* for Imperial Tobacco Company shares; Aerated Bread Shares were *Breads*, while fractions of these shares were *Bread Crumbs*.

Traders have always enjoyed slang terms with sexual references. In the 1960s, according to magazine articles, Wall Streeters dubbed Simmons Mattress Company *America's Playground* and Italian Development Bonds *Lolas*. Southern Bell Telephone was known as *Scarlett O'Hara* and Continental Can was *Zsa Zsa Gabor*. Traders still talk about the nicknames for two companies that are no longer traded: Welbilt Corporation, *Marilyn Monroe*, and Pittsburgh Screw and Bolt Corporation, *Love 'em and Leave 'em*. Currently heard at the New York Stock Exchange are *Huge Tool* for Hughes Tool and *Dildo* for Snap-On Tool, Inc.

As these examples illustrate, traders refer to many stocks by women's names. Londoners traded *Floras, Berthas, Claras, Clarettes, Coras, Noras*, and *Saras*. In the U.S., Wall Streeters have dealt in stocks named *Becky, Amy, Old Mona, Maggie, Pamela, Jennie Tel, Weeping Mary, Rebecca, Minnie, Alice, Annie*, and *Molly* ...

A popular stock market proverb also treats stocks as feminine, with some as prostitutes: 'When the paddy wagon comes, they take the good girls with the bad' – when the market crashes, strong stocks fall along with weak ones.

Traders may *goose Jennie Tel, ride Pamela*, or *pull out of Becky*. The market also is portrayed as female and subject to sexual maneuvers. Traders *straddle* the market when they execute *spreads*; they perform *in-and-out trading*. Among the orders traders carry out are *touch but don't penetrate* the market and *participate but don't initiate* ...

The derogatory aspect of many nicknames for stocks – *Slob* for Schlumberger, *Murder Burgers* for McDonalds, *Bare Ass* for Boeing – is part of the macho, rebellious persona traders cultivate. True to this image, commodity traders in Chicago refer to their work as the *Last Frontier*, as though their lives were as free and rough as a cowboy's. Similarly, high-powered Wall Streeters have been known as *gunslingers* and *hipshooters* ...

Even the once proper world of investment banking has adopted a body of slang in the last two decades that portrays corporate takeovers as a fight over female corporations. In the *takeover wars, raiders* come to metaphoric blows with *white knights* over attractive corporations that both would like to acquire, known as *sleeping beauties* or *damsels in distress*. The raiders have employed such tactics as *strong bear hugs, blitz-kreig tender offers*, and *Saturday Night Specials*. These *takeover artists*, who use junk bonds to finance takeovers, meet at the annual conference known as the *Predators' Ball* to learn the latest junk bond techniques ...

The theme running through the slang, whether violent or sexual, is dominance. The image Wall Streeters want to project is one of being in control, winning the war or conquering the female, doubtless because they have so little control over the main force in their world – the market ...

One also hears that 'the market climbs a wall of worry,' or that the market is a cruel force that *blows out* speculators, *burns* them and *kills* them. In return, traders *hammer* the market, *jackscrew* it, and *dump* stocks on it. They *pound* stocks and *slaughter* them, *fill* and *kill* orders, and execute *strangles*. But since the market is ultimately unpredictable, it is no wonder that some Wall Streeters try to control it through illegal maneuvers. In the highly publicized cases of *insider trading* during the 1980s, Wall Streeters acquired information about imminent takeovers in order to trade with certainty. Current investigations of the Chicago commodities market have revealed that traders have been illegally securing profits at customers' expense in a maneuver known as *bag trading*. Stories also appear in the news periodically about brokers *churning* customers – depleting their accounts through numerous trades solely to produce commissions for the broker.

Such crimes do immeasurable harm to the image that the public holds of Wall Street by reinforcing the longtime perception of it as shady, the result of many swindles and scandals in the market's history. Although presumably only a small percentage of Wall Streeters are guilty, the reputation of the whole profession suffers, as two jokes, one from the 1960s, the other from the 1980s, illustrate:

> Dear Abby, I've met the most wonderful man. We're engaged and plan to be married, but I have a terrible problem. He doesn't know about my family. My father's in jail, my mother's running a whorehouse, my sister's a prostitute there, and my brother is a stockbroker. Dare I tell him about my brother?

and

> Q: What happens when you cross a Wall Streeter with a pig?
> A: There are some things even a pig won't do.

The public's attitude towards Wall Street is one not just of distrust but of hostility. When the market slumps or crashes, even those who have no investments suffer. As Will Rogers said in 1929, 'Let Wall Street have a nightmare and the whole country has to help get them back in bed again.' The public bitterly resents it when the stock market harms the general economy.

For their part, brokers have traditionally used slang to vent hostility against customers behind their backs. Disappointed investors rant at their brokers, but brokers who would like to respond in kind must restrain themselves because they rely on their customers' goodwill. At brokerages, as elsewhere, 'the customer is always right,' but brokers can joke with each other about *churning and burning* customers or *blowing them out after a point*, that is, making trades for the sake of commissions, or selling a *cemetery spread*, a trading combination guaranteed to kill any possible profit.

Slang terms for unsuccessful, gullible investors have proliferated throughout market history, including *suckers, mullets, lilies, barefoot pilgrims, Aunt Janes,* and *widows and orphans*. In the late 1700s in England, a popular term for an investor who suffered large losses was *lame duck*. As William H. Ireland cautioned in 1807:

> If to the Stock Exchange you speed
> To try with bulls and bears your luck
> 'Tis odds you soon from gold are freed
> And waddle forth a limping duck.

Wall Street adopted the term, and added the variation *dead duck* to describe a speculator who had lost everything. (*Lame duck* had gained its political usage by 1863.)

Money itself has a dark side, as stock market slang and general slang reveal. It is associated with dirt, as in *filthy rich*, and losing money is expressed in terms of getting cleaner. A person who *takes a bath*, gets *taken to the cleaners*, or gets *put through the financial wringer* loses money. To be *wiped out* or *cleaned out* leaves the person metaphorically cleaner – and financially worse off. At a stock market *laundry*, victims got swindled out of their money in a maneuver known as the *laundry business. Washing the market*, another illegal maneuver, takes money out of the market and puts it in the swindler's pocket. Money obtained illegally seems to be dirtier than other money and needs to be *laundered*, moved through a number of financial channels until it appears to be respectable.

Wealthy people wallow in luxury the way pigs wallow in mud. Freud noted the link between money and feces in dreams and folklore, also found in the old proverb, 'Money, like dung, does no good till it is spread.' In the same vein, millionaire J. Paul Getty commented in 1967, 'Money is like manure. You have to spend it around or it smells.'

Source: Odean, 1990, pp. 224–31

Reading C
PROFESSIONALS AND CLIENTS: FORM FILLING AND THE CONTROL OF TALK

Jo Longman

Introduction

In the course of our everyday lives most of us will at some time or other have to take part in an 'interview': an encounter between a person acting in a professional capacity and a member of the public.

My own research (e.g. Mercer and Longman, 1992, 1993; Longman and Mercer, 1993) has been done on interviews in which professional advisers in occupational training (whom I call 'counsellors') are talking with their 'clients', who are people (usually unemployed) at the point of entering an occupational training scheme. The research has involved the transcription and analysis of many hours of interview talk, recorded in many locations throughout Britain. In this paper, however, I use data from just one such interview to illustrate some of the features of 'interview talk' and explain how the English language, spoken and written, is used to define, construct and maintain the roles of the counsellor and the client and the relationship between them.

Background to the interview

The interview in question involved a counsellor who was a young woman and a client who was a man in his thirties. For both people, English was their first and main language. The interview lasted for 45 minutes, and took place within a British national vocational training scheme called Employment Training which operated from 1988 until 1993. This scheme was designed to facilitate the return of long-term unemployed people to the workforce by placing them in a suitable course of training. For clients entering the scheme, the first substantial contact was an interview with a counsellor whose job it was to:

1   elicit the client's preferences for specific kinds of work;

2   identify the client's relevant vocational strengths and weaknesses, special needs and so on;

3   propose suitable training.

One of the outcomes of the interview was a completed form which contained the information listed above. The form then had subsequent audiences: it went to a provider of training (known as a training manager) to see if they would accept the client on to their training programme; and it was also often used to 'sell' the client to an employer for a work experience placement at some point during their training. The completed form was officially meant to be owned and used by the client during their training.

This interview has a number of features which are typical of the interviews I recorded, and also of many other kinds of encounter between 'professionals' and 'clients'. These are:

- talk is the central vehicle for getting the business of the interview done;
- the participants have different 'internal' status within the interaction, i.e. one is a professional and the other is a member of the public;
- the participants have different 'external' status – in this case this is perhaps most noticeable in that the professional is employed and the client is unemployed;
- the participants follow certain conventions of English language use which distinguish the event from many other kinds of conversation.

Transcript

(The transcript begins about 40 seconds into the interview.)

Transcription conventions

- [indicates simultaneous speech

- the dialogue has been punctuated to aid understanding

- [*n secs*] indicates a noticeable pause (i.e. at a point or for a duration which it did not seem appropriate to represent by standard punctuation)

	Client	**Counsellor**
1		Right, okay. What what what
2		prompted the interest why cars,
3		why motor
4	Uhh [*3 secs*] I just	
5	like tinkering about	
6	with cars more or less	
7	you know what I mean	
8		Do you do you own a car or, no
9	Not at the moment no	
10		But have you in the past?
11	Oh aye yeah	
12		Right so have you got a driving
13		licence?
14	Yeah I have yeah	
15		[*4 secs*] And you say you tinker
16		about with cars. Is that a sort
17		of like servicing and things?
18	Er well yeah just you	
19	know repairing them	
20	when they need it,	
21	y'know	
22		What sort of things have you done
23		you have done brake shoes,
24		oil changes?
25	I've more or less done,	
26	practically anything,	

	Client	**Counsellor**
27	on a car I can more or	
28	less do anything on a	
29	car as long as it	
30	isn't, y'know, one of	
31	these new fuel injected	
32	[things I'm a bit lost	[Mm
33	on the electrical side	
34		Right
35	When it comes to taking	
36	an engine out and	
37	putting another engine	
38	in I can do that sort	
39	of stuff. As long as	
40	it isn't, you know too complicated	
41	or anything	
42	you know	
43		*[5 secs]* What what I'm trying to
44		do with you, it's an opportunity
45		for you to actually look at
46		Employment Training, you've
47		been through the basics. What I
48		need to go through with you is
49		the sort of area you need to go
50		into and then tie up any
51		previous experience you might
52		have which we can build on and
53		say he's this, he's done servicing
54		of cars, he's done brake shoes
55		etcetera, etectera […] so we go
56		through the form and then I'll
57		write down the sort of bits and
58		bobs of what you've serviced [*6*
59		*secs*] it's in your spare time I
60		suppose
		[30 seconds later]
61		So if I put when you were working
62		as a taxi-driver you serviced,
63		your own car and, carried out
64		general maintenance
65	It may come to, er if I	
66	get on a motor mechanic	
67	course I'd maybe prefer	
68	to do that [. I aren't	
69	really sure yet. I'd	[Mm
70	like to go back in	
71	taxis more or less,	
72	there's more money in	
73	it, y'know [. I could	[Yeah, yeah
74	do with the extra money	

Three concepts are useful for analysing how the relationship between the counsellor and the client is defined, constructed and maintained through the use of spoken language: 'filtering', 'reformulation' and 'accountability'.

Filtering

One of the major themes throughout the whole of this interview is the client expressing doubts about his ability and level of experience. This includes not only his expertise in the central topic of car servicing and general maintenance (lines 4–7, 18–21, 25–33) but even his entire commitment to the idea of commencing training (in the last few lines). However, nearly all the information about his lack of knowledge and his uncertainty is 'filtered out' by the counsellor in that it does not find its way into the written record of the interview. What she actually recorded on the form (not included in the transcript here) were the following words:

> John is awaiting the outcome of an application for a taxi-driver licence and is considering a back-up plan in case this does not occur. His present experience as a motor mechanic has encouraged him to consider a career in mechanics or body repair. This he feels could be used as an alternative or supplementary income to taxi-driving.

Reformulation

The short extract from the written form quoted above is also interesting because the language is so strikingly different in style from that used by the client. Of course, any rendition of the meaning of English speech into writing, other than transcription, is likely to effect some change of meaning. But remember that the completed form is meant to represent the client's past and present situation, to communicate this to trainers and possible future employers, and to be *owned* by the client. Throughout the interview, the language the client uses is hesitant and uncertain (*I've more or less done, more or less, as long as it isn't, I'm a bit lost*, etc.). The counsellor's written version makes him sound better organized than how he represents himself during the interview. So, as well as filtering out information about the client's uncertainty, the counsellor recasts or *reformulates* the client's statements, recording the information he provides in a way that makes it more 'suitable' (from the counsellor's perspective) for the form. In this case (as in many others I have observed), this means choosing words that are more definite, positive, formal or technical than the words that are spoken by the client. For example, the client in this interview initially describes his experience with cars as *tinkering* (line 5) and the *just* at the beginning of the sentence has the effect of making his experience seem less formal or technical. The counsellor attempts to reformulate the words that the client has used to describe his experience by suggesting *Is that a sort of like servicing and things?* (lines 16–17). The use of the word *servicing* in this instance has the effect of making the client appear to be more technically and professionally competent than someone who simply tinkers around with cars in his spare time.

Reformulation is symbolic of the relative power that the counsellor has over the final words that are written down as the material outcome of the interview.

Accountability

Reformulation of clients' words by counsellors is a very common occurrence in these interviews, and highlights the importance of the completed form for the professional accountability of the counsellor. Counsellors know that the form may reach professional audiences – trainers, possible employers, possibly future counsellors in the client's projected future. They know that these audiences will judge them, as may the client, by the quality of form they produce. Of course, counsellors are also accountable to their clients, and every client will be expected to agree and sign the form at the end of the interview. For this reason, one sometimes finds counsellors *accounting for* their form filling to the client in the talk of the interview. A good example is the long statement by the counsellor in lines 43–60.

The complexity of the counsellor's role in handling information provided by the client is apparent from the contents of the official manual of practice for these interviews (Training Commission, 1988). There it says: 'Your job is to be the client's advocate: to encourage each individual to present him or herself in the best possible light' (Training Commission, 1988, p. 9). There is an implication here that in completing the form the counsellor *is expected* to filter out and reformulate information wherever necessary so as to create on the client's behalf a suitably positive image of the client as a potential worker.

Conclusions

Throughout these kinds of interview the way in which spoken and written language is used reflects a tension for the counsellor between achieving the institutional language business of the interview (i.e. getting the form completed, showing the client in the best light to other audiences, etc.) while at the same time keeping the interview process 'client centred' so that the client's concerns are addressed, all within very constrained time limits. Overall, however, the responsibility for resolving this tension, and the power to achieve that resolution, can be seen to rest with the 'professional' rather than the 'client'.

The above analysis also highlights the relationship between spoken and written language in these interviews. Some very influential theories of language use have treated spoken and written language as though they were two completely separate modes with separate purposes and traditions (e.g. Saussure [1916], 1959; Halliday, 1985). However, the interviews are neither spoken events nor written events, but events in which the two modes are 'intertwined' (as Czerniewska, 1992, put it). As other recent research (e.g. Medway, this chapter (Reading A); Bergmann, 1992; Linell and Jonsson, 1989; Jonsson and Linell, 1991; and Heath, 1992) has shown, this intertwining of oral and literate modes is a common feature in the use of English and many other languages today.

References

BERGMANN, J.R. (1992) 'Veiled morality: notes on discretion in psychiatry' in DREW, P. and HERITAGE, J. (eds) *Talk at Work: Interaction in Institutional Settings*, Cambridge, Cambridge University Press.

CZERNIEWSKA, P. (1992) *Learning about Writing*, Oxford, Blackwell.

HALLIDAY, M.A.K. (1985) *Spoken and Written Language*, Victoria, Deakin University Press.

HEATH, C. (1992) 'The delivery and reception of diagnosis in the general-practice consultation' in DREW, P. and HERITAGE, J. (eds) *Talk at Work: Interaction in Institutional Settings*, Cambridge, Cambridge University Press.

JONSSON, L. and LINELL, P. (1991) 'Story generations: from dialogical interviews to written reports in police interrogations', *Text*, vol, 11, no. 3, pp. 419–40.

LINELL, P. and JONSSON, L (1989) 'Suspect Stories: on perspective setting in an asymmetrical situation' paper presented at 'Conference on Dialogical and Contextual Dominance', 23–5 November 1989, Bad Homburg, Studiengruppe die Dynamic des Dialogs.

LONGMAN, J. and MERCER, N. (1993) 'Forms for talk and talk for forms: oral and literate dimensions of language use in employment training interviews', *Text*, vol. 13, no. 1, pp. 91–116.

MERCER, N. and LONGMAN, J. (1992) 'Accounts and the development of shared understanding in employment training interviews', *Text*, vol. 12, no. 1, pp. 103–25.

MERCER, N. and LONGMAN, J. (1993) 'Language events with two dimensions: the relationship between talking and writing as exemplified in a set of counselling interviews', *Changing English*, vol. 1, no. 1, pp. 154–67.

SAUSSURE, F. ([1916] 1959) *Course in General Linguistics*, trans. W. Baskin, New York, McGraw Hill.

TRAINING COMMISSION (1988) *The Employment Training Interview: identifying personal strengths and past achievements*, Sheffield, Training Commission.

This reading was specially commissioned for this book.

4 RHETORIC IN ENGLISH

Robin Wooffitt

4.1 INTRODUCTION

In this chapter I describe some of the ways in which the English language can be used to persuade, convince and elicit support: for example, to convince others of the merit of an argument or an opinion, or to establish the credibility of a reported event. Such uses of a language are commonly called rhetorical uses. I begin by looking at classical Graeco-Roman studies of oratory which formed the original basis for the study of **rhetoric** in English. I then go on to examine more contemporary analyses of English rhetoric. In the early part of the chapter, the focus is on the speeches of politicians, and I describe some of the linguistic devices that public speakers use to elicit and orchestrate support from their audiences. Some of these devices, however, are not confined to political discourse; as I demonstrate below, there are similar patterns in other kinds of public speaking in English, such as the sermons of Christian evangelists. Finally, I look at a more intimate kind of persuasive speech – conversations in which people describe their paranormal or supernatural experiences to a researcher.

What is rhetoric?

The *Collins Shorter Dictionary* provides four definitions of rhetoric:

1   The study of the technique of using language effectively.

2   The art of using speech to persuade, influence, or please; oratory.

3   Excessive ornamentation and contrivance in spoken or written discourse; bombast.

4   Speech or discourse that pretends to be significant but lacks true meaning: *mere rhetoric.*

(Hanks (ed.), 1993, p. 997; original emphasis).

The last two definitions probably more accurately reflect what most British people today understand by rhetoric: that it is a superficially clever but ultimately shallow type of speaking where the use of words is concerned more with effect and style than with content and meaning. Indeed, the phrase 'a rhetorical question' – a question which requires no answer – seems to encapsulate the common belief that rhetoric is somehow an empty and insubstantial form of speech.

This negative view of rhetoric, however, is perhaps a particularly British phenomenon, and even in Britain a comparatively recent development. (Rhetoric used to be taught in British universities until the latter part of the nineteenth century.) For nearly 2,000 years, people throughout the world have viewed rhetoric and the study of rhetoric positively, an attitude reflected more accurately by the first two definitions presented above. In some parts of the English-speaking world, such as the United States, 'rhetoric' is still an established subject or component of English studies in secondary school and university timetables.

In classical ancient Greek civilization, there were three types of rhetoric. First, there was *judicial* rhetoric, or the use of language to argue legal cases. Secondly, there was *deliberative* rhetoric which was used to persuade an audience to take a certain course of action, or to adopt a set of beliefs. And thirdly, there was *demonstrative* rhetoric which occurred in more formal public ceremonies. The principles of Greek rhetoric were taken up and developed by Roman orators, and this Graeco-Roman tradition has strongly influenced how the subject of rhetoric has been taught in Europe and North America. But other rhetorical traditions have also made their mark on how English is used in public speaking today. Later in this chapter, we examine evidence of the continuing influence of African and Indian traditions on the speech of politicians and preachers.

Many of the analytic and presentational skills that were taught as part of classical rhetoric are still used today by public speakers and lay people alike, albeit tacitly. Equally, academic concern with the ways in which we use language to persuade, incite and entertain other people still flourishes in a range of analytic approaches – for example, sociolinguistics, critical linguistics, literary theory and conversation analysis.

For a comparison of such approaches, see Chapter 7 of *Describing Language* (Graddol et al., (1994).

In this chapter I draw mainly on one of the most recently developed approaches to the study of rhetoric, that of **conversation analysis**, which uses as its data talk recorded in actual social events. I apply the methods of conversation analysis to reveal structural patterns and techniques in the way that the English language is used to persuade and convince, and to try to discover why such techniques seem to be so successful.

First, however, I want to return to the classical rhetorical tradition of the ancient Greek and Roman civilizations. Cicero (106–43 BC) was a Roman orator who (drawing on the ideas of the earlier Greek rhetoricians) formulated sets of recommendations as to the most effective ways of representing arguments in judicial settings. By examining Cicero's suggestions we can illustrate a traditional European perspective on rhetoric.

4.2   CLASSICAL GRAECO-ROMAN ORATORY

In ancient Greek society judicial rhetoric was important because it was expected that all citizens would be able to represent themselves in legal debate. Consequently, ordinary citizens needed to be able to develop skills of rhetoric and argument. Let us consider the kind of advice Cicero offered about the most effective way to present a case in a speech in law court.

Cicero argued that legal presentations of this type should have six parts: exordium, narration, partition, confirmation, refutation and conclusion. The exordium should prepare the audience and make them receptive and amenable to the speaker (and, if the speaker is representing someone else, the client). The narration should provide a brief, clear account of the case and may include some attacks on an opposing argument. The partition is a description of what is to be proved; this also should be clear and brief. The confirmation is the basic argument for the points that the speaker wishes to prove. The refutation, as the term suggests, involves undermining an opponent's argument. The conclusion should consist of three parts: summing up the speaker's argument, inciting indignation against the opponent, and ensuring that the speaker or the speaker's client is perceived sympathetically. These simple recommendations formed the basis for courses in rhetoric for many centuries.

The main points we can draw from Cicero's analysis are:

- that rhetorical speech designed for use in specific contexts (such as the law courts of ancient Greece) may have some common, distinctive structural features;

- that it may be possible to identify some specific, effective techniques for convincing and persuading.

Cicero offers a way of analysing rhetorical speech that might be applied to contemporary English. His concern is with the structure of the language and the various techniques that are used. However, this kind of traditional rhetorical analysis has a serious limitation: although we can identify the ways that a speech may be organized, and can identify certain techniques, it does not show us what effects these techniques achieve or how successful they are in achieving a speaker's goals.

In the next section we look at a sociological study of political speeches which not only identifies the kinds of rhetorical technique used by public speakers, but which also indicates why some of these techniques seem to be particularly effective in soliciting audience support.

4.3   POLITICAL RHETORIC

Political speeches are designed to hold the attention of the members of the audience and gain their approval and support for the politicians and the messages and sentiments being expressed in their speeches. An audience can display approval (or disapproval) in many ways, for example by cheering, booing and heckling; but probably the most common kind of display is the clapping of hands. Clapping can occur either at the end of a speech, or in shorter bursts during the speech. Intuitively, it seems reasonable to assume that such applause which appears during the speech is a display of the audience's approval of a specific point or sentiment expressed by the speaker: that is, the applause is a response to the content of the speech. However, research by a British sociologist, Max Atkinson (1984a; 1984b), suggests that the way in which a point is presented may also influence the likelihood of applause.

Atkinson studied video and tape recordings of political speeches, and the transcripts of those recordings. He began by noting bursts of applause in the speeches. Atkinson was relying on applause as a kind of barometer of the effectiveness of speeches, and consequently he felt it was important to try to transcribe it in some detail. He derived a way of taking account of three crucial features of applause: the varying intensity of applause, the precise moment that a round of applause begins and ends, and the length of applause. These features are illustrated in the following extract, in which a point made by the British Labour politician Peter Shore during the 1979 UK general election seems to receive only half-hearted approval: there is a one-second gap after the end of the point before the audience begins to applaud (indicated in Atkinson's transcripts by the row 'xxx' and the number of seconds in brackets), and even then the clapping is rather weak and hesitant, lasting for only five seconds.

For an explanation of the transcription conventions used in this and subsequent extracts please refer to the appendix to this chapter (pp. 143–4). Note for these extracts particularly: capitals are used to indicate spates of talk/applause which were louder, and underlining indicates those words or parts of words which have been stressed.

Extract 1

Shore   … it's one thing to sell to sitting tenants (0.7)
               and it's quite an↓other (0.2) to keep hous↑es ↓empty (0.4)
               while they're ↓HAWKED ar↓ound (0.2) to find ↑some
               ↓purch↑aser
               (0.2) who could just as well ↓buy (0.7) in the open market
               (0.2) like any ↓other (0.2) owner occupier ↓does.
               (1.0)
                              |———(5.0)———|
Audience   -x- (0.2) x-xx- xxxxxxxxx -xx-x
(Adapted from Atkinson, 1984a, p. 77)

In the next extract, however, we can see Margaret Thatcher (who was British prime minister at the time) eliciting much more enthusiastic applause from an audience during the 1980 Conservative Party conference:

Extract 2

Thatcher   Soviet marxism is ideo↑logically pol↑itically and mor↓ally
            bank↓ru ⌐pt |———(9.0)———|
Audience   └xx XXXXXXXXXXXXXXX-x
(Adapted from Atkinson, 1984a, p. 63)

In this case, the audience begins to show its approval even before Thatcher has finished speaking. (The precise moment at which the audience's applause begins during Thatcher's utterance is marked by the deep bracket). Also the applause is loud and continues for more than nine seconds before dying away.

Atkinson began to study his data to see if those parts of speeches that seemed to precede enthusiastic applause had any recurrent, common features. He identified various rhetorical formats that seemed to be particularly effective at soliciting audience applause. We now consider two of these: 'three-part lists' and 'contrast devices'.

Three-part lists

A **three-part list** is simply a point made via the use of three specific components. We have a good example of a three-part list in Extract 2 in Thatcher's denunciation of Soviet Marxism: she claims it is bankrupt ideologically, politically and morally. Extracts 3 and 4, both from the 1980 Conservative Party conference, provide further examples produced by Thatcher.

The three parts of the list are here numbered 1, 2, and 3

Extract 3

Thatcher   I am however (0.2) very fortunate (0.4) in having (0.6) a
            marvellous deputy (0.4) who's wonderful (.)
            1 in all places (0.2)
            2 at all times (0.2)
            3 in all things. (0.2)
               Willie White ⌐law |———(8.0)———|
Audience   └x-xx XXXXXXXXXXXXXXXXXXX-x
(Adapted from Atkinson, 1984a, p. 50)

Extract 4

Thatcher   This week has demonstrated (0.4) that we are a <u>party</u>
                <u>united in</u>
    1   ↑<u>purpose</u>
        (0.4)
    2   strategy
        (0.2)
    3   and re↓sol ⌐ve
Audience   └Hear ⌐hear |————(8.0)————|
Audience   └x-xx XXXXXXXXXXXXXXXXxxx-x
(Atkinson, 1984a, p. 61)

Atkinson observes that politicians tend to produce specific intonational shifts as they present the three parts of their lists. In Extract 4, for example, the upwards and downwards arrows indicate upwards and downwards intonational shifts. We can see that Thatcher says the first part of the list with a marked upward intonation, maintains that pitch through the second part, and then produces a downward intonation before the second syllable of the third item. This pattern of intonational shifts is a quite common feature of three-part lists. The following extract, from a speech by the British Labour politician Eric Heffer at a fringe meeting of the 1980 Labour Party conference, exhibits the same features.

Extract 5

Heffer   The National Executive decided (0.8) that w*e agr*eed   * in this extract indicates
                                                                                the lowest point reached by
                in <u>PRINCIPLE</u> (0.8) that we <u>MUST</u> <u>AGAIN</u> <u>TRY</u> AND   the hand in a downward-
                                                                                pointing gesture.
                <u>GET</u> SOME <u>CONSTITUTIONAL</u> <u>AMENDMENTS</u>
                (0.5)
    1   BE↑<u>FORE</u> YOU
        (0.2)
    2   <u>AT</u> CONFERENCE
        (0.2)
    3   <u>THIS</u> ↓<u>WEEK</u>
        ⌐ SO THAT YOU CAN <u>STILL</u> MAKE YOUR <u>MINDS</u> UP
Audience   └ xxxxxxxxxxxxxxxxxxxxxxxxxxxxxxxxxxxxxxx
                [the TV editor cut the film at this point – the
                applause may have continued for longer]
(Atkinson, 1984a, p. 64)

Here again the speaker raises his intonation on the first part of the list, maintains it for the second part and then drops it on the third part of the list. It is interesting to note that the combination of the three-part list and these intonational patterns is so effective that the audience begins to applaud immediately after the end of the third item, despite the fact that Heffer has not finished. Consequently he has to battle against the audience's enthusiastic applause to finish his point.

    One of the reasons why three-part lists are so successful at soliciting audience applause is that their structure allows speakers to amplify and strengthen more general points. (Note how Thatcher emphasizes the concept of party unity in

Extract 4.) Later, we will look at some of the more structural or organizational features of three-part lists to see if we can find out more about what makes them so effective as a way of packaging a political point. But before that we examine a second powerful technique: the contrast structure.

Contrasts

Politicians often criticize other political parties and politicians in their speeches. Pointing out the deficiencies of other groups is an effective way by which speakers can implicitly affirm the value of their own party or approach. But of course, politicians can positively evaluate their own position in a much more explicit way, while at the same time still criticizing another position or set of policies. This can be done through **contrast devices**, in which one argument or approach is compared to another, so that the speaker's favoured position is seen to be superior. In the following extract the British Labour politician Helen Osborn is advising her own party on the best way to oppose Thatcher's government. (The two parts of the contrast are indicated by the letters A and B.)

Extract 6

Osborn	The wa:y to fight Thatcher
	(0.4)
	A is not through the silent conformity of the graveyard,
	(0.5)
	but by putting party policies (0.2) powerfully
	B and determinedly from the front bench.
Audience	hear ⌈hear
Audience	⌊hear ⌈hear
Audience	⌊Applause (8.2 seconds)

(Heritage and Greatbatch, 1986, p. 124)

The next extract also provides a good illustration of a well-constructed contrast. It comes from a debate at the 1981 Labour Party conference, where a member of Parliament called Alf Morris was talking about the needs of disabled people in society.

Extract 7

Morris	Governments will argue: (0.8) that resources are not
	available: (0.4) to help disabled people.
	(1.3)
	A The fact is that too much is spent on the munitions of
	war::,
	(0.6)
	B and too little is spent ⌈(0.2) on the munitions of peace.
Audience	⌊Applause (9.2 seconds)

(Heritage and Greatbatch, 1986, p. 123)

Nonverbal aspects of political rhetoric

In his research, Atkinson also examined nonverbal components of political rhetoric – gestures, intonational features and so on which are an intrinsic part of such speech making.

Activity 4.1   *(Reading A)*

Read 'Extract from *Our Masters' Voices'* by J.M. Atkinson (Reading A) noting the nonverbal components.

Some other research has provided evidence about the effectiveness of the techniques Atkinson describes. In 1986 two British sociologists, John Heritage and David Greatbatch, published a study of the speeches made at the annual conferences of the Conservative, Labour and Liberal parties in 1981, from which Extracts 6 and 7 come. By simply recording the televised broadcasts of these conventions, they were able to acquire nearly 500 speeches, which lasted for a total of approximately 40 hours.

Heritage and Greatbatch found that the most effective technique for producing applause was the contrast structure, which was responsible for nearly 25 per cent of all applause. The three-part list was the third most effective and was responsible for 6.5 per cent of applause. The second most effective device was what they called a 'combination', in which devices such as lists and contrasts were interwoven. Here is an example of a combination, used by the British politician and veteran public speaker Tony Benn in the 1980 Labour Party conference.

Extract 8

Benn		... and I make not too much of that (.) <u>save</u> for one thing.
		(1.0)
	A	If you have a <u>veto</u> (0.3) those who op<u>pose</u> (.) <u>policies</u> (0.2) don't <u>bother</u> (0.2) to <u>argue</u> (0.2) with conf↓erence
		(0.4)
	B	because they ↑<u>wait</u> to the Clause ↑*Five* ↓meeting and they ↑<u>kill</u> it (0.2)
		1 <u>SECRETLY</u>
		(0.2)
		2 <u>PRIVATELY</u>
		(0.2)
		3 with↓out↓ <u>debate</u> ⌈now MY RESENT –
Audience		⌊x-xxXXXXXXX ...

(Atkinson, 1984a, p. 95)

Here the second part of the contrast is composed of three points, at the end of which the audience begins to clap, regardless of the fact that Benn is still speaking. Atkinson has commented that audiences seem predisposed to clap at the end of three-part lists: 'if speakers are groping for a third item in a list, they will not be interrupted ... But they will be interrupted if they are searching for a fourth' (Atkinson, 1984a, p. 58). It might seem strange that a veteran speaker like Benn does not take account of this tendency. However, Atkinson suggests that speaking while the audience is clapping may have strategic presentational benefits, in that the speaker is able to convey the impression of a politician concerned only with the issues at hand, rather than with achieving public acclaim.

In fact contrasts, and combinations which involved contrasts, were responsible for a third of all applause in Heritage and Greatbatch's study. Their basic finding was that political messages which are packaged in one or more of these limited range of rhetorical formats are more likely to be applauded than messages which are not so packaged.

Activity 4.2   *(Allow 20 minutes)*

Listen to any political speech given by a politician from any country on the radio or television. Instead of listening to *what* he or she says, try to focus on the *way* the points are made.

But what about the relationship between the form of a speech and its content? Earlier, we raised the common-sense idea that an audience will applaud those parts of speeches that express political sentiments with which members of the audience agree. But the findings about the effectiveness of rhetorical devices suggest that the organization and presentation of a message may be equally influential in soliciting approval. Heritage and Greatbatch tried to assess the relative importance of political sentiments and the way in which they are packaged and presented.

To do this, they looked at political debates where it was obvious that the majority of the audience supported a specific position. For example, in 1981 the Conservative Party thoroughly endorsed the economic policies which later came to be known as Thatcherism after its then leader, Margaret Thatcher. Consequently, it was uncontentious to assume that during the debate on economic policy the majority of the audience would be fervent supporters of Thatcherite economics. Heritage and Greatbatch also examined speeches produced at the Labour Party's debate on defence policy. Here too there was an overwhelming consensus; in this case, in favour of unilateral nuclear disarmament.

Heritage and Greatbatch found that sentiments that echoed the beliefs of the majority tended to be applauded regardless of the kind of rhetorical format in which they were delivered. But the intensity and extent of applause for popular sentiments were enhanced greatly if they were packaged rhetorically. And there was a high incidence of rhetorical formats in those anti-majority messages which were applauded. So it seems that the use of these kinds of devices increases the likelihood of support for alternative or anti-consensus ideas; and approval for popular ideas is enhanced when they are expressed in three-part lists, contrasts and so on.

Why are these devices so effective?

Let us look more closely at the function of three-part lists and contrasts. Imagine a large political meeting at a rally or a party conference. The audience is composed of hundreds, perhaps thousands, of people who do not know each other and whose behaviour is unrehearsed and, therefore, likely to be unco-ordinated. This is an uncomfortable position for members of the audience to be in, because social psychological research (and introspection about our own experiences) tells us that when we are part of a group, we feel pressure to act as a whole. Consequently, individuals who make up the audiences for political speeches face a tricky dilemma: how do they know when to applaud? How can they ensure that they won't start clapping when no one else does? In short, how can they organize a collective response?

It is this problem that is solved so effectively by lists and contrasts. Used at mass gatherings, they are audience management devices. They provide the audience with a cue for when to clap and thus allow collective displays of support. And that in part explains why these devices are so frequently followed by applause: the audience is simply responding to the signal to applaud which is built into these devices. So lists and contrasts are successful at eliciting applause because they project their own completion: as they are being built, they signal when they are going to end.

An audience can see that a politician is making a list, and their experience of conventions of everyday conversation will lead them to expect that it will be completed not after two points, not after four, but after three. Each individual member of the audience can therefore predict the end of a specific point and can co-ordinate his or her behaviour with the other audience members to provide a collective response.

That is how lists project the ends of specific points in a speech. But how do contrast devices do it? The most effective contrast devices tend to have both parts built and presented in the same ways; for example, some words or phrases may even be used in both parts. Quite often the second part of a contrast is almost a mirror image of the first part. Look at the two parts of the contrast in Extract 7 (repeated here as Extract 9).

Extract 9

Morris   Governments will argue: (0.8) that resources are not
                      available: (0.4) to help disabled people.
                      (1.3)
                  A   The fact is that too much is spent on the
                      munitions of war::,
                      (0.6)
                  B   and too little is spent ⌈(0.2) on the munitions of peace.
Audience   ⌊Applause (9.2 seconds)

(Heritage and Greatbatch, 1986, p. 123)

There are several points where the second contrasting part mirrors the first:

too much is spent on the munitions of war
too little is spent (0.2) on the munitions of peace

This is useful for audiences. Their awareness that certain words and phrases are being repeated will alert them to the fact that a contrast is being set up; they can recognize that what is being said now echoes the structure of what was just said before. (Indeed, in Extract 9 the audience begins to clap after the speaker has produced only half of the second part of the contrast.) But more importantly, because there is the tacit convention that the second parts of contrasts tend to mirror the first parts, and because they have already heard the first part, members of the audience can predict exactly when the second part of the contrast will end.

It is quite important to make sure that both parts of the contrast device are similar. If there are differences, the effect on audience applause can be striking.

The audience will have monitored the first part, and will be expecting the second part to have roughly the same structure. If the second part doesn't mirror the first, then the audience may not be able to anticipate when the point being made is complete. In the following example from the 1979 UK general election, Edward Heath, the former British Conservative prime minister (1970–4), is arguing that the influence of the trades unions on government policy should be restrained. This anti-union stance was a central theme of Conservative government policy throughout the 1980s. As he was speaking to an audience of Conservative party members and supporters, we might expect Heath's remarks to receive unequivocal support and enthusiastic applause.

Extract 10

Heath	A	... it is right that the government should consider these matters and take them into account.
		(1.0)
	B	What is entirely unaccept↓able (0.8) is the view that parliament never can (0.6) and never should (0.6) approve any legisl↓ation (0.8) unless first of all the trade unions them↓selves (.) approve ↓of it.
		(0.5)
		THAT is en↓tirely unac↓ceptable
Audience	Hear	⌐hear |————————(0.8)————————⌐
Audience		└x-xx XXXXXXXXXXXXXXXXXXXXxxx-x

(Atkinson, 1984a, p. 78)

Despite the fact that Heath is espousing a sentiment widely supported by the audience, the end of his point is greeted with silence. Indeed, it is only when he summarizes his view, thereby indicating to the audience that he has finished making a point, that the audience show their appreciation.

The absence of any applause may well be due to Heath's failure to build a symmetrical contrast. The first part of the contrast is neat and short. The second part, however, meanders somewhat and clearly does not match the first part. (The first extract in this chapter was an illustration of lukewarm audience applause; if you look at it again, you will find that the preceding bit of talk was a poorly constructed contrast structure, with much the same kind of 'design faults' as Heath's example.)

Rhetoric in Indian English

The analysis of political speech presented so far has depended heavily upon examples from speeches made by British politicians, most of whom were recorded in the early 1980s. The analysis used has also focused on the rhetorical techniques identified by the British conversation analyst Max Atkinson. Reading B by Julu Sen, Rahul Sharma and Anima Chakraverty, which accompanies this chapter, broadens the perspective on English rhetoric in two ways. First, it offers an example of a political speech from another English-speaking country, India, which is also from a different historical period (the late 1940s). We can consider how relevant Atkinson's categories are for analysing this speech by Jawarharlal Nehru. Secondly, Sen et al. provide an analysis of a rather different kind from Atkinson's, one which shows how some of the principles of an Indian rhetorical tradition are embodied in the speech.

Activity 4.3   *(Reading B)*

The Indian politician Jawarharlal Nehru was one of the main founders of an independent India in the period after the Second World War. The most famous and influential political figure of the Indian struggle for independence, however, was Mahatma Gandhi. In the appendix to Reading B, 'The light has gone out', you will find a transcript of the speech that Nehru made to the Indian nation on the death of Gandhi. Read that speech now. As you read it, consider whether or not Nehru uses either of the two rhetorical techniques we have been discussing, that is, three-part lists and contrasts.

Then read the rest of Reading B by Sen et al. Note the kind of analysis that the authors offer, and their references to Indian rhetorical traditions.

Comment

Sen et al. point to the essentially oral character of Nehru's speech, with its effective use of cohesive devices (such as the use of 'and') and 'purposeful repetition' (as with the repetition of the phrase 'the light has gone out'). They also suggest that Nehru, like other Indian political speakers, drew on established Indian rhetorical practices, such as the 'factors of effective communication' established by Kautiliya. So the reading offers a glimpse of another analytic perspective on the rhetorical use of English, one which might be complementary to those we have presented in the chapter. Although Sen et al. do not draw attention to them, you may have noticed that Nehru's speech contains a three-part list ('We must face this poison ...', lines 34–6) and a contrast ('But that does not mean we should be weak ...', lines 47–9).

The ubiquity of three-part lists and contrast pairs

We have seen that three-part lists are not confined to the speeches of British politicians. There is indeed evidence that they are used more widely, and they seem to be common in political speech in several English-speaking countries. For example, here is one (of a number) in a speech made by Malcolm X, the American 'Black Power' leader, at the University of Oxford in 1964.

Extract 11

Malcolm X   And I say, I'm speaking as a Black man from America,
                 which is a racist society. No matter how much you hear
                 it talk about democracy
           1 it's as racist as South Africa
           2 or as racist as Portugal,
           3 or as racist as any other racialist society on this earth.
                 (Malcolm X, 1991, p. 23)

Three-part lists and contrast pairs occur in public speeches other than political ones, where speakers are trying to be persuasive or build a strong case for their claims. For example, in their study of the selling techniques of market traders, Pinch and Clark (1986) found that one of the most common rhetorical devices used by the traders was to contrast the value of the goods being sold with the actual selling price at which they were being offered.

Here is just such an example, recorded in a market in Maidstone (a town in south-east England): the trader was selling a device used in dressmaking, called a 'tailor tacker'.

Trader   While I demonstrate, I don't charge £2.25, like they do in the shops and stores on the mail order. In fact I save you 75p on the price: I charge you £1.50.

(Open University, 1980, p. 10)

Three-part lists are not confined to spoken forms of rhetoric. Look at the example below (Figure 4.1) of a form of rhetoric that we examine later in the chapter, that of Christian evangelism. The particular leaflet 'Sin: am I guilty' from which this extract comes was distributed through letterboxes in Milton Keynes in 1995 by New City Baptist Church.

What is sin ?

It is breaking God's laws, doing what he forbids, neglecting what he commands.

It is failure to put God first, failure to care about other people.

It is not something that only others do but rather it is my personal problem.

Figure 4.1   What is sin?

Three-part lists are not only found in speeches addressed to mass audiences; they are a common phenomenon in ordinary conversation. The following extracts come from Jefferson's (1991) study of the interactional properties of lists. All occurred in everyday conversation, either on the telephone or in face-to-face interaction.

Extract 12

Sidney   While you've been talking tuh me, I mended,
    1   two nightshirts,
    2   a pillow case?
    3   enna pair'v pants.

(Jefferson, 1991, p. 64)

Extract 13

Maybelle   I think if you
        1   exercise it
        2   an' work at it'
        3   n studied it
            chu do become clairvoyant.

(Jefferson, 1991, p. 64)

Often when people repeat words in conversation they'll be repeated three times.

Extract 14

Carol: Did this phone ring? I dialed twice en it n-rang'n rang'n
            rang

(Jefferson, 1991, p. 64)

In these next extracts speakers have produced two parts of a list, but either have exhausted the relevant items which could be used to extend the list, or cannot find an appropriate word with which to complete it. In each case they use an item such as 'or something' or 'things like that', so as to complete the lists as a three-part unit.

Extract 15

Heather   And they had like a concession stand like at a fair
              where you can buy
        1   coke
        2   and popcorn
        3   and that type of thing.

(Jefferson, 1991, p. 66)

Extract 16

Sy   Take up
        1   m:Metrecal er,
        2   Carnation Slender
        3   er something like that.

(Jefferson, 1991, p. 66)

Extracts 15 and 16 are important because they tell us something very interesting about three-part lists. Note that in each case the third part is not actually another item as in the two extracts that went before. Instead, it is a general term. By using general phrases such as 'like that', these speakers seem to be displaying their tacit understanding that lists should have three parts. That is, where a specific third component does not come to mind, they are using a general term to make sure the list has three parts. It is as though there is a normative principle underlying people's communicative activity which runs something like: 'if presenting information in a list, try to do it in three parts'. (Note how in Extract 11, from a speech by Malcolm X, the third part of his list functions as a generalized list completer.) But the rhetorical power of three-part lists is not simply that of effectively eliciting applause, because we have seen that they are used in some situations (evangelical texts, informal conversations) where applause would be quite inappropriate.

There is a sense of completeness or roundness about these devices which gives them an air of persuasiveness. The persuasive character of three-part lists in particular has not been lost on the advertising industry. It is remarkably easy to find advertisements that are built around three-part lists. Perhaps there is a deeply embedded cultural significance about organizing activity into three parts: the Christian faith has the Holy Trinity (Father, Son and Holy Ghost), jokes routinely have three characters or three distinct components, and many fairy tales have three central episodes. This brings us to another genre of rhetorical English: the language of Christian evangelists.

4.4   RELIGIOUS RHETORIC

First, we examine one study of preaching styles found in black Pentecostal church services in Britain, as studied by Sutcliffe and Tomlin (1986). They suggest that the use of English by Pentecostal preachers embodies rhetorical traditions found in African cultures. We then trace the influence of these same traditions in some extracts from the speeches of the US civil rights leader Martin Luther King.

During the 1950s and 1960s many thousands of people migrated to Britain from the Caribbean, and it has been estimated that approximately 70 per cent of these were regular church-goers. Consequently, forms of Pentecostalism which were popular in Jamaica began to take root in the United Kingdom.

Although the spiritual content of black Pentecostal church services draws heavily on Judeao-Christianity, Sutcliffe and Tomlin suggest that some of the ways in which this content is communicated reflect traditional African religious ceremonies. Sutcliffe and Tomlin focused on three features of Pentecostal services: preaching, testimony and prayer. Their study set out to relate the organization of these verbal activities to patterns of speaking found more generally in the language practices of people whose culture had African roots. Pentecostal preachers' performances depend on verbal eloquence and spontaneous creativity in the use of the English language. While preparation for a sermon will certainly involve study of the Bible, little may be written down in advance. In keeping with the Pentecostal belief in the power of the Holy Spirit, instead preachers rely on divine guidance and performative skills. This in turn allows them to vary their presentation according to the mood or composition of their congregation. Sutcliffe and Tomlin argue that there are a number of factors which make this Pentecostal preaching style quite distinctive. Moreover, they suggest that it draws on styles of language use which are commonly found in communities with African cultural roots. They note, for example, that a feature of this preaching style is the use of proverbs. Proverbs are used to illuminate and emphasize specific points in the sermon. For instance, the negative consequences of sin and temptation will be underscored by saying 'Wha sweet nanny goat wi run him belly' (what a nanny goat desires will upset her stomach). Sutcliffe and Tomlin make the point that the use of proverbial expressions in church services invokes features of more traditional African forms of speaking. They say:

> Proverbs and proverbial expression ... have their roots in the African cultural linguistic pattern and have been retained by West Indians ... Concrete imagery and fable both shade into proverbs and proverbial expressions. A preacher likens the Christian life to a journey on the motorway. A pastor compares the true Christian not with the hen who gives her eggs but with the pig who, in giving, gives its all. A young British-born woman, in a devotional sermon, says that the aspiring Christian

travels a road with detours, wrong turnings, road works and missed signs but with true determination to reach the end of the journey, come what may. She builds the images one by one, to end amid tremendous applause.

(Sutcliffe and Tomlin, 1986, p. 21)

The use of proverbs, parables and metaphors for life's events may well be common in many African societies, as Sutcliffe and Tomlin suggest, but it is questionable as to whether this is the only, or main, reason why they are commonly found in Pentecostal church rhetoric. The use of parables and journey metaphors is a common feature of Christian pulpit rhetoric in general, and perhaps of rhetoric in other religions too. For Christian preachers, certainly, the use of such devices can be traced back to their frequent appearance in the text of the New Testament.

Activity 4.4   *(Allow 15 minutes)*

Consider whether the use of proverbs, parables and metaphors is a feature of any religious rhetoric with which you are familiar.

Sutcliffe and Tomlin also describe another common feature of the Pentecostal church services, which is usually referred to as the **call and response**. This refers to the way the congregation will echo the words of the preacher or even add words of their own: for example, the audience may say 'Amen', 'Preach it preacher', 'Yes', 'Come on now preacher' and so on. Because of this, the members of the audience are not passive recipients of the preacher's sermon, but are actively engaged in its performance. Indeed, if the congregation's response seems weak or intermittent, preachers may encourage the audience's participation by using prompts such as 'You gone quiet on me church'.

This call-and-response pattern of communication does seem to be a distinctive feature of public performance rhetoric in many parts of the Afro-American world (as described, for example, by Smitherman, 1986).

An interest in call and response informed Keith and Whittenberger-Keith's (1988) study of the speeches of the black American community leader and preacher, Martin Luther King. They adapted the analytic perspective on political rhetoric developed by Atkinson (discussed earlier). They studied King's speech to see how it was designed to manage the interaction between him and the audience. Specifically they wanted to answer the following questions:

- What kinds of responses are typically produced by the audience?
- In the absence of an explicit call, what features of the speech can function as a call?
- Are there recurrent patterns in call and response?
- What kinds of communicative functions are served by patterns of call and response?

Keith and Whittenberger-Keith found two basic categories of responses. First, and most common, there are **affirmations,** such as 'Yeah', 'Alright' and 'Amen'. A second and less common form of response they call **commentaries**, such as 'I like it', 'talk about it' and 'yes it is'. Both types of response provide positive evaluations of the speech. However, whereas affirmations tend to mark the audience's approval of a line of argument, commentaries tend to occur in response to specific devices.

Figure 4.2   *Martin Luther King addressing his followers*

This research suggests that there are three kinds of device in King's speeches which operate as inexplicit 'calls' for an audience response. First, there are devices which are embedded in very short segments of the text of King's speech, such as three-part lists and contrasts. The second set of devices includes those which structure larger passages of the text. For instance, King often repeats specific phrases to produce call and responses. The phrase 'I have a dream' is an example, as is 'now is the time'; this latter phrase is illustrated in the following data extract.

In this extract audience responses are coded as: 'Affirmation' to mark applause, and 'Commentary' to mark a verbal response.

MLK   now is the time ⌜ (1.0) to make real the
Audience   ⌞ [Commentary]

MLK   promises of democracy   ⌜ (1.5) n::ow is the time (1.0) to
Audience   ⌞ [Affirmation]

MLK   rise from the dark and desolate valley of segregation to
           the sunlit path of racial justice (0.5) <u>no:w</u> is the time
               ⌜ (3.5) to lift our nation from the quicksands of
Audience   ⌞ [Affirmation]

MLK   racial injustice to the solid rock of brotherhood and <u>now</u>
           is the ⌜ time (3.5) to make justice a reality
Audience   ⌞ [Commentary]

MLK   for all of God's children

(Adapted from Keith and Whittenberger-Keith, 1986, pp. 127–8)

Keith and Whittenberger-Keith claim that the repetition of these kinds of phrases establishes a form of 'instant tradition' in the course of the speech which the audience members quickly come to recognize as a cue for a response.

Keith and Whittenberger-Keith use the word 'musical' to describe the final set of devices to initiate audience response. This refers to specific rhythmic or

tonal patterns in the way King delivers his speech. They also make the methodological point that traditional rhetorical analysis, which largely examines written
representations of public speeches, is not able to address the significance of such
paralinguistic features.

Figure 4.3
Popular evangelism in
the written mode

Of course, political and evangelical speakers do not always have a physically present
audience to provide feedback on their performances, to applaud at the end of lists, or
to join in call-and-response sequences. They may be performing on one of the mass
media, as is the case for the television evangelists studied by John Thompson.

❖   ❖   ❖   ❖   ❖

Activity 4.5   *(Reading C)*

Read 'Televangelical language: a media speech genre' by John Thompson
(Reading C). As you do so, consider the following questions:

•   Why does Thompson suggest that it is functional for televangelical talk to
    have easily recognizable, distinctive features?

•   What distinctive features of the talk does he identify?

•   What established rhetorical techniques does he describe 'televangelists' as
    using?

Comment

Thompson argues that the distinctive genres of television talk are recognized as such by TV audiences. Moreover, he suggests that they may be attracted and reassured by the familiarity of genres. He notes that televangelical talk is typified by such features as switching from formal, religious address to more intimate, informal talk to viewers. Although the talk has distinctive features, the televangelists also draw on rhetorical techniques described earlier in this chapter.

4.5   REPORTING EXTRAORDINARY EXPERIENCES

A recurrent theme of this chapter so far has been the various ways in which English can be actively used to be persuasive. However, with the exception of Cicero's recommendations for legal discourse, the kinds of discourse we have looked at tend to occur when there is some doubt that the recipients of the discourse actually need to be persuaded. For example, the audience of a politician's speech will almost certainly support the party represented by the politician. And the congregation in a church service does not need to be persuaded of the importance of worship. On such occasions, the aim may be to encourage or reinforce loyalty, rather than to change people's beliefs. However, there are occasions when the people we are speaking to may be less than sympathetic to our claims, and when the event is not a public speech-making occasion but an everyday conversation in which formal rhetoric would be inappropriate. On these occasions, the ability to produce a convincing, plausible account is a more pressing issue. And in these cases there is a variety of rhetorical techniques that people use to establish the credibility of the claims they are making. It is this persuasive use of English that I focus on for the rest of the chapter.

I start by drawing on the research of the conversation analyst Gail Jefferson (1984). She made a study of reports of events such as shootings, hijackings, accidents and so on made by witnesses who were quite 'ordinary people'. Witnesses to these extraordinary events often employ a format she identifies as 'At first I thought … but then I realized'. A well-known example is the way that witnesses to the shooting of J.F. Kennedy reported a loud bang, which they first thought to be a firecracker or a car backfiring, but which they then realized was gunfire. The following example comes from Sacks's (1984) initial identification of the phenomenon:

> I was walking up towards the front of the airplane and I saw the stewardess standing facing the cabin and a fellow standing with a gun in her back. *And my first thought was he's showing her the gun, and then I realized that couldn't be, and then it turned out he was hijacking the plane.*
> (Sacks, 1984, p. 419; emphasis added)

In her analysis of this kind of rhetorical device, Jefferson notes that speakers typically begin by describing their initial assessment of what was going on – an assessment which, crucially, turns out to be wrong. However, she also points to the fact that the incorrect first thoughts are often themselves quite unusual. In the extract cited above, for example, the speaker reports that his first thought was that the man was showing the stewardess the gun. But had the speaker really drawn this conclusion then his reasoning processes must have been informed by gross naivety or a staggeringly optimistic view of human nature. That is, he appears to be reporting that he found nothing strange about a man with a gun on an aeroplane and that he assumed that by putting the gun against the stewardess's back, the man was showing it to her.

Jefferson argues that however extraordinary these formulations are, they are not so extraordinary when compared to what was actually happening: for instance, a hijacking is a much more dramatic event than someone simply showing something to someone else. Jefferson argues that what speakers are doing with the first part of the 'At first I thought … ' device is to present, as their normal first assumption, an innocuous reading of the state of affairs on which they are reporting. Through their 'first thought' formulations they display that they did not immediately assume that anything untoward was happening. They are presenting themselves as having had the kind of initial assumptions about the event that any normal person might have. In so doing, they are rhetorically invoking their social identity as ordinary people.

Describing paranormal experiences

There is an even greater need to appear normal when reporting paranormal experiences, such as telepathy, apparitions, UFOs, visions of the Virgin Mary and so on, because the strangeness of paranormal events derives from the fact that they present an implicit challenge to scientific declarations about the world and, moreover, they undermine common-sense knowledge of what sorts of things are possible. In the light of the scepticism in western societies about anomalous phenomena, people who claim such experiences place themselves in an inauspicious position. The mere act of claiming to have had a paranormal experience can lead to assumptions of at best crankiness, or worse, some form of psychological problem. It is interesting, then, to see how people construct their reports of their experiences to take account of the potential scepticism with which their claims may be met. What communicative resources can they use to show that the event being described actually happened?

In the first chapter of this book, Janet Maybin talks about the way that people can use reported dialogue or incorporate other people's 'voices' into their own accounts and stories. She points out that using other people's voices in our accounts allows us to convey particular evaluative perspectives. In that sense, reported speech can be an interactional resource: it is in fact also a rhetorical tool.

In accounts of paranormal experiences, speakers often use reported speech: words that they said, words that other people said, or reported dialogue between themselves and other people. The use of active voices can perform a variety of tasks. Look at the following extract, in which the speaker is describing the first of a series of apparitions which appeared in her bedroom. In this extract she is reporting the appearance of the figure of a young girl.

```
1    she stood there at the side of the bed
2    (1.3)
3    she had her hand like this (.) and she was
4    looking down at me like that
5    (1.0)
6    and ah looked ah wo- my eyes were open
7    'nd I looked at her
8    (0.5)
9    than ah jumped up ah sat up in hh (0.3) (    )
```

10 I just said
11 (0.7)
12 'however did you get in'
13 (0.5)
14 just like that

(Wooffitt, 1992, pp. 157–8)

Let us look at what the speaker is able to convey with the use of her reported remark 'however did you get in'. First, she conveys her reaction: her surprise at being disturbed by the figure. Secondly, the reported speech is a question which asks how the figure got into her home. This is very important: to produce a credible account of a paranormal experience, it is important to be seen as a credible witness. It is necessary therefore to demonstrate that one's reasoning and assumptions about the world are quite normal. 'Ordinary' people do not interpret every stimulus in their environment as the product of non-normal, non-material causes. Even stimuli that are not part of the routine features of daily life are not immediately accorded any supernatural status. The speaker's use of the question 'however did you get in' displays her 'normal' first assumptions about the nature of the intruder: that it was a human being who would have had to overcome the kinds of locks and bolts which secure doors and windows, and not a paranormal entity, for which human security measures would present no obstacle. In this, the use of reported speech allows the speaker to demonstrate her identity as an 'ordinary person'. Finally, the reported utterance also provides information about the appearance of the figure. So, for the speaker to have assumed it was a human being, it must have been particularly vivid, lifelike and three-dimensional. This in turn undermines the possible suggestion that the speaker's experience was the product of misperception; for example, mistaking the shadows of a dimly lit bedroom for an apparitional visitor. Thus one short segment of reported speech allows the speaker to accomplish a range of subtle inferential tasks.

One powerful argument which can be made about a claim to have encountered an anomalous experience is to suggest that the phenomenon was in some way the product of the claimant's own imagination, or simply a perceptual error. Reported talk can be used to undermine the basis for this claim by demonstrating (and substantiating) the objectivity, or 'out-there-ness', of the phenomenon. In the following extract a different speaker is describing one of a series of encounters with a malevolent spirit:

1   that:t night:
2   (1.5)
3   I don't know what time it was:
4   (1.3)
5   my: husband (.) and I both woke up: (0.7)
6   with the mo:st (.) dreadful (0.5) feeling of
7   (1.7)
8   hhh °well° being (nyrie) smothered (0.3) but the
9   powerful smell ˙h and a blackness (0.3) that ws
10 that was (0.2) blacker than black I can't describe it
11 like (.) anything else (.) ˙hh it was the most
12 penetrating (0.3) type of blackness ˙hh

13 and there was this
14 (1.7)
15 what I assumed to be th- the shape of a man (.)
16 in a cloak
17 (2.0)
18 it was the most (0.3) formidable
19 (1.2)
20 sight
21 (1.0)
22 my husband said 'my God what is it'
23 (.)
24 an' I just said 'now keep quiet and say the Lord's prayer'

(Wooffitt, 1992, pp. 163–4)

Here the speaker invokes the urgency of the encounter by dealing with three evocative and dramatic features of the experience: the smell, the 'blackness' and the description of the figure itself. Immediately after this elaborate description, she introduces her husband's utterance, 'my God what is it?', which establishes that he could also see the figure. The alarm and shock conveyed by her husband's question confirm that the thing in the room, and the associated sensations, were as powerful and disturbing as the speaker had described. This in turn confirms the speaker's reliability as an accurate reporter of the event.

Reported dialogue thus offers a resource which can be exploited, rhetorically, by speakers in subsequent retellings.

4.6 CONCLUSION

I began this chapter with a brief discussion of the classical, Graeco-Roman approach to the analysis of rhetoric. We saw that the Graeco-Roman tradition encouraged people to believe that effective rhetoric could be achieved through the careful structuring of a speech and through the use of specific techniques.

Drawing heavily on the research of Max Atkinson, I first showed how the rhetorical devices of the three-part list and the contrast pair are commonly and effectively used by political speakers to emphasize the main points of their messages and to elicit – and manage – audience responses. I went on to show that these devices are not limited to political rhetoric, or even to spoken language, but are found in other kinds of verbal performance and persuasive text.

You will have seen that the rhetorical use of English reflects a variety of cultural traditions. The reading by Sen et al. illustrated how Indian rhetorical traditions may be embodied in English. I also discussed Sutcliffe and Tomlin's analysis of preaching styles in black Pentecostal churches in the United Kingdom, and the continuing influence of African rhetorical traditions in those settings (as in the use of call-and-response sequencing). I also drew attention to rhetorical features which may be typical of Christian pulpit rhetoric, and perhaps of religious rhetoric on a wider scale. In Reading C Thompson's research revealed some distinctive features of 'televangelical talk', while also helping to emphasize the ubiquity of some rhetorical techniques. Finally, I have shown that even in more informal, intimate conversations speakers use rhetorical techniques to be persuasive: even apparently simple descriptions of events can be designed to have a persuasive rhetorical force.

APPENDIX   TRANSCRIPTION SYMBOLS

The transcription symbols listed below are conventional for the method of analysing talk known as conversation analysis. Many, but not all, of the symbols listed appear in those extracts of transcribed speech included in the chapter which have been taken from conversation analytic research (authors however do sometimes differ in their use of the various transcription symbols). A more detailed description of these transcription symbols can be found in Atkinson and Heritage (1984, pp. ix–xvi).

See also Chapter 1 of this book and Chapter 7 of *Describing Language* (Graddol et al. (eds), 1994) for more about conversation analysis.

(1.0)	The number in brackets is a time gap in seconds.
(0.5)	The number in brackets is a time gap in tenths of a second.
(.)	A dot enclosed in a bracket indicates a pause in the talk of less than two-tenths of a second.
˙hh	A dot before 'h' indicates the speaker's in-breath. The more hs, the longer the in-breath.
(( ))	A description enclosed in a double bracket indicates a nonverbal activity. For example, ((banging sound)).
-	A dash indicates the sharp cut-off of the prior word or sound.
:::	Colons indicate that the speaker has stretched the preceding sound or letter. The more colons, the greater the extent of the stretching.
( )	Empty parentheses indicate the presence of an unclear fragment on the tape.
(guess)	The words within a single bracket indicate the transcriber's best guess at an unclear fragment.
.	A full stop indicates a stopping fall in tone. It does not necessarily indicate the end of a sentence.
,	A comma indicates a continuing intonation.
?	A question mark indicates a rising inflection. It does not necessarily indicate a question.
Underline	Underlined fragments indicate speaker emphasis.
↑ ↓	Pointed arrows indicate a marked falling (↓) or rising (↑) intonational shift. They are placed immediately before the onset of the shift.
CAPITALS	With the exception of proper nouns, capital letters indicate a section of speech noticeably louder than that surrounding it.
° °	Degree signs are used to indicate that the talk they encompass is spoken noticeably quieter than the surrounding talk.
Thaght	A 'gh' indicates that the word in which it is placed had a guttural pronunciation.

> <   'More than' and 'less than' signs indicate that the talk they
            encompass was produced noticeably quicker than the
            surrounding talk.

=   The 'equals' sign indicates contiguous utterances. For example:

            Speaker 1 yeah September ⌐seventy six=
                                      [
            Speaker 2   ⌐September

            Speaker 1 =it would be yeah that's right

[Square brackets spanning adjacent lines of concurrent speech
]   indicate the onset and end of a spate of overlapping talk.

Reading A
EXTRACT FROM *OUR MASTERS' VOICES*

J.M. Atkinson

The general importance of intonation and associated variations in volume and rhythmic stress is underlined by the fact that it is sometimes possible to anticipate where an audience will applaud in the course of speeches made in languages we do not understand. The process of recognition is also greatly assisted by the way speakers produce their talk in conjunction with a variety of precisely timed non-verbal activities. By combining these different techniques to package and deliver their messages, orators can communicate to their audiences that a change of mood or tempo is taking place. They can signal that they are, as it were, 'changing gear', and launching into a sequence which will be worthy of closer attention and perhaps even applause. [An] obvious case of this ... is the excerpt from Mr Heffer's fringe-meeting speech at the 1980 Labour Party conference.

* indicates the lowest point reached by the hand in a downward-pointing gesture.

(Fringe meeting, Labour Party conference, 1980)

Heffer   The National Executive decided (.08) that we agreed in
PRINCIPLE (0.8) that we MUST AGAIN TRY AND
GET SOME CONSTITUTIONAL AMENDMENTS (0.5)
BEfORE YOU (0.2) AT CONFERENCE (0.2) THIS ↓WEEK
⌈SO THAT YOU CAN STILL MAKE YOUR MINDS UP
Audience ⌊xxxXXXXXXXXXXXXXXXXXXXXXXXXXXXX

[the TV editor cut the film at this point – the applause may have continued for longer]

At the exact point where the first 'we' signals the start of the applaudable message, Mr Heffer produces the first in a series of sharp downward-pointing gestures with his right hand. He raises his voice, first at 'principle' and then again at 'must', after which he continues to shout out the rest of his message at the same volume. More pointing gestures follow, each one being timed to coincide precisely with stressed vowel sounds. This gives the general impression that he is beating out the rhythm of the words with a view to making absolutely sure that his point is well and truly driven home. When it comes to producing the three-part list [see Extract 5, p. 126], each stage in its delivery is clearly marked out by the use of a progressively longer stabbing gesture. His arm finally reaches its maximum point of extension in the middle of the third item, and his hand then changes direction and sweeps sideways across the front of his body [see Figure 1].

From quite an early stage in this sequence, the audience is positively bombarded with a variety of different signals, all of which point in the same direction: 'this week' is projected as the place for an audience response by the fact that it comes at the end of an applaudable message which began with a noticeable increase in volume, gestural activity and rhythmic emphasis. It is also the third item in a list, and is marked as the final one both by falling intonation on the last beat, and by the most sweeping stabbing gesture so far. The techniques deployed by Mr Heffer were thus so numerous and unmistakable that it is hardly surprising that the audience responded so promptly.

' … before you … '   ' … at conference … '   ' … this week … '

Figure 1   Mr Heffer's gestures become progressively more expansive with each item in a list of three

One reason why Mr Heffer was able to deploy such expansive gestures is that he was not speaking from a written text. By contrast, speakers who rely on scripts are much more restricted when it comes to using non-verbal signals. This is because gestures look very unnatural when not co-ordinated with talk that is spontaneous or 'off the cuff'. From the speaker's point of view, it is extremely difficult in sheer practical terms to produce flamboyant movements of the hands and arms at the same time as referring to a script. If he looks up from his text and then produces a gesture, it is almost certain to appear badly timed, and might even arouse suspicions among the audience that the gestures themselves had actually been written into the script. The speaker who strays too far from his text also runs a serious risk of losing his place. This can be an embarrassing enough experience in itself, but is even worse if the speaker finds himself stranded in the middle of a series of gestures without being able to remember what to say next.

The importance of being seen to be able to speak confidently without continually referring to a text is such that some politicians have made a practice of learning their scripts by heart before giving speeches. More recently, technology has come to their aid by making it possible for them to read their scripts from transparent teleprompter screens. The words, which are transmitted from a back room on to flat perspex screens, can be clearly seen by the speaker, but are invisible to the audience. Speaking with the aid of this technology, politicians can appear to be continually addressing their audience, as they move their heads from side to side (i.e. screen to screen) and look 'through' the screens. Interestingly, it has been dubbed the 'sincerity machine', and was first used in Britain by President Reagan in his speech to members of parliament at Westminster in 1982 [see Figure 2]. The only British politician to have used it extensively is Mrs Thatcher who relied heavily on it during the 1983 general election.

Previously, Mrs Thatcher was a very 'script-bound' orator, and was unable to make much use of expressive non-verbal actions. However, this is not to say that script-bound speakers are prevented from using any non-verbal signals at all, as can be clearly seen by looking a little more closely at the way Mrs Thatcher speaks when reading her text from papers on a lectern rather than transparent teleprompter screens.

Like most speakers who seldom stray from their prepared scripts, Mrs Thatcher continually moves her head up and down from lectern to audience and back again. When video tapes of her speaking are played at faster speed than normal, it emerges that the timing and direction of her glances are remarkably rhythmic, and go through a cycle of movements that keep recurring at very regular intervals and in much the same order. After looking up from her script, she hardly ever looks straight ahead at the audience, but directs her gaze at those to her left or right. The usual pattern involves about three glances to the left

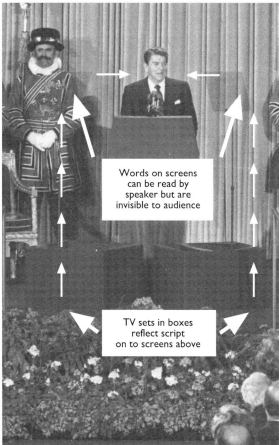

Words on screens
can be read by
speaker but are
invisible to audience

TV sets in boxes
reflect script
on to screens above

Figure 2   Ronald Reagan using the 'sincerity machine' to deliver his speech at Westminster in 1982. The words on the transparent screens (arrowed) can only be seen by the speaker and are invisible to the audience. They are reflected on to the screens from TV sets facing upwards from the floor (concealed in arrowed boxes). Behind the scenes, an assistant winds the script in front of a TV camera which relays it into the hall

' ... Willie ... '   ' ... White- ... '   ' ... law.'

Figure 3   *Audience and television production staff respond on cue as Mrs Thatcher commends her deputy [Extract 3, p. 125]*

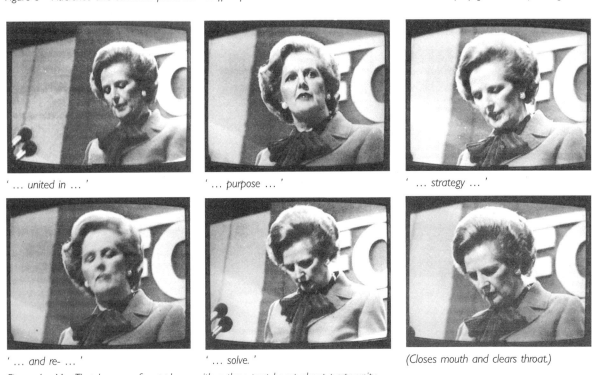

' ... united in ... '   ' ... purpose ... '   ' ... strategy ... '

' ... and re- ... '   ' ... solve. '   *(Closes mouth and clears throat.)*

Figure 4   *Mrs Thatcher goes for applause with a three-part boast about party unity*

followed by one to the right, and the sheer regularity of these movements may be one of the factors which has contributed to the view held in some quarters that her public-speaking style has a tendency to be rather monotonous.

A hint as to what typically happens when she is going for applause is given in the second frame [of Figure 3], where her head started to move down to the text as she started to say the first syllable of 'Whitelaw' [the text for this part of her speech is given in Extract 3, p. 125]. In fact, this retreat to the lectern after a glance to her left occurs extremely frequently during her last one or two syllables prior to an audience response. But because the picture switched to Mr Whitelaw before she had finished saying his name, and before her head had reached its destination, it was in that case impossible to see two other things that regularly happen immediately after she reaches such completion points. They are, however, visible on the video tapes of [Extracts 2 and 4, pp. 125 and 126], and are illustrated [in Figure 4].

These show that, after bringing her head down from the left, Mrs Thatcher visibly closes her mouth, and then promptly clears her throat. As these things are usually done after the first few claps have already started, they appear to be retrospective signals, or confirmations, that the time has indeed come for the audience to show their approval: by closing her mouth so noticeably she indicates that she has finished for the time being, and by clearing her throat she shows that she is putting the few seconds break to good use in getting herself ready to carry on once the applause is over. Anyone in the audience who has still failed to notice that it is time to applaud is therefore provided with two final reminders as to what should now be done.

It might seem that a slight head movement of this sort is too subtle a signal to play any significant part in the delivery of a successful claptrap. But there are at least two reasons for thinking otherwise. One is the sheer regularity with which the [head-down] [mouth-close] [throat-clear] sequence occurs at completion points that precede bursts of applause during Mrs Thatcher's speeches. The other emerges from a case where things nearly went badly wrong as she was producing a boast about her government's achievements. As can be seen from the extract below, the audience, or rather a small portion of it, produced a brief flutter of applause just after the third item in a list, but withdrew when it turned out that she had quite a lot more to say:

(Conservative Party conference, 1980)

Thatcher		As you know we've made the first crucial
		changes in trade union law
		(0.4)
	1	to remove the worst abuses of the closed shop
		(0.2)
	2	to restrict picketing to the place of work of the parties in
		dis↑pute
		(0.2)
	3	and to encourage secret bal↓lots
		⌈hhhh Jim Prior has carried <u>all</u> these ⌉=
Audience		⌊x-xx-xxxxxxxxxxxxxxxxxxxxxxxxx-xx-x-⌋
Thatcher		=measures through with the support
		of the vast majority of trade union
		memb ⌈ers ⊢————(10.0)————⊣
Audience		⌊x-xx XXXXXXXXXXXXXXxx-x

Source: Atkinson, 1984a, pp. 63–71

Reading B
'THE LIGHT HAS GONE OUT':
INDIAN TRADITIONS IN ENGLISH RHETORIC

Julu Sen, Rahul Sharma and Anima Chakraverty

Although English has been used in India since 1600, and we are familiar with
Indian writing in English, we have only recently begun to study the speeches in
English of well-known Indian orators, such as Gandhi and Nehru. Since India is a
multilingual country, most of the broadcasts to the nation are in Hindi as well as in
English. Although Gandhi spoke mostly in Hindi or Gujarati, his speeches
delivered in south India and in South Africa were generally in English.

While studying these speeches, we have discovered that spontaneous impromptu speeches were very different from prepared addresses. The formal
written addresses of both Gandhi and Nehru resemble their writing in English,
while in their impromptu speeches we find features of oral speech – additive,
aggregative, redundant, conservative, close to human life world, empathetic and
participatory. Their transcribed speeches also show evidence of the influence of
Indian rhetorical traditions. We will illustrate and discuss some of these features
here, with reference to one famous impromptu speech by Jawarharlal Nehru,
entitled 'The light has gone out' (as transcribed in Gopal, 1987).

Figure 1   Nehru, Indian prime minister, addressing a public meeting (May 1957)

The assassination of Mahatma Gandhi on 30 January 1948 was a national catas-
trophe. The brutal murder of the Father of the Nation, barely a few months after
independence, sent shock waves throughout the country and plunged millions of
Indians into gloom and mourning. In this hour of crisis, Nehru, the then prime
minister of India and a trusted lieutenant of Gandhi, addressed the nation on the
radio. Widely regarded as one of Nehru's immortal speeches, this spontaneous

address to the nation made an indelible impact on the hearts and minds of millions of Indians. (We recommend that you read now the complete speech, reproduced here as an appendix to this reading.)

The influence of Indian rhetorical traditions

A salient feature of this speech is that the expression of 'grief' is accomplished without the use of the word 'grief' or any of its synonyms. This is because the feeling is too deep to be directly expressed in conventional words. It can only be evoked or suggested indirectly, and Nehru expresses the inexpressible in the following manner:

> The light has gone out from our lives and there is darkness everywhere.
> (lines 2–3)

This manner of dealing with grief indirectly is in accord with one of the principles of Indian aesthetics, *dhvani*, 'the use of poetic or dramatic words to suggest or evoke a feeling that is too deep, intense and universal to be spoken' (Coward, 1980, p. 148). *Dhvani* forms part of a theory of language propounded by the fifth-century Sanskrit grammarian and philosopher of language, Bhartrahari, and has also been drawn on by other Indian scholars in the analysis of figurative speech.

The speech also embodies several principles of effective communication that can be traced back to the *Artha Sastra*, a series of books dealing with politics, thought to have been written by the scholar Kautiliya in the fourth century BC. Kautiliya advises his readers that:

> Arrangement of subject-matter, connection, completeness, sweetness, exaltedness and lucidity constitute the excellences of communication. Among them, arranging in a proper order, the statement first of the principal matter, is *arrangement of subject-matter*. The statement of a subsequent matter without its being incompatible with the matter in hand, right up to the end, is *connection*. Absence of deficiency or excess of matter, words or letters, description in detail of the matter by means of reasons, citations and illustrations, (and) expressiveness of words, is *completeness*. The use of words with a charming meaning easily conveyed is *sweetness*. The use of words that are not vulgar is *exaltedness*. The employment of words that are well-known is *lucidity*.
> (Kangle, 1988, pp. 92–3; emphasis added)

Later in the same chapter Kautiliya refers to two further principles: *relevance* and *empathy* with the audience. We shall give examples of these principles in Nehru's speech, beginning with *arrangement of subject matter* and *connection*.

In a spontaneous speech like this, unlike in a written/prepared speech, one has to think on one's feet, and the textual order reflects the order in which impressions occur in the mind. Despite the fact that this is a spontaneous speech, it is a good example of arrangement of subject matter and connection, as described by Kautiliya. These can be seen in the sequence of topics in the speech:

> assassination – funeral – homage

Nehru starts with the principal matter of Gandhi's assassination by articulating his deep sense of dismay bordering on helplessness:

> I do not know what to tell you and how to say it.
> (lines 3–4)

This is how he identifies himself with the Indian masses and shares their sorrow. At the same time, however, as their undisputed leader, he is conscious of his responsibility to warn them of the dangers of communalism, and to impress upon them the need to strengthen the bonds of unity to face challenges boldly. With all the force at his command, he reminds his people that the likes of Gandhi never die and that the best homage to Gandhi would be a solemn pledge to work for peace, unity and brotherhood. In the midst of all this, Nehru keeps his cool, pauses, and finds time to give details of the funeral arrangement:

> May I now tell you the programme for tomorrow?
> (line 59)

Finally he advises his listeners on how they can best pay homage to Gandhi.

Nehru is concerned about the welfare of India so he repeats this concern before turning to the funeral arrangements and afterwards at the very end of his speech. Compare these two sentences:

> As in his life, so in his death he has reminded us of the big things of life, the living truth, and if we remember that, then it will be well with us and well with *India*.
> (lines 56–8; emphasis added)

> That is the best prayer that we can offer to *India* and ourselves.
> (lines 95–6; emphasis added)

The speech illustrates other principles suggested by Kautiliya. One of these is *completeness*. Although it is an impromptu speech, Nehru has chosen his words very carefully, whether they concern bringing the first news of the assassination to the nation (lines 1–23), his own reactions (lines 24–58), his plans for the funeral arrangements and advice on paying homage (lines 59–95) or finally the 'prayer' (lines 95–7). We can't strike out any part, claiming it is irrelevant, or deficient. It seems *complete* in all respects.

Sweetness can be found in Nehru's choice of words, word order, sentence construction, elegant variation and purposeful repetition. The first two sentences of the speech comprise a virtual string of 25 monosyllables. This aptly reflects the speaker's deep sense of anguish and helps create an atmosphere of mourning. However, this is soon followed by a little drama and the element of suspense. 'Bapu … is no more. Perhaps I am wrong to say that … The light has gone out, I said, and yet I was wrong' (lines 4–13). (*Bapu*, meaning 'Father', is the affectionate name Indians gave Gandhi.)

One of the best examples of Nehru's oratorical skill can be found in:

> The light that has illumined this country for these many, many years will illumine this country for many more years, and a thousand years later that light will still be seen in this country, and the world will see it, and it will give solace to innumerable hearts.
> (lines 15–19)

This rather extraordinary construction effectively illustrates the 'extraordinariness' of Gandhi, and places him far above not only common mortals but also most leaders of men and women. The magnitude of Gandhi's contribution to India's freedom struggle and the eternal relevance of his teachings is communicated most effectively through expressions like 'these many, many years', 'many more years' and 'a thousand years later'.

Nehru concludes the speech with the words:

> That is the best prayer that we can offer him and his memory. That is the best prayer that we can offer to India and ourselves.
> (lines 95–7)

The use of repetition here not only emphasizes the fact that the best prayer would be a life-long commitment to Gandhi's ideals of non-violence and communal harmony but also (by equating 'him' with 'India') acclaims Gandhi as the architect of India's freedom and the Father of this Nation.

The speech also shows great *dignity*. Nehru has not uttered a single word that could be termed socially offensive. That he had suffered a great blow may be gauged from the expression: 'A *madman* has put an end to his life, for I can only call him *mad* who did it' (lines 30–31; emphasis added). And 'We must face this *poison*, we must root out this *poison*, and we must face all the perils that encompass us, and face them, not *madly* or *badly*, but rather in the way that our beloved teacher taught us to face them' (lines 34–7, emphasis added). Yet he advises his people to be strong and determined. He maintains the dignity of his state and office, as prime minister, and talks about the funeral arrangements in a very calm manner.

The speech is *relevant* to the needs of the moment because in the hour of 'grief', through his 'love for his country', Nehru is making an appeal to his people to remain calm. The style is *lucid*, expressed in simple language so that this request reaches the masses. And finally, anticipating and sharing their love for Bapu, he can *empathize* with the audience. His use of the term *Bapu* itself is an illustration of this.

References

COWARD (1980) *The Sphoth Theory of Language – a philosophical analysis*, Delhi, Motilal Banarasidass.

GOPAL, S. (ed.) (1987) *Selected Works of Jawaharlal Nehru:* second series, volume 5, New Delhi, Jawaharlal Nehru Memorial Fund.

KANGLE, R.P. (1988) *The Kautiliya Artha Sastra – Parts 1 and 2 – an English translation with critical and explanatory notes* trans., from the Malayalam manuscript of the twelfth century AD, Delhi, Motilal Banarasidass.

Appendix to Reading B

On 30 January 1948 at about 5 p.m., Mahatma Gandhi was late by a few minutes for the prayer meeting in the grounds of Birla House, New Delhi, because he had been held up by a meeting with Vallabhbhai Patel. With his forearms on the shoulders of his grandnieces, Abha and Manubehn, he walked briskly to the prayer ground where about 500 persons had gathered. He raised his hands and joined them to greet the congregation who returned the greeting in a similar manner. Just at that moment Nathuram Vinayek Godse pushed his way past Manubehn, whipped out a pistol and fired three shots. Mahatma Gandhi fell instantly with the words *He Ram* (Oh God!) on his lips.

The following speech is Nehru's broadcast to the nation announcing the death of Gandhi (30 January 1948, All India Radio tapes).

The Light Has Gone Out

1   Friends and Comrades,

The light has gone out from our lives and there is
darkness everywhere. And I do not know what to tell
you and how to say it. Our beloved leader, Bapu, as we

5   called him, the Father of the Nation, is no more.
     Perhaps I am wrong to say that. Nevertheless, we will
     not see him again as we have seen him for these many
     years. We will not run to him for advice and seek
     solace from him; and that is a terrible blow, not to me
10   only, but to millions and millions in this country. And
     it is a little difficult to soften the blow by any advice
     that I or anyone else can give you.

     The light has gone out, I said, and yet I was wrong. For
     the light that shone in this country was no ordinary
15   light. The light that has illumined this country for these
     many, many years will illumine this country for many
     more years, and a thousand years later that light will
     still be seen in this country, and the world will see it,
     and it will give solace to innumerable hearts. For that
20   light represented something more than the immediate
     present; it represented the living, eternal truths
     reminding us of the right path, drawing us from error,
     taking this ancient country to freedom.

     All this has happened when there was so much more
25   for him to do. We could never, of course, do away with
     him, we could never think that he was unnecessary, or
     that he had done his task. But now, particularly, when
     we are faced with so many difficulties, his not being
     with us is a blow most terrible to bear.

30   A madman has put an end to his life, for I can only call
     him mad who did it. And yet there has been enough
     of poison spread in this country during the past years and
     months, and this poison has had effect on people's
     minds. We must face this poison, we must root out this
35   poison, and we must face all the perils that encompass
     us, and face them, not madly or badly, but rather in the
     way that our beloved teacher taught us to face them.
     The first thing to remember now is that none of us dare
     misbehave because we are angry. We have to behave
40   like strong, determined people, determined to face
     all the perils that surround us, determined to carry out
     the mandate that our great teacher and our great leader
     has given us, remembering always that if, as I believe,
     his spirit looks upon us and sees us, nothing would
45   displease his soul so much as to see that we have
     indulged in unseemly behaviour or in violence. So we
     must not do that. But that does not mean that we
     should be weak, but rather that we should, in strength
     and in unity, face all the troubles that are in front of us.
50   We must hold together, and all our petty troubles and
     difficulties and conflicts must be ended in the face of
     this great disaster. A great disaster is a symbol to us to
     remember all the big things of life and forget the small

55   things of which we have thought too much. Now the time
     has come again. As in his life, so in his death he has reminded
     us of the big things of life, the living truth, and if we remember
     that, then it will be well with us and well with India.

     May I now tell you the programme for tomorrow? It
60   was proposed by some friends that Mahatmaji's body
     should be embalmed for a few days to enable millions
     of people to pay their last homage to him. But it was
     his wish, repeatedly expressed, that no such thing
     should happen, that this should not be done, that he
65   was entirely opposed to any embalming of his body,
     and so we decided that we must follow his wishes in
     this matter, however much others might have wished
     otherwise.

     And so the cremation will take place tomorrow in
70   Delhi city by the side of the Jumna river. Tomorrow
     morning, or rather forenoon, about 11.30, the bier will
     be taken out from Birla House and it will follow the
     prescribed route and go to the Jumna river. The
     cremation will take place there at about 4.00 p.m. The
75   exact place and route will be announced by radio and
     the press.

     People in Delhi who wish to pay their last homage
     should gather along this route. I would not advise too
     many of them to come to Birla House, but rather to
     gather on both sides of this long route, from Birla
80   House to the Jumna river. And I trust that they will
     remain there in silence without any demonstrations.
     That is the best way and the most fitting way to pay
     homage to the great soul. Also, tomorrow should be a
     day of fasting and prayer for all of us.

85   Those who live elsewhere, out of Delhi and in other
     parts of India, will no doubt also take such part as they
     can in this last homage. For them also let this be a day
     of fasting and prayer. And at the appointed time for
     cremation, that is 4.00 p.m. tomorrow afternoon,
90   people should go to the river or to the sea and offer
     prayers there. And while we pray, the greatest prayer
     that we can offer is to take a pledge to dedicate
     ourselves to the truth and to the cause for which this
     great countryman of ours lived and for which he has
95   died. That is the best prayer that we can offer him and
     his memory. That is the best prayer that we can offer to

Jai Hind roughly translated   India and ourselves. *Jai Hind.*
means 'Long live India'.
                                    (Cited in Gopal, 1987, pp. 35–6)

This reading was specially commissioned for this book.

Reading C
TELEVANGELICAL LANGUAGE:
A MEDIA SPEECH GENRE

John O. Thompson

In this reading I present some examples of an interesting genre of spoken English which is now a common feature of broadcasting in the USA. This is the talk of TV evangelists – people who may or may not be formal ministers of a Christian church, but who all present programmes whose apparent aim is to convert viewers to (or to sustain viewers' belief in) their version of 'born-again' Christianity. Other aims of TV evangelists are also apparent: they often solicit cash donations to their church or movement from viewers, and they may also try to sell their published works. It is at least partly because of the obvious link between sacred and commercial interests that the phenomenon of TV evangelism exists in a strongly polarized judgemental field, a field of a 'we–they' sort. How far can I count on my readers to recoil somewhat from the broadcasting genre in question? This will certainly depend on their own cultural expectations of how religious broadcasting should sound and look. Certainly when the development of religious broadcasting is discussed in Britain, trouble is always taken to distinguish anything new that is proposed from 'US-style' Christian television or radio.

One of my own interests in American TV evangelism is with its distinguishing features as a genre of spoken English. What features typify it? Does it share features with other 'persuasive' genres such as TV advertising or political speech making? I argue here that, despite some similarities, it has some distinctive qualities. Moreover, I suggest that this distinctive nature is important for the communicative function of the evangelical broadcasts.

The basic point is this: on television, but also on radio, in the cinema and in the pages of newspapers and magazines, a large repertoire of distinguishing modes of delivery exist, so that, almost independently of what is actually 'being said' semantically in the sentences produced, the hearer/reader is able to tell what kind of discourse – what *genre* of spoken language – he or she is dealing with.

I could invoke any number of cases of this – think, for instance, of that most curious delivery that was once used for the scripts of newsreels on both sides of the Atlantic, or of the 'sound' of the sentences that emanate from the pages of the tabloid press – but it may be best to discuss a subtler instance.

In a mid 1980s British advertisement for soap powder, a little scenario is set up of the most typical kind: a woman approaches another woman, offering her a chance to try out this soap powder, which is not her regular brand. The housewife at first demurs but then tries the product and is 'converted'. Here is the final bit of dialogue.

DS   Tricia, we persuaded you to try Daz in the hot whites wash.

C   I was absolutely amazed. This sheet, for instance, my eldest son is very fond of playing ghosties with it and dragging it all over the floor, and it's come out beautifully white. And these pillow-slips: my youngest son has had a cold, and you try giving him medicine at two o'clock in the morning and it goes everywhere but in their mouth, but Daz has brought it out beautifully white. And being that much cheaper, it does save me money.

DS = Daz spokesperson
C = consumer

DS   So will you swap your packet of Daz for two packets of your old powder?

C   No, I'm going to stick with Daz.

DS   Try biological Daz yourself in a hot whites wash. Most women agree: Daz
     gives unbeatable white at a price that's right.

What is not predictable, just reading the words on the page, is how the vocal styles
of the two women differ. C delivers her lines with 'naturalistic', conversational
intonation. What she says is unlikely to be unrehearsed, but it is spoken with a
convincing air of spontaneity ('recognized' by DS with a little laugh at its most
vivid moment, the mention of the son 'playing ghosties' with the sheet). DS,
however, speaks in a distinctly different 'this is an advertisement' tone. Such a
tone is, arguably, required by her last lines, spoken directly to audience and
involving the clearly nonconversational rhyming jingle of the final sentence.
What is more puzzling is why she should adopt it in conversing with C. Perhaps it
would be less fitting for her to change register than for her to keep to 'advertising'
register at the cost of lack of conversational verisimilitude; equally, keeping the
whole thing conversational and eliminating the final lines to the audience would
take the ad 'out of genre' unacceptably.

DS's delivery is equivalent to the small-print message 'ADVERTISEMENT' that is
required to appear in print media when the layout of an advertisement is such that
an unwitting reader might confuse it with 'real' editorial content. The televisual
equivalent might well be, quite generally, not a subtitle but a tone of voice. And
viewers might well, while believing themselves to be mildly scornful of the
'obvious' this-is-an-ad sound, actually find the ad's self-proclamation as such an
orienting, comforting aspect of it.

A distinctive register which signals 'this is religious' could be equally useful
for the television viewer. Moreover, presenting viewers with a genre they can
recognize may (as with advertisements) not necessarily undermine the evangelical programme's communicative, persuasive functions. Viewers may again be
orientated, comforted and reassured by this recognition.

In the next part of the reading, I discuss three examples of the discourse of TV
evangelism. (These examples were collected for me between December 1994 and
January 1995 in the San Francisco area by Nancy Roberts and Robin Beeman.)

In my first example, the evangelist Charles Stanley is speaking to a large
audience, with a choir arrayed behind him. He then expounds the doctrine of
God's unconditional love:

> And you see, it is by loving each other that God uses all of us to meet each
> other's needs: emotional needs, material needs, physical needs, learning
> to love Him and receive it, loving ourselves: you see, the reason we don't
> love each other much is because we are so entangled with getting
> ourselves and our own sense of self-worth and value straightened out, we
> don't have any time to give – you see – we don't have anything to give
> away. If you don't love yourself, you don't have anything to give. Here's
> what it's like. It's like, here's your heart; and when you received the Lord
> Jesus Christ, God came into your life, and the love of God's in there. Now,
> if my whole life is wrapped up in getting, in getting me straightened out
> and checking out my sense of self-worth and my value and – 'I don't, I
> don't like myself', I don't, I don't have anything to give away. Because it's
> all locked up. But when the spirit of God sets me free, when I am liberated
> by the spirit of God, and He begins to work in my heart, what happens?
> Then I am no longer the important one; but now what happens is, my life
> is open to others and the love of God comes gushing out all over
> everybody around me, and you see, that is the goal of God. He says, he

says you are to love one another, that's the way the Church functions best. He says, now this love is to be all-inclusive – You remember what Jesus said in the Sermon on the Mount and people say, 'Well, I believe in the Sermon on the Mount' … Well, how many of your enemies do you love? 'I don't love any of my enemies.' Well, you don't believe in the Sermon on the Mount. He says we are to love our enemies, if we're only to love our friends, he says then you're no more than a Pharisee, we're to love our enemies, and he says we're to love our neighbours

This is a relatively brief stretch of Stanley's speech, artificially detached from the impressively continuous flow of the whole discourse, which iterates and tirelessly reiterates the argument that only someone with healthy self-love can love others, and only the unconditionality of God's love can ground such self-love.

Lengthy continuous speech is itself not 'normal television', and other aspects of Stanley's presentation make it immediately recognizable as religious. The voice is urgent, with a gestural vocabulary to match (e.g. quick, extravagant movements of the hands). It can also incorporate a quaver of emotion, as it does when, later, Stanley recounts a personal experience of suddenly and surprisingly feeling love for a fellow minister whom he had not thought he liked.

Especially striking here is a moment of metaphor, starting at 'It's like, here's your heart'. The words themselves are startling ('the love of God comes gushing out all over everybody around me'), but they are complemented by a gestural image, with Stanley's hands first knotted together and then unfolded and put in motion to represent 'gushing out'. The effect is to propose a very concrete image of love and the heart. Where else in everyday television is such a deployment of arms and eyes allowed?

Having focused on some distinctive features of evangelical talk, we might also note that, especially in continuous monologues of the kind illustrated above, evangelists often use techniques such as three-part lists and contrasts of the kind noted in the performances of other 'persuasive' public speakers such as politicians (Atkinson, 1984). Thus in the early part of the above example, we can see Stanley reminds us that we have:

- emotional needs
- material needs
- physical needs

The later part of the extract is an elaborated contrast between life without a healthy self-love, and life with it.

In my second example, a viewer sees the evangelist Kenneth Copeland sitting at a table, a kitchen table (complete with salt and pepper shakers), with a book in front of him: not the book he will later urge us to buy, but the Book, the Bible. He is 'speaking to' a text, rather as a jazz musician might develop a melody.

Copeland's delivery is much more stylized than Stanley's. He punctuates his speech with 'Amen'. While Stanley's accent is mildly southern, Copeland's is more pronouncedly so, and more 'rural'. He paraphrases in a punchy manner which it would be possible to read as condescending but which is crucially saved from this by something in the delivery style that can only be described as 'eccentric'. Having got himself slightly muddled, 'getting ahead of myself', Copeland retells the last bit of the parable he is dealing with thus:

> But he [the 'man which had not on a wedding garment'], he was not there for the same purpose, and he was not anointed, he, he had on no wedding garment, and the king [C. prolongs the word, with falling, 'sing-song' intonation over the 'i'] had all of him he could take [C. chuckles],

boy, he said, 'Throw him [dramatic arm movement] out the back door! And out there where it's dark, let him sit out there and chew on his tongue.' Amen. Now ...

The king's aggression is taken over by Copeland, sitting slightly hunched forward, eyes making direct contact with the camera to startling effect at times. At the same time, he seems somehow to retreat into the world of the story; 'let him sit out there and chew on his tongue' is almost thrown away, a musing on the scene the biblical account evokes. The eyes and the mouth are both mobile, but hardly smoothly so, in a generally 'set' face; similarly, gestures are abrupt, even jerky. Awkwardness and passion register.

Copeland turns out to be someone who works in mimicry, using 'funny voices' for those in error:

One thing we have to be really, really careful of is making light of what God did in Jesus for us. 'Oh Lord, you know I'm just so unworthy – Oh God, I don't deserve Heaven – Oh Lord, yes, Amen, I'm just so unworthy, I'm just a little worm': you're making light of the blood, you're making light of the name of Jesus, you're making light – 'But, but, I didn't intend to make light –' I know you probably didn't intend to do it, but you cannot receive from God, making light of this gospel. You cannot receive from God, making light of what Jesus did for you on the Cross. 'Well, you know how it is, brother, I mean uh, whuw, it looks like the whole world's going to hell in a handbasket.' Well, the whole world's not going to hell, we're reaching out to the world, the Bible said the whole world would be filled with his glory. 'Well, I mean, I didn't mean it.' Well, stop saying that junk if you don't mean it.

Note that Copeland also uses the rhetorical technique of the three-part list ('you're making light of the blood ...'); the interruption of the repenting sinner prevents the list being marred by the addition of a fourth part. He also offers stark contrasts, as between the sinner's view of the future ('it looks like the whole world's going to hell in a handbasket') and God's reassurance ('Well the whole world's not going to hell ...'). Note too the use of the rhetorical technique of *repetition* in the use of the phrase 'the whole world'.

We can also see Copeland here satirizing, pointedly and successfully, both a 'dumb-humble' approach to God and a 'dumb-gloomy' approach. He is about to move into an apocalyptic reading of what is in store for us in these last days, but by using one 'funny voice' (the 'little worm') for an unthinkingly pessimistic view and another soon after for a defeatist, abject view, he distinguishes his own position from those he mocks, and in an entertaining way. It is interesting to note that the 'little worm', as Copeland renders him, looks up as he humiliates himself. Copeland himself looks up at times, in his own serious address to God, but he is prepared to mock looking up as savagely as any unbeliever might in order to make his point.

The divine is apart, 'up there', distant: this is the Christian tradition. If Copeland and Stanley, and the televangelists generally, appear to some viewers as tasteless, as kitsch, it is no doubt because their register is an intimate one. They speak of, and to, God in a distinctive style, certainly (these intonation patterns, choice of words and so forth would sound very strange applied either in everyday conversation or to a media simulacrum of everyday conversation). But the awayness of the divine is subordinated to the nearness to the viewer/listener which the televangelist is devoted to establishing. And, after all, there is a real, physical distance between broadcaster and viewer to be overcome, whatever status we, as unbelievers or as believers, accord the metaphysical distance between the human and the divine: the televangelists may be speaking *of* God, but they are speaking *to* men and women watching a smallish image of them at home.

Dean and Mary Brown are a married couple who present an evangelical programme, *Music that Ministers*, together. They intermix back-chat with religious speech and song in a manner which, at a first or even a second glance, might disconcert. The couple address us from a set which simultaneously declares itself to be 'living room' (shelves, pictures on walls) and 'stage' (huge flower arrangements, overall sense of performing space). 'We have a great day planned for you,' Dean enthusiastically begins, and speaks of the day's guest performers: 'a special guest … by special demand – great demand'. But then Mary continues, with even greater enthusiasm: 'But a *more* special guest, in even *greater* demand for this guest to be here – it talks about him in the Ninety-first Psalm, the fourteenth verse …' She reads from a small Bible.

God is the guest of the television hosts, then; but what guest on 'everyday television' has ever been introduced by (constituted by?) reading from a book? Mary continues after reading the text in question:

> I tell you, that gives us an overwhelming sense of – the awe and wonder at God's *continued* provision for us. [Dean: 'Yes!'] Thank God He is a provision, a fortress in the time of trouble, He's going to deliver us, He'll protect us – that's your promise …

This is delivered in a manner that grows in force, 'exaltation': it is a lead into something, and that something turns out to be a Dean and Mary rendition of 'A Mighty Fortress Is Our God'.

The transition is very striking, because Dean and Mary are good singers and the hymn, in itself a distinguished marriage of religious language and melody, responds wonderfully to a spirited, robust delivery. A possible experience of the transition (my own, I should say) is from kitsch into quality. (I imagine that the programme's intended audience would experience something more continuous; as might, in negative mode, a thoroughly unsympathetic viewer.)

The last line of 'A Mighty Fortress' is: 'His kingdom is forever'. Having concluded the singing with a mighty 'Amen', the Browns reiterate the word 'forever'; even as Mary moves on to describe what is to happen on the rest of the programme – 'We're going to talk about and we're going to worship that almighty and forever God' – Dean echoes her echo of the song: 'He *is* an almighty and a forever God.' They invite viewers to sit down for the rest of the programme, and themselves sit down: this becomes the occasion for a bit of by-play about Mary's not sitting on her glasses; it turns out she has pairs of glasses all over the house ('$7 at the drugstore', she assures us, lest this look like a sign of wealth); Dean's mention of this prompts her to counter-tease, 'And guess who wears them sometimes!' Dean responds to this charge of ocular cross-dressing slightly sheepishly: 'Well, some days I do, some days I can't see, but I believe God's going to heal me. But anyway …' The phrase about God's healing is thrown away, not emphasized; there is an eerie air of its being a joke, and Mary certainly utters a little laugh. Here, as elsewhere with the Browns, a sense is generated of their speech running away with them, not being under full control. 'But anyway,' Dean continues, moving back into verbal focus, 'I'm thankful for the kingdom of God and the fortress and the deliverer that he is.' Mary continues: 'And he's always, always and for sure.' ('Always' takes over from 'forever' now, while 'for sure' is delivered idiomatically, with the intonation it has in the USA when it is used to mean 'Yes', even though it is also stressed so as to bring out the 'surety' of God.) She continues:

> Lord, remind us, every person that listens today [note that she speaks of listening, not of watching or viewing], remind us that you are – *always* there. Where we can't see you, when it's dark, when it's night inside of us, that you're always there. When circumstances are overwhelming, that you're not overwhelmed, God, that you're present, and you're always there ...

The transition from the jokiness of 'And guess who wears them sometimes' to the seriousness of 'when it's night inside of us' is carried through seamlessly, but what allows the transition is a sustained tone of excitement and of, as with Copeland, eccentricity.

Conclusion

I am suggesting, then, that despite some obvious diversity in personal style and programme format, the rhetoric of various televangelists has some common, though not universal, features. Televangelists use a register which is typified by emotional, intimate appeals to the viewer by the speaker through direct, intimate address, and often through fairly lengthy monologues, but which also incorporates formal references to, and quotes from, the Bible. They can often be seen to use some rhetorical techniques also favoured by other kinds of public speakers. But one particular distinguishing characteristic is that they often make rapid transitions to and from formal 'biblical' declamations, or from hymns, into more casual 'everyday' styles of speech.

In stylizing themselves so unmistakably, the televangelists accept a 'place' in the overall system of television which allows viewers to categorize them and thus feel at home with television as usual. However, their place is a deviant one in its emphasis on the non-televisual, both in the reference 'upward' to the divine, directly and via the Book, and in the reference 'outward' to concrete effects for the audience and concrete manners of participation which the audience can 'buy into'.

Much more can be done to specify the 'televangelical voice' than I have attempted here. But what begins to emerge is a distinctive tension between *familiarity* with the divine, as an ongoing, everyday part of the life of the believer, and the more traditional sense of *distance* from the divine which is what distinguishes faith from secularity in the first place. The televangelical style of delivery both incorporates signs of that distance, in harking back to earlier preaching styles and in registering God gesturally as 'elsewhere' (above, inside), and annuls that distance, as the televangelist uses television to 'come close' (with God) to his or her audience.

References

ATKINSON, J.M. (1984) *Our Masters' Voices: the language and body language of politics*, London, Methuen.
(The source material for this reading was first presented at a conference on 'The Nature of Religious Language' held at Roehampton Institute on 11–12 February 1995. A written version closer to that presentation appears in Porter, S. (ed.) (1996), *The Nature of Religious Language*, Sheffield, Sheffield Academic Press.)

This reading was specially commissioned for this book.

5 WHAT MAKES ENGLISH INTO ART?

Lesley Jeffries

5.1 INTRODUCTION

The earlier chapters of this book have explored mainly functional uses of English. In the second half of the book, we focus more on what might be seen as language for its own sake, although it may emerge that this distinction is not always as clear as it seems. In this chapter we examine what is special about the way English is used in poetry, novels, plays, stories, songs and various kinds of live performance which makes them into a form of art. Is it a question of particular linguistic techniques cleverly used by accomplished authors, or is there something more difficult to define about the creative and artistic uses of language? Can we talk about art purely in terms of a text or performance, or do we also need to look beyond the text at cultural expectations and conventions? How far should we consider art as a particular kind of social practice rather than in abstract aesthetic terms? In Activity 5.1, you have the opportunity to reflect on your own ideas on such topics before continuing with the chapter.

Activity 5.1   What makes English into 'art'?   *(Allow about 10 minutes)*

Which of the following might you describe as 'art'? (For the purposes of this activity, it is not necessary to be familiar with all of these texts.) What factors seem to be important in deciding whether an oral or written text counts as art?

1 Shakespeare's *Romeo and Juliet*
2 a poem written in dialect
3 a list of immigration laws
4 the song *Sergeant Pepper's Lonely Hearts Club Band* by The Beatles
5 an anonymous traditional ballad
6 Jane Austen's *Pride and Prejudice*
7 Wole Soyinka's *Ake* (twentieth-century Nigerian dramatist's autobiography)
8 an improvised twentieth-century theatre piece
9 a conversation with a friend while shopping together

Comment

You probably immediately identified numbers 1 and 6 from the list as 'art'; as part of the English literature canon, their quality and value seems incontrovertible. You may have decided that although the song by The Beatles and the traditional ballad might not have been accepted by everyone as 'art' when they first appeared, they have now stood the test of time and can safely be included. You probably wanted to know more about numbers 2 and 8 in order to decide whether they can be counted as art. They also raise issues about whether an artistic text can be written in any variety of English and whether a work of art in English needs a permanent script. What counts as art is influenced by conceptions of 'literature', which often means printed fiction (poetry, plays and novels), but it is already clear that language often combines with other media to produce artistic effects. What about texts on the borders of fiction and non-fiction, like number 7?

Numbers 3 and 9 are not immediately obvious as art in themselves but, as we see later in the chapter, technical documents and everyday talk can be contextualized within artistic performances.

You may have found in this exercise that the factors determining whether a text is art were not as distinct as you expected. Often, when we try to categorize our experience, we find that we are left with many grey areas. Art is a term which has many different and sometimes contentious interpretations, but there are a number of linguistic and social factors which can help us answer the question: What makes English into art? These are explored throughout the rest of the book.

In this chapter we look from a linguistic point of view at some of the ways in which English has been used to achieve special artistic effects. We also examine the way artistic uses of English are shaped by the contexts in which they are created and also by the contexts in which they are received. Our focus in this chapter is mainly on poetry, novels and drama. Later chapters in the book look in more detail at the uses of English with other media in popular culture, for example, songs and comedy routines (Chapter 6); the history and controversy surrounding the English literature canon (Chapter 7); and how the language and cultural background of individual writers affect the way they use English (Chapter 8).

5.2   LANGUAGE ART IN WRITTEN ENGLISH TEXTS

Focusing on language

In this section we draw on a form of linguistic analysis known as **stylistics** to try to pinpoint a number of language features commonly found in artistic uses of English. Stylisticians have focused mainly on written texts, partly because these are more accessible for detailed study. However, the emphasis on written texts also arises because those theories of language dominant in the western world in the twentieth century have, at least until recently, treated language as a self-contained symbolic system which is revealed more clearly in writing than in speech.

One key idea used by stylisticians, which comes from the Russian formalists of the 1920s and 1930s, is the notion that literary language is different from everyday language because it draws attention to some property of the language itself, and highlights or foregrounds it. This **foregrounding** surprises the reader into a fresh perception and appreciation of the subject matter. Foregrounding can be achieved by focusing on sounds, grammar, or meanings, and will be a central theme throughout this chapter.

Rhyme, rhythm and repetition

One fairly obvious example of foregrounding is the way in which literary language, especially poetry, uses regular controlled patterns of rhythm, rhyme and repetition.

Activity 5.2   Rhyme, rhythm and repetition   *(Allow about 10 minutes)*

The poem below, by the English poet William Blake, was published in 1789 in his collection *Songs of Innocence*. In what ways does his use of rhythm, repetition and rhyme foreground particular qualities of language? (Reading the poem aloud may help you recognize these features.) How do they appeal to the senses and give some kind of form to the ideas and meaning in the poem?

The Tyger

Tyger! Tyger! burning bright
In the forests of the night,
What immortal hand or eye
Could frame thy fearful symmetry?

In what distant deeps or skies
Burnt the fire of thine eyes?
On what wings dare he aspire?
What the hand dare seize the fire?

And what shoulder, & what art,
Could twist the sinews of thy heart?
And when thy heart began to beat,
What dread hand? & what dread feet?

What the hammer? what the chain?
In what furnace was thy brain?
What the anvil? what dread grasp
Dare its deadly terrors clasp?

When the stars threw down their spears,
And water'd heaven with their tears,
Did he smile his work to see?
Did he who made the Lamb make thee?

Tyger! Tyger! burning bright
In the forests of the night,
What immortal hand or eye
Dare frame thy fearful symmetry?

Comment

Let us look first at the rhythm; every line has four stressed syllables alternating with three or four unstressed syllables – a rhythm associated in English with songs or ballads, as in the traditional nursery rhyme '*Jack* and *Jill* went *up* the *hill*'. This, together with the repetitive string of questions, gives the lines an unusually obvious 'beat', like the beating of a drum, or in this case, the beating of an anvil, or the powerful tread of a dangerous animal. This apparently excessive emphasis on rhythm actually enhances the sensory appeal of the poem, by imitating the frequency of a hammer striking an anvil, or an animal's foot hitting the ground. The 'beat' is also emphasized by the sounds of the words themselves with their frequent plosive /d/, /t/ or /p/, all suggestive of sounds made by hammering or hitting.

In each four-line stanza, the first two and last two lines rhyme in the pattern aabb. The symmetry of the rhyme scheme in each stanza reflects the 'fearful symmetry' in the design of the tiger which Blake describes. Rhymed or repeated words increase their emphasis and develop in the reader a sense of expectation or inevitability. The last stanza and the first are identical except for one word; this break in the pattern provides the sense of closure, and of a powerful design fulfilled.

Rhythm, rhyme and repetition also contribute to the imagery in the poem: the fire, the blacksmith and the darkness. The formalists saw these different, specialized uses of language working together to create a self-contained and complete work of art. The meaning was believed to be contained within the text, so that the social or historical context in which it was written, or facts about the author's life, or the reader's experience, were all irrelevant.

Practical criticism is
discussed in Chapter 7.

This belief that a work of language art is complete in itself, with a definitive
meaning waiting to be discovered, also underpins what has been the dominant
twentieth-century British–US approach to literary criticism, known as **practical
criticism** (although there is no evidence of contact between the British and US
critics and the formalists).

(I am grateful to Robert Abel for permission to draw on his unpublished
material in the analysis of 'The Tyger'.)

Rhyme and alliteration

Rhyme is a kind of 'phonetic echo'. In English verse, the most frequently occurring
rhyme is the 'end rhyme': units at the end of metrical lines have identical stretches of
sound from the vowel to the end of the word (usually stressed), with the initial sound
varied, for example, *sight/night*. Rhyme usually depends on phonemes rather than
spelling (for example, *ewe* rhymes with *too*), although sometimes 'eye-rhymes' are
used, which are based on sight rather than sound (*bough/cough*). Rhymes within a
metrical line are called 'internal rhymes'. Since the nineteenth century, poets have
also used 'half rhymes', in which the final consonants are repeated (*bend/sand*).

Before the Norman conquest, Anglo Saxon used alliteration (repeated initial
consonants) rather than rhyme for poetic cohesion, a style which reappeared in the
poetry of fourteenth-century England, as for example, in the following lines from
Sir Gawain and the Green Knight:

The snaw snitered ful snart, that snayped the wilde

(The snow came shivering down very bitterly, so that it nipped the wild
animals)

(Cited in Wales, 1989, p. 18)

Alliteration is still widely used in poetic language, as is assonance which is based on
the repetition of vowel sounds in adjacent words, for example, the *far star*.

(Based on Wales, 1989)

You may have noticed the foregrounding of repeated sounds, in addition to
rhyme, in 'The Tyger'; for instance, the repetition of the sound /t/ at the end of
the first two lines of the first and last stanza (brigh*t* nigh*t*), which symmetrically
reflects the initial sound /t/ in '*T*yger!, *T*yger!' with which each verse opens. Blake
also uses alliteration in '*d*istant *d*eeps'. Like rhythm, alliteration and assonance
(repeated vowel sounds) give poetry its musical effect and contribute to the
overall mood and meaning. For instance, in the following extract from *The Prelude*
(Book 1) by English poet William Wordsworth, the alliterative use of a number of
sibilant sounds shows how a build-up of one type of consonant can echo the action
being described, in this case the sound of ice-skates on winter ice:

All shod with steel.
We hissed along the polished ice in games
(Wordsworth [1850] 1991, p.26.

An example of assonance can be seen in the following line from Ruth Padel's
poem 'Still Life with Bible' in which she describes the artist (perhaps Van Gogh)
painting his madness:

If the sick sun came now it couldn't purge
the mad grappling sky.
(Padel, 1993, p. 20)

The open front vowel, /a/, is repeated in quick succession and is therefore foregrounded, with the effect that the vowel evokes a 'scream' or blood-curdling cry of despair. If you doubt this, see what kind of cry is evoked if you replace the phrase 'mad grappling' with words containing closed vowels like /ɪ / as in *hit* or /u:/ as in *fool*.

Breaking the rules of English

So far we have been concentrating on how language in poetry highlights or foregrounds particular properties of sound and rhythm. Foregrounding also occurs when particular language rules are played with, or broken.

Every language has rules for combining sounds and words and linguists have pointed out **syntagmatic** and **paradigmatic** relations between words. First, a language has rules for the way words are syntactically combined in phrases or sentences; for example, English is a 'determiner adjective noun' language (Graddol et al., 1994, p. 5). Secondly, words have paradigmatic relations with other words which could grammatically and semantically replace them. For instance, in the line 'Did he smile his work to see?', *he* has a syntactic relationship to *smile*, while *work* has a paradigmatic relationship with *creation*, *product*, or other words of the same word-class which could replace it (Graddol et al., 1994, pp. 73–5). These syntagmatic and paradigmatic rules are often exploited and broken in literary language. In fact, as we shall see, rules governing the sound system (phonology), the writing system (graphology), word structure (morphology), grammar and paragraphing, can all be broken, individually or in combination.

Let us look at some examples where authors and poets deliberately manipulate, or break rules at various levels. The following passage is from the opening chapter of *The Sound and the Fury* by US novelist William Faulkner. It is narrated by Benjy, a character whose cognitive development is stuck in babyhood, although he is thirty-three years of age when the book opens:

> Through the fence, between the curling flower spaces, I could see them hitting. They were coming toward where the flag was and I went along the fence. Luster was hunting in the grass by the flower tree. They took the flag out, and they were hitting. Then they put the flag back and they went to the table, and he hit and the other hit.
> (Faulkner [1929] 1989, p. 1)

In this first section of the novel, Faulkner's aim is to show what might be going through Benjy's mind, even though Benjy does not actually speak. This use of English to represent a stream of thought which looks strange in written English, is a challenge which requires the reader to be 'shocked' out of feeling comfortable with the language. For instance, Benjy constantly uses a transitive verb (one that expects to be followed by an object) with no object, for example, *he hit*. This simple device gives us some insight into the way that Benjy fails to make connections between cause and effect; Benjy does not realize that the golfers are hitting the balls into the holes. Benjy visits the golf course frequently, because he likes to hear the name of his beloved sister, Caddie, when the golfers shout to their caddy (the assistant who transports the golf-clubs). The power of Faulkner's text lies in the way it reveals a limited and unrefined mind through language which recreates the freshness and vividness of a human perception unrestricted by learned cultural and social structures.

Some writers make a particular feature of breaking the rules of English morphology and syntax. For instance, the American poet e e cummings refuses to use upper-case letters (as in the spelling of his own name), changes word classes, adds morphological endings to words that do not normally have them and plays with negation. What is interesting about such radical rule breaking is that cummings's stylistic tendencies are repetitive and thus once accustomed to his ways, we can understand the poetry quite well. A familiar structure that cummings plays with is where a word is repeated with *by* in the middle, as in the everyday examples: 'one by one', 'side by side', 'year by year'.

In the following extract from the poem 'anyone lived in a pretty how town', cummings uses this structure but subverts paradigmatic rules by choosing words that normally belong in another word-class:

> busy folk buried them side by side
> little by little and was by was
>
> (cummings, 1969, p. 44)

Here cummings sets the scene with a conventional phrase, *side by side.* He then moves on to the phrase, *little by little,* which normally means 'gradually'. However, since one can hardly bury a body 'gradually' we are forced to understand *little* as a noun. The last phrase turns the past tense form of the verb 'to be', into a noun in *was by was.* The echoes of another noun derived from the verb 'to be', 'has-been', perhaps suggest that these people were never very 'present' in their lives, even before they died.

Activity 5.3   Breaking writing conventions   *(Allow about 5 minutes)*

The extracts below come from the opening passages of two novels; the first, from *Bleak House by* Charles Dickens, is set in nineteenth-century England; and the second, from *Midnight's Children* by Salman Rushdie, in twentieth-century India. In each case, what conventions of formal written English are being broken, and to what effect?

1   Fog everywhere … Fog on the Essex marshes, fog on the Kentish heights. Fog creeping into the cabooses of collier-brigs; fog lying out on the yards, and hovering in the rigging of great ships; fog drooping on the gunwales of barges and small boats. Fog in the eyes and throats of ancient Greenwich pensioners, wheezing by the firesides of their wards; fog in the stem and bowl of the afternoon pipe of the wrathful skipper, down in his close cabin; fog cruelly pinching the toes and fingers of his shivering little 'prentice boy on deck.

   (Dickens [1850] 1948, p. 1)

2   I must work fast, faster than Scheherazade, if I am to end up meaning – yes, meaning – something. I admit it: above all things, I fear absurdity.

   And there are so many stories to tell, too many, such an excess of intertwined lives events miracles places rumours, so dense a commingling of the improbable and the mundane!

   (Rushdie, 1982, p. 11)

Comment

In the first extract, Dickens omits the main verb from each clause, painting a scene in the present tense, drawing the reader into the actual context of the novel. The clauses describing the fog build up and accumulate to create the effect that there is not a corner, nor a person, that can escape its stifling damp and cold. If you know *Bleak House,* you may remember that this fog is a metaphor for the crippling and all-pervasive effects of the nineteenth-century English law courts which are a central theme of the novel. Dickens highlights the importance of particular qualities of the fog (and the legal system), by breaking syntactic rules to catch and focus the reader's attention right at the beginning of the novel.

In the second extract, the way Rushdie addresses the reader as an intimate friend is an unusual and striking aspect of his style. The aberrant starting of a new paragraph (let alone a new sentence) with *And* contravenes traditional written conventions, but is in keeping with the highly colloquial and rather chaotic opening of the novel. This chaos is echoed when Rushdie breaks the graphological convention of putting commas between the listed items in the last sentence. The reader is surprised into recognizing the lack of separateness of these items; they are, as Rushdie says, densely intertwined and intermingled.

Metaphor and collocation

We have looked at different ways of highlighting the sounds, rhythms and grammatical patterns of English. Another important aspect of literary language is the way in which it plays with, and subverts, relationships of meaning, through metaphors, similes and puns.

The *burning* of the tiger's eyes and the stars' *spears* in Blake's poem, and the fog of the British legal system in Dickens's novel, are metaphors used to highlight particular qualities through direct comparison, sometimes in a surprising way. Metaphors exploit the networks of meaning invoked by particular words and many of the most effective metaphors are 'slipped in' to the text by way of a small deviation from traditional patterns of word combination. This can just as easily happen in spontaneous conversation as in a poem or a short story, but is particularly common in poetry.

An example of metaphor comes from Carol Ann Duffy's poem 'Litany', where she condemns the lives of her parents' generation in the lines:

> The terrible marriages crackled, cellophane
> round polyester shirts.
> (Duffy, in France, 1993, p. 117)

Duffy uses metaphorically the verb 'crackled' which normally follows an inanimate subject (for example, sticks crackling in a fire). This, together with her metaphoric comparison of the marriages with cellophane around polyester shirts, evokes images of relationships which are dry, brittle and somehow 'synthetic' – just like the materials which were at that time first being produced and which were replacing natural materials in every area of life.

Simile and metaphor

Simile refers to a device that makes a comparison explicit, as in this example from the American writer Toni Morrison's novel *Jazz* (emphasis added):

> Washing his handkerchiefs and putting food on the table before him was the most she could manage. A poisoned silence floated through the rooms *like a big fishnet* that Violet alone slashed through with loud recriminations.
> (Morrison, 1992, p. 5)

The effect of **metaphor** is akin to that of the simile, but the comparison is not made explicit, for example, *crackled* in the example from Duffy, and, on a broader level, the comparison of God to a blacksmith in 'The Tyger' and the fog in *Bleak House*.

In 'Litany' Duffy is relying on the reader's knowledge of the **collocations** of the word 'crackle' to make sense of her unusual choice of verb. When we hear or read a word a whole range of possible associations may be invoked, drawn from our experience of its use in other contexts. The artist juxtaposes particular words or phrases to highlight unusual and striking associations of meaning. Here is another example of this kind of juxtaposition (notice also the use of alliteration and assonance), taken from Samuel Beckett's *Footfalls*:

> Some nights she would halt, as one frozen by some shudder of the mind, and stand stark still till she could move again.
>
> (Beckett, 1984, p. 242)

Beckett exploits the reader's familiarity with the common collocations 'stock still', 'stark naked' and 'stark staring mad', to make the phrase *stand stark still* particularly concise, evoking both madness and nudity as well as the stillness it conveys more directly.

The effect is achieved by exploiting the reader/hearer's usual collocational expectations. For example, the verb *awaken* is normally constrained to occur with an animate object such as a person or an animal. The effect of placing an inanimate object after it, as the poet Sujata Bhatt does in the following lines from 'The Langur Coloured Night', is to suggest that the cry was loud enough to wake objects normally considered unwakeable:

> It was a cry
>   to awaken the moon
>
> (Bhatt, 1991, p. 11)

Collocation

Collocation refers to the combining tendencies of words. We know, for example, that *coffee* and *dining* are often to be found in the company of *table*. Some words are subject to slightly looser restrictions. For example, *eat* normally requires an object that is edible such as *sandwich* or *apple* while *snap* requires an object brittle enough to break in this way. Poetic effects often depend on unusual juxtapositions of words where collocations are invoked to create a metaphor, as in *marriages crackled* and *stark still*.

More systematic study of the collocations of words has been made possible through the amassing on computer of large numbers of spoken and written English texts, which can then be analysed to show the kinds of context in which particular words are likely to occur. The extraction from a large collection of texts of all the instances where a particular word appears is called a **concordance**. Concordancing can throw up some surprising results; for instance, some apparently neutral words can be shown to have consistently negative, or consistently positive, connotations. Sinclair (1987) describes how the phrase *set in* almost always refers to a negative set of affairs, being commonly found in association with words such as *decay, ill-will, impoverishment, bitterness, rigor mortis*, and *disillusion*, for example (cited in Louw, 1993).

Analysts claim that concordances can explain some of the more subtle nuances that particular words or phrases may have for us. Bill Louw has used computer concordancing to investigate the semantic associations of phrases used by Philip Larkin, whose poetry is well known for its ironic melancholy. Louw computed a concordance for the phrase *days are* in Larkin's poem 'Days', by extracting all the instances where the phrase appears from an 18 million-word corpus of English texts:

Days

What are days for?
Days are where we live.
They come, they wake us
Time and time over.
They are to be happy in:
Where can we live but days?

Ah, solving that question
Brings the priest and the doctor
In their long coats
Running over the fields.

(Larkin, 1964, p.27)

Concordance for 'days are'

1	t it yourself the prices these	days are	absolutely astronomica
2	ite 'The world is wide, no two	days are	alike, not even two ho
3	ays are gone whenel. But those	days are	almost twenty years go
4	glass extinction when the grey	days are	done but who are reaso
5	o men for unequal pay. But the	days are	gone whenel. But those
6	or do I. The big beer drinking	days are	gone. They drank becau
7	nd cry for peace. My political	days are	good and over. I'm not
8	ople making these things these	days are	making money out of th
9	erage trawler when its fishing	days are	over – as the Morning
10	it was before. Those good old	days are	over because trout fis
11	Lourenco Marques. Alas those	days are	over. What did he die
12	o walk means that his babying	days are	over. The stroking cea
13	ade me regret that my dancing	days are	over. Rudolph couldn't
14	fate of Czechoslovakia. These	days are	over, and that is what
15	ng after me Grandad's working	days are	past walk along with m
16	a black black sky. But those	days are	rare and usually to be
17	f I had a striking clock. The	days are	stretching out again a
18	ness and constancy of country	days are	the very qualities tha
19	e the only movies I see these	days are	these nights, on the 1
20	finances of old people these	days are	very much better than
21	rate that situation. The hard	days are	with us and they are c

(Louw, 1993, p. 162)

Activity 5.4 *(Allow about 10 minutes)*

The line *Days are where we live* might be expected to produce happy associations, yet it leaves the reader with inexplicable feelings of sadness, foreshadowing the theme of death in the second verse. How might the evidence from the concordance explain the feeling of sadness evoked by the second line?

Comment

Louw points out that in more than two-thirds of the concordance, the phrase *days are* is followed by words like *past, over* and *gone*. As he puts it, 'Days are not so much *where we live* as where we *have lived* and where we are likely, possibly sooner rather than later, to die' (Louw, 1993, p. 162). Louw did a further concordance using a 37 million-word corpus of texts where the term *days are* appeared 104 times, and found the same kind of profile as in the concordance above.

This kind of analysis challenges both the idea that a literary work should be treated as a self-contained piece of art, and the belief that literary analysis should focus on how literary language is different from that in other texts. Louw shows that our unconscious understanding of the associations of particular words and phrases in a poem is built up through our previous experience of them in many different kinds of other texts. In 'Days', these collocations are a central vehicle for the poem's effect; the meanings associated with the intertextual collocations swarm into the poem, colouring our reading of *days are*, so that its juxtaposition with *where we live* becomes deeply ironic.

In the margin:
Chapter 6 discusses punning in popular language art in some detail.

In addition to exploiting the collocations of words, writers sometimes play on different meanings of the same word. You may recall examples of **punning** in extracts earlier in the chapter: the two meanings of *Caddie* in the Faulkner novel tell us that although Benjy is simple, he is capable of strong human attachment; and the word *Lamb* in Blake's poem refers to an animal associated with gentleness and weakness, but which is also a common metaphor for Jesus Christ.

Punning highlights particular relationships between two different sets of meaning, for dramatic effect, as shown in the following extract from *My Children! My Africa!*, by South African playwright Athol Fugard:

Thami   But you were good!

Isabel Because I happen to feel very strongly about what we were debating. But it was also the whole atmosphere you know. It was so ... so free and easy. The debates at my school are such stuffy affairs. And so boring most of the time. Everything is done according to the rules with everybody being polite and nobody getting excited ... lots of discipline but very little enthusiasm. This one was a riot!

Thami   [*Finger to his lips*] Be careful.

Isabel Of what?

Thami   That word.

Isabel Which one?

Thami   Riot! Don't say it in a black township. Police start shooting as soon as they hear it.

Isabel Oh ... I'm sorry ...

Thami   [*Having a good laugh*] It's a joke, Isabel.

Isabel Oh ... you caught me off guard. I didn't think you would joke about those things.

Thami   Riots and police? Oh yes, we joke about them. We joke about everything.

(Fugard, 1990, p. 7)

The extract explores a culture clash in South Africa where two high school children, one black and one white, begin to find out about each other's lives when they meet in an interschool debate. The irony here lies in the two opposing meanings of the word *riot* that are being juxtaposed. The more obvious and literal meaning is a real and often frightening experience for township dwellers, while the privileged white girl is brought up sharply when she realizes that she uses the same word lightly to mean 'great fun'. The solemnity of her reaction is turned round again by Thami's ironically humorous response.

Iconicity

We have been looking at the way in which meaning can be played with, and highlighted, by invoking particular connotations. Writers also manipulate another layer of meaning by highlighting the manner in which a word relates to the object or process it is representing. For most words, this relationship is purely **symbolic**. There is no intrinsic reason, for example, for calling a tiger 'tiger' – it could just as well be called something else, so long as everyone in the speech community understood. But there are two other kinds of relationship which a sign can have with the object or event it is representing. The relationship may be **indexical** where there is some direct cause and effect: for example, smoke is a sign of fire, and, in the English language, an accent or dialect is a sign that the speaker comes from a particular geographical area or class. The third type of sign, which is particularly significant in literary language, is the **iconic**, where the sounds and shapes of words and phrases imitate particular objects or processes. Words can often function as more than one kind of sign simultaneously. For example, in 'The Tyger', the phrase *What dread hand and what dread feet* iconically imitates the sound of the beating of an anvil, while individual words have a symbolic relationship with the thing they are representing (hand, feet).

One of the most easily recognizable examples of iconicity in literary language is **onomatopoeia**, where the sound of a word echoes the action it is describing; for example, in the extract from *The Prelude* we looked at earlier in this chapter, Wordsworth uses the sibilant /s/ sound of the words to describe skating on ice. Another kind of iconicity is the way the patterns of rhyme in 'The Tyger' mirror the symmetry of its stripes.

Iconicity can also be achieved through the manipulation of grammatical rules. In another extract from *The Prelude* (Book 1) Wordsworth describes skating on a frozen lake in midwinter. Notice how he invokes the childhood pleasure of making oneself dizzy. Again, the effect is more marked if you read the poem aloud.

> ... and oftentimes,
> When we had given our bodies to the wind,
> And all the shadowy banks on either side,
> Came sweeping through the darkness, spinning still
> The rapid line of motion, then at once
> Have I, reclining back upon my heels,
> Stopped short; yet still the solitary cliffs
> Wheeled by me – even as if the earth had rolled
> With visible motion her diurnal round!
> (Wordsworth [1850] 1991, p. 26)

Wordsworth's language imitates the movement and dizziness of the narrator so effectively that we can not only remember, but almost feel, the childish exhilaration of the skater. How is this effect achieved? The passage consists of a single, rather long, sentence, whose main subject and verb, *I* and *stopped*, occur very late in its structure. This late placing of subject and verb, the two obligatory clause elements in English, contravenes a general 'rule' of English sentences, in which commonly the main verb appears early in the sentence, with any lengthy and complicated phrases occurring after the verb. The result of this general tendency in English sentences is that speakers of English expect the verb sooner rather than later. When it fails to occur, there is either a feeling of frustration and expectation, or (as in this case) a breathless, headlong rush towards the verb.

Wordsworth's description gives us four adverbial elements, the second of which is very long:

oftentimes

when we had given our bodies to the wind ... motion

then

at once

They almost begin to spin out of control until suddenly the auxilliary verb and subject, *have I,* seem to pull the structure back into line. However, there is one more adverbial element, *reclining back upon my heels,* before the main verb finally arrives. It is as though the skater is first of all abandoned to the movement, then decides to take control, but finds this takes a little longer than expected. When he does at last manage to stop, the short, sharp plosives of *stopped short* just have time to echo in the sudden stillness before the sentence continues, like the apparent movement of the landscape to a dizzy skater, for a further two and a half lines.

Iconicity

Iconic describes a word, phrase or other symbol which has some non-arbitrary relationship with the thing it represents. So while the words *male toilets* are arbitrary (symbolic), the sign in the margin is iconic, because it looks like a man. Iconicity at the level of phonology, where a word imitates the sound it represents, is known as **onomatopoeia,** for example, *buzz, miaouw, plop.* Iconic words may echo the sound they are representing within their form, for example *quick* has a short vowel and a final plosive consonant while *slow* has a long diphthong and no final consonant. Patterns of rhythm and syntax may mime or enact meaning as in, for example, Wordsworth's description of skating, the symmetrical patterns in 'The Tyger', or the rhythm of the train in W.H. Auden's poem 'Night Mail': 'This is the night mail crossing the border/Bringing the cheque and the postal order'(Auden, 1969, p. 83). Within narrative, chronological sequencing may iconically mimic the order in which participants experience events.

5.3 NARRATIVE AND DIALOGUE

So far we have been focusing on how particular aspects of English are highlighted and exploited in poetry. In this section we look at narrative, and the kinds of foregrounding used in this genre. Narrative is basically a story of events which the narrator considers important. Narratives are found in newspapers and histories (non-fiction), and in epic poems, ballads, comic strips, novels and short stories (fiction). They can be oral or written, enacted on stage, or envisioned in film and mime (Wales, 1989, p. 313). We look particularly at the use of detail and dialogue in novels, short stories and plays.

Plot and detail

The formalists distinguished between the series of events on which a narrative is based (which they called the 'fabula'), and the way those events are turned into a story (the 'sjuzhet'). The sjuzhet may include significant emphases, omissions, inferences and flashbacks, for example, which are all part of the narrator's art. The relationships between these two levels can be more or less complex. For instance, the film *Dr Zhivago* begins with an event which occurs long after the main portion of the narrative, and introduces a 'narrator' who is only very peripheral to the main events in the film. We only become aware of the significance of who the narrator is as the plot unfolds, and his interest at the beginning of the film in a particular factory girl is only explained at the very end. The fabula, the basic chronology of events, is like a skeleton, given a body and life by the way the sjuzhet is used to explore the relationships between the characters, and the intricacies of plot.

Another aspect of foregrounding in prose writing is the very explicit or concrete nature of descriptive language use, in contrast to the generally inexplicit nature of English in everyday speech (see Chapter 1).

Activity 5.5   *(Allow about 10 minutes)*

Read the extract below from the opening of Ambrose Bierce's short story 'Occurrence at Owl Creek Bridge'. What might be the author's purpose in providing such precise details about the height of the bridge, and the nature of the stream?

> A man stood upon a railroad bridge in northern Alabama, looking down into the swift water twenty feet below. The man's hands were behind his back, the wrists bound with a cord. A rope closely encircled his neck. It was attached to a stout cross-timber above his head and the slack fell to the level of his knees. Some loose boards laid upon the sleepers supporting the metals of the railway supplied a footing for him and his executioners – two private soldiers of the Federal army, directed by a sergeant who in civil life may have been a deputy sheriff …
>
> Beyond one of the sentinels nobody was in sight; the railroad ran straight away into a forest for a hundred yards, then, curving, was lost to view …
>
> The man who was engaged in being hanged was apparently about thirty-five years of age …
>
> His face had not been covered nor his eyes bandaged. He looked a moment at his 'unsteadfast footing,' then let his gaze wander to the swirling water of the stream racing madly beneath his feet. A piece of dancing driftwood caught his attention and his eyes followed it down the current.
>
> (Bierce, 1970, pp. 305–6)

Comment

Here are comments on Bierce's opening from a contemporary US novelist, Robert Abel:

> One purpose of this explicitness is 'authenticating detail', to draw us into the story, so we feel we are actually there … Bierce goes to the extreme of even giving us precise measurements to help dissolve the barriers between the world he is creating and our own awareness that it is 'only a story', after all. He tells us not that the bridge is 'high above the water', or even 'quite a distance from the water', but 'twenty feet' above. The precision of this detail makes the scene quite vivid. Notice also that the stream beneath the bridge is not just any stream, but contains 'swift water', 'racing madly', which can carry driftwood logs along. All these details seem innocent enough, vivid as they are, but in fact they serve at least two important purposes at this point in the story. One is that the stream's turbulence reflects the psychology of the situation – it is war time, and a man is being hanged for attempted sabotage. His state of mind is also in turmoil. The second purpose these details serve is to make

it possible to believe what happens – or seems to happen – in the rest of the story. Such a raging little stream could carry a man along as well as a log, and at a fast pace. Such a little stream, we don't need to be told, but can already sense, could, with a little bit of luck, carry a condemned man to safety. The carefully selected details, therefore, give us not only a sense of time and place, but prepare us nicely to accept and believe what happens next in the story. You might like to play with the details of the story, to see what the consequences would be for the reader. Suppose, for example, the stream was shallow and not so fast moving. Suppose the bridge was only ten feet from the water, or fifty feet above it. Even these apparently trivial adjustments in the 'facts' of this fictional world would make it almost impossible to persuade us that the condemned man would have any chance at all of getting out of his predicament. Caught in a narrow, muddy stream, he would surely be an easy target for the sharpshooters. If he fell fifty feet, he would surely be injured too badly to make a successful flight into the woods beyond. So there is nothing really innocent or haphazard about these details – they establish secretly what is possible in this fictional world, and 'authenticate' the reading experience which follows.

(I am grateful to Robert Abel for his permission to use material from his unpublished work *The Characteristics of Literary English.*)

Constructing dialogues

Authors make explicit decisions about the kind of details they are going to foreground in their descriptions. They also have to make decisions about the ways in which they represent natural speech, in their characters' dialogue. They usually conform to a number of conventions that distinguish dialogue from 'real' speech. These include using the minimum of overlaps and interruptions, very few hesitations and almost no self-corrections. Speakers in novels or plays often use complete sentences, as in the next example from *The Radiant Way*, a novel by the twentieth-century British writer, Margaret Drabble:

> 'Well, I don't know,' said Liz. 'I don't know why Charles doesn't move out, until he goes to New York. Wouldn't that be more orthodox, Charles?'
>   'I think I've lost my grip of orthodoxy. It's too late to be orthodox now,' said Charles: not quite believing his own words.
>   'Has Henrietta got any children?' asked Aaron. 'Are we about to acquire some new stepbrothers and stepsisters?'
> (Drabble, 1987, p. 122)

However, although written dialogue is often 'tidied up', writers can also exploit our knowledge of the apparent inconsistencies and non-sequiturs in ordinary conversation in a fairly direct way, as in this extract from *Minna*, a play by the contemporary British dramatist, Howard Barker:

> Minna   Go away!
> Francisca If you insist.
> Minna   No, don't go away …
>   [*She hesitates, then flings herself into Francisca's arms*]
>   I don't like dancing, I only think I do!
> Francisca Very well, don't dance –
> Minna   But that is true of everything.
> (Barker, 1994, p. 95)

From our experience of everyday conversation, we know that people in distressed states of mind sometimes contradict themselves in succeeding utterances, as Minna does at the beginning of this extract. And we understand that the apparently irrelevant last line must be interpreted as a general 'truth' of which the dancing is just one example.

Activity 5.6   (*Allow about 10 minutes*)

The following extract is taken from *Night School,* a play by the twentieth-century British dramatist Harold Pinter. In what ways does the dialogue here differ from 'natural' conversation? You might like to glance back at some of the examples in Chapter 1.

> Walter   Marvellous cake.
> Milly   I told her to go and get it.
> Walter   I haven't had a bit of cake like that for nine solid months.
> Milly   It comes from down the road.
> Walter   Here you are, Aunty, here's some chocolates.
> Milly   He didn't forget that I like chocolates.
> Annie   He didn't forget that I don't like chocolates.
> (Pinter, 1979, p. 201)

Comment

Pinter uses no overlaps, interruptions, hesitations or self-corrections. He writes in complete sentences and, while he parodies the tendency of people to repeat each other's words, he stylizes these repetitions to create a rhythmic and mesmeric pattern. This pattern implies that people's everyday lives are made up of such humdrum, pointless repetitions.

In prose writing, stretches of dialogue are usually 'framed'. There are particular narrative or aesthetic reasons for the points at which the author chooses to begin and end the dialogue, relating for instance to character, plot, or communicating information to the reader. In the extract below, from *Things Fall Apart,* the Nigerian novelist Chinua Achebe provides just enough direct dialogue to convey the ritual politeness commonly used at the beginning of a visit in the community depicted in his novel. Okoye has come to ask Unoka to give him back the quite considerable sum of money Unoka owes him.

> One day a neighbour called Okoye came in to see him. [Unoka] was reclining on a mud bed in his hut playing on the flute. He immediately rose and shook hands with Okoye, who then unrolled the goatskin which he carried under his arm, and sat down. Unoka went into an inner room and soon returned with a small wooden disc containing a kola nut, some alligator pepper and a lump of white chalk.
> 'I have kola,' he announced when he sat down, and passed the disc over to his guest.
> 'Thank you. He who brings kola brings life. But I think you ought to break it,' replied Okoye passing back the disc.
> 'No, it is for you, I think,' and they argued like this for a few moments before Unoka accepted the honour of breaking the kola.
> (Achebe, 1958, pp. 4–5)

This dialogue 'enacts' the beginning of Unoke and Okoye's encounter and gives us the flavour of the ritual exchange, the rest of which Achebe summarizes: 'they argued like this for a few moments'. After this point, Achebe summarizes the content of most of the encounter, switching back into direct speech for the final confrontation concerning the money.

In the examples so far, there has been a fairly clear boundary between the author's voice, and those of the characters. Sometimes, however, we are particularly aware of the author's voice behind the character, putting words into their mouth for particular ironic effect. For example, when Uriah Heep in Dickens' *David Copperfield* keeps telling David how humble he is, the reader suspects, because of what Dickens has hinted about Uriah, that this is in fact quite opposite from the truth. Conversely, we can also sometimes hear the voice of a character within the authorial voice. This happens, for instance, in 'stream of consciousness' novels, where the narration is ostensibly in the third person, but reflects the thought processes of particular characters.

In the next example, taken from *To the Lighthouse*, Virginia Woolf uses a kind of internal monologue to describe Minta's feelings:

> Besides, she knew, directly she came into the room, that the miracle had happened; she wore her golden haze. Sometimes she had it; sometimes not … Yes, to-night she had it, tremendously; she knew that by the way Mr Ramsey told her not to be a fool. She sat beside him, smiling.
>
> (Woolf [1927] 1977, p. 133)

Woolf's novels are renowned for consisting of a series of different perspectives, usually reflecting the thoughts of the major characters in turn. The author does not intervene, but tells the story through the emotions and reactions of the characters themselves. The result is that there are differences of vocabulary and syntax that approximate to the style of whichever character is currently the 'narrator'; for example, the terms *golden haze* and *tremendously* are typical of Minta's speech.

The use of English vernaculars

The use of strongly vernacular language would seem to go against the idea that literary language represents the best or most prestigious forms of English, and is distinctly different from everyday usage. Vernacular English is not particularly widespread in traditional English literature, although there are some famous examples of dialect in characters' speech, for example in Dickens's *Hard Times* and Emily Brontë's *Wuthering Heights*. More recently there has been a considerable increase in the number and range of writers who feel free to use their own variety or some other nonstandard variety of English for characters' voices, or even for whole poems and novels.

The Singaporean writer Catherine Lim, for example, uses vernacular Singaporean English in her short stories to convey a realism that also addresses the issue of linguistic oppression. In her story entitled 'The Teacher', she portrays a teacher obsessed with 'correctness' (that is, with Standard English) and a secondary-school girl who is clearly very unhappy:

> The teacher read, pausing at those parts which he wanted his colleague to take particular note of. '*My happiest day it is on that 12 July 1976 I will tell you of that happiest day. My father want me to help him in his cakes stall to sell cakes and earn money. He say I must leave school and stay home and help him. My younger brothers and sisters they are too young to work so thay can go to school. My*

mother is too sick and weak as she just born a baby.' Can anything be more atrocious than this? And she's going to sit for her General Certificate of Education in three months' time.'

In the story Lim tells how in a later essay under the title 'The stranger', the same girl wrote about her father:

> *He canned me everytime, even when I did not do wrong things still he canned me and he beat my mother and even if she sick, he wallops her.*

and the teacher comments:

> This composition is not only grossly ungrammatical but out of point. I had no alternative but to give her an F9 straightaway. God, I wish I could help her!
>
> (Lim, cited in Platt et al., 1984, p. 191)

The irony (for the reader) of the teacher's comment is underlined at the end of Lim's story when, on hearing of the girl's suicide, he complains, 'If only she had told me of her problems'.

Another writer who directly addresses the subject of linguistic equality is Tony Harrison, a British poet whose Yorkshire dialect was in danger of getting in the way of a 'good' education. In one of his poems on the subject of his dialect and identity, 'Them & [uz]', he recalls his schooldays at Leeds Grammar School, where he was among a minority of boys with a local dialect:

> I doffed my flat a's (as in 'flat cap')
> my mouth all stuffed with glottals, great
> lumps to hawk up and spit out ... *E-nun-ci-ate!*
>
> (Harrison, 1987, p. 122)

This poem is also discussed in Chapter 7 of the first book in this series *English: history, diversity and change* (Graddol et al. (eds), 1996).

Other poets have also made the decision to write in their own variety of English as a way of making a point about the validity of different varieties within literature. There are, for example, many writers of Caribbean backgrounds, who write at least some of the time in creole. The following example is from Louise Bennett's poem, 'Independance':

> Independance wid a vengeance!
> Independance raisin Cain!
> Jamaica start grow beard, ah hope
> We chin can stan de strain!
>
> (Bennett, in Burnett (ed.) 1986, p. 35)

The editor of the *Penguin Book of Caribbean Verse in English*, Paula Burnett, argues that 'it is only in the twentieth century (with one or two exceptions) that poets in the literary, Standard English tradition have begun to explore ways of working the rich ore of dialect in literary contexts'.

Activity 5.7   *(Reading A)*

Read 'In the vernacular' by Rib Davis (Reading A). What various purposes do authors have, in the different ways they reconstruct vernacular Englishes in written form?

Comment

Davis shows that the choice to use a nonstandard variety of English, and the way in which the author represents it on paper, is never 'innocent'. It is not a simple matter of transcribing the sounds and forms of speech; there is always a selection and focus on particular aspects of nonstandardness to construct a character or advance a plot. Writers' purposes vary enormously; for instance, they may use an eye-dialect to mark a character as the kind of person who would use nonstandard English (with all the social connotations that conveys). In the example from Hoban, we see an invented vernacular variety being used to symbolize iconically the degeneration of a whole society. It could be that use of the vernacular is a new kind of foregrounding, in presenting language which looks strange in the context of established literary conventions.

The stylistic landscape

We have already begun to explore the consistent use of particular forms of English which constitute a genre or, at a more specific level, the personal styles of individual authors. While this has always been an area of interest in literary criticism, the development of fast computers has enabled us to examine in far more detail cumulative effects of style; that is, those effects which are not localized in a phrase or a paragraph but are the result of a gradual build-up of grammatical and semantic choices which characterize the style of an author, rather like an individual fingerprint. It is now possible, for instance, to compare authors' works with databases of texts ranging from the literary to the functional, as a genuine basis of comparison.

Computer studies have shown that many of these 'topographical' features of the textual landscape can only be seen as the researcher rises above the details of a text in order to gain a bird's-eye view. For instance, it has often been assumed that the small words which knit phrases and sentences together, such as articles, pronouns and conjunctions, are not particularly significant in achieving artistic effects. They are often regarded as a kind of inert medium, against which artistic uses of English are highlighted. But the assumption that these 'grammatical' words are of no consequence to a writer's style is challenged by John Burrows (1987), who carried out a computer analysis of the frequency and pattern of occurrence of these words in Jane Austen's novels. Burrows shows that the patterns of use for these grammatical words, which make up between a third and a half of Austen's written output (depending on where one draws the line), are far from arbitrary in her novels. For example, there is a distinct contrast between two of the main protagonists in *Northanger Abbey*, Henry Tilney and Isabella Thorpe, in terms of the number of times they use *the*, *of*, *I* and *not*. These kinds of differences contribute to each character's **idiolect**, or individual speech style.

Table 5.1   Differences of incidence: four words in three idiolects

	Catherine	Henry	Isabella	Mean[1]	Mean[2]
the	16.34	35.29	25.81	24.61	26.45
of	15.91	29.92	17.32	20.71	23.69
I	56.68	24.56	52.86	43.69	38.75
not	26.99	12.69	19.62	19.12	16.14

Mean[1]: overall incidence in dialogue of *Northanger Abbey*
Mean[2]: overall incidence in dialogue of Jane Austen's six novels
(Burrows, 1987, p. 3)

Burrows argues that the effects of these differences must colour every speech the characters make, and leave some impression in the mind of the reader. Using information about the incidence of common grammatical words, he builds up a picture of the individual speech styles of particular characters, and tracks how these change during the course of the novel, sometimes moving further apart from the idiolects of other characters, and sometimes almost converging with them, as the characters come together within their own lives in the story.

Some literary scholars are very suspicious of the results produced by computer analysis of texts, because it tends to ignore the kinds of features that generations of critics have identified as the crowning achievement of literary style. However, there is increasing evidence to show that quantitative analyses give us indications of the overall pattern of usage in particular writers, even in texts from different periods of their writing careers.

Leech and Short arrive at the following compromise:

> So let us see quantitative stylistics as serving a role in the 'circle of explanation' as follows. On the one hand, it may provide confirmation for the 'hunches' or insights we have about style. On the other, it may bring to light significant features of style which would otherwise have been overlooked, and so lead to further insights; but only in a limited sense does it provide an objective measurement of style.

(Leech and Short, 1981, p. 47)

Grammatical and lexical words are discussed in Chapter 2 of this book and in Chapter 8 of the first book in this series English: history, diversity and change *(Graddol et al. (eds), 1996).*

5.4 AUTHORS, AUDIENCE AND CONTEXT

We looked in the last section at writers' use of vernacular Englishes, how an author's purpose affects the choice of language, and how that choice reflects the society within and about which they write. Although traditional approaches to literary criticism have tended to treat a novel, play or poem as a self-contained work of art with fixed meanings, more recently, there has been a growing interest in how the context and process involved in creating language art, and the contexts in which it is read, listened to, or viewed, affect meaning and interpretation.

Context and meaning

We saw in Chapter 1 how selective people are in their reporting of events in everyday conversation. The world is not reflected in talk, but refracted, as speakers or writers shape an account according to their own perspective, values and motives. It could be argued that literary language, in its simulation of the language of other discourses and its focus both on what is being represented and on itself, adds additional refractive layers. In this sense all texts, including literary ones, are 'ideological'; they present the reader with a particular view of the subject matter, which is usually the author's view and is deeply embedded and often implicit in the language of the text. In this respect the text cannot help but be a distorting refraction; but it also follows that there is no such thing as the 'perfect' mirror, a text with no ideological basis.

Overt or coercive propaganda in a text is not as common as the more hidden 'common-sense' or 'naturalized' ideologies that take for granted the reader's agreement on certain points. Authors may make implicit assumptions about the 'normal' needs and aims of men and women. Jane Austen played on this technique in the famous opening sentence of *Pride and Prejudice*: 'It is a truth universally acknowledged, that a single man in possession of a good fortune, must be in want of a wife.'

See Chapter 7 for a discussion of this in relation to the English literary canon, and Chapter 8 for accounts of how the language and cultural backgrounds of particular writers have affected the way they use English in their work.

Such statements normally mean that the reader is not in a position to doubt their truth, since their truth is precisely what the sentence asserts. Austen, however, clearly has her tongue in her cheek in presenting the reader with assumptions made by a society where mothers and daughters spend their lives scheming to win the latter the richest husband possible.

The basis for the perception that all texts are ideological is that language (spoken and written) is now usually seen as being shaped by its context, both linguistic and sociopolitical. No text is produced which is not in some way affected by texts, both spoken and written, literary and nonliterary, that have gone before it. Based on Bakhtin's idea that every utterance has some kind of dialogic relationship with other utterances which have preceded it (see Chapter 1), **intertextuality** in literature refers to the way in which a text may invoke other texts through the use of particular words, phrases or ideas, so the reader or listener's knowledge of that other text comes into play in their interpretation of what the current author is saying.

Activity 5.8   *(Allow about 10 minutes)*

Read the following extract from the opening of the novel *A Chain of Voices* by André Brink, a contemporary South African author writing about the slave trade in nineteenth-century Afrikaaner society. Consider the kinds of connection this text has with its context, and any references it makes to other texts. The narrator is a woman, Ma-Rose.

> To know is not enough. One must try to understand too. There will be a lot of talking in the Cape these days, one man's word against another's, master against slave. But what's the use? Liars all. Only a free man can tell the truth. In the shadow of death one should walk on tiptoe, for death is a deadly thing.
> (Brink, 1982, p. 19)

Comment

What knowledge of the world or of other texts do you find yourself using in interpreting the passage? You may have noticed a number of hints about the context and intertextual relationships, some of which would be more apparent when you were familiar with the whole book. For example, the word *Cape* conjures up associations with the southern part of South Africa. These associations may be contemporary thoughts about the establishment of democracy in the country and the abandoning of apartheid, but the reference to masters and slaves may also, depending on the reader's historical knowledge, bring to mind the early nineteenth century and the days of Afrikaans rule.

The phrase *the shadow of death* is evocative to those familiar with the Christian liturgy, and the twenty-third psalm: 'Yea, though I walk through the valley of the shadow of death, I will fear no evil: for thou art with me; thy rod and thy staff they comfort me'. As we discover later in the book, Ma-Rose is resistant to the white person's religion, preferring to take counsel from her traditional spiritual world. Here, however, the words so evocative of the Christian 'comfort' are undermined by the rest of the sentence, *one should walk on tiptoe, for death is a deadly thing,* underlining the cultural difference between the white and black participants in the drama that is to unfold in the novel. Ma-Rose would advise caution where the psalmist reassures with knowledge of the after-life. We shall also discover in the story that Ma-Rose is a woman in a man's world, so the repeated use of the masculine generic *man* may be an intentional irony.

A similar interextuality is exhibited in the poem 'Spring Cleaning' by Jean 'Binta' Breeze, who intertwines extracts from the twenty-third psalm with a description of a woman spring cleaning.

> de Lord is my shepherd
> I shall not want
> an she scraping
> de las crumbs
> aff de plate
> knowing ants will feed
>
> Maketh me to lie down in green pastures
> leadeth me beside de still waters
>
> (Breeze, in France, 1993, p. 71)

In this case the juxtaposition of the two styles underlines the gulf that exists between the words of comfort of the Psalm and the hard drudgery of the woman's life.

In the previous paragraphs, almost without noticing, we have taken for granted that the context of any text is the context of its production. We would probably agree that writers are influenced by their background (education, family, wealth) and their social context (country, period, history, tradition). However, many literary and linguistic theorists have also pointed out the importance of the context in which a text is 'received'; for instance, a South African with intimate and direct knowledge of the country's history may respond differently to Ma-Rose than might a student in a far-off place encountering the book on a literature course. And individual South Africans and students will vary in their reaction to the book, depending on their own personal histories and political beliefs. The 'meaning' of any text, then, is a kind of negotiation between producers and receivers, both of whom are to some extent constructed by their own cultural positioning.

The reading of texts is also historically conditioned, as particular periods attach value to particular styles of writing. Once-maligned writers may come back into fashion and be re-established as great 'artists'. For example, the work of English seventeenth-century poet John Donne went out of fashion in the eighteenth century because the expectation of 'correct' or 'polite' usage in literature was not met in his more rugged expression.

Particular cultures place value on different kinds of English language art. Oral literature has lost much of its currency in the dominant literate society of England. But in other cultures, irrespective of literacy, there are highly regarded forms of storytelling with stylistic features deriving from their oral delivery. In Ireland, for example, the tradition of storytelling survives despite the high literacy of the population. Loreto Todd (1989) shows that some features of storytelling also occur in everyday conversation in Ireland including, for example, the Irish love of hyperbole:

> He has a tongue that would clip a hedge
> She could cut beef that thin, you could a blew the slices over a mountain.
> (Todd, 1989, p. 53)

Storytelling is also highly valued in many parts of Africa. In the box below is the opening of one of the stories collected by Loreto Todd in West Africa. It was told in Kantok, an English-related pidgin language that is widely spoken and accepted as a lingua franca in Cameroon; Todd has added a Standard English translation. Notice the use of repetition in the last four sentences, echoing the oral delivery of the story.

Cameroon Folktale

Sehns no bi foh daso wan man

(Wisdom belongs to everyone)

Sohm taim bin bi we trohki bin disaid sei sehns pas mohni, so, i bin bigin foh gada sehns. i tek smohl sehns foh ehni man wei i mitohp. i swipam foh graun an i kasham as i fohl foh di skai. ehni taim we i fain sohm smohl sehns, i tekam, putam foh sohm big pohl. i gada di ting foh plenti dei. i gadaram foh plenti yia. i gadaram sotei i poht dohn fulohp foh sehns. trohki tink sei i geht ohl di sehns foh di hol graun foh i poht.

At one time Tortoise decided that wisdom was more precious than wealth, so he began to collect wisdom. He took a little from everyone he met. He swept it up from the ground and caught it as it fell from the sky. Every time he found a piece of wisdom he took it and put it in a large pot. He gathered it for many days. He gathered it for many years. He gathered it until his pot was full of wisdom. Tortoise believed he had all the wisdom of the world in his pot.

(Todd, 1979, pp. 84–5)

Some contexts have seen a transmutation of oral tradition into modern settings. The African tradition of oral songs and rhymes was exported to the Caribbean and America with the slaves, and on the plantations the ability to improvise satirical lyrics ridiculing the slave-owners was highly prized. This tradition has influenced more recent phenomena such as 'dub' poetry, a highly rhythmical improvised verse form where performers are admired for their ability to invent witty and often politically astute verses to the accompaniment of instrumental music.

Activity 5.9   *(Reading B)*

Read 'Feminist theatre: performance language as art form and communicative gesture' by Lizbeth Goodman (Reading B). In what ways do these performance pieces question traditional practices in the theatre?

Comment

Goodman shows how these three performances question and break down generic distinctions between fact and fiction, and bring everyday intimate forms of experience and language to the public stage. None of the plays was written by just one playwright and the two unscripted pieces produce performances which are flexible and provisional. All three pieces question the boundary between actors and audience, both in addressing the audience directly, and in urging them, through the plays' messages, to some sort of political action. Most radically, these pieces raise questions about the boundary between text and context (what 'counts' as a text?). Some of the examples of literature we looked at earlier foregrounded and manipulated particular aspects of the English language system; the plays here foreground and interrogate aspects of language practices and their contexts, in both art and everyday life, by highlighting and breaking conventional boundaries.

5.5   CONCLUSION

We have looked in this chapter at some of the ways in which English is used to achieve specific artistic effects in literary texts, through different kinds of fore-grounding, the manipulation of rules, iconicity and the exploitation of relations of meaning within the English language system. We have looked at particular artistic techniques within narrative, including different ways of representing and framing vernacular dialogue. We have also explored how various aspects of context and intertextuality are invoked by authors, and how they influence the reader/au-dience's understanding and appreciation of oral and written artistic texts.

Activity 5.10   *(Allow about 15 minutes)*

Figure 5.1 shows the different levels of language in the organization of a text. Many of the examples we have discussed in this chapter have involved fore-grounding or breaking the rules and conventions of English in relation to one or more of these levels.

Choose two examples from the chapter and, if possible, a couple of examples of your own and consider how they illustrate artistic uses of language, using any of the levels shown in the figure.

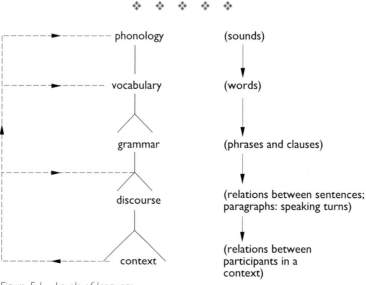

Figure 5.1   Levels of language
(Carter and Nash, 1990, p. 9)

We have seen through the course of this chapter that artistic uses of English achieve their effect by creating meanings on a number of different levels simul-taneously, for example, through collocation, iconicity, metaphor and irony. A further layer of meaning may be added through invoking intertextual references, or through the combination of language with visual effects, body language and movement. We can't explain art, or a particular style, with reference to any one of these levels on its own. It is the complex combination of manipulating the properties of language and context at different levels that turns English into art. This is then interpreted by readers and viewers, who bring a whole range of new contextual information to bear in their appreciation of the text and its meaning.

Reading A
IN THE VERNACULAR

Rib Davis

> 'Why do you speak Yorkshire?' she said softly.
> 'That! That's non Yorkshire. That's Derby.'
> He looked at her with that faint, distant grin.
> 'Derby, then! Why do you speak Derby? You spoke natural English
> at first.'
> 'Did ah though? An' canne Ah change if Am'm a mind to't? Nay, nay,
> let me talk Derby if it suits me. If you'n nowt against it.'
> (Lawrence [1928] 1970, p. 254)

In this extract from *Lady Chatterley's Lover* it was not in fact the 'Derby' speech of Mellors which offended his upper-class lover's sister: it was that he was clearly using it out of choice. Here was a working-class man, a gamekeeper – but nevertheless one with some education – *choosing* to use the vernacular of that part of the north Midlands of England when he was capable of using 'Standard English': it was an insult to the woman's language, to her class and thus to her, and at the same time was an infuriating statement of his control of the situation. So in this novel which created such a furore over another aspect of its language – the use of everyday 'slang' terms for sexual matters – we are at once involved with some of the key issues connected with use of the vernacular language as a reflection of class, as a statement of identity and as a means of control. Language, and in particular the use of Standard and nonstandard English, operates in all these ways in our everyday lives. When it is used as the vehicle for fiction, for the utterances of character or narrator which have emerged from the writer's imagination, then these elements of language take on yet further layers of complexity.

Representing regional speech

The focus of this reading is the representation of vernacular English in fictional prose (rather than poetry or drama, though many of the observations below must of course also apply to those genres). English is spoken in different ways by people in Newcastle, Aberdeen, Belfast or Swansea, in Perth, Cape Town, Toronto or Kansas City. There is a wide variety of English *accents*, so that the English sounds different, and there is a range of *dialects* – varieties of English with distinctive local vocabulary and nonstandard grammar. There are also various kinds of 'slang', which may or may not be regionally defined. Yet despite what is *spoken* by most people in those places (and regardless of where the authors come from) in these places, the *written* language of most fictional writing (and, indeed, in non-fiction) is Standard English. A surprising amount of dialogue, representing the speech of 'ordinary' people, is not written in an obviously vernacular form. However, some authors have attempted to represent the speech of their characters in ways which reflect particular aspects of accent, dialect and idiom. To most authors – as for Mellors – the use of Standard or nonstandard English on each occasion is a matter of choice. The choices that the writer makes, and the apparent reasoning behind those choices, as well as the results, reflect not only upon those individual writers and their work but also on the societies from which they have emerged. But before examining further the possible reasons for writing in nonstandard forms, let us look at a few more examples of how it is done. The first is from *Trainspotting* by Irvine Welsh, a contemporary novel set in Scotland.

> Ali's doon tae see aboot her rent arrears. She's pretty mad, like, screwed-up and tense; but the guy behind the desk's awright. Ali explains that she's oaf the gear n she's been for a few job interviews. It goes quite well. She gits given a set amount tae pay back each week.
> (Welsh, 1993, p. 274)

The second is a depiction of black American life, *The Color Purple* by Alice Walker.

> Dear God,
>
> Me and Sofie work on the quilt. Got it frame up on the porch. Shug Avery donate her old yellow dress for scrap, and I work in a piece every chance I get. It a nice pattern call Sister's Choice. If the quilt turn out perfect, maybe I give it to her, if it not perfect, maybe I keep.
> (Walker, 1983, p. 53)

The third is from one of Thomas Hardy's novels set in 'Wessex' (the rural Dorset of nineteenth-century England), *Under the Greenwood Tree*.

> 'Mayble's a hearty feller enough,' the tranter replied, 'and will spak to you be you dirty or be you clane. The first time I met en was in a drong, and though 'a didn't know me no more than the dead 'a passed the time of day.'
> (Hardy [1872] 1985, p. 92)

In each of these extracts the writer has gone to some lengths to convey the vernacular. In *Trainspotting* we have a first-person narrator, using both in his own speech and in his narration essentially the same language as the other characters in the book. Here, unusually, there is no distinction between the language of narration and the language of dialogue. The invented spelling conveys the sound of spoken language and, in the process, the very particular identity of this group of people, which includes the narrator. In the extract from Alice Walker's *The Color Purple*, on the other hand, we have a character, Celia, who is writing letters to God. Here the character's own pronunciation cannot be deduced: there is no modified spelling as she is writing letters rather than conveying the sound of speech. But her grammar is nonstandard, reflecting her black working-class background in the southern states of America (though her better educated sister, whose letters form the rest of the book, writes in a style much closer to Standard English, indicating the variation of written and spoken language even within one family). In *Under the Greenwood Tree* we have a third-person narrator represented in Standard English, but a number of the characters speak in a dialect which the author attempts to write 'as it sounds'. As in the first extract, the spellings are of course not completely altered to represent the sounds of speech: in *Trainspotting* 'pretty' is not spelt 'pritty', as it would probably be pronounced, and 'enough' does not become 'enuff'. It seems that only where the author considers pronunciation to differ significantly from Received Pronunciation (RP) is the spelling changed and therefore highlighted.

Speech and characterization

There are a number of different ways, then, to represent nonstandard accents and dialect in fictional writing. As well as giving regional authenticity to a character, use of vernacular can convey particular messages about the kind of person that character is. The Scots writer William McIlvanney presents the vernacular in a number of different forms. In *Waving*, for example, almost the whole touching story is presented in Standard English, but the character of Duncan has a very gently noted vernacular speech, which seems to add to his naivety. Indeed, a certain naivety or simplicity seems to be one of the stock character aspects which writers emphasize through use of written-out vernacular. Others include roughness, earthiness, a certain naturalness or lack of education, an unintended capacity to amuse, and exoticism. McIlvanney, however, is also aware of the subversive power of the nonstandard:

> 'McQueen.'
> 'Sur!'
> The governor felt that McQueen's respect was subtly disrespectful. He invariably addressed the governor as 'Sir' but he invariably used the inflection of his West Scotland dialect, as if reminding him that they didn't quite speak the same language. 'Sur' was the fifth-column in the standard English McQueen affected when speaking to the governor.
> (McIlvanney, 1990, p. 58)

In an entirely different example, Richmal Crompton uses nonstandard speech for William and his friends in her 'William' novels (enduringly popular among British children, even though they are set in a lost middle-class world of the 1930s).

> 'Gotter bit of money this mornin',' explained William carelessly, with the air of a Rothschild.
> (Crompton, 1972, p. 12)

The representation of William's speech as nonstandard (in contrast to that of the rest of his family) is part of his characterization as a nonconformist rascal.

Some authors give a character what is called an 'eye-dialect', where a word is written as nonstandard, when its pronunciation is actually the same as the spoken standard, for example, *wot* and *what*. *wot* is then a symbol, rather than an accurate representation, of nonstandardness, and is often used by authors for less intelligent, less socially prestigious characters. Conversely, Dickens uses flawless Standard English for Oliver in *Oliver Twist*, despite the fact that he was brought up in poverty in the workhouse. Oliver's standard speech conveys an impression of his innate respectability and incorruptible goodness – and of course at the end of the novel he does indeed turn out to have been of high birth.

Here is an example of a vernacular being used for a different purpose again, in Raymond Chandler's depiction of the archetypal American private eye, Philip Marlowe, in *The Big Sleep*.

> I let my breath out so slowly that it hung on my lip. 'Regan?' I asked.
> 'Huh? Who? Oh, you mean the ex-legger the eldest girl picked up and went and married. I never saw him. What would he be doing down there?'
> 'Quit stalling. What would anybody be doing down there?'
> 'I don't know, pal. I'm dropping down to look see. Want to go along?'
> 'Yes.'
> 'Snap it up,' he said. 'I'll be in my hutch.'
> (Chandler, 1948, p. 47)

Here we are in an utterly different world. There is little resort to modified spelling, but the vocabulary and the snappy sentences create a fictional vernacular which helps to authenticate the world created by Chandler. Perhaps we don't care whether this is really how the 'cops' and private eyes speak – it's what we expect and enjoy listening to.

Invented vernaculars

We have looked so far at some examples of authors' representation of regional and social vernacular in nineteenth- and twentieth-century British and American fiction, and examined some of their purposes for highlighting the nonstandard. Other writers have invented a new vernacular, as part of a futuristic world. In Russell Hoban's *Riddley Walker*, English in a post-holocaust future has undergone a frightening transformation – it has degenerated, and become corrupted in its vocabulary, its grammar, its spelling, and its meaning. The eponymous narrator presents us with a written version of it, but it is a language which clearly was used for some time almost exclusively in its spoken form; and even then the words which lived on were only partly understood; new meanings had to be created for words and new explanations found.

> Wunnering who ben the las to look at Greanvine befor me. That red and black stripet hard clof it wer old but not as old as Greanvine. Did it come from a Punch mans fit up or a Eusa show mans? Ben there Punch back then in what ever time Greanvine come from? How far back did Greanvine go? Ben he there when them jynt music pipes ben making ther music?
>
> (Hoban, 1982, p. 163)

Just as the language of the culture has mutated, so have its myths; the people are now coming to terms with their existence through new myths strangely forged from, among others, the traditional tale of Punch and Judy and the Christian legend of St Eustace (referred to in 'a Eusa show mans'). Riddley Walker is trying to make sense of both his own language and his own culture, totally intertwined as they are. Sometimes we can guess the meanings of his words without difficulty; the significance of others we only gather after a number of uses. This is not an easy world to enter, but, like other linguistic worlds, once we are in it and have gained a little confidence then the overcoming of further difficulties only makes us feel more a part of the whole experience, an initiate. And there is a real pleasure in divining the rules. Yet for all the logic of corruption (nouns mutating into verbs, the fairly regular shifting of one consonant to become another) this is a story about a disintegrating society. The language both tells us about that disintegration and represents it in the forms of words and phrases. As Jean-Jacques Lecercle has pointed out in *The Violence of Language*, this strange language is continually reminding the reader of the processes of corruption, and of the relationship between past and present (Lecercle, 1990).

Hoban's vernacular has something in common with the use of language in Anthony Burgess's *A Clockwork Orange*, a novel which shocked many with the violence of both its language and action when it first appeared in the 1960s. Here too we are in the future, but *nadsat*, the Russian-sounding vernacular of Alex and his 'malchicks', does not represent the new standard, the mutation of a whole culture, as does that of *Riddley Walker*; rather, as in earlier, more conventional writing, this is a vernacular expression that emphasizes wilful defiance. *Nadsat* is contrasted in the novel with something very close to Standard English – it has not superseded it.

> The Doctor said:
>   'Come on, gentlemen, we don't want any trouble, do we?' in his very high-class goloss, but this new prestoopnick was really asking for it. You could viddy that he thought he was a very big bolshy veck …
>
> (Burgess, 1965, p. 70)

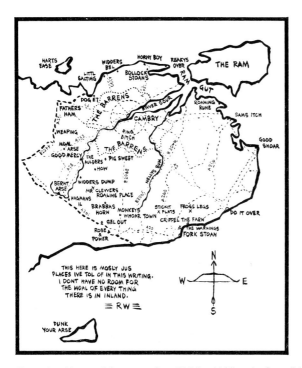

On my naming day when I come 12 I gone front spear and kilt a wyld boar he parbly ben the las wyld pig on the Bundel Downs any how there hadnt ben none for a long time befor him nor I aint looking to see none agen. He dint make the groun shake nor nothing like that when he come on to my spear he wernt all that big plus he lookit poorly. He done the reqwyrt he ternt and stood and clattert his teef and made his rush and there we wer then. Him on 1 end of the spear kicking his life out and me on the other end watching him dy. I said, 'Your tern now my tern later.' The other spears gone in then and he wer dead and the steam coming up off him in the rain and we all yelt, 'Offert!'

The woal thing felt jus that littl bit stupid. Us running that boar thru that las littl scrump of woodling with the forms all roun. Cows mooing sheap baaing cocks crowing and us foraging our las boar in a thin grey girzel on the day I come a man.

The Bernt Arse pack ben follering jus out of bow shot. When the shout gone up ther ears all prickt up. Ther leader he wer a big black and red spottit dog he come forit a littl like he ben going to make a speach or some thing til 1 or 2 bloaks uppit bow then he slumpt back agen and kep his farness follering us back. I took noatis of that leader tho. He wernt close a nuff for me to see his eyes but I thot his eye ben on me.

Coming back with the boar on a poal we come a long by the rivver it wer hevvyer woodit in there. Thru the girzel you cud see blue smoak hanging in be tween the black trees and the stumps pink and red where they ben loppt off. Aulder trees

Figure 1   *Map and first page from* Riddley Walker *by Russell Hoban*

From representation to reconstruction

We have looked at authors' representation of 'authentic' dialects, and their use of invented vernaculars. In some ways the boundary between these is not as clear-cut as it might at first seem, as this final example illustrates. *Huckleberry Finn* is one of the most influential models of nonstandard usage in English literature. It has a first-person narrator, the young white American boy, who draws us into the world of a homeless, rootless child on the edges of respectable society in the USA of the late nineteenth century. Here he describes part of his wanderings, aboard a raft on the Mississippi:

> It must 'a' been close on to one o'clock when we got below the island at last, and the raft did seem to go mighty slow. If a boat was to come along we was going to take to the canoe and break for the Illinois shore. And it was well a boat didn't come, for we hadn't ever thought to put the gun in the canoe, or a fishing line, or anything to eat. We was in ruther too much of a sweat to think of so many things. It wasn't good judgement to put *everything* on the raft.
> (Twain [1884] 1976, p. 41)

Although it has always been assumed that Huck spoke poor white nonstandard American (Twain himself claimed the book's dialogue was based on painstaking research), Fishkin (1993) raises some interesting questions about Twain's sources for the character. Through a detailed analysis of the language used by Huck and an investigation into Twain's sources, she presents a convincing case that the model for Huck and Huck's language was in fact a black boy, a certain 'Sociable Jimmy' whom Twain met in the early 1870s. There were, of course, elements of the speech of other, white, boys mixed into this, yet it seems that Huck's energetic,

EXPLANATORY

In this book a number of dialects are used, to wit: the Missouri Negro dialect; the extremest form of the backwoods Southwestern dialect; the ordinary "Pike County" dialect; and four modified varieties of this last. The shadings have not been done in a haphazard fashion, or by guesswork; but painstakingly, and with the trustworthy guidance and support of personal familiarity with these several forms of speech.

I make this explanation for the reason that without it many readers would suppose that all these characters were trying to talk alike and not succeeding.

THE AUTHOR

CHAPTER I

Civilizing Huck–Miss Watson–Tom Sawyer waits

You don't know about me without you have read a book by the name of *The Adventures of Tom Sawyer;* but that ain't no matter. That book was made by Mr. Mark Twain, and he told the truth, mainly. There was things which he stretched, but mainly he told the truth. That is nothing. I never seen anybody but lied one time or another, without it was Aunt Polly, or the widow, or maybe Mary. Aunt Polly–Tom's Aunt Polly, she is–and Mary, and the Widow Douglas is all told about in that book, which is mostly a true book, with some stretchers, as I said before.

Now the way that the book winds up is this: Tom and me found the money that the robbers hid in the cave, and it made us rich. We got six thousand apiece–all gold. It was an awful sight of money when it was piled up. Well, Judge Thatcher he took it and put it out at interest, and it fetched us a dollar a day apiece all the year round–more than a body could tell what to do with. The Widow Douglas, she took me for her son, and allowed she would sivilize me; but it was rough, living in the house all the time, considering how dismal regular and decent the widow was in all her ways; and so I lit out.

I got into my old rags and my sugar-hogshead again, and was free and satisfied. But Tom Sawyer he hunted me up and said he was going to start a band of robbers, and I might join if I would go back to the widow and be respectable. So I went back.

The widow, she cried over me and called me a poor lost lamb, and she called me a lot of other names, too, but she never meant no harm by it. She put me in them new clothes again, and I couldn't do nothing but sweat and sweat and feel all cramped up. Well, then the old thing commenced again. The widow rung a bell for supper, and you had to come to time. When you got to the table, you couldn't go right to eating but had to wait for the widow to tuck down her head and grumble a little over the victuals, though there warn't really anything the matter with them–that is, nothing only everything was cooked by itself. In a barrel of odds and ends it is different; things get mixed up, and the juice kind of swaps around, and the things go better.

After supper she got out her book and learned me about Moses and the Bullrushers, and I was in a sweat to find out all about him. But by and by she let it out that Moses had been dead a considerable long time; so then

Figure 2   Explanatory and opening page of Chapter 1 from Huckleberry Finn *by Mark Twain*

powerful, utterly memorable nonstandard speech is based on nineteenth-century black American vernacular speech, not on the speech of poor whites.

We do not know if Twain was reluctant to make a black boy the hero of his novel, or whether he shared the general reluctance among whites to acknowledge the influence of black language on their speech. What the example does illustrate, however, is the power of the vernacular in fiction-writing to add a very special kind of authenticity to the characters, the setting and the story which may not directly map on to the 'real world' being depicted. In this example, as in others throughout this reading, the author's representation of speech reflects not just the features of a particular variety of spoken English, but also specific authorial purposes, to do with plot and character development as well as imaginative authenticity. And the way in which authors use vernacular to represent a particular kind of character, or a particular sort of setting, reflects both their own attitudes and values towards different varieties of spoken English, and also those values of the society from which they have sprung.

References

BURGESS, A. (1965) *A Clockwork Orange*, Harmondsworth, Penguin.

CHANDLER, R. (1948) *The Big Sleep*, Harmondsworth, Penguin.

CROMPTON, R. (1972) *Just William*, London, Collins.

FISHKIN, S.F. (1993) *Was Huck Black?*, Oxford, Oxford University Press.

HARDY, T. ([1872] 1985) *Under the Greenwood Tree*, Oxford, Oxford University Press.

HOBAN, R. (1982) *Riddley Walker*, London, Picador.

LAWRENCE, D.H. ([1928] 1970) *Lady Chatterley's Lover*, Harmondsworth, Penguin.

LECERCLE, J-J. (1990) *The Violence of Language*, London, Routledge.

McILVANNEY, W. (1990) *The Prisoner in Walking Wounded*, London, Sceptre.

TWAIN, M. ([1884] 1976) *Huckleberry Finn*, Maidenhead, Purnell.

WALKER, A. (1983) *The Color Purple*, London, The Women's Press.

WELSH, I. (1993) *Trainspotting*, London, Secker and Warburg.

This reading was specially commissioned for this book.

Reading B
FEMINIST THEATRE: PERFORMANCE LANGUAGE AS ART FORM AND COMMUNICATIVE GESTURE

Lizbeth Goodman

What is feminist theatre?

Feminist theatre is an art form and a platform, a form of entertainment and a forum for communication of feminist political ideas. Because theatre is performed, it is a public medium. Because it is performed live (not pre-recorded for broadcast or film) its impact on individual people is immediate. Thus, feminist theatre can be seen as a dialogue between performers and audiences, about issues of gender and power (Goodman, 1993, 1996b, 1996c). In this reading, we consider the impact of feminist theatre in English as a form of 'performed political language', and how it questions the values and assumptions of mainstream theatre.

Let's consider three contemporary women's performance pieces, all of which 'speak out' in very different ways, drawing on gesture and body language, as well as spoken and scripted English and other languages, to communicate personal and political ideas on stage. Two of the pieces discussed are performance works, with no written texts to support them. Only the video recordings of the live performances, and the memories of audience members who saw the work, remain to chronicle this work. The first example, *Have You Seen Zandile?*, however, does have a script which has been published. But even this play is not in any sense traditional. It was not written by one author in isolation, but created and devised by several people in a collaborative process of storytelling, role play and direction. The written text which became the permanent record of the piece, or 'the play', is the last stage of the creative process.

As we shall see, all three of these pieces share features which are distinctive of feminist theatre.

Gcina Mhlophe's Have You Seen Zandile?

Have You Seen Zandile? is based on Gcina Mhlophe's own life, and was devised and performed by her with Maralin Vanrenen and Thembi Mtshali in Johannesburg, and later in England. It tells the story of a young girl, Zandile, who at the beginning of the play is living happily with her beloved grandmother in Durban. The story opens with Zandile calling goodbye to her school friends, then playing hopscotch with some stones on the path as she walks home. She is speaking Zulu as well as English:

Zandile   Nabaya omame, bethwel' imithwalo
           Nahaya omame, bethwel' imithwalo
           Ngcingci bo, ngcingci bo, nabaya omame
           Sabona ngoricey, sabona ngonyama
           Sabona ngokhekhe, sabona ngoswitie

           Mhhhm swities! I wonder if my grandmother will bring me some
           sweets today … lucky if she does because she will bring me my
           favourite icemints! That's what I like. I could be standing here
           like this and my gogo would say to me – Zandi, I have a surprise
           for you. Close your eyes, open your mouth …

The play is presented mainly in English in order to communicate to white South
Africans and a broader international audience, but African languages are interwoven throughout (Zulu in the first half and Xhosa in the second half, when
Zandile moves to the Transkei). The audience can pick up the general meaning of
the phrases in Zulu and Xhosa from their context on stage. For those who read the
play in its printed version, translations into English are listed at the end of the text.

*Figure 1   Book cover:
Have You Seen Zandile?*

Have You Seen Zandile? depicts a world of women and children, and their language
practices reflect the hybrid culture of their everyday lives. At different points
Zandile refers to a popular western song, a Barbara Cartland novel, Christian
prayers and hymn singing, and numerous African oral forms from lullabies and
urban jazz songs to a praise poem for a respected teacher (Walder, 1992). Above
all, this is a play based on storytelling; not the great male sagas of war and

conquest, but the intimate stories of women's everyday lives. Here, for instance, is the first time we meet Gogo, the grandmother, who is unpacking shopping bags in the house while Zandile plays outside.

Gogo   Oh, my grandchild. What did she say to me the other day when I bought this doll? Hawu Gogo, I love this doll but why do they always make them pink? [*She laughs*]

I hope Zandile is happy living with me. Oh, I could not bear to see the child playing all by herself looking so subdued. And there I was, with all the time in the world. Why could my grandchild be lonely? And yes, I have been lonely too since my husband died and my son Tom moved out with his family.

I would not talk badly about Tom, but he is the one who should take care of Zandile. His wife's hands are full – she has to take care of their six children. Zandile's own mother lives in the Transkei with her husband and four children. So Zandile is nobody's responsibility it seems. Well, she's welcome to be my responsibility. Oh, she's such a delight to cook for. [*Pauses, thinking*]

Zandile and Gogo's life together is rudely interrupted when Zandile is kidnapped and taken to live with her mother in the rural Transkei. She is terribly unhappy, and misses her grandmother. Gradually, however, she learns that her mother too has a tragic personal story to tell, and genuinely cares for her daughter. Meanwhile, we see Gogo searching desperately for her granddaughter, asking the audience directly, 'Have you seen Zandile?'. When she is eighteen, Zandile returns to Durban to look for Gogo, but the old lady has died. She has, however, left Zandile a suitcase full of little parcels, saved for her over the years. The play ends with Zandile opening these, and holding the children's dresses they contain up against her now adult body.

The play is made up of short scenes about intimate details of Zandile's life, where the actors use an extensive range of facial expressions to convey different emotions – pleasure, sorrow, understanding, contentment, confusion and loss. But it also explores universal themes of loss and continuity between different generations of women. And the stories told about themselves by Zandile, her mother and Gogo are highly political in the way they depict the effects of the brutal apartheid regime, and urge the audience, implicitly, to take some kind of action. This is not just art for art's sake, but art with a political message and purpose.

Midnight Level 6, by the Magdalena Project

The Magdalena Project is an international women's theatre network based in Cardiff, Wales. While *Have You Seen Zandile?* presents fragments from one girl's life, *Midnight Level 6* weaves together the stories of a large number of women, fictional and non-fictional. It is a large-scale performance piece which puts twelve women on stage (a rare thing in itself); there is no script and indeed, the director, Jill Greenhalgh, argues that the piece can only retain its integrity as a feminist statement and piece of art in live performance.

Midnight Level 6 tells the story of a Cardiff prostitute, Lynette White, who was brutally murdered on Valentine's Day in 1988. The text of the play draws on both factual and fictional sources. It includes newspaper headlines about the murder and storytelling around this incident which links Lynette White to mythical and historical figures such as Mary Magdalene and Medea, interwoven with fragments of the personal stories of the performers who collaborated in devising the piece. The performers experiment with representations of women, naked from the waist up, carrying crosses which they throw from one to another. The movement of the crosses in the air, the swaying of skirts and hair and bodies, contrast starkly with the dark image of the cross. In this way, the piece subverts biblical imagery; the performance is deliberately provocative yet appropriate (in the company's view) as a metaphor for the 'sacrifice' of women in society today.

The audience is positioned as an active spectator and listener, hearing confessions, seeing that which is normally too personal to be seen in public, including the bodies of the performers who communicate with each other and the audience through dance, body language and gesture, as well as with words.

For example, in one scene a young women is alone on stage, exhausted with her baby's tireless crying. She begs the baby to be still, and the audience is trapped in the moment of desperation with the young mother who pleads for silence, for time to collect her thoughts. She appeals to the audience, crying out for help, yet the confines of the theatrical event – which keep one set of people, the audience, from intervening in the acts of another set of people, the performers – leave this woman alone in her despair. The young mother cries out her own name, but the only reply is the wail of the child, demanding comfort. In desperation the mother stabs the baby, to silence it, to allow her own voice to find itself again. The mother becomes Medea. And each of the eleven other performers, and the audience, is complicit with her in their failure to intervene.

Figure 2
Scene from Midnight Level 6

In this deliberately shocking scene, *Midnight Level 6* offers a disturbing image which resonates across the 'extra-scenic' barrier between stage and audience. When the child is stabbed, the audience, with the performer is left to wonder why no one helped, why this woman had to suffer alone, why this tragedy could not have been prevented. While the scene is fragmentary and surreal (not 'realistic') in style, the anguish of the young mother and the horror of her act are very 'real' indeed.

The story of Lynette White and her solitary, anonymous death comes back, like a refrain. What is most important about *Midnight Level 6* as a feminist piece is its inclusion of many women's voices. The collective identity expressed is complex. It does not imply any sameness to the many different women represented, but does suggest that women living in the world today may share some stories in common, may share experiences which aid communication across cultures, and across the gap between theatre and audience.

Anna O's Twenty Ways to Learn a Language

Performances like *Have You Seen Zandile?* and *Midnight Level 6,* which begin with women's autobiography, incorporating personal experience and direct communication with the audience, have been common in British and American theatres since the rise of the womens' liberation movement in the late 1960s and early 1970s, when consciousness-raising techniques were employed in the theatre by explicitly feminist performers and directors. Since then, these techniques have shifted focus from agit-prop and social realism to more experimental and theoretically sophisticated forms. The last performance piece discussed has no text or script, not even a fragmented story as in *Have You Seen Zandile?* or intersecting narratives as in *Midnight Level 6.* This third piece makes demands on the imagination of the audience for its interpretation. 'Anna O', named after the pseudonym of one of Freud's most infamously silenced female patients, is a three-person team: Janet Hand, John Gange and Tessa Speak. *Twenty Ways to Learn a Language* is a multimedia performance, projecting English letters, words and messages on to screens, boards, television sets, the floor, and the performers' bodies. Huge single letters are projected on to a screen at the opening of the play, then two women appear, who explore and interact with the letters, and with other words and messages which appear projected around them. They write letters and words themselves, including a list of topics which the play is going to address. Using performers' bodies to mirror, interrogate and erase the words, as well as to speak and write them, the performance piece from the outset raises questions about our relationship with language, how we use it, and the ways it writes and constructs ourselves. The power of words is represented in the stage set, where they are scribbled graffiti-style on the walls and floors, projected on screens and spoken and analysed verbally by performers. Fragments of different genres, from poetic material to immigration laws, are interwoven.

A series of stories or incidents is presented around the theme of language. For instance, an event which prevented a fourth person joining the team who co-devised *Twenty Ways to Learn a Language* is presented. Mutsumi Yagi, a Japanese woman, was denied entry to the UK when she was detained at British Customs, and her diary confiscated, translated and read. Mutsumi had written the letters 'R.T.' several times alongside a notation of minor sums, and this was interpreted as proof she had been working illegally. On stage, this event is related by a British woman who stands at a podium as if to deliver a lecture. She is dominated by the enlarged photograph of a Japanese woman's face projected on screen, and the

Figure 3   Twenty Ways to Learn a Language

audience becomes aware that although the account is true, the woman speaking the words is not their author, and the loudest voice at this point is that of an absent, silenced performer represented in the photograph. This highlighting of Mutsumi Yagi's enforced absence raises questions about who has the right to speak for and represent another, or to read and interpret or misinterpret another's words. The performance encourages each spectator to consider his or her right to be present, free to write and speak without censure.

Evaluating feminist theatre as a form of communication

In the non-traditional format and aims of all three pieces we have discussed, we can identify common features of much feminist theatre:

- Feminist theatre, as a political form, tends to address the audience directly (Gogo searching for Zandile, the distraught mother crying for help, the silenced voice of the Japanese actor).

- It tends to assume a female 'gaze' in its audience, and an interest in issues of relevance to women in all audience members, female and male (the attachments and pain of motherhood, female experience of sexuality, the minutiae of everyday domestic life).

- It often makes a point of focusing the audience's attention on the function of language within the piece, to label or confine or enable and empower characters, as the case may be (the newspaper articles about Lynette White's death, the use of Mutsumi Yagi's diary as evidence).

- Feminist theatre questions the nature of language and of the status of any text, asking: is a text a script, or a performance, or a reading, or an idea collaboratively devised but never recorded? How do we define the relationship between texts and contexts? Is the performer's body a text of sorts? If so, who is in the best position to 'interpret' it?

- When feminist theatre crosses cultural boundaries, to what extent is written language and translation into English (as in *Have You Seen Zandile?*) a necessary form of political communication or a compromising of artistic and political purposes?

- Is there a language or set of experiences, communicable in some form, which is common to women across borders of culture and spoken language? If so, can it be inscribed as a 'text'? Can body language and gesture, or storytelling, or even silence, be implemented as forms of communicative performance to bridge cultural gaps?

- Feminist theatre, with its collaborative techniques and emphasis on process rather than text as product, challenges the notion of the 'great individual author', so central to the English literary canon.

The most effective feminist theatre draws on the resources of the English language, within performance, to effect social change, whether on a large or an individual scale. It does so by making people think, by asking questions of itself and its audience. These questions will be differently posed from one culture to another, from generation to generation. And different answers will be worked out, within the playing space.

References

Plays

MHLOPE, G., VANRENEN, M. and MTSHALI, T. (1990) *Have You Seen Zandile?* London, Heinemann/Methuen. The play was first produced at the Market Theatre, Johannesburg, 6 February–8 March 1986 and revived at the Market Theatre in 1987; winner of the Edinburgh Fringe First Award 1988, and performed in England as part of the London International Festival of Theatre (LIFT), 1991.

Midnight Level 6 was devised and directed by Jill Greenhalgh for The Magdalena Project, Cardiff, Wales, 1991. It was then workshopped and revised for international production. The company also took part in educational workshops and talks about the piece, and the social conditions which inspired it.

Twenty Ways to Learn a Language, devised and presented by Anna O, Oval House Theatre, London (and tour), 1994.

Other

GOODMAN, L. (1993) *Contemporary Feminist Theatres: to each her own*, London, Routledge.

Interviews with Jill Greenhalgh (Magdalena) and Anna O. in GOODMAN, L. (ed.) (1996a) *Feminist Stages: interviews with women in contemporary British theatre*, Harvard Academic Press, Gordon and Breach.

Interviews with Gcina Mhlophe in GOODMAN, L. (ed.) (1996b) 'Gender, Politics and Performance in South African Theatres Today'. Theme issue of *Contemporary Theatre Review*.

GOODMAN, L. (1996c) *Sexuality in Performance*, London, Routledge.

WALDER, D. (1992) 'South African literature today' in WALDER et al., *Post-Colonial Literatures in English: study guide*, Milton Keynes, The Open University.

This reading was specially commissioned for this book.

6 LANGUAGE PLAY IN ENGLISH

Guy Cook

6.1 INTRODUCTION

Play with language is usually studied as a feature of the discourse of children, or of literature. Yet it is also a common feature of adult discourse and we come across it regularly in unremarkable settings. This chapter considers examples of five everyday discourses in which language play is prominent: comedy, song, graffiti, newspapers and advertisements.

Earlier chapters of this book discuss the ways we use the English language to collaborate in managing the world around us; and to form and maintain extensive social networks, to carry out our social lives at home, at work and elsewhere. Yet once these aims have been achieved we do not, like machinery, fall silent; we all keep talking and writing. Even where there is no immediate task to fulfil, and where relationships are clearly and firmly established, talking and writing continue. We use language to fill up the spaces between necessary activity: for recreation, relaxation and pleasure.

There are many types of discourse, both spoken and written, in which language is employed in this way. Casual conversation is an example. Although it does serve practical purposes, there is often an element of talking for talking's sake, motivated by more complex forces.

A similar use of language can be found in literature, one of the most highly valued of all discourse types, the paradigm case of language art. As with casual conversation, it is possible partly to explain the function of literature by saying that it conveys information, or enables us to explore hypothetical situations; but these utilitarian explanations do not seem sufficient. From a practical point of view, literary language is superfluous.

Both literature and conversation can be described as space-filling discourses, ways of using English or other languages that we indulge in when there is nothing more pressing to do. Strangely, however, such discourses are very highly valued. Two challenging lines of enquiry are therefore to investigate:

- the way English is used in such discourses;
- why people enjoy and value these apparently useless uses so much.

Literary language is often described as creative. It generates imaginative fictional worlds, expresses original insights into the real world, and skilfully manipulates language to create patterns and new usages. Apparently, it is this creativity which earns it such high social status as a form of 'art'. Yet English and other languages are also used creatively in other, less exalted, more everyday discourses.

In Chapter 5, Lesley Jeffries considers what kinds of uses of English are commonly held up as representative of 'art'. In this chapter I consider some other equally creative ways of using language which are commonly excluded from this status.

There are a number of different conclusions to which this investigation may lead:

- we should widen our definition of art to include at least some instances of these more everyday discourses;
- though *like* art, these discourses are nevertheless *not* art;
- they are not even like art, but are categorically different.

Whatever the final conclusion, the investigation itself can be entertaining and informative. It can make each of us think harder about how we, as individuals, define and recognize art and what kinds of language use we identify with it.

There is one argument against the artistry of these everyday discourses, which is best tackled at the outset. This cites the worst instances of these discourses as evidence against the artistic merit of the whole. But this approach does not stand up to scrutiny; it could be used to disqualify even literary genres. My reasoning is as follows. As is made clear in Chapters 5 and 7, 'art' and 'literature' are terms of positive evaluation rather than merely mechanical criteria which can be applied without the subjective (and therefore disputable) intervention of individual judgements. The term literature is normally used to refer to poetry, novels, short stories and drama, but not every instance of these genres is necessarily literature. If we define a novel, for example, as an extended fictional narrative, many texts which fit this definition are not regarded as literary. It follows, therefore, that just as one could not bar poetry in general from being art simply by drawing attention to a few bad poems, then similarly, for other genres, it must be the best rather than the worst examples which are considered. For instance, the fact that the majority of graffiti (an interesting form of language art, which I discuss later in this chapter) are linguistically unoriginal expressions of banal or narrow-minded ideas does not exclude the possibility that there are also linguistically skilful graffiti reflecting mental agility and imagination.

6.2   ON PAGE AND STAGE: COMEDY, POETRY AND SONG

Activity 6.1   *(Allow about 30 minutes)*

Read the following transcript of a comedy monologue performed by the British comedian Victoria Wood. It is set out in lines, with the ends of lines corresponding to pauses.

Figure 6.1   Victoria Wood

> Listen, a terrible thing happened to me.
> I've got acne.
> What's going on?
> I'm 33, I've got a mortgage, I go to the Garden Centre.
> I shouldn't have acne.
> Apart from which – what with the lipstick and the wrinkles –
> There's hardly room for any.
> What are we going to get next?
> Loon pants?
> Crushes on the Men from Uncle?
> I had acne the first time round.
> I was covered in it.
> I had to take on a paper round just to pay for the Clearasil.
> There were two sorts of Clearasil – do you remember?
> There was a white sort,
> That used to take the skin off the tips of your fingers.
> Then there was the other sort,
> Which they used to call 'flesh-coloured',
> Which was for those very unfortunate people who'd been born with orange faces.

I wouldn't be an adolescent again
If you bumped my pocket money up to three and six.
You're going along quite happily – 9, 10, 11 –
Then suddenly this dial inside you clicks over from fun to grease.
Everybody in my school had really greasy hair.
It even made seal skin look 'dry and unmanageable'.
Because nobody used to wash it.
Well they washed it once a week on Friday nights.
So by Wednesday dinner time there was enough oil about to heat six radiators
and a towel rail.
And if we went swimming in the sea without our caps on, they were hosing
down seagulls with Fairy Liquid for weeks.
Nobody used to take showers after Games.
So many people had body odour
They had to make it part of the school uniform.
And Games kit – I never knew airtex was washable.
I used to have to hit my gym blouse with a hockey stick to get it to crack at the
armpits.
Oh but Games – what a nightmare.
We used to do cross-country running –
Thirty three enormous girls lumbering around the streets of Greater
Manchester.
They stopped that after we dented a viaduct.
And before any Games lesson there would be this procession of girls crawling
to the Games mistress,
Hoping to be pronounced sick enough to be let off.
It was like a sort of Lourdes in reverse.
I didn't mind swimming,
Except we shared our swimming pool with the boys next door.
And somebody told me you could get pregnant if you swam backstroke in the
same lane as a boy who'd just done the butterfly.

- How does this differ from literature, such as poetry? Is it the subject matter?
  The choice of language? The structure? Or the imagery?
- Victoria Wood is talking in the 1980s about her adolescence in Britain in the
  late 1960s. There are a number of very specific references to teenage life in
  Britain at that time: to the education system, to TV programmes (*The Man
  from Uncle*), to products like Clearasil and to well-known advertisements such
  as the one for shampoo which describes hair as 'dry and unmanageable'. This
  makes the humour much more accessible to a particular age group from a
  particular country or social background. Do you think that popular comedy
  (perhaps unlike literature) is necessarily exclusive in this way?

❖   ❖   ❖   ❖   ❖

A Martian anthropologist visiting Earth might be forgiven for confusing a poetry
reading and a stand-up comedy performance. They have many features in
common. An audience assembles to listen to an individual who stands isolated on
stage and speaks words which he or she has composed. If the performance is
successful, the audience will admire this individual's originality and way with
words, value the penetration of the observations and relate what they hear to the
personal circumstance of their own lives. Of course, there are also striking
differences. In the poetry reading the words may be declaimed rhythmically; in

the comedy act they may resemble an extended conversational turn. Reactions can be different too; appreciation at a successful poetry reading may well be reflected in sombre and serious faces, whereas for successful comedy it erupts in spontaneous laughter.

Another event with marked similarities to a poetry reading is a performance by a singer-songwriter. Here the obvious difference is that the words are sung rather than spoken, but again the similarities in both text and performance can be striking. Perhaps the greatest difference is in reception. The attitude and the composition of audiences for poetry and song are very different. In Britain today, for example, poetry audiences are often small and mostly middle-class, while those for song can be very large and socially mixed.

However, the characteristics commonly associated with poetry in some places may reflect a contemporary localized attitude rather than universal defining features. Poetry is not always serious (think of the bawdy *Canterbury Tales*), or always for the socially privileged (the Russian poet Mayakovsky read his poems through megaphones on factory floors). Nor is it necessarily isolated from music accompaniment (the ancient Greeks and medieval troubadours recited their verse to music). And poets can, in some times and places, inspire mass emotion:

> Crowds of people of all ages and professions paid homage to his memory. Women, old men, children, students, ordinary people in sheepskins and some even in rags, came to pay homage to the body of their national poet … That day I am told over twenty thousand people … passed through the church in reverent silence and deep sorrow … The whole square before the church was filled to overflowing with a huge crowd, which made a rush at the church as soon as the service was over and the gates were opened.
>
> (A contemporary account of the death of the Russian poet Pushkin in St Petersburg in 1837, quoted in Magarshack, 1967, pp. 303–5)

Activity 6.2   *(Allow 20 minutes)*

In his book *ABC of Reading* Ezra Pound ([1951] 1961, p. 61) claims that 'Music rots when it gets *too far* from dance. Poetry atrophies when it gets too far from music.' Do you agree?

How does your answer affect your evaluation of the following two poems? (The first is by the British Jamaican poet Linton Kwesi Johnson, the second (untitled) by the American poet e e cummings.) Read each one silently, and then read each one aloud.

Time Come

it soon come
it soon come
look out! look out! look out!

fruit soon ripe
fe tek wi bite,
strength soon come
fe wi fling wi mite

it soon come
it soon come
look out! look out! look out!

wi feel bad
wi look sad
wi smoke weed
an if yu eye sharp,
read di vialence inna wi eye;
wi goin smash de sky wid wi bad bad blood
look out! look out! look out!

it soon come
it soon come:
is de shadow walkin behind yu
is I stannup rite before yu
look out!

but it too late now:
I did warn yu.

when yu fling me inna prison
I did warn yu
when you kill Oluwale
I did warn yu
when yu beat Joshua Francis
I did warn yu
when yu pick pan de Panthers
I did warn yu
when yu jack me up gainst de wall
ha didnt bawl,
but I did warn yu

now yu see fire burnin in mi eye
smell badness pan mi breat
feel vialence, vialence,
burstin outta mi;
look out!
it too late now:
I did warn yu.

(Johnson, 1975, p. 25)

    I

l(a

le

af

fa

ll

s)

one

l

iness

(cummings, in Firmage (ed.), 1973, p. 673)
❖   ❖   ❖   ❖   ❖

The maxim in Ezra Pound's *ABC of Reading* suggests that the difference between poetry and song may be seen as a continuum. A feature distinguishing poem and song, however, is the widespread dissociation of a poem's value from any actual performance. Though it may be performed and interpreted in the context of a particular situation and audience reaction, a poem may also be treated as written text, preserving its identity in varying situations. In this respect, it resembles a novel or short story, which in most circumstances we read privately and to ourselves, without the intervention of an interpreting performer. This primacy of the written form is emphasized by the facts that we refer to a poetry *reading* not a poetry *speaking* and that many performers of poetry do actually hold a book in their hands and read from it, rather than relying on memory. Improvisation and adaptation, which would be praised in a comedian, might well disturb a poetry audience, for in poetry the exact wording is regarded as important, and is fixed and consequently protected by being in print.

Although a poem may build into its text certain sound effects that depend upon its being read aloud (or at least sounded in the mind's ear), as is the case with the piece by Linton Kwesi Johnson, there are also many poems deploying visual effects (such as layout, unusual punctuation or capitalization) which can only be appreciated when the poem is read rather than heard. In the poem by ee cummings the insertion of the parenthesis in midsyllable which allows the creation of a pun depends on typeface rather than handwriting ('one' and lower-case L are both represented by 1). These devices mean that the poem cannot be read aloud.

cummings's poem is an extreme example, at the far end of Ezra Pound's continuum. Yet today the perception of English poetry (at least in academic circles) has tended to move towards writing and away from speaking. More and more, the accolade 'good' poetry describes 'good' written text. If performance is added, it is regarded as an optional extra.

A 'good' comedy routine, on the other hand, is inseparable from the skill of the delivery of an individual performer. Victoria Wood, in the transcript in Activity 6.1, uses timing, laughter, intonation and posture to create humour, while her Manchester accent, appearance and clothing signal (at least within Britain) a lack of pretentiousness and help to create an atmosphere of solidarity with the audience. (It is the loss of such features which can make the written text of a comedy seem so dead.) In this respect the comedy act is closer to verbal art in an oral culture where language – without writing to freeze and decontextualize it – is inextricably involved with a particular speaker, hearer, situation and delivery.

Activity 6.3   *(Allow 5 minutes)*

The blues singer Big Bill Broonzy once gave the following introduction to a song:

> This is one that I wrote back in nineteen and um forty five I think it was – forty five yeah – I did use the word 'wrote' but I don't know whether I 'wrote' it or 'writ' it or what I done. But anyway I sings it.

As he said earlier in the same performance, he never learned to read or write. To what extent do you think this makes the songs he 'wrote' different in kind from songs which were (in a literal sense) written?

Comment

As a form of language art, 'song' falls somewhere between poetry with its fixed written texts, and an oral performance art such as stand-up comedy with its variable routines. A song may come into existence through performance and never be written down by its author (as Big Bill Broonzy reminds us). The representation of the text of a song may also be modified by the way the words are sung, or by the way they are musically accompanied.

Activity 6.4   *(Reading A)*

Read 'Songs in Singlish' by Marie Tan (Reading A). It is a linguistic analysis of the songs of Dick Lee, a contemporary Singaporean songwriter and performer who uses the varieties of English heard in Singapore to comic and satirical effect. The 'Singlish' referred to in the reading is a vernacular form of English which includes elements of other languages used in Singapore (particularly Mandarin Chinese), and SSE (Standard Singaporean English) is the variety normally used in print and formal speech in Singapore.

As you read through it, bear in mind the following questions:

- Lee's songs are in English; but does it seem that his intended audience is English speakers everywhere?

- How does Lee ensure that the Singlish elements of his lyrics are represented not only on record, but also on the printed page?

Comment

Tan notes that Lee uses features of Singlish (pronunciation and vocabulary) to represent aspects of Singapore's culture. Much of the humour of his songs appears to depend on 'insider knowledge' – not only of linguistic variation, but also of the cultural practices, images and stereotypes which are a familiar part of life in Singapore. As playful uses of English, then, Lee's songs appear to be relatively inaccessible in their full intended meaning to English speakers outside Singapore. As I mentioned earlier, comedy often does not travel well. But later in this chapter, I consider some songs which, while clearly also drawing on the language and life experience of particular ethnic groups, have transcended such local cultural boundaries.

You will also have seen that Lee is able to represent his Singlish lyrics through modified spellings – a technique used by many other writers with an interest in oral vernacular traditions, as discussed in Reading A by Rib Davis in Chapter 5.

As words can be written and music scored, a song can be abstracted from both singer and situation. It may even begin life on paper and generate many performances in many places, none more authoritative than another. Or it may fall somewhere between the two extremes. There are songs which are valued independently of singer and singing, although good performance may be needed too. These are more like poetry: texts with potential for performance. On the other hand, there are songs where singer and performance seem essential to their value (some of the songs of Elvis Presley or of the French singer Edith Piaf, for example), and the words alone can seem quite lame.

Literary art is distinguished from comparable discourses such as popular song and comedy by being seen primarily as written text, having virtues independent of its realization. Yet there is nothing intrinsic to literature which compels us to treat it in this way. This is clear in the case of drama. Although novels and short stories are written to be read silently, and poetry to be either read silently, spoken or sounded in the head, plays are written to be performed. As with comedy and song, value may arise from elements added in performance rather than something intrinsic to the text itself. There are occasions when good actors make texts that appear banal in writing seem profound or moving, in much the same way as a good singer or melody can inject mundane words with the power to move and inspire. Nevertheless, drama, strangely yoked with the novel and poetry under the single superordinate term of 'literature', is commonly treated in educational establishments primarily as written text. On the school literature syllabus, a play is a book; a trip to see a performance is an optional extra.

As the case of drama illustrates, the textual nature of literature is sometimes a convention rather than an intrinsic feature. Drama is *treated as* writing, but it does not have to be. Conversely, the words of popular songs or comedy can be treated as texts. There are books containing the texts of songs or the scripts of comedies: the lyrics of Bob Dylan, for example, or the screenplays of Woody Allen. These are read independently of their performance (though they are perhaps only appreciated by readers who have experienced the original performance and can still recall it, prompted by the written word, in their mind's ear). Equally, there are poems (like Kwesi Johnson's 'Time Come') which seem to depend on performance (whether actual, remembered or imagined) for their effect.

6.3   A SINGULAR SONG

Ezra Pound's maxim implies that there is a continuum from poetry to song. Some poems, like cummings's on loneliness, exist on the page and cannot be read; others, like Linton Kwesi Johnson's incantation, need to be declaimed in a particular rhythm. Between the two extremes are poems demanding varying proportions of dependence on writing and performance. In a similar way, there are some songs in which words seem unimportant, a mere vehicle for the human voice employed as a musical instrument. There are others which aspire to be more like written poetry, and whose words can be dissociated from both music and performance and yet still retain an intrinsic merit as text. And there are, of course, many songs which fall between these two extremes.

The advent of rock and roll in the mid 1950s initiated a major new departure for popular music, one whose influence continues worldwide to this day. The growing international appeal and influence of rock and roll (and its progeny) have a close relationship with the spread of English as a world language; one of the common vehicles for carrying English (mainly US English) into the lives of young people the world over has been the popular song. In the 1960s, in parallel to rock, there emerged in North America a kind of song which focused attention upon words, encouraging listeners to assess song as text. In some early performances, singers such as Bob Dylan and Leonard Cohen (and their many imitators) downplayed both musical accompaniment and visual presentation, thus foregrounding the potential literariness of their lyrics. Delivered by a casually dressed, static figure on stage, singing in a hoarse (and, in the view of many people, unmusical) voice with resonances somewhere between speech and song, the performance inevitably emphasized the words of the song – with the result that (even when the musical accompaniment *was* polished and intricate) the fashion of the time was to reflect upon and discuss the song as text. In addition, the growing acceptance, distribution and improvement of recordings meant that songs could use words which were not absorbed on first hearing and took on some of the permanence of writing. Records could be taken home and played in solitude, replayed when words were missed, repeated as often as desired, stacked on shelves, handled and generally treated – in many ways – like books.

Significantly, many songwriters of this period, such as Cohen, Dylan and John Lennon, published poems and fictional prose in addition to their songs.

On either side of this phase in western pop music came periods when it was performance that was foregrounded and words that were made secondary. In the 1950s limited technology and restricted media access made early rock music both intimately tied to live performance and divorced from performance as a visual spectacle. Recording techniques were not yet sophisticated enough to allow the mixing and double-tracking which would later produce recordings (such as those of the later Beatles songs) that could not be performed live. There is a parallel here to the way some poems cannot be read aloud. The record was still a relatively new phenomenon and in many ways was regarded as a substitute for presence at a live performance in which the audience would be actively involved, dancing, clapping and applauding: a relationship captured in Chuck Berry's song 'Round and Round' from the late 1950s:

> Oh it sounds so sweet
> Got to take me a chance,
> Rose out of my seat
> Just had to dance,
> Started moving my feet
> Well and clapping my hands.
> Well the joint started rocking,
> Going round and round,
> Yeah reeling and a rocking,
> What a crazy sound.
> Well they never stopped rocking
> Till the moon went down.

With this emphasis on song as sound, text could often seem unimportant, at times even dispensing with conventional language and meaning altogether, creating or stringing words together just to keep singing, as in the Little Richard song 'Tutti Frutti' which begins:

> Wo bop a loo bam a lop bam bam

Yet despite the evocation of live performance, the fan who had only the record was often starved of the visual images that went with it. Video was not yet widely available, and recording was only of sound. Neither television nor cinema were as responsive to the demands of a younger audience as they are today. Establishment disapproval and censorship, moreover, restricted access to the sight of the stars: Elvis Presley's hip gyrations and Chuck Berry's duck walk – so exciting on stage – were simply not shown on television.

From the 1970s onwards, changes and advances in technology again relegated lyrics and brought performance to the fore, although this time with an emphasis upon the visual. The growing importance of the 'pop video', often employing elaborate computerized images, and the immense investment of money and technology in ever more dazzling stage shows (also recorded and distributed on video), encouraged the presentation of songs as multifaceted mixtures of dance, film, drama, music and singing that were quite different from the raw rock and roll of the 1950s, or the minimally accompanied words of the 1960s singer-poets. Dancing again predominated, although this time it was the carefully choreographed and highly skilled dancing of performers such as Michael Jackson, Madonna and their professional ensembles, rather than that of the audience. In addition, the prevalence of the visual combined with a relaxation in censorship led to an emphasis on erotic movement and dress.

Despite their considerable differences, then, both the early rock bands and the superstar ensembles of the 1980s and 1990s share an emphasis on song as performance in which words are only part of a larger whole. In both these cases song is far removed from poetry. If we wish to examine the nature of language art in popular song, I believe it is better to examine material from one of these two performance-oriented periods, rather than from the intervening phase in which lyrics were emphasized in a highly self-conscious attempt to occupy a middle ground between poetry and song – for there we find the devices of poetry itself rather than anything distinctive to song.

Let us consider in some detail a song from the first of these periods, '(What A) Wonderful World', as recorded by Sam Cooke in the late 1950s. In a sense it belongs to the second period too, for in 1985, 30 years after its initial release, it was used in 'Bath', a television commercial for Levi 501 jeans (see Plate 9 in the colour section). This was one of two advertisements that increased annual sales of these jeans in Britain from 85,000 to 650,000 within two years. Re-released at the same time, the original recording again became a hit record. It is clearly a very popular song.

The apparently simple words and melody and the repetitive structure of the verses ensure that the song is memorable and hummable:

Don't know much about history,
Don't know much biology,
Don't know much about a science book,
Don't know much about the French 'I took';

But I do know that I love you,
And I know that if you love me too,
What a wonderful world this would be.

Don't know much about geography,
Don't know much trigonometry,
Don't know much about algebra,
Don't know what a slide rule is for;

But I do know one and one is two,
And if this one could be with you,
What a wonderful world this would be.

Now I don't claim to be an A student,
But I'm trying to be;
For maybe by being an A student baby,
I can win your love for me.

Don't know much about history,
Don't know much biology,
Don't know much about a science book,
Don't know much about the French 'I took';

But I do know that I love you,
And I know that if you love me too,
What a wonderful world this would be.

La ta ta ta ta ta history,
Mmm mm mm mm biology,
Wa wa cha cha cha cha cha science book,
Mm mm mmm mmm mmm mm French 'I took' yeah,

But I do know that I love you,
And I know that if you love me too,
What a wonderful world this would be.

This is a recording where words and music seem largely a vehicle for a gifted individual rendering. Sam Cooke's mellifluous voice is exquisite; the accompaniment and backing vocals are accomplished and suave. Released in the sound-oriented 1950s and re-released (with powerful advertising images superimposed) in the vision-oriented 1980s, this song seems the epitome of the performance-oriented recording. In such circumstances it might seem appropriate for words to be subordinated to music and performance, and not to interfere with the overall effect by being too striking. Semantically, the words of this song, because they plead sincerity over cleverness, seem ideally suited to this role. They assert the simplicity of the singer and, iconically, they seem to be simple themselves. The song is endearing precisely because it eschews the threat inherent in assertions of cleverness. The repeated structures of the verses, the clichéd declaration of love, seem to bear this out.

And yet these words, without foregrounding the fact, are far more accomplished and complex than at first appears. The lyrics depict and alternate between two different value systems: the public world of the school, where personal worth is measured by knowledge and assessed by grades (A, B, C, etc.); and the private world of love, where worth is measured by sincerity and depth of feeling. The two worlds are incompatible and in conflict. The sweetheart addressee is faced with a simple plea: I'm not successful in the world of school, but I love you, so please love me. Right at the heart of the song, however, are two devices, one metaphorical and one phonological, which bring the two separate worlds together through language play:

> Don't know much about algebra,
> Don't know what a slide rule is for;

> But I do know one and one is two,
> And if this one could be with you,
> What a wonderful world this would be.

Here, something from the world of school (1 + 1 = 2) becomes a metaphor for the world of love (lonely individual + lonely individual = happy couple), as though the singer sees images of his passion even when looking at the most passionless schoolbooks which are the cause of his failure. The equation 1 + 1 = 2 is also a common-sense fact, reliable and constant like the singer, contrasting with the dangerous sophistries of education. All in all, it is an ingenious and striking metaphorical conceit (a poetic figure of speech, often associated with metaphysical poetry, that establishes an elaborate parallel), which makes a play to win over by the very intellectual ingenuity that the singer explicitly denies he possesses. It offers a bridge between the two separate worlds, creating a harmony represented in the alliteration and consonance of the line:

> *What* a *won*der*ful* *world* this *would* be

This harmony through sound patterning continues in the four lines following the second refrain. If the singer is not an A student, perhaps he is a B student, and the sounds of these letters (/eɪ/ and /biː/) occur in stressed syllables throughout the lines:

> /eɪ/   /biː/   /eɪ/
> Now I don't claim to be an A student
>   /biː/
> But I'm trying to be
>   /eɪ//biː/   /biː/   /eɪ/   /eɪ//biː/
> For m a y be by being an A student ba by

creating an alternating pattern of these sounds:

abab ab baab

as harmonious as the metaphorical 'one and one' or the alliterative 'wonderful world', or the melody, rhyme scheme and balanced structure of the song itself.

Such analyses of pop lyrics as the one that I have just carried out are often perceived as pretentious, overdone or simply 'reading too much into it', and it may be argued (with some justification) that millions of people have listened to and enjoyed this song on many occasions without subjecting it to any structural analysis of the patterns and parallels which I have described above. It may also be argued (though without any hard evidence) that the three songwriters (Campbell, Adler and Alphert) are unlikely to have been conscious of, or to have deliberately deployed, the symmetrical and punning sound alterations or the complex and disarming 'one and one' metaphor. If this lack of awareness by both the senders and the receivers of the song is actually the case, then it seems to follow that the structures had no existence before I described them and were not therefore part of the song. This reasoning has some force, although I do not agree with it myself, but it also has two important implications which I believe cannot be avoided if it is adopted. First, if it is applied to the interpretation of songs, there is no reason why it should not also apply to the interpretation of high literature such as poetry, where stylisticians often point out intricate linguistic features of which appreciative readers, and very probably the poet too, had no conscious awareness. Secondly, if we begin with the premise that the words of this song give pleasure, and investigate why this may be, the argument against analyses such as mine has to insist that the causes of pleasure must always be conscious and that the mind can neither produce nor perceive patterns subconsciously. In the case of language this seems to be manifestly untrue, as we are all constantly producing and receiving phonologically and grammatically structured utterances without any conscious access to the rules which govern them, and it may well be that the pleasure listeners feel when hearing the words of this song – like the sense of 'rightness' that the composers may well have felt when they put words and music together – derives from the subconscious perception of exactly the kind of patterns that I have described.

You must reach your own conclusions, and they may well be different from mine, but the problem is a useful one for helping us to focus on what exactly we do believe about how language works, and why certain uses of it are experienced as beautiful and enjoyable.

Meaning in '(What A) Wonderful World' is achieved through a combination of words, music and performance. Words are less readily detached from the music than they are in the case of some 1960s songs or, more recently, in the case of 1990s rap. It is not that the words lack complexity – far from it – but they are not foregrounded: they work in conjunction with, rather than independently of, their nonverbal context, and their meanings are enriched by it. In these respects their qualities are more quintessentially song-like, and less literary, than their more 'poetic' cousins. Like advertisements, to which we turn later, they exploit the interaction of language with music. In this dependence of words on context, they have something in common with the next discourse type we analyse – graffiti. This is perhaps surprising, for as the names themselves make it tautological to observe, graffiti must be written and songs must be sung.

6.4   GRAFFITI

Write on! We are together.

(Part of a graffiti dialogue from Nigeria, analysed by Nwoye, 1993)

Activity 6.5   *(Allow about 10 minutes)*

Which of the following do you think are graffiti? What factors influence your judgement? If they are not graffiti, what kind of writing are they?

1   Who's afraid of Virginia Woolf?

2   Glory to God in the High St.

3   When a man has married a wife, he finds out whether
     Her knees and elbows are only glued together.

4   Even such is Time, which takes in trust
     Our youth, our joys, and all we have,
     And pays us but with age and dust;
     Who in the dark and silent grave,
     When we have wandered all our ways,
     Shuts up the story of our days;
     And from which earth and grave and dust,
     The Lord shall raise me up I trust.

5   Letting rip a fart –
     It doesn't make you laugh
     When you live alone.

Comment

If by graffiti we mean any illicit writing in public places on surfaces such as walls, (1) and (2) are graffiti, though (1) was borrowed by Edward Albee for the title of a play. Item (3) is a poem by William Blake. There is a tradition (not, unfortunately, supported by historical evidence) that (4) was carved with a diamond ring by Sir Walter Raleigh on the window of his cell the night before his execution; if this were true, though undoubtedly a poem, the piece would also, technically speaking, be graffiti. Item 5 is the translation of an eighteenth-century Japanese *senryu* – a kind of poem very similar to the *haiku* (Bowans, 1964).

If you were misled, this exercise illustrates two very important points. The first is that graffiti are not reliably identified as such by their language or subject matter, but rather by their physical situation and realization. The second is that their low status sometimes derives from the authors we assume to have written them. A knighted Renaissance explorer-scholar is not a prototypical graffiti writer.

Of all the discourse types considered in this chapter, graffiti have (in the English-speaking world today) the lowest status. Because they can damage and disfigure, graffiti are regarded as antisocial and illegal. Many are objectionable in subject matter, banal and clumsily expressed. Yet there is no discourse type which offers such an opportunity for the disinterested, individual voice. Here is language anonymous, unsolicited, unrewarded, uninfluenced by reactions, repercussions or payment. It is significant that Sir Walter Raleigh is supposed to have turned to this genre when he was deprived of power and privilege. While modern society denigrates graffiti, one could imagine another age in which they might be accorded extreme reverence, as the most disinterested expression of individual feeling.

Unlike comedy and song, which preserve features of an oral culture, graffiti are even more closely tied to literacy than the quintessentially written literary genres, the novel and short story. Those that use language (rather than pictures) must be written rather than spoken; they are literally space-filling as well as time-filling. Etymologically the word *graffiti* (from the Italian *graffiare*, to scratch), like the word *literature* (from the Latin *littera*, a letter), is intimately connected to the act of writing. Yet whereas, in general, writing allows the abstraction of a message from a particular situation or realization, for graffiti the place and circumstances of production are definitive. Graffiti are necessarily written illicitly on a surface in a communal or public place (bridge, bus shelter, wall, cell, school desk, toilet door) and are thus typically short, rushed, careless and handwritten rather than printed. Taken away from their situation and reproduced legitimately in print (as on the cover of Edward Albee's play), although the linguistic form and the meaning remain the same, they lose their edge and in a sense cease to be graffiti. (So one valid answer to the question in Activity 6.5 about which texts are graffiti could be 'none', as all now have moved out of that context.) This situation-bound nature explains the futility of attempts to divert graffiti away from the valued surfaces that they disfigure, to specially provided ones where they do no harm. When a pub in north London placed chalk and a blackboard headed Please write your graffiti here in one of its toilets, the only graffiti this act inspired was No I fucking wont, violently carved into the wall beside it.

From data collected in Germany and Britain, Blume (1985) concludes that the degree to which the chosen surface is enclosed or open correlates with subject matter. She observes that the most enclosed spaces (toilet cubicles) yield the highest numbers of graffiti concerning sex, and are addressed by a single individual either to no one in particular or to another single interlocutor, while the most public places (such as bridges) yield graffiti about politics or religion addressed to society in general by the (self-appointed) representative of an interest group within it. But is this always the case?

Figure 6.2
Political graffiti in Northern Ireland. The UDA (Ulster Defence Army) and the UVF (Ulster Volunteer Force) are Protestant paramilitary groups

Activity 6.6 *(Reading B)*

Read the extract from *Social Issues on Walls: graffiti in university lavatories'* by O.G. Nwoye (Reading B).

You will see that Nwoye observes that in situations where expression of political opinion is banned or may lead to persecution, it is often political graffiti which are written in the safety of enclosed spaces.

In addition to this *general* situational determination of content, there are also graffiti whose meaning depends upon a particular setting: Beanz Meanz Fartz on a toilet door; Cymru Rhydd (Free Wales) on an east-facing cliff at the Welsh–English border; Looking into darkness in a cell below the high court in Pretoria, South Africa; Jesus loves you on the wall of a London street used by prostitutes and kerb crawlers; The DPP crawled here at the other end of the same street, where a Director of Public Prosecutions, the head of the British legal service, was once cautioned by the police for 'kerb crawling' past prostitutes.

Many graffiti are the expression of a single wish, opinion or thought by a single individual, sometimes quite specific in reference. In Tracey go out with me (written on a house wall in Leeds in England), both 'Tracey' and 'me' presumably refer to individuals.

In the collections of graffiti by Rees (1980, 1981) the average length of each item is between seven and eight words. None are less than two words but few are more than eighteen words long.

It might be argued that it is *only* simplistic ideas that can be expressed in so few words. Yet, surprisingly, some of the best graffiti achieve their impact not by intensifying or enriching an individual voice, but by deploying two contradictory voices at once. Glory to God in the High St (see Activity 6.5) is a case in point. Here, through the inspired deletion of a single letter from the Christmas angels' message to the shepherds ('Glory to God in the highest', Matthew, 2.14), the writer invokes simultaneously, and thus juxtaposes, both this original text and the new one derived from it, thus satirizing the distortion of the original Christmas angels' message by the commercialism of its contemporary celebration, for 'the High St' is a current metonym for the buying and selling of goods. As in cummings's untitled poem (see Activity 6.2), this effect depends upon the message being written down, as the two texts that are simultaneously suggested in the graffiti are closer graphologically than phonologically.

graphology	**phonology**
High St	/haɪ striːt/
highest	/haɪəst/

Such extraordinary compression of meaning is rare but not unique. Write on! We are together (the line of Nigerian graffiti used as the introduction to this section) contrasts through the pun the world of public protest (where 'Right on' is a spoken expression of solidarity) and the individual written protest made by the graffiti writer who at the point of creation is not 'together' with anyone. Beanz Meanz Fartz invokes and mocks the 'voice' of advertising by distorting a well-known slogan ('Beanz Meanz Heinz'), playing further with the word play which already exists. Who's afraid of Virginia Woolf (see Activity 6.5) invokes the 'voice' from a well-known children's song, 'Who's afraid of the big bad wolf?', thus over-riding the orthographic difference between Woolf/wolf and identifying the speaker with a child and the Bloomsbury intellectual with the wolf. The DPP *crawled here* ironically exposes the contradiction inherent in the head of the legal profession being cautioned by the police, as well as the polysemy of 'crawled' (kerb crawled; indulged in masochistic sex acts; behaved in a low way; was sycophantic to the police; was humiliated).

Some graffiti are also capable of extremely rich, compressed expression. This is the case with *Looking into darkness* in the Pretoria cell. Other examples are *Neither work nor leisure* as a description of unemployment and *Mr Work and Mrs Home* as a description of the traditional nuclear family.

The generation of multiple meanings, rich connotations and associative resonances through very few words is implicitly applauded as a virtue in academic criticisms of literature by such critical movements as New Criticism and stylistics. Yet because we are encouraged and trained to perceive multiple meanings in poetry, we can often overlook them in 'lower' discourse types such as graffiti.

❖   ❖   ❖   ❖   ❖

Activity 6.7   *(Allow about 1 hour in total)*

Over the next couple of weeks, note down any graffiti which you encounter, in both open and enclosed places. Classify them by topic, place, probable sender, implied receiver, and any notable linguistic features such as dialect, misspelling, unusual grammar, etc. How many different types can you identify?

❖   ❖   ❖   ❖   ❖

The commonest evocation of two contradictory voices is created through a particular sub-genre of graffiti: additions to public notices and to other graffiti. Here the authority, sentimentality, prejudice or pomposity of a message is subverted by being incorporated as a part of a longer one, the whole of which contradicts the original. Consider the following examples. (With the exception of the Uniroyal advertisement, these graffiti are from Rees, 1980 and 1981.)

Addition to a notice:

> Warning. Passengers are requested not to cross the lines
> *It takes hours to untangle them afterwards*

Addition to a book:

> To my father and mother (dedication in law book)
> *Thanks Son, it's just what we wanted*

Additions to advertisements:

> If it [this car] were a lady, it would get its bottom pinched
> *If this lady was a car she'd run you down*

> He only knows three words of English: Boy George and Uniroyal
> *He only knows three words of English: Yankee Go and Home*
> (slogan on an advertisement for Uniroyal tyres showing a Mexican boy listening to a tape recorder in the desert next to two tyre tracks)

Additions to graffiti:

> *Are you a man?*
> *No I'm a frayed knot*

> *Ave Maria*
> *Don't mind if I do*

> *Women like simple things*
> *Like men*

The wit, inventiveness and effectiveness of such criticism through calm and controlled irony are striking.

On occasion, additions to graffiti may themselves provoke further additions, as is well demonstrated in Reading B.

❖   ❖   ❖   ❖   ❖

Activity 6.8   *(Allow about 5 minutes)*

Look back at Reading B, and read again Nwoye's example (3) of a wall writing with thirteen turns by different contributors. In what ways does it assume shared knowledge among its readers? Also note the shift between righteous, reflective, humorous and flippant voices among the contributors.

❖   ❖   ❖   ❖   ❖

Another class of graffiti combines iconic and symbolic meaning. (See the box on iconicity in Chapter 5.) In other words, they do what they say:

> Dsylexia rules KO
> I am damaging your property but you are damaging my mind
> (on a wall in Cambridge University)
> I never use to be able to finish anything but now I
> Amnesia rules er ...

or, in a twist to this, they create contradictions between what they say and what they do:

> Everybody writes on the wall but me
> (From first-century Pompeii, quoted in Rees, 1980, p. 137)

Many of the effects in graffiti are only evident in writing, creating puns by using phrases that are homophones (words that sound alike) but not homographs (words that look alike), as in 'Write on', 'Woolf' and 'frayed knot', or near homographs but not homophones, as in 'High St' and 'Ave'. This technique seems to play off the tensions between orality and literacy, and although graffiti are by definition written rather than spoken, they often seem to use writing in a way which perpetuates a rebellious oral tradition challenging the authority of the establishment by humorously and deliberately abusing the rules of writing. Whereas the writing system tends to reduce all dialects to one standard written form, graffiti often orthologically represent nonstandard forms, thus asserting by implication the viewpoint of the groups which speak them (as shown in Reading B). In this, and in many other ways, graffiti have a great deal in common with the next discourse type we examine: the tabloid newspaper.

6.5   PIN-UPS AND PUNS DOWN: THE POPULAR PRESS

Language play in newspaper headlines has become fashionable in many countries. The following, for example, are headlines from the southern Indian broadsheet newspaper the *Deccan Herald* (6 November 1994):

> SENSE AND CENSORSHIP (cinema review, p. 7)
>
> HOW CLEAN IS SOAP (television review, p. 7)
>
> A SITE FOR SORE HIGHS (article on refuse disposal, p. IV)
>
> NEGATIVE SIDE OF HIV POSITIVE (p. I)

In British tabloid journalism such punning and play are more than incidental and similar uses of language in news reporting can be found in other English-speaking countries. 'Tabloid' newspapers have a small page format, and are usually less 'serious' in their style than the larger 'broadsheet' papers. The explanation I give below of the popularity of the tabloids is a rather unconventional and controversial one.

At first sight, it may seem strange to include tabloid journalism under the heading of language art. Most attention to the tabloids, whether critical or supportive, has centred upon the information they convey and the opinions they express. On both counts their approach is striking. It is in the nature of tabloid journalism to be insular in its approach both by focusing upon national concerns and by depending upon quite narrow cultural knowledge.

Activity 6.9   *(Allow about 15 minutes)*

Choose a news report from a serious newspaper, television or radio programme. Write a tabloid headline for the story. Do you find this easy? Do you think the editor of the tabloid would continue to employ you?

In the *Sun*, Britain's most successful tabloid (and the one used in the analysis here), the majority of articles concern sex scandals, the private lives of the famous or trivial (if bizarre) events. (As a representative headline, I'VE GOT TAPES OF DIRTY DUKE BONKING ME combines all three strands.) Political opinions are strongly, briefly and simplistically expressed. One *Sun* editorial concludes, for example:

> It's a replay of Britain in the Seventies. The question then was: Who runs the country? The answer was: The unions. Thank goodness those days are over. May they never return under Labour.
>
> (*Sun*, 26 October 1993)

This uncomplicated and self-confident tone is applied not only to party political issues, but to broader social and international issues too:

> You don't have to be barmy to be a teacher. But it sure helps.
> (*Sun*, 26 March 1994)

> [B]it by bit, our sovereignty is being whittled away by the empire-builders in Brussels.
> If we're not careful, there'll soon be nothing left worth fighting for.
> (*Sun*, 21 March 1994)

It is hardly surprising that such attitudes and presentation absorb critical academic attention and that feelings run high. The tabloid approach to news, with its alleged distortion of facts (rather than creation of fiction), apparent insensitivity towards people in the news, simplification of complex issues and incessant hectoring political campaigning, seems incompatible with either popular or academic notions of art. While academic commentary often seeks to identify popular art forms with subversive or alternative culture, the tabloid press is, on many issues, manifestly conservative and mainstream. It is seen as a voice *to* the people rather than *of* the people: an institution imposed upon them, rather than an expression of their own thoughts and values.

So what is it that makes this newspaper and others like it so popular? Is it the choice of news stories? To some degree it may be so. Bizarre crimes are interesting (the fact, for example, that a farmer murdered his wife by training a bull to trample her). There is also the possibility that it is the attitude to events as much as the events themselves that appeals to so many people. However, it may be neither the news itself nor the attitude to it that exerts such a compelling attraction, but the way both news and opinion are represented in language – a representation that is remarkably similar to that in the other discourse types we are considering here, and a way that may have a distinct function of its own, related neither to the reporting of events nor to the manipulation of opinion.

Just as it is easy to conflate the viewpoint of the writer with the viewpoint of the reader, assuming that one necessarily follows from the other, so it is also easy to conflate simplicity of opinion with simplicity of expression. Commentary on the language of the tabloids often does exactly this. It is frequently asserted without much discussion that their language is 'simple'. Yet the issue of what makes language simple is itself anything but simple. We may be referring to the size and type of vocabulary, to the formal structural complexity of sentences, to the kind of background knowledge required, or to accessibility for a particular type of reader.

By formal criteria the language of the tabloids undoubtedly is 'simpler' than that of the broadsheets. In the serious British newspaper, the *Independent*, for example, lead stories are at least three times longer, with twice as many sentences per paragraph. On average, sentences are one-third longer, containing twice as many subordinate clauses; while noun phrases contain three times as many relative clauses. Yet these statistical measures – which seem to hold with remarkable consistency no matter how many lead stories from the two newspapers are compared – do not reflect some important aspects of tabloid language.

Although the size of vocabulary in the tabloids may not be large in comparison with that in the serious press, making sense of deliberately cryptic headlines demands considerable cultural knowledge and awareness of colloquial and dialect uses, together with interpretative skill. Word counts are unlikely to reveal such difficulties for they assume knowledge of a word to be a simple fact, a case of either knowing it or not, and are unlikely to do justice to assumed knowledge of specialized, connotational or metaphorical meanings. A headline such as

GEORGE: I'LL FIRE MY FLOP GUNNERS can hardly be described as simple, when it is incomprehensible even to many English speakers. (It introduces a report of how manager George Graham has warned the strikers of Arsenal football club, nicknamed the 'Gunners', to improve their goal-scoring record or risk dismissal.)

As with many poetic texts, the skilful compression of information in these headlines is witnessed by the fact that a paraphrase demands many more words than the original. Indeed one could argue that the formal simplicity and brevity of tabloid prose indicate greater rather than lesser linguistic skill, for such prose demands considerable powers of compression and is disciplined by the need to conform rigorously to house style. In many ways, it is easier to write in the style of the *Independent* than the style of the *Sun* (as Activity 6.9 was intended to reveal).

The most obvious complexity of tabloid language not reflected by statistical measures is its constant and ubiquitous punning. The following are examples from the *Sun*:

> WEDDING PREZ (President Clinton unexpectedly attends a wedding)
>
> BELLY NICE (model Naomi Campbell with bare stomach)
>
> OCTOBER SET FOR RECORD FRRREEZE (cold-weather predictions)
>
> SCRUM-TIOUS (rugby player wins cookery prize)
>
> I'M IN A PICKLE BUT I WASN'T PICKLED SAYS JUDGE PICKLES (a British judge accused of being drunk on television)
>
> BRIDE AND ZOOM (rushing bride Zouhour Zabaar, aged twenty-six, bought her wedding dress and accessories in one store minutes before marrying Ian Hedly in Brighton)

Such uses of language as these cannot be incorporated into the linear counts and comparisons referred to above, for they defy description in terms of the conventional grammar to which the serious press generally conforms. They coin words and combinations which allow a single linguistic unit to be classified simultaneously in two ways: 'Belly Nice' is a noun (belly) post-modified (unconventionally) by an adjective (nice), and it also evokes the phrase 'very nice' in which an adjective (nice) is pre-modified by an adverb (very). The key words in 'Bride and Zoom' are either two coordinated nouns or a noun and verb. 'Pickle' is both a verb and a noun.

This persistent language play is something which the tabloids share with comedy, song, graffiti, advertisements and of course literature. The broadsheets may be better news than the *Sun*, but they are not candidates for consideration as language art; conversely, the tabloids may be awful news, but it may be their playfulness with language which attracts so many millions of regular readers.

Consideration of language play in the tabloids may help us to confront some of the central issues concerning the circumstances in which language play deserves to be called language art, for the tabloid combination of linguistic inventiveness and dexterity with banal subject matter or objectionable opinion highlights the question of the degree to which clever form should serve content, and the degree to which form may even become content. Current opinion in linguistics and stylistics seems strongly to favour a view in which literary form exists only to give extra dimension to content, rather than one in which form is an end in itself (Hasan, 1989, p. 105). Thus, inspired by opposition to the political viewpoint and social stance of the tabloids, most academic attention to tabloid language has centred upon the way it can be used to manipulate opinion by weaving together fact and opinion. Where language play is noted it is treated as a minor and distracting phenomenon (Fowler, 1991, pp. 44–5).

An alternative view might regard language play as something which neither obviously entails nor is entailed by subject matter or political opinions, and might justifiably be detached from these other aspects as a separate and parallel feature of the discourse – or might even be in conflict with them. If that were the case, then the interesting question would be to find out why so many people find such disembodied play so compelling.

Language play is not evenly distributed in the *Sun*, either according to topic or to position. The paper arranges its news in a similar way every day. Though puns may occur in the one or two front-page stories, they are far less in evidence in the several short reports of serious topics (about wars, tax changes, terrorism, serious accidents) on page two. On page three, where less momentous events are described, however, punning dominates, with often the majority of features headlined with a pun. In the arrangement of editorial paragraphs on page six, the same order is followed: the serious is succeeded by the light-hearted, often marked as such by language play. It is almost as though the arrangement of topics and the shift of emphasis from language as a transparent medium to language as something self-reflexive, combined with the greater salience of right-hand over left-hand pages, serve deliberately to elevate both trivial subject matter and language play above more serious subjects and more sober language.

Activity 6.10   *(Allow about 20 minutes)*

Take a popular English-language newspaper from any country (other than the *Sun*). Is there any discernible pattern to the way that examples of language play are distributed throughout the text?

The relation between subject matter and language play is complex. Even if a degree of separation between topic and language is acknowledged, there is also clearly interplay between them. While in general there is a tendency for language play to be reserved for less consequential events and avoided in the reporting of more weighty matters, there is also a sense in which the degree of language play *creates* rather than *reflects* the levity or seriousness of the item. Thus there are grave matters which are presented with puns. I'M BLACK AND BLUE headlines a report of the alleged beating of a black policeman by Anti-Nazi League protesters. OUT WITH A BANG headlines the story of how a faulty pacemaker exploded inside a corpse during a funeral service. And the *Sun* editorial on a farmer's use of a bull to murder his wife (mentioned above) concludes with the observation 'Who said marriage was for heifers?' (a pun on 'ever'). In these cases punning indicates a refusal to become involved in the serious implications of the event, and a humorous effect may result from a sense of relief when this becomes apparent. The BLACK AND BLUE quadruple pun (blue colour of police uniform; sad) is used to make a rather cheap and self-righteous political point; it also uses the incident in a way which would probably have been avoided had the officer been white.

A similar use of punning to diminish the seriousness of the topic can be seen in the headlines from the *Deccan Herald* quoted at the opening of this section. A SITE FOR SORE HIGHS, for example, relegates the issue of waste disposal to an occasion for humour. The degree of language play, in other words, is not entailed by an aspect of any independent reality, the 'facts': puns and *double entendres* may be used to describe anything. Events in the world and the language which reports them are in this respect quite separate.

These issues are particularly well illustrated by the language accompanying one of the most famous and controversial features in the *Sun*: the 'page 3 girl', a picture of a naked or topless young woman. Regarded by many as degrading and offensive, these pictures have attracted considerable opposition, including an attempt to introduce legislation against them in 1986. The reaction of the *Sun* has been defiant (although at the time of writing it is rumoured that page 3 models are soon to be dropped – *Guardian*, 25 March 1994). Each picture is accompanied by a short paragraph of around 30–40 words, in which punning is intense, more so than anywhere else in the newspaper (or indeed in any other kind of nonliterary text that I am aware of). In the following (randomly chosen but typical) instances, for example, there is an average of one pun every six and a half words (BT and Mercury are UK telephone companies; GCSE is a secondary school examination).

> SHE'S A DIALLING
>
> Call blimey! Anna Maria, 22, had a tiff with BT and switched to Mercury. Telecom lads must be ringing their handsets in dismay. Of course, our telephone belle from Cardiff isn't totally unobtainable. They can still see her hot lines on Page 3.
> (*Sun*, 18 February 1994)
>
> CLASSY LASS
>
> Clever Debra Turpin is to sit exams at college – and she's sure to pass. The 17-year-old Liverpool lass is a re-vision in pink. GCSE for yourself!
> (*Sun*, 20 October 1993)

Opposition to the page three girls centres upon the pictures themselves rather than the captions which accompany them, and would presumably continue whether or not these captions were published. Conversely, the captions add nothing to the pictures. Any topic or picture could be used as a nominal starting point for such language. Even if the names and ages of the models are correct, the other 'information' seems to be invented or embellished (it matters little which) solely as a vehicle for the puns. Punning here is not even remotely an incidental ornamentation of something with an independent purpose (as might be argued about the 'Bride and Zoom' story above). It is an end in itself. This raises a number of very interesting questions.

❖ ❖ ❖ ❖ ❖

Activity 6.11   *(Allow about 20 minutes)*

Consider the following questions about the page 3 captions.

- Is there a relationship between the nature of the picture and the nature of the language, or is it that there is nothing to say about the picture, and language play fills up the space?

- Can picture and language be evaluated separately? Could one disapprove of the picture but enjoy the language?

- If the language carries no information, what is its purpose?

- If we were to assume a connection of some kind between the popularity of the *Sun* and the high frequency of puns, what is it that makes puns so popular?

6.6   THE SLIP OF THE PUN

All languages contain meaningless coincidences of form (Brown, 1991, p. 133), and the punning which is enabled by this is probably a feature of all cultures.

There are even cross-linguistic puns. Below are a couple of examples of these that play on the fact that Nair is a typical surname for the Malayalees (the people of Kerala in India):

What do you call a rich Malayalee?
Milaya Nair (millionaire)

What do you call a handsome Malayalee?
Debu Nair (debonair)

Bilingual speakers can play on the fact that a word in English has a similar form to (but different meaning from) a word in another language. Because there is no meaning in such coincidences, punning focuses attention away from meaning and on to form, but quite why it is so popular and so widespread deserves some investigation, which is the purpose of this section.

Most instances of word play in the tabloids are puns of one sort or another (and in the above analysis of them, as you may have noticed, I have gradually narrowed the focus of attention from word play in general down to puns in particular). Puns are a prominent feature of the other discourse types we have examined too: 'I'm a frayed knot', etc. In the contemporary science-dominated western world, punning is kept at arms' length; people frequently apologize for punning (by saying 'no pun intended') and the ritual response to puns is a groan, even when their wit is also simultaneously enjoyed or admired. Puns are regarded as childish trivia, unsuitable for serious subjects or discourses, and in a sense all puns, even good ones, are bad puns. While other forms of word play that force incongruous juxtapositions of semantically separate concepts (rhyme, alliteration, metaphor, irony) receive serious and respectful attention in literary criticism, punning is largely ignored or scathingly dismissed. In this atmosphere, it is not surprising that when puns are in the company of opinions or attitudes of which we disapprove, it is easy to link meaning and form together. Tabloids' nationalism, chauvinism and xenophobia are, in many people's opinion, integrally related to their use of language and especially the pun. The bigoted opinions seem to threaten calm intelligent debate, and the punning language which accompanies them seems to disrupt the form/meaning correlations of the language on which that debate depends. The silly 'facts' about the page three girls and the 'silly' language which delivers them seem inseparable. Opponents of the tabloids thus indulge in a double groan: both at what is said, and how. But is the association so straightforward? Let us investigate a little further.

Opposition to, if not fear of, puns has a long and respectable history. Aristotle saw them as a danger to philosophy (Ulmer, 1988); Dr Johnson regarded them as 'the fatal Cleopatra' which spoiled Shakespeare's plays (Redfern, 1984); the literary critic William Empson described them as not 'manly' (Ahl, 1988). Yet this rationalist disquiet and disapproval, the downgrading of puns to the realm of childish play, is in no way a universal or historically consistent phenomenon. The oracles of ancient Greece used puns as prophecy, and classical Roman poetry is often structurally dependent upon puns (and anagrams, which are their visual equivalent – see Ahl, 1988). In the Bible, the verse which provides the authority for the Roman Catholic belief in the apostolic succession, Christ's charge to Peter:

Thou art Peter, and upon this rock I shall build my church.

(Matthew 16:28)

is a pun in the original Greek, where the Greek name 'Petra' also means 'rock' (the pun survives in French, where both Peter and rock are *pierre*). Yet it is hardly a light or culturally unimportant utterance. Shakespeare was a dedicated punster, not only for comic but also for tragic purpose, though this is often obscured by etymological change and needs explication by glossaries and notes. An example is Hamlet's cry:

> Is thy union here?
> (*Hamlet*, v. iii. 340)

when he realizes that his mother has drunk the wine laced with a poisoned pearl (a *union*) by the man she has joined in *union* or marriage, thus bringing about her *union* with death. Here a pun compresses meanings and emotions in a powerful and poignant manner. The pearl was an established symbol for the soul, and Gertrude's life is slipping away as the pearl dissolves in the wine, just as her virtue (in Hamlet's view) was destroyed by her intoxication with her brother-in-law Claudius, who was himself addicted to wine. Although since the eighteenth century puns have often been treated by critics as slips of taste (or even of the pen), there has never been a time when the 'best' writers have avoided them. In modern(ist) times they have resurfaced with a vengeance in high literature and art, visually as well as verbally in surrealist poetry and painting, most notably in James Joyce's *Finnegan's Wake*. In the twentieth century puns have also gained respectability from their importance in psychoanalysis. Freud ([1905] 1952) saw unintentional puns as reflections of people's covert thoughts and motivations. In some cultures, puns have traditionally been given higher status (they are regarded, for example, as a navigator of thought in Zen Buddhism – see Redfern, 1984, p. 146). The pun is ubiquitous in all the discourses examined in this chapter.

Why are puns so controversial and why do they arouse such widely differing responses: of pleasure and a sense of profundity on the one hand, and of contempt and derision on the other? Why do they figure so prominently in the tabloids and in the other discourse types we have been examining? Perhaps some insight may be gained by examining particular instances more thoroughly and contrasting a modern light-hearted use of a pun with more serious uses in the past. In his excellent book *Puns*, Walter Redfern gives (without further comment) the following example of a modern punning joke:

> A man always bought his wife her favourite flowers, anemones, for her birthday. One year, he arrived at the flower shop late, and, as they had run out of anemones, he bought her some greenery. When she received the bouquet she commented: 'With fronds like these, who needs anemones?'
> (Redfern, 1984)

This is a classic punning joke, using the slightest phonemic substitution and addition to yield virtual homophony. It is also a story in which the pun is the point itself, rather than some additional embellishment or decoration. If, therefore, the reader does not like puns, or does not like this particular pun, then he or she will not like the whole story, for there is nothing else there: the pun does not emerge from a fictional world; the fictional world is constructed in order to create the pun. If we reconstruct the creation of this story, it is very likely to have proceeded backwards, beginning with the set utterance 'With friends like these, who needs enemies', proceeding to the spoof substitutions, and then creating the man, his wife and her birthday in order to lead to the conclusion. Why is her favourite flower anemones rather than tulips? Why had the flower shop run out of them? Why does it have only greenery instead of, say, daffodils? The answer to all these questions is clear: to enable the punchline to take the form it does. This illustrates both the nature of the pun and its disruptive anarchic power. For not only does the composition of the story run backwards, but the whole functioning of language is thrown into reverse. Meanings are there to create forms rather than forms to create meanings. The orthodox view in linguistics, reflecting both popular wisdom and the standard outlook of a rationalist scientist world view, is that language serves to represent the world. Within a language, signifiers ('anemones', 'friends') have an arbitrary but socially conventional and shared relationship to concepts (Saussure, [1916] 1960, p. 16), which in turn represent both the external and internal world. This enables language to perform, in a fairly orderly way, its main functions of conveying information – the **ideational function** – and the establishing of social relationships – the **interpersonal function** (Halliday, 1973, pp. 22–46).

The concepts of ideational function and interpersonal function are also discussed in Chapters 1 and 3 of this book.

The code is there to serve a purpose, not to take on a life of its own. There are, however, confusions, crossovers and coincidences within the code. Homonyms (both homographs and homophones) – the stuff of puns – are obvious instances of such crossovers, though the sense intended is usually clear from the context (see Graddol et al., 1994, Chapter 4). If it is not, clarification is made by the sender or sought by the receiver of the message, all in an orderly manner. In the story above, however, this is overturned. Confusion and meaningless coincidence are not only *not* avoided but deliberately sought out and created. Signifiers do not *represent* events and people but, through a chance association, *create* them. Rather than conveying any information about the world, language says something useless about itself. Although the story may be used interpersonally to create phatic communion when there is nothing else to say, this does not explain why a punning story should be used to do this rather than something else.

In the case of the fronds and anemones, all this may seem rather trivial. This story can be taken or left as we please; punning uses of language and more rational ones can be kept apart. Though punning may have the *potential* to overturn the rational empiricist view of language, it is not through stories such as this one. When we turn to other examples, however – Christ's words to Peter, or Hamlet's to his mother – the issue is less easily dismissed. If both the choice and the qualities of the apostle seem to emerge from a chance and apparently meaningless coincidence; and if the themes and images of what is considered to be one of the greatest works of English literature can be so focused in four words, then puns seem to be of quite a different order: the most extreme instance (and therefore the least tolerated) of language which creates reality rather than only reflecting it. Regarded in this light, puns can appear as the remnant of a different cosmology in which language not only creates new realities but does so in a random, uncontrollable, dreamlike and magical manner. In punning, we allow language itself to take charge and to guide our thoughts. These weighty considerations may seem a long way from the 'telephone belle' and 're-vision in pink' in the *Sun*, but they may help us to reach conclusions about the function of language play. The situation is by no means as clear as it may seem at first, and there may be no simple conclusion to be reached. A number of points, however, can be made. They lead in two opposite directions, and whether one or both may be true is for each reader to decide. First, the potential of puns to derail the socially sanctioned uses and nature of language may account for the atmosphere of unruliness, disrespect and boisterous insolence which they seem to create. In most contemporary English-speaking societies, puns are more often the expression of insubordination by the less powerful (naughty children, football fans, graffiti writers) than a feature of the declarations of oracles, gods, God or dying princes. Tabloid newspapers and graffiti writers certainly seem to take advantage of this effect, by using puns to taunt and disparage those they oppose, though avoiding (as schoolchildren might do) direct confrontation or rational argument in which they might lose.

We have looked at language in four disparate space-filling discourses and discovered in all of them a disposition to use language in original and playful ways. The code is exploited to expose contradictions, create multiple meanings and generate unconventional messages. Yet there are also important differences. Song, comedy and news have clearly prescribed slots in society and are kept very much under control. Although song and comedy as a whole are universally popular, songs and comedians in particular are sought out by particular audiences. Similarly, the tabloid press, though thrusting itself forward at the newsstand, is bought and read by choice. The fact that these discourses are commodities is important. We have to pay for comedy, song and news; and what we don't choose to pay for, we don't get. Graffiti of course are different. They turn up uninvited all over the place, and they are free. But for this they are despised, and also removed.

6.7   ADVERTISEMENTS

'Your fish is our command'
(sign in a London fish shop)

Our fifth and last discourse type – advertisement – is different again: uninvited, ubiquitous, often intrusive, but, unlike graffiti, quite legal. Advertisements appear in almost all inhabited environments. They line our streets, arrive in our post, wait for us at work, punctuate our newspapers, interrupt our television programmes. If the term 'advertisement' is interpreted broadly to include logo brand names on products, then advertisements are also on almost every object we use. We are hardly ever out of sight of an advertising text.

Such dominance and prominence are hardly surprising in a world market economy which believes that advertisements sell goods. Expenditure on advertising is astronomic and the care and craft expended on its production are correspondingly distinguished. Given that most advertisements have a very specific purpose – to sell goods or promote services or social behaviour – it seems strange, on reflection, that it is perhaps the discourse type with the most prominent use of language play in contemporary society. Perhaps, like the uninvited guest who wins us over with a joke, they are making amends for their intrusiveness?

Walter Redfern points to the frequent use of puns in advertising:

> Advertising is all about association: associating a particular product with a particular firm and with an idea of quality; and so word and thought associations (echoes, jingles, puns) obviously come into useful play. There is a kind of situational punning in many adverts which forces distinct things together, e.g. the one for White Horse Whisky. There is no inevitable link between horses and whisky, but the slogan establishes one, to punch home by baroque juxtaposition the message 'You can take a white horse anywhere.'
> (Redfern, 1984, p. 13)

Advertisements do not only make extensive use of puns. They also use language in other markedly literary ways to create rhymes, rhythms, sound effects, parallelisms, metaphors, neologisms, intertextual echoes, emotive resonances and entire fictional worlds. Advertisements manipulate all levels of language, from pronunciation and letter shapes through morphology and grammar to discourse structure, combining the levels both in dynamic interaction with each other, and with music, photographs, cartoon and film.

It is surprisingly hard to define advertisements, but perhaps two fairly constant features are their brevity and their dependence upon other discourse types or activities. They occupy either a short time or a limited space. Television commercials generally last for less than one minute and often only 20 or 30 seconds; print advertisements rarely occupy more than the equivalent of a single page. (Roadside hoardings are very large but limited to a single rectangle nevertheless.) As with graffiti and the tabloid headlines, limited space and competition for reluctant attention have encouraged skills in linguistic compression, allowing the simultaneous rendering of more than one voice, more than one meaning. Yet despite this focus on text, advertisements are also performances. Their impact does not reside in the abstracted words (as it might with a poem) but is integrally related to the physical realization of those words and to the situation in which they occur. Most advertising language carries its context of situation around with it in the form of pictures, and needs to be interpreted in interaction with this context. Even in advertisements which appear to be purely verbal (let us say a printed advertisement with no pictures) it is very often the shape and colour and positioning of letters which matter, rather than the abstract linguistic structures to which these letters give rise. Such advertisements (unlike most poems) would not survive being scribbled on to a piece of paper.

In this dependence on physical realization, advertisements have something in common with graffiti (where surface and writing implement are part of the meaning) and with tabloid headlines (where typeface, size and position 'shout out' the message just as much as the linguistic choices). Yet the range of meaningful choices open to advertisements are infinitely more sophisticated and varied (Cook, 1992, pp. 23–97). Like graffiti and headlines, advertisements often depend upon linguistic effects which are only perceptible in writing, yet like song and comedy they also maintain characteristics of an oral tradition at variance with the dominant establishment emphasis on literacy and text. This is not only because of the alliance of language with performance, pictures and music. There are many other factors creating this atmosphere of orality too. Advertisements have some of the ephemerality of speech, as most individual advertisements are exposed for only short periods of time before being replaced. Together with songs, prayers and children's rhymes, they are one of a small but potent class of 'oral texts' which are repeated verbatim over and over again (although of course by using recording rather than actual repetition). Another feature which they share with orality is the low esteem in which they are held. The reasons for this may be partly in the nature of advertisements themselves, but factors that contribute to this at least may also be a puritanical objection to the idolization of material objects and possessions, and a degree of snobbery about 'trade'. There is something strangely contradictory in the simultaneous elevation and repudiation of advertisements. This would no doubt be immediately apparent to the Martian anthropologist whom, as you may remember from section 6.2, I imagined attending a comedy performance and a poetry reading. He or she (or it) might well assume that advertisements are the highest status and most valued artistic discourse types of the modern world. I suspect that future archaeologists will agree.

As advertisements strive to succeed by differing from each other – and only succeed in so far as they *are* different – no successful advertisement can be, by definition, typical. An analysis of a television ad for P&O Scottish Ferries, however (shown as still pictures in Plate 10 in the colour section) helps to draw attention to the ways in which advertisements make use of language. Even by advertising

The fourth book in this series, *Redesigning English: new texts, new identities* (Goodman and Graddol (eds), 1996), discusses further these aspects of printed texts.

standards, this advertisement is extremely brief, both in time (20 seconds) and in its number of words (ten). The text is as follows:

>Lorries go
>Drills go
>Lambs go
>Caterpillars go
>Cargo
>P&O

Each line is spoken over an animated image, the pictures being composed of the letters of the word. And each moving image is accompanied by the sound of the thing in question (a lorry revving, a drill drilling, a lamb bleating, a caterpillar bulldozing, a ship's siren blaring). The words are spoken in a Scottish accent.

Advertisements often exploit or make use of existing discourse types. There are many which are stories, jokes, cartoons, even soap operas. In this case, the discourse of a toddler's book is evoked by the nature of the pictures, the subject matter of animals and vehicles and the short grammatically simple sentences. This generic context, combined with the noise of the vehicles, gives the verb *go* a very particular and limited sense which is more or less confined to language directed to small children, where *go* means 'to make a noise' (as in the sentence 'Cows go moooo'). The four grammatically parallel sentences (each one is noun + verb) set up both a pattern and an expectation. They also phonologically echo each other (by ending with /go/). All this makes the fifth line – *Cargo* – stand out (in formalist poetic terms it is foregrounded). First, it is a single noun rather than a noun + verb sentence; secondly it is neither an animal nor a vehicle. Yet, given the expectations set up in the lines before, the fact that the first syllable is *car* and the second *go* is likely to make us attempt to process it as a deviant version of the sentence 'Cars go'. (The lack of agreement between noun and verb is itself reminiscent of child grammar.) Only with the last line – another noun – and with the realization that the advertisement is for P&O ferries can we retrospectively make sense of the whole, by re-reading and this time interpreting *go* to mean 'travel by'. Thus, through a manipulation of all the levels of language working in concert, the advertisement is a puzzle to be solved, a language game. The fact that a viewer is likely to see an advertisement many times makes second and subsequent viewings very different from the first.

Activity 6.12   *(Allow about 40 minutes)*

Choose two or three advertisements in which you find the language or overall effect interesting. Consider how these make use of:

- speech and writing (and for television advertisements, combinations of the two);

- the use of particular letter shapes, sizes and arrangements; and (on television) voice features (consider such factors as the age, sex and accent of the speaker(s) and the mood and speed of their words);

- the ways in which the effect or meaning of the language is altered by combination with pictures and (on television) music;

- any 'poetic' uses of sound such as rhyme, rhythm, alliteration;

- any neologisms or conversions of grammatical word class;

6   uses of individual words in an unusual, metaphorical or emotive sense;

7   grammatical patterning or deviation from conventional (Standard) English grammar;

8   switching from English to any other language;

9   assumed knowledge of any other advertisement or kind of advertisement, or reference to an instance of another discourse type such as a film;

10   adoption of another generic form (as the P&O advertisement imitates a children's book).

One of the main outcomes of Activity 6.12 may have been to raise your awareness of how complex many advertisements are. Why are advertisements like they are, and why do they share so many features with art – both verbal and nonverbal – and with space-filling discourses such as song, comedy and graffiti? I should like to suggest some answers to these questions. You may well disagree, but the ideas may nevertheless give pause for reflection and, if not accepted, at least provoke alternative hypotheses.

Clearly both the manufacturers who finance advertisements and the agencies which create them wish to attract our attention, impress the existence of their product upon us and associate it in our minds with something positive and pleasurable. They are driven therefore by consumer response (our fish is their command). A good advertisement is what its recipients like, not what the sender wants the recipient to like. In the early days of television advertising, advertisers adopted the technique of the hard sell: constant repetition, pronouncements by authoritative figures, attempts at deception and appeals to selfish emotion over intellect (suggestions that certain products would make people more successful, sexy or appreciated). The use of language was correspondingly brutal. But in some parts of the English-speaking world, at least, the hard sell has been replaced in all but small-budget advertisements. The contemporary advertisement on British television, for example, spends little time telling us what the product is or giving us (even spurious) information about it. This frees the space of the advertisement – small or short as it may be – to be filled with whatever seems to please people most. Driven by a large and heavily financed brigade of psychological researchers, constantly monitoring audience responses, the advertising industry has increasingly filled this space with what it perceives people to enjoy: play with the codes of communication themselves. Play with language is something which people need, value and – perhaps most importantly of all – find pleasurable. This perhaps explains the strange fact that graffiti, the least financially or economically motivated discourse, have much in common with advertisements, the most heavily financed. In a materialist, puritanical and conformist society we tend to denigrate play to the status of an activity for children, or for times when we have 'nothing better to do'. Yet its constant appearance in very different discourse types suggests a more important role. We depend upon language for everything that we know about the world and society, for our relationship, and for our sense of individual identity. Not only does play with language demonstrate that it is *within* our control, but it is also a celebration of an infinite potential and unexpected creative power which, though *beyond* our control, is also the key to change and freedom *from* control.

6.8   CONCLUSION

This chapter has analysed examples of five common types of discourse in order to describe the nature of language play in English and to speculate about reasons for its popularity and prevalence. We have looked at examples of comedy, song, graffiti, tabloid journalism and advertisements.

It has been suggested that, despite their obvious differences of form, function, prestige and social origin, the five discourse types here have a lot in common. In particular I have claimed that they are all characterized by language play as an end in itself and by their dependence on performance, context and physical realization. Moreover, in the techniques employed by their creators as well as some of the functions they perform, these kinds of discourse have much in common with other kinds of language 'art' (as discussed in Chapter 5). I set out on page 198 some possible conclusions one can draw about the relationship between commonly recognized forms of language and the kinds of language play that I have considered here. My own conclusion is that maintaining a strong distinction between the forms of 'art' and 'play' is inappropriate and unnecessary. What is more, representations of language play I have discussed and illustrated preserve aspects of our relationship with language which are often disparaged in the modern world, with its emphasis on language as the repository of facts.

Reading A
SONGS IN SINGLISH

Marie Tan

Introduction

Dick Lee is one of Singapore's best-known singer-songwriters. As the 'creator of Singlish pop' he started the trend of writing and singing songs with a distinctive Singaporean flavour. See Plate 7 in the colour section for a picture of him.) Dick Lee claims that his music is unique because he has injected the Singapore element into his songs. This injection, I suggest, is achieved by:

1   references to Singaporean life – the national symbols, the places, the historical figures, the food, etc. which reveal what it means to be a Singaporean;

2   the use of Singlish, with its own syntax and lexicon – reflecting how English in Singapore has developed into a unique variety;

3   the use of several languages (Chinese dialects, Malay, Tamil, etc.) – which reflects the multilingual nature of Singapore and also the way Singaporeans codeswitch.

I will briefly describe some linguistic features of Lee's songs, with reference to three aspects of Singapore's cultural life – Indian movies, eating and shopping – and to the way in which the phonology of Singapore English is used.

Indian movies

References to Indian movies in relation to the Singapore element may seem an oddity. On the contrary, they bring back memories of a favourite pastime of many Singaporeans – watching Indian films and laughing at the exaggerated love scenes, in which the male and female leads sing love songs to each other while chasing each other around trees. These memories are evoked in two songs, 'Mustapha' and 'Chin Chin Choo', in which Indian love scenes are 'acted' out by Dick Lee and Jacintha, another Singaporean singer. The chasing scenes are alluded to in the following verses:

> J   But to take a sip,
>   you have to catch me first.
> D   I am going to be catching you,
>   you little curry puff.

Both singers even sing in a strong Indian-accented English, emphasizing especially the Indian English stereotype of realizing /w/ as [ʋ] – for example, in the line 'what's the time, what's up, what's news?' Like many kinds of language play, this humour depends heavily on shared experience. The references to Indian movies are only hilarious if listeners have shared in the experience which Dick Lee wants to evoke.

Singaporean likes: eating and shopping

Eating – the pastime Singaporeans indulge in with consummate passion – has a special place in Dick Lee's songs, appearing in at least three songs, including

'Fried Rice Paradise', 'Rasa Sayang' and 'Mustapha'. A list of the food items mentioned includes prata, mee pok, satay, nasi goreng, kway teow, sambal belachan, papadam and putu mayam. Another favourite Singaporean pastime, shopping, is also mentioned. The two main passions of Singaporeans are captured most succinctly in these two lines from 'Rasa Sayang':

> We can eat, eat, eat till we nearly drop
> Then we all get up and we shop, shop, shop.

A number of lexical items have developed new meanings in Singapore English. Occurrences of such lexical items include 'hawker centre'. As used in Singaporean Standard English (SSE), this means 'an area set aside for cooked food stalls'. Its meaning has developed from the general English meaning of 'hawker' as 'an itinerant salesman' (Platt and Weber, 1980, p. 88).

Use of nonstandard spelling

Another interesting feature of Lee's songs is the (nonstandard) pronunciation of Singapore English speakers in the spelling of words, as represented in the lyrics printed on the covers of his recordings. Features such as consonant cluster simplification, palatalization and the realization of /θ / as [t] are exemplified below. (SSE translations of Singlish are given in square brackets, and the particular songs referred to in round brackets.)

Palatalization

> For example: 'Can I *hepchew*?' [Can I help you?]
> ('Say Lah!')

[T] substituted for /θ /

> For example: '*Tingwat*?' [What do you think?]
> ('Say Lah!')

Consonant cluster simplification

> For example: 'Oi, why you all *dowan* to say?' [*dowan* = don't want]
> ('Rasa Sayang')

> For example: '*Wen*, lah – must let off steam, what!' [*wen* = won't]
> ('Rasa Sayang')

These spellings thus represent stereotypical features of pronunciations commonly heard in Singapore. They are considered by Lee to be part of Singlish (he refers to them as Singlish features in 'Say Lah!').

The examples I have presented show how, in what seems to be a self-conscious, playful use of features of Singaporean English that have strong cultural connotations, Dick Lee is successfully able to represent aspects of Singaporean life in ways that are – to his intended audience – both immediately recognizable and hilarious.

References

PLATT, J.T. and WEBER, H. (1980) *English in Singapore and Malaysia: status, features, functions*, Kuala Lumpur, Oxford University Press.

(This reading is a revised and abridged version of TAN, M. (1992/3) 'Language play in Dick Lee's songs – the Singapore element', unpublished BA (Hons) thesis, Department of English Language and Literature, National University of Singapore.)

Reading B
EXTRACT FROM *SOCIAL ISSUES ON WALLS: GRAFFITI IN UNIVERSITY LAVATORIES*

O.G. Nwoye

Wall writings were used early in human history to record and preserve the activities of humankind. The invention of writing, and later printing, led to more permanent methods of such record-keeping. Apart from advertising and other such purposes, wall writing is no longer a recognized method of preserving records by mainstream society. Nevertheless, groups prohibited from, or denied, avenues of public expression seek other outlets, with graffiti on walls of public places as a favoured option. One such group is the student population in most parts of the world. In particular, Nigerian university students have been seen as agents of destabilization by successive governments in Nigeria. Within the individual universities, they are not involved in decision-making in matters that affect their academic and social life as students. Nationally, they are not allowed to contribute to discussions of socio-economic and political issues. Even where campus newspapers exist, they are often subject to censorship by university authorities. A few daring publications run by individual students and organizations are proscribed as soon as they run foul of the authorities by publishing what are considered to be inciting or inflammatory articles. The young, in their impatient idealism, see most leaders as inept, uncaring and therefore unconcerned with their well-being. In Third World countries in particular, students can constitute the most articulate opposition to bad governments and oppressive regimes. They are often, if not always, on collision courses with established authorities both within and outside their campuses. Denied the means of expressing their views on matters they feel they should be involved in, they resort to graffiti, and on college campuses all over the world, lavatory walls and other public places are used extensively for this purpose …

At the University of Benin, the walls of the lavatories in the faculty buildings, as well as other semi-public places like walls of stairways, are covered with graffiti. Chalkboards are also used for this purpose, but these lack the relative permanence of the lavatory walls. Graffiti thrive in lavatories because they afford the 'authors' relative privacy in which to express their views without fear. Second, the lavatory walls have not been painted over since 1980 when the faculty building was erected. It is therefore possible, given limitations of space, to record 'dialogues' that run for a long time. 'Authors' do compete for the available space, and often wipe out previous 'dialogues' to create space for new ones.

The materials for this paper were collected and transcribed between July and September 1991 from men's lavatories in faculty buildings at the main campus of the University of Benin, Benin City, Nigeria ...

Analysis

The subject matter of the graffiti can be divided into the following broad topics: politics, socio-economic issues and others. Politics (national and international) accounts for 113 graffiti or 48.09 percent and socio-economic issues for 81 or 34.47 percent. National political issues are those directly related to the internal affairs of the country and its governance, while international political issues deal with global matters in which Nigeria may or may not be directly involved. Of the political issues, some of the graffiti show evidence of being out-dated, since their topics were no longer relevant, or had been overtaken by events. One such topic is 'Free Mandela' (Mandela was released from prison in 1989).

The following extract was obtained from the walls of a lavatory in the Social Sciences building:

(1) (a) – Free Mandela

(b) – Jail De Klerk

(c) – and Buthelezi, his stooge.

These graffiti must have been written some time before Mandela was released from prison, but since the lavatory walls have not been painted since the building was completed in 1980, this text remained *in situ*. It is interesting to note that this piece has survived frequent erasures by other writers seeking space for initiating new topics.

Related to the Mandela issue is the following, which appeared almost next to it:

(2) (a) If Winnie is jailed ...

(b) – Soweto will burn again.

(c) – De Klerk will die.

The above graffiti (1) are representative of the many others on the same topics and are characterized by the terse nature of the contributions. The style of these graffiti is that of the 'banner-headline' as used in newspapers. Coherence is achieved by linkages. The 'jail' in 'Jail De Klerk' thus makes for cohesion between the first 'turn' and the subsequent ones, particularly when it is appropriated and used in the third 'turn' (c), thus dispensing with its repetition. The *and* in (c) functions as an additive marker of cohesive relationship (Halliday and Hasan, 1976, p. 234) between (c) and the two previous moves. Such a rhetorical device contributes to the terseness and brevity of the graffiti. In (2), the first 'turn' opens with a hypothetical statement, marked syntactically by a preposed *if* clause and is followed by consequences (b) and (c). The conditional, *if*, is thus used to express 'a dependency between two hypothetical events' (Schiffrin, 1992, p. 165). The listing of the consequences was stated (Brown and Yule, 1983, p. 133) in the opening contribution by the incompleteness of the remark marked by the ellipsis. These seem to invite the subsequent contributors to supply the possible consequences of the predicted event. The terseness of the contributions gives the graffiti a poetic feature. It is tempting to suggest that the brevity of the contributions was triggered by the initiating contribution. Contributors seem to take a cue from what they are responding or contributing to ...

In (3) below, a long initiating contribution elicits long responses.

(3) (a) OAU should form an African High Command for the liberation of South Africa.

    (b) – Fool, that country is called AZANIA.

    (c) – Who will lead the High Command, IBB?

    (d) – No, he can't even shoot.

    (e) – Does he fire blanks?

    (f) – Be serious! Let's chase all whites out of Azania.

    (g) – I suggest all students from next semester should volunteer to fight the Apartheid regime in SA.

    (h) – Good suggestion, but I suggest it should take effect after I have graduated.

    (i) – Not me o, SA has atomic bomb!

    (j) – Coward.

    (k) – No, he is a traitor.

    (l) – He should be shipped to SA, where he will use Blacks only loo.

    (m) – Not funny.

OAU = Organization of African Unity

The above graffiti covered a large space on the wall of a lavatory. Unlike (1) and (2) above, the structure is characterized by a long initiating contribution and fairly long responses. The structure of the initiating contribution which invited a 'dialogue' was responsible for eliciting the type of contributions that followed … By opening the extract with a proposition (a), the writer has invited a discussion of that proposition. The rhetorical device used in turns (c) and (e) is a question–answer format. The play on the words 'shoot' and 'fire' moves the discussion from serious and formal to non-serious and informal and therefore merited the call for a return to the seriousness which the subject matter demanded. The call for a return to seriousness after the comic relief introduced by the sexual allusions (d) and (e) serves as an overt indicator of 'return-to-topic' (Yule and Mathis, 1992, p. 208) and resembles such spoken, face-to-face discourse strategies as, 'seriously speaking', 'and so, anyway'. There is, however, no shift from standard English to non-standard to correspond with the shift in seriousness as one would expect. Supportive discourse strategy is present in 'turn' (h) (Good suggestion), even though the contributor made a suggestion that differed slightly from that of the previous contributor. A style shift, from standard to non-standard Nigerian English, occurred in 'turn' (i) (Not me o, …), marking the first of such style shifts. Repetition as 'a strategy toward the pragmatic goal of persuasion' (Johnstone, 1983, cited in Rains, 1992, p. 253) is employed here to give support to a proposition. Thus a suggestion (g) that students volunteer to fight in South Africa is taken up (h) and the words 'suggest' and 'suggestion' used twice in one move. This creates the effect of reinforcing the suggestion and advancing the proposal in (a).

Apart from the first response, which sought to correct the first contributor's use of the name South Africa instead of the unofficial Azania, all other contributions advanced the discussion in some way. There was, therefore, a steady progression in the development of the argument. Both the scepticism about the OAU chairman's ability to lead the High Command (c) and the sexual response (e) are evidence of the type of regard in which he is held by the students, and evidence of the not too cordial relationship between the two. The use of the word 'loo' [in (l)] for lavatory or toilet is strange and unusual, since the word is rare in students' repertoire. Abbreviations (SA for South Africa) are common. Their frequency in graffiti may be explained by the need to economize space and because they are a response to previous usages. It seems to be the case that if an item has been referred to in an abbreviated form by a previous contributor, subsequent contributors tend to adopt and use that form. The use of 'coward' (j) which a later contributor changed to 'traitor' (k) is significant in the context of students' politics. Those two lexical items are synonymous for many students in a restricted area of usage. During student demonstrations and strikes, lecture boycotts are frequent, and those students who do not take active part are labelled cowards because they are afraid of the results of physical confrontations with the police and the Army, who are invariably brought in to quell the 'riots', as these demonstrations are labelled by university authorities and government. The students who fail to take part in these activities are also perceived as traitors to the cause of student unionism and the fight against social injustice. ...

Not all the graffiti on these walls deal with political and socio-economic matters. We expected to find, and found, those that were concerned with the more mundane issues of student interpersonal relationships, comments on academic courses and professors. The graffiti on students' interpersonal relationships were romantic in nature, most of them sexual in tone. Some were declarations of love for some female, most probably a student, as in the following:

(12) (a) Uche loves Ngozi

(b) – Does she love you?

(c) – Love is dead.

The initiating contribution has a heart drawn around each of the names. The use of this additional pictorial device is aimed at enhancing the romantic nature of the message, hearts being icons universally recognized and associated with love. In some other graffiti of the same subject matter, two hearts with names written inside them sufficed as the entire communication. Such personal declarations of love were not expected to attract rejoinders, but many of them did, as the extract above indicates. The rejoinders were often found to be contradictions of the stated propositions or some other propositions denying the content of the first, such as the declaration that love is dead. If love is dead, then nobody can claim to be in love.

Very uncomplimentary remarks on courses and their teachers were also made, and opposing viewpoints expressed.

(13) (a) SAA 324 is a joke, the guy has no stuff.

(b) – A hint for an A – memorize his notes.

(c) – You are the problem, not the Prof.

(d) – If you don't buy his handouts, you qualify for an F.

(e) – He just copies textbooks.

(f) – Where do you want him to get it from, from his garden?

(g) – From his empty head [followed by a drawing of an oversized head].

In the extract above we find a discourse feature, mutual support and encouragement, in the hint given by a contributor on how to make an A in the course ... Cole (1991, p. 405) found such mutual support devices in her study of women's graffiti in an American university campus. She attributes them to politeness features said to characterize women's discourse. It might be that mutual support is a feature of all groups which perceive themselves as minorities and which are in need of mutual bonding for protection from perceived oppressive groups. The student body fits into such a group, bound in solidarity against an 'oppressive' group (university administration, lecturers), who, they argue, have forgotten all they ever learnt, and are busy producing handouts for sale to their students, who are bound to buy them to prevent getting failing grades. Such a view of lectures is very widespread and, given the relative lack of freedom to articulate them openly, graffiti become a ready avenue for so doing. ...

The use of graphics (drawing), for emphasis and effect is another rhetorical device employed here. The picture of an oversized head said to be empty does much to reinforce the intended message that the lecturer under reference has nothing in his head.

One significant feature of the language of this graffiti item is Americanization. The use of such lexical items as 'guy' and 'stuff' is a strong feature of Nigerian English as used by undergraduates and high school students. Although British standard is taught in schools and some teachers rate American English negatively and tend to discourage its use in both speech and writing, it is the preferred [variety] for these classes of Nigerians.

Conclusion

The samples of graffiti analysed show that graffiti, far from being mere vandalism, as many people like to regard them, are, in fact, expressive modes adopted by subgroups that have been denied other avenues of self-expression.

References

BROWN, G. AND YULE, G. (1983) *Discourse Analysis*, Cambridge, Cambridge University Press.

COLE, C.M. (1991) 'Oh wise women of the stalls...', *Discourse and Society*, vol. 2, no. 4, pp. 401–10

HALLIDAY, M.A.K. and HASAN, R. (1976) *Cohesion in English*, Harlow, Longman.

JOHNSTONE, B. (1983) 'Presentation as proof: the language of Arabic rhetoric', *Anthropological Linguistics*, 25, pp. 47–60.

RAINS, C. (1992) '"You die for life"': on the use of poetic devices in argumentation', *Language in Society*, vol. 21, pp. 253–76.

SCHIFFRIN, D. (1992) 'Conditionals as topics in discourse', *Linguistics*, vol. 30, pp. 165–97.

YULE, G. and MATHIS, T. (1992) 'The role of staging and constructed dialogue in establishing a speaker's topic', *Linguistics*, vol. 30, pp. 199–215.

Source: Nwoye, 1993, pp. 419–42

7 AN ENGLISH CANON?

Janet Maybin

7.1 INTRODUCTION: WHAT IS A CANON?

Throughout history the process of creating a **canon** – the identification of a body of indispensable and authoritative writings – has been a central part of cultural and intellectual life in the English-speaking world. In the field of English studies, a 'great tradition' of English literature has emerged during the twentieth century, and until recently seemed well established. The canon can either mean a broad literary intellectual heritage, including a wide range of fact and fiction (reflecting the older, broader meaning of the term 'literature' as 'learned writing'), or can focus more narrowly on the poetry, fiction and drama which currently constitute the main **genres** within English literature. For instance, most university courses in English studies today include works by Chaucer; poetry by Spenser and Milton; plays by Shakespeare; a selection from romantic poets such as Wordsworth and Keats; nineteenth-century novels such as those by Thomas Hardy, Charles Dickens, George Eliot and Jane Austen; and the works of twentieth-century poets and novelists like T.S. Eliot and D.H. Lawrence. For many, this collection of texts represents the highest existing form of English literary art.

Activity 7.1   *(Allow about 10 minutes)*

Make a list of ten works of literature which you would include in the English literature canon. What are the reasons for your choices? How does your choice compare with the following lists?

- When asked by *The Times* newspaper for a 'list of essential reading for an educated person', the British novelist Kingsley Amis suggested the following:

    The poems of Edmund Spenser
    The works of John Milton
    The works of John Dryden, including his [translation of] Virgil's work
    The works of Samuel Johnson
    The poems of William Wordsworth
    The poems and letters of John Keats
    The poems of Alfred, Lord Tennyson
    The novels of Charles Dickens
    The novels of George Eliot
    The works of T.S. Eliot

    (*The Times Higher Education Supplement*, 24 January 1992, p. 17)

- The writer and television presenter, Melvyn Bragg, believes that English literature in British schools should include study of:

    William Shakespeare: *King Lear*
    Thomas Hardy: *Jude the Obscure*
    Jane Austen: *Pride and Prejudice*
    Charles Dickens: *Great Expectations*
    William Golding: *Lord of the Flies*
    D.H. Lawrence: *Sons and Lovers*

Evelyn Waugh: *Decline and Fall*
William Wordsworth: *The Prelude*
Henry Fielding: *Tom Jones*
George Orwell: *Animal Farm*
(*The Times Education Supplement,* 18 September 1992, p.15)

• For the purposes of this chapter, we asked a similar question of S.K. Verma, Vice-Chancellor of the Central Institute of English and Foreign Languages in Hyderabad, India. He supplied the following list of the ten most frequently studied writers of literature in English at school and university level in India, based on the analysis of a number of official documents:

Ernest Hemingway
Robert Frost
William Shakespeare
John Keats
Emily Brontë
Thomas Hardy
T.S. Eliot
E.M. Forster
Raja Rao
R.K. Narayan

❖   ❖   ❖   ❖   ❖

Why is the canon so important? It is obviously the backbone of English literature, but its significance extends far beyond the field of literature studies to language generally, and to ideas about culture and national identity. Canonical texts have always been important for definitions of what counts as **Standard English**. For instance, when Samuel Johnson was compiling his first English dictionary in the eighteenth century, he based it on books which he believed illustrated authoritative uses and meanings in the language. And histories of English languages in the nineteenth century focused not on spoken language, but on what were believed to be the most important written works. Currently, debates about canons are closely tied up with arguments about Standard English and the role of English in relation to other languages.

The traditional canon has also been associated with 'Englishness' and nationality. Shakespeare, the national bard, is as much of a British cultural symbol as the Union flag, or tea at four o'clock. The canon thus acts as an authority for both language and cultural identity: indeed the word itself carries connotations of rule-making and authorization, with its derivation from the Greek *kanon*, meaning 'rule', and its first use in England to mean ecclesiastical law and those works of the Bible that were accepted as genuine and inspired.

The canon is by definition exclusive: it is defined as much by the genres, the uses of language and the cultural experience that are omitted as by those that are authorized. So what exactly is a great piece of writing and how can it be recognized? How do texts achieve a place in the canon, and who decides this? What is its significance for speakers of English in different parts of the world? And how relevant is a collection of written texts from previous centuries to a rapidly changing, multicultural, multimedia world? As this chapter demonstrates, arguments and controversies about the canon are as much to do with its social and political functions as with the literary qualities of its contents. Contrasting views of the function of the English literary canon from three academics in the field of English literature are shown in the box on p. 238 You may like to come back to these again at the end of the chapter when you are assessing your own conclusions.

*Figure 7.1   (opposite)
The opening of the prologue to Chaucer's* The Canterbury Tales *(1484), one of the oldest texts of 'English literature'*

Prologue

Han that Apryll wyth hys shouris sote
The droughte of marche hath percydr the rote
Andr bathydr euery veyne in suche lycour
Of whyche vertue engendrydr is the flour
Whanne zephirus eke wyth hys sote breth
Enspyrydr hath in euery holte andr heth
The tendyr croppis / andr the yonge sonne
Hath in the ram half hys cours y ronne
Andr smale foulis make melodye
That sleppyn al nyght wyth opyn eye
So prykyth hem nature in her corages
Than longyn folk to gon on pylgremages
Andr palmers to seche straunge strondis
To serue halolwys couthe in sondry londis
Andr specyally fro euery shyris ende
Of engelondr to Cauntirbury thy wende
The holy blyssful martir for to seke
That them hath holpyn when they were seke
Pfyl in that seson on a day
In Suthwerk atte tabardr as J lay
Redy to wenden on my pylgremage
To Cauntirbury wyth deuout corage
That nyght was come in to that hostelrye
Wel nyne andr twenty in a companye
Of sondry folk by auenture y falle
In feleshyp andr pylgrymys were they alle
That tolwardr Cauntirbury wolden ryde
The chambrys andr the stablys were wydir
Andr wel were we esidr atte beste
Andr shortly whan the sonne was at reste
So hadr J spokyn wyp h hem euerychon
That J was of her feleshyp anon
Andr made forlwardr erly for to ryse
To take our wey ther as J you deuyse
But natheles whyles J haue tyme andr space
Or that J ferthyr in thys tale pace
Me thynketh it accordaunt to reson
To telle you al the condicion

a iij

The function of the canon

A shared cultural heritage

[Marilyn Butler, speaking in an Open University radio discussion]

Shakespeare, the eighteenth-century novelists and the romantic poets are among the most readable, wide-ranging and humane of writers … [This literary heritage is] a bonding force, a uniting force in a populace. It's not imposed from on top, it has nothing to do necessarily with the State's purposes, it's something which you are brought up knowing, just as fairy tales are. You don't have to have read or studied these works in detail to have a huge pool of shared knowledge which makes us different in the British Isles from people who belong in France or Germany.

(Open University, 1991)

A way of organizing the history of literature and art

[Frank Kermode]

Canons are complicit with power, and canons are useful in that they enable us to manage otherwise unmanageable historical deposits. They do this by affirming that some works are more valuable than others, more worthy of minute attention … whether one thinks of canons as objectionable because formed at random or to serve some interests at the expense of others, or whether one supposes that the contents of canons are providentially chosen, there can be no doubt that we have not found ways of ordering our thoughts about the history of literature and art without recourse to them. That is why the minorities who want to be rid of what they regard as a reactionary canon can think of no way of doing so without putting a radical one in its place.

(Kermode, 1988, pp. 115–17)

A social construction for particular purposes

[Terry Eagleton]

… the so-called 'literary canon', the unquestioned 'great tradition' of the 'national literature', has to be recognised as a *construct*, fashioned by particular people for particular reasons at a certain time. There is no such thing as a literary work or tradition which is valuable *in itself*, regardless of what anyone might have said or come to say about it.

(Eagleton, 1983, p. 11)

In this chapter I briefly trace the development of the traditional English literature canon in Britain, subsequently exported to other parts of the world, and its relationship with a particular critical method and theory of literature. I then discuss how this canon has been challenged in various parts of the English-speaking world by writers with different kinds of cultural and gender experience, and by new theories about language. Lastly, I focus on recent discussions about the canon and cultural literacy in the USA. Although processes of canonization have been going on for centuries, the relatively recent common use of the term 'canon' in the area of English and cultural studies suggests that it has a particu-larly interesting and controversial role to play at this point in history.

Genres in English literature

The modern distinction between poetry, fiction and drama can be traced back to Aristotle's three-part division, established during the Greek classical period but rooted in an earlier, oral culture:

- *Poetic / lyric*: a text uttered as if in the author's voice throughout.

- *Epic / narrative*: a text including the author's voice, and also characters speaking for themselves.

- *Drama*: a text in which the characters do all the talking.

Since classical times critics have also identified many more specific genres; for example, tragedy, comedy, satire and ballad and, more recently, novel, essay, biography.

From the Renaissance to the eighteenth century, recognized genres were believed to be fixed literary types (following the model of species in the biological order of nature), and rules were developed that stipulated subject matter, style, structure and emotional effect for each type. Like the English social classes, genres were arranged hierarchically, running from epic and tragedy at the top to the short lyric and epigram at the bottom.

This rigid structure was weakened in the eighteenth century by the development of a new genre – the novel – and by the increasing prestige of the short lyric poem during the rise of romanticism. Genre mixing was used to produce new forms, such as the lyrical ballads of Wordsworth and Coleridge. Qualities such as 'sincerity', 'intensity', 'high seriousness' and 'organic unity' became more important than generic purity.

Recently, there has been a revival in genre theory, using the idea of genres not as fixed literary types, but as changing cultural conventions which are evolved through reading and writing practices and through institutional processes. Generic terms are still, however, commonly used loosely to describe a particular style of writing; for example, comedy, science fiction and romance.

7.2   THE TRADITIONAL ENGLISH LITERATURE CANON

In Britain today, the traditional canon of English literature is often invoked as an image of a better past, a set of standards from which the British have sadly fallen. Here is John Marenbon, Director of Studies in English at Trinity College, Cambridge, arguing for a return to a more traditional English curriculum in schools:

> A few decades ago, those who took 'O' and 'A' Levels in English received a good introduction to the heritage of English Literature. Those who gave up English before the sixth form would have had the chance to study works by Shakespeare and Milton, eighteenth-century dramatists and essayists, the romantic poets and the nineteenth-century novelists; and English specialists left school with a knowledge of their literary heritage which would shame most graduates in English today (for instance, in 1950 candidates for the Cambridge Board Higher School Certificate … chose from a syllabus which covered – among other writers – Chaucer,

Sidney, Spenser, Marlowe, Shakespeare, Bacon, Johnson, Milton, Bunyan, Pepys, Swift, Gibbon, Fielding, Defoe, Wordsworth, Byron, Shelley, Lamb, Hardy, Browning and Shaw).

(Marenbon, 1987, p. 27)

The heritage Marenbon is invoking, like the English literature canon of my own schooldays in Northern Ireland, gives the impression of a long-established roll-call of authors and scholars extending back over hundreds of years to the Middle Ages. It can be something of a shock therefore to discover that although ideas about what constitutes good literature in English have been around since the sixteenth century, this particular construction of the canon has only really emerged in the twentieth century, through the work of a group of critics in Cambridge in the 1930s, of whom the best known are F.R. Leavis, I.A. Richards and T.S. Eliot. In order to set their work in historical context, we need to look briefly at how English literature itself began emerging as a school and university subject in Britain in the nineteenth and early twentieth centuries.

The term 'literature' came into currency around the fourteenth century, when it meant 'learned writing'. It was only in the late eighteenth century, with the influence of European romanticism, that its meaning began to shift towards the more specialized modern concept of imaginative and creative writing (Williams, 1976). Although a growing literature in English existed, it was not considered a subject for serious study. In the eighteenth and early nineteenth centuries, literature education for boys from the upper classes still meant classical writings in Greek and Latin. Their sisters' education, focusing on the accomplishments which might attract a husband, did not include any serious academic study (see Purvis, 1987). The idea of a specifically English literature as a serious subject emerged in the nineteenth century, in the wake of a growing national consciousness and profound social change. As the British empire grew and Britain became the most powerful industrial nation in Europe, industrialization brought with it the emergence of new middle classes. At the same time, developments in scientific knowledge were increasingly undermining the religious institutions which had bolstered the old social order. During the second half of the nineteenth century, a growing middle-class women's movement demanded equal access to educational institutions, including universities. The 1870 Education Act introduced compulsory elementary education for all children in England and Wales, and by the end of the nineteenth century, with mass secondary education, syllabus reform and the provision of academic places for women, a different base for the curriculum was needed to replace the traditional elitist foundation of Greek and Roman classics.

The promotion of English literature to provide that base is closely associated with the ideas of Matthew Arnold, the nineteenth-century poet, critic and school inspector. Arnold believed that literature, particularly poetry, could fill the spiritual and social gap left by the demise of religion. He argued that literature was morally uplifting, and would ennoble the minds and spirits of the middle and lower classes, thus drawing the nation together. Arnold identified key writers (in English and the classics) whom he believed set the standards for all other writing, and he referred to their work as 'touchstones'.

The first book in this series, *English: history, diversity and change* (Graddol, et al. (eds), 1996), discusses the emergence of literature in English in more detail.

Arnold's touchstones

For Arnold the classical writers were Homer, Dante, Shakespeare and Milton. He recognized other writers as great, but placed them slightly lower in the literary hierarchy. For instance, Chaucer was 'the father of our splendid English poetry', with his 'divine liquidity' of diction and movement. But Chaucer, for all his 'largeness, freedom, shrewdness, benignity', did not achieve the high seriousness identified by Aristotle as one of the grand virtues of poetry. Dryden and Pope were classics of prose rather than poetry, Gray and Burns were also important but, using the great classics as a touchstone, did not achieve true greatness (Arnold, 1880).

His examples of touchstone passages from Shakespeare and Milton are:

If thou didst ever hold me in thy heart,
Absent thee from felicity awhile,
And in this harsh world draw thy breath in pain
To tell my story ...

(From Shakespeare's *Hamlet*, where the dying Hamlet addresses Horatio)

Darken'd so, yet shone
Above them all the archangel; but his face
Deep scars of thunder had intrench'd, and care
Sat on his faded cheek ...

(From Milton's *Paradise Lost*)

Activity 7.2   *(Allow about 20 minutes)*

The table of English literature overleaf comes from *A Manual of our Mother Tongue*, a school textbook on the English language by Marmaduke Hewitt and George Beach, which was published in Britain in 1894. Different typefaces show the ranking of authors and works (the most important are in **bold**, then *italic*, then plain text).

How does this list compare with the 'English literature' of your own school-days? Is there anything you find surprising about it?

Comment

One of the most striking things for me about this list is the range of different genres included, from sonnets to sermons and translations of Greek and Latin classics, to histories and political economy. In contrast, my own school literature syllabus was restricted to poems, plays and novels. The writers included in the 1894 table are almost all English, but 'literature' is still being interpreted in its older, broader sense. Some of the works listed are probably unfamiliar to today's literature students; on the other hand, I was surprised that Jane Austen (who died in 1817) was not included. Indeed, you may have noticed that very few women writers at all appear in the table. I look at the issue of gender in relation to the canon in more detail later in this chapter.

English literature became established as a school subject and later, in the 1920s and 1930s, it achieved recognition in Britain at university level. Victorian ideas about the uplifting effects of literature and its social importance were taken up and reshaped in the 1930s by a group of Cambridge critics, including F.R. Leavis. Like Arnold, Leavis believed literature could have a positive, regenerative effect on the British nation. In the 1930s this meant for him saving British society from

Table 7.1   Table of literature from 1588 to present time

Authors	Works
Lord Sackville (1536–1608)	The Induction, a poetical preface to the Mirror for Magistrates. Gorboduc, *first regular tragedy in blank verse.*
Sir Walter *Raleigh* (1552–1618)	*History of the World*
Edmund **Spenser** (1553–1599)	**Faery Queen**; and Shepherd's Kalendar (Poetry).
John Lyly (1553–1600)	Euphues, a fantastic romance.
Richard Hooker (1553–1600)	Ecclesiastical Polity; and Sermons.
Sir Philip Sidney (1554–1586)	Arcadia, a euphuistic, prose, heroic romance; Sonnets.
Lord **Bacon** (1561–1626)	**Advancement of Learning; Essays; Novum Organum.**
Michael Drayton (1563–1631)	Polyolbion (Poem of 30,000 lines).
William Shakespeare (1564–1616)	**DRAMAS**, Poems (Sonnets).
Ben Jonson (1574–1637)	*Dramas,* Songs, English Grammar.
Archbishop Usher (1581–1656)	Annals; Chronologia Sacra (Prose).
Thomas Hobbes (1588–1679)	Leviathan, and Behemoth, both works on Ethics and Politics.
Izaak Walton (1593–1683)	Compleat Angler (Prose).
George Herbert (1593–1632)	The Temple (Poetry); The Country Parson (Prose).
Edmund Waller (1605–1687)	An Amatory Poet.
Thomas Fuller (1608–1661)	Church History; Worthies of England.
John **Milton** (1608–1674)	Comus, Lycidas, **Paradise Lost**, Sonnets (Poems); Areopagitica (Prose).
Lord Clarendon (1609–1674)	History of the Great Rebellion.
Samuel *Butler* (1612–1680)	*Hudibras,* a mock heroic poem.
Richard Baxter (1615–1691)	Saint's Rest; Call to the Unconverted (Prose).
John **Bunyan** (1628–1688)	**Pilgrim's Progress**, Holy War, Grace Abounding.
John **Dryden** (1631–1700)	Virgil's Georgics and Eneid (Translated); Plays; Absalom and Ahithopel: Hind and Panther (Poetry).
Samuel Pepys (1632–1703)	Diary (Prose).
John *Locke* (1632–1704)	*Essay on the Understanding*; Letter concerning Toleration.
Isaac **Newton** (1642–1727)	**Principia**, Optics, Observations on the Prophecies.
Daniel **De Foe** (1661–1731)	**Robinson Crusoe**; History of the Great Plague.
Richard Bentley (1661–1742)	Dissertation on the Epistles of Phalaris.
Dean *Swift* (1667–1745)	*Gulliver's Travels;* Tale of a Tub; Drapier's Letters (Prose).
Sir Richard *Steele* (1671–1729)	The Conscious Lovers (Drama); Papers in Tatler, **Spectator**, and Guardian.
Joseph **Addison** (1672–1719)	Cato (Drama); Papers in Tatler, **Spectator**, and Guardian.
Edward Young (1681–1765)	Night Thoughts (Poetry).
Bishop Berkeley (1684–1753)	The Minute Philosopher (Metaphysical) (Prose).
Alexander **Pope** (**1688–1744**)	**Translation of Iliad**; Essay on Man; Rape of the Lock (Poems).
Samuel *Richardson* (1689–1761)	Pamela; Clarissa Harlowe, Sir Charles Grandison (Novels).
Bishop Butler (1692–1752)	Analogy of Religion; Sermons.
James Thompson (1700–1748)	The Seasons; Castle of Indolence.
Henry *Fielding* (1707–1754)	Joseph Andrews; Tom Jones (Novels).
Dr. **Samuel Johnson** (1709–1784)	**Lives of the Poets, English Dictionary,** Rasselas (Prose); Vanity of Human Wishes (Poetry).
David *Hume* (1711–1776)	*History of England.*
Laurence Sterne (1713–1768)	Tristam Shandy; Sentimental Journey (Prose).
Thomas **Gray** (1716–1771)	Odes; **Elegy** in Country Churchyard.
William Collins (1720–1756)	Ode on the Passions.
Tobias *Smollett* (1721–1771)	Continuation of Hume's History; Roderick Random (Novel).
Adam **Smith** (1723–1790)	**Wealth of Nations** (Political Economy).
Oliver Goldsmith (1728–1774)	The **Traveller, Deserted Village** (Poems); She Stoops to Conquer, Good-natured Man (Plays); Vicar of Wakefield (Prose).
Edmund *Burke* (1730–1797)	*French Revolution* (Political); On the Sublime and Beautiful (Philosophical).
William *Cowper* (1731–1800)	The *Task,* Olney Hymns, Translations (Poetry).
Horne Tooke (1736–1812)	Diversions of Purley (On Language).
Edward *Gibbon* (1737–1794)	*Decline and Fall of the Roman Empire.*
Sir Philip Francis (1740–1818)	Letters of Junius (Political Invectives). Authorship doubtful.
William *Paley* (1743–1805)	*Evidences of Christianity; Natural Theology.*
Jeremy **Bentham** (1748–1832)	**Theory of Legislation.**
Thomas Chatterton (1752–1770)	Poems of Rowley.
Dugald *Stewart* (1753–1828)	Philosophy of Human Mind; Outlines of *Moral Philosophy.*
Robert **Burns** (1759–1796)	**Tam o'Shanter**, and other Poems.
Sir James Macintosh (1765–1832)	Progress of Ethical Philosophy; History of England.
William **Wordsworth** (1770–1850)	**Excursion**; The Prelude; **Lyrics**.
Sir Walter **Scott** (1771–1832)	Lay of Last Minstrel, Marmion, Lady of the Lake, Rokeby (Poems); **Waverly Novels**.
Samuel Taylor *Coleridge* (1772–1834)	The Ancient Mariner, Christabel, Genevieve (Poems); Aids to Reflection, *Lectures on Shakespeare* (Prose).
Robert Southey (1774–1843)	Thalaba, Roderick, Curse of Kehama (Poems); Life of Nelson (Prose).
Charles Lamb (1775–1834)	Essays of Elia.
Thomas Campbell (1771–1844)	Pleasures of Hope, Gertrude of Wyoming (Poems); Life of Petrarch (Prose).
Henry **Hallam** (1778–1859)	**Europe during Middle Ages; Constitutional History of England.**
Thomas Moore (1779–1852)	Lalla Rookh; Irish Melodies.
Thomas De Quincey (1785–1859)	Confessions of an English Opium-Eater (Prose).
Sir William Hamilton (1788–1854)	Lectures on Metaphysics and Logics.
Lord **Byron** (1788–1824)	**Childe Harold**, Corsair, Lara, Don Juan, Manfred, etc. (Poems).
Percy Bysshe *Shelley* (1792–1822)	Queen Mab, Revolt of Islam, Prometheus Unbound, *The Cloud* (Poems).
Thomas **Carlyle** (1795–1881)	**French Revolution**; Oliver Cromwell; Frederick the Great; **Sartor Resartus**.
John Keats (1796–1820)	Endymion, Hyperion, Eve of St. Agnes, Lamia (Poems).
Thomas **Hood** (1798–1845)	*Song of the Shirt*, and other poems; Up the Rhine (Prose).
Lord **Macaulay** (1800–1859)	**History of England; Essays** on Clive, Milton, etc.; **Lays** of Ancient Rome.
Nathaniel Hawthorne (1804–1864)	Twice Told Tales; History of New York (**American**).
Lord Lytton (1805–1873)	Lady of Lyons (Poem); My Novel; The Caxtons, etc.
Earl of Beaconsfield (Benjamin Disraeli) (1805–1882)	Henrietta Temple; Coningsby, etc.
John Stuart **Mill** (1806–1873)	**Political Economy; Logics.**
Henry Wadsworth *Longfellow* (1807–1887)	Golden Legend, Evangeline, Tales of a Wayside Inn (Poems) (American).
William Makepeace **Thackeray** (1811–1863)	Colonel Newcombe, Vanity Fair (**Novels**); The Four Georges.
Charles *Dickens* (1812–1870)	Pickwick Papers, Bleak House, Dombey and Son, etc. (Novels).
Charlotte *Brontë* (1815–1855)	Villette, Shirley, etc. (*Novels*).
Mary Evans (**George Eliot**) (1820–1880)	**Adam Bede**, Middlemarch, Mill on the Floss, etc. (Novels).

(Cited in Durant and Fabb, 1990, pp. 10-11)

mass production, advertising and popular culture. While Arnold had been keen for literature to educate and tame the middle and lower classes through state-established schools, Leavis concentrated on drawing together and reviewing existing ideas about what should actually count as great English literature; in fact, on establishing a definitive canon. In the course of this, he and his associates developed a method of literary criticism which replaced the existing rather dilettante approach that allowed any work written in elegant English to count as 'good literature'.

Leavis argued that only a small cultural minority were capable of making authentic judgements about literature, and that this group had a particular responsibility both to the English language and to the nation:

> Upon this minority depends our power of profiting by the finest human experience of the past; they keep alive the subtlest and most perishable parts of tradition. Upon them depend the implicit standards that order the finer living of an age, the sense that this is worth more than that, this rather than that is the direction to go, that the centre is here rather than there. In their keeping ... is the language, the changing idiom, upon which fine living depends, and without which distinction of spirit is thwarted and incoherent.
>
> (Leavis, 1943, pp. 143–5)

Believing that he and his associates represented such an important minority, Leavis set to work reviewing existing literature, elevating particular texts into the canon and discarding others, through the pages of the critical journal *Scrutiny*. To do this, the Leavisites developed a critical method of 'close reading' and **practical criticism**, which involved a careful scrutinizing of individual texts to analyse their use of language and uncover their authentic meaning. Practical criticism (the term was coined by I.A. Richards) became an influential form of literary criticism in the 1930s and 1940s, consolidated in schools and universities through the examination system. It was also an intrinsic part of constructing the English literary canon, since this depended as much on authoritative readings of texts as on the texts themselves (see Richards, 1929).

Practical criticism

Practical criticism treats literary texts as independent, self-contained objects, with a fixed meaning waiting to be discovered by the skilful reader. Knowledge about the author's life, or the circumstances of the text's creation, is therefore not particularly relevant. What is important are the words on the page and the way in which they contribute to the coherence of the text theme. For example, G. Wilson Knight, in his influential commentary on Shakespeare called *The Wheel of Fire* (1949), describes in his chapter 'Macbeth and the metaphysic of evil' how in this play Shakespeare's tense, nervous, insubstantial language reflects the mesmeric, nightmarish plot. The constant references to blood (on Macbeth's sword, his hands, Lady Macbeth's hands, Duncan's body, Banquo's murderer's face, Banquo's ghost), together with the brilliant fire imagery (for example, the thunder and lightning, the green glint of the spectral dagger, the glaring eyes of Banquo's ghost), produce a poetry of 'intense darkness shot with the varied intensity of pure light or pure colour' which mirrors the contrast between moral darkness and bright purity and virtue in the play (Wilson Knight, 1949, p. 148)

[61]

Spent in Difcourfe does but defer his Death,
And but delays our Vengeance,
　　Macd. Come let's go.
The fwifteft haft is for Revenge too flow.
　　　　　　　　　　　　　　　　　　　[*Exeunt.*

　　　　Enter *Macbeth, and Souldiers.*
　　Macb. Hang out our Banners proudly o're the Wall,
The Cry is ftill, they Come: Our Caftles Strength
Will Laugh a Siege to Scorn: Here let them lie
Till Famine eat them up: Had *Seaton* ftill
Been ours, and others who now Increafe the Number
Of our Enemies, we might have met 'em
Face to Face.　　　　　　　　　　[*Noife within.*
What Noife is that?
　　Ser. It feems the Cry of Women.
　　Macb. I have almoft forgot the Tafte of Fears,
The time has been that Dangers have been my Familiars;
Wherefore was that Cry?
　　Ser. Great, Sir, the Queen is Dead.
　　Macb. She fhould have Di'd hereafter,
I brought Her here, to fee my Victines, not to Die.
To Morrow, to Morrow, and to Morrow,
Creeps in a ftealing pace from Day to Day,
To the laft Minute of Recorded Time:
And all our Yefterdays have lighted Fools
To their Eternal Homes: Out, out that Candle,
Life's but a Walking Shaddow, a poor Player
That Struts and Frets his Hour upon the Stage,
And then is Heard no more. It is a Tale
Told by an Ideot, full of Sound and Fury
Signifying Nothing.　　　　　　　[*Enter a Meffenger.*
Thou comeft to ufe thy Tongue: Thy Story quickly.
　　Meff. Let my Eyes fpeak what they have feen,
For my Tongue cannot.
　　Macb. Thy Eyes fpeak Terror, let thy Tongue expound
Their Language, or be for ever Dumb.
　　Meff. As I did ftand my Watch upon the Hill,
I lookt towards *Birnam,* and anon me thoughts
　　　　　　　　　　　　　　　　　　　　　　　The

Figure 7.2　The robust vitality of 'English English': an extract from Shakespeare's Macbeth *(1674)*

(Folger Shakespeare Library)

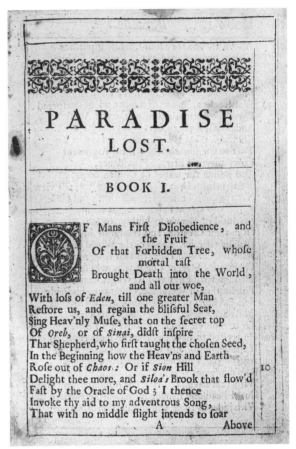

PARADISE LOST.

BOOK I.

OF Mans Firft Difobedience, and
　　　　the Fruit
Of that Forbidden Tree, whofe
　　　　mortal taft
　　Brought Death into the World,
　　　　and all our woe,
With lofs of *Eden,* till one greater Man
Reftore us, and regain the blifsful Seat,
Sing Heav'nly Mufe, that on the fecret top
Of *Oreb,* or of *Sinai,* didft infpire
That Shepherd, who firft taught the chofen Seed,
In the Beginning how the Heav'ns and Earth
Rofe out of *Chaos:* Or if *Sion* Hill
Delight thee more, and *Siloa's* Brook that flow'd
Faft by the Oracle of God; I thence
Invoke thy aid to my adventrous Song,
That with no middle flight intends to foar
　　　　　　　A　　　　　Above

10

Figure 7.3　The opening of Milton's Paradise Lost *(1668). Although this provides one of Arnold's 'touchstones', it was criticized by Leavis for the heavy Latinate phrasing and vocabulary (notice the passage above is just one sentence), and by Eliot for its 'magniloquence'*

(Bodleian Library)

One impulse from a vernal wood
May teach you more of man,
Of moral evil and of good,
Than all the sages can.

Sweet is the lore which nature brings;
Our meddling intellect
Mis-shapes the beauteous forms of things:
We murder to dissect.

Enough of Science and of Art;
Close up those barren leaves;
Come forth, and bring with you a heart
That watches and receives.

Figure 7.4　An extract from Wordsworth's poem The Tables Turned: *an evening scene on the same subject (1798). For Leavis, Wordsworth's writing portrayed the moral centrality of rural England*

Thou on whose stream, mid the steep sky's
　　commotion,
Loose clouds like Earth's decaying leaves are shed,
Shook from the tangled boughs of Heaven and
　　Ocean,

Angels of rain and lightning: there are spread
On the blue surface of thine airy surge,
Like the bright hair uplifted from the head

Of some fierce Mænad …

Figure 7.5　An extract from Shelley's Ode to the West Wind *(1820). For Leavis these verses were proof of Shelley's vague, unacceptably ethereal use of English; he complains that although Shelley uses the terms 'bough' and 'leaves', it is not clear what the tree, to which they must belong, is meant to be*

In order to be admitted into the Leavisite canon, texts had to display particular kinds of moral, aesthetic and 'English' qualities which would arm readers against the moral, social and commercial degeneration of the age. Aesthetics and English identity were intertwined: the Leavisites searched for what they saw as truly 'English' writing, where the rich language recalled the lost golden age of an organic, rural utopia, in contrast to the abstract anaemic language of contemporary commercial society and popular culture. Their goal was to safeguard the robust vitality of 'English' English, classically demonstrated in Shakespeare's work, from the debased language of the popular press and from language which was too abstract or Latinate (the influence of Latin and the romance languages was seen as somehow non-English).

These criteria were used to demote some writers (for example, Milton, who was too Latinate, and Shelley, who was not concrete enough) and to promote others. Favoured writers included Donne, whose voice was believed to embody the living nerve of Englishness, and Wordsworth, whose poetry was thought to demonstrate a deep rural social-moral consciousness (Eagleton, 1983). Leavis, like Arnold, started with poetry, but moved on to deal with drama and the novel as well.

This is how the Marxist critic, Terry Eagleton, describes the work of the Leavisites in their journal *Scrutiny*:

> With breathtaking boldness, *Scrutiny* redrew the map of English literature in ways from which criticism has never quite recovered. The main thoroughfares on this map ran through Chaucer, Shakespeare, Jonson, the Jacobeans and Metaphysicals, Bunyan, Pope, Samuel Johnson, Blake, Wordsworth, Keats, Austen, George Eliot, Hopkins, Henry James, Joseph Conrad, T.S. Eliot and D.H. Lawrence. This *was* 'English literature': Spencer, Dryden, Restoration drama, Defoe, Fielding, Richardson, Sterne, Shelley, Byron, Tennyson, Browning, most of the Victorian novelists, Joyce, Woolf and most writers after D.H. Lawrence constituted a network of 'B' roads interspersed with a good few cul-de-sacs. Dickens was first out and then in; 'English' included two and a half women, counting Emily Brontë as a marginal case; almost all of its authors were conservatives.
>
> (Eagleton, 1983, pp. 32–3)

Activity 7.3   *(Allow about 10 minutes)*

The texts in the Leavisite canon, like Arnold's touchstones, were seen as providing criteria against which to judge new work. Jot down your own views about using comparisons with texts in an existing canon to decide on the quality of new writing.

Comment

For some, canons are necessary to organize the past and to provide enduring standards; for others, they are an unnecessarily conservative and rigid force stifling new and different forms of creativity. T.S. Eliot, although he believed that English language and literature had degenerated from the eighteenth century onwards, did suggest that when a really great new piece of writing was admitted to the canon, the 'existing monuments' as he called them, shifted slightly so that our perception of the canon, and of literature, would be subtly altered (Eliot, 1932). It was important, however, for new literature to stand the test of time. Thus Leavis announced in the first sentence of his 1948 volume *The Great Tradition* (with uncharacteristic gender balance): 'The great English novelists are Jane Austen, George Eliot, Henry James and Joseph Conrad – to stop for a moment at that comparatively safe point in history' (Leavis, 1948). Interestingly, two of these great English novelists, Henry James and Joseph Conrad, were of North American and Polish origin, respectively.

The Leavisite canon has been criticized for its conservatism, restrictiveness and elitism, for the way in which works were selected for inclusion, and for the construction of singular authorized readings. However, it still affects our current perception of what counts as great English literature and how the canon functions in a number of important ways. The Leavisite approach can be summarized as follows:

- Great literature is believed to have a humanizing effect on individuals, and its study develops a sensitivity to the higher values of life.
- It embodies a truly English use of the language, seen as non-Latinate and somehow 'concrete'.
- It puts the reader in touch with a past golden age which existed before the debasement of language, literature and human values in modern industrial society.
- Texts contain a literary essence which will endure over time. The precise social and historical context of their production is thus relatively unimportant.
- These texts should be analysed through close reading, in relation to literary standards established in the canon.

And, rather more controversially:

- Literary value can only be appreciated by a small cultural elite, whose duty it is to preserve and guard great literature, and the English language, against foreign influences, degeneration and popular culture.
- We need to look to the past for truly great literary uses of the English language.

What are the implications of the Leavisite canon for those whose experience and writing falls outside it? It has been argued that the experience of women, and of black and working-class people, is not adequately represented in many canonical texts, and that the very concept of a past golden age providing the moral heart of the canon is heavily biased. The utopias of old England and the American south invoked by Leavis and Eliot, respectively, may not have seemed so golden to landless English serfs, or to slaves on the American plantations.

I now explore some of the arguments which have provided a powerful challenge to the Leavisite literature canon.

7.3   WOMEN AND THE CANON

Why are there so few women authors in the examples of canons in section 7.1 and in the table of English literature (Table 7.1)? Is this because women write less well than men? Do they find it more difficult to have their work published? Or is there something about the process of canonization itself which excludes women's writing?

In many ways women in the past simply did not have the opportunity to produce canonical texts, particularly in the areas of poetry or drama. Poetry, with

its privileged and prestigious position within the canon, has been closely connected to the Greek and Roman classics. In Britain these were taught to boys at
public school and university, where girls were not admitted until the end of the
nineteenth century. Major women poets are difficult to find (can you think of
anyone as well known as Milton or Keats or Eliot?). Even those who are celebrated
are often better known for their association with a male poet; for example,
Elizabeth Barrett's elopement with Robert Browning, or Sylvia Plath's marriage
with Ted Hughes (Birch, 1992). In the area of drama, women writers are even
rarer. As part of the public commercial world, theatres were not considered
appropriate places for respectable women to work, either as actresses or as
writers. For instance, the English dramatist Aphra Behn (1640–89) achieved
notoriety rather than respect during her lifetime and is only now being taken
seriously as an important writer.

Two out of three of the main literary genres, then, were virtually inaccessible
to women. The writing of novels, which did not depend on a classical education or
access to public institutions, was the one area where women did begin to make
headway, but even here women often had to use male pseudonyms in order to be
published; for example, Charlotte Brontë wrote as Currer Bell and Mary Evans as
George Eliot.

In the past, then, women have had restricted access to education and to the
public world with its theatres and publishers, and male publishers and critics have
been unwilling to take their writing seriously. Is this still true today? Pam Morris
(1993) argues that men continue to dominate the institutions of literary criticism,
publishing and education, through which the canon is established and sustained.
Male critics tend to marginalize women's writing by censoring its subject matter
(no nice woman would write about such things) or calling it trivial. Some feminist
writers argue that most literary criticism is shaped and dominated by a specifically
male world view. At their most extreme, very masculine-centred readings of texts
(by male and female authors) have been dubbed 'phallic criticism'.

Phallic criticism

Feminist critic Elaine Showalter identifies one example of phallic criticism in the
comments by the critic Irving Howe on the opening scene of Thomas Hardy's *The
Mayor of Casterbridge*, where the hero sells his wife and daughter at a country fair.
Howe writes:

> To shake loose from one's wife; to discard that drooping rag of a woman, with
> her mute complaints and maddening passivity; to escape not by a slinking
> abandonment but through the public sale of her body to a stranger, as horses
> are sold at a fair; and thus to wrest, through sheer amoral willfulness, a second
> chance out of life – it is with this stroke, so insidiously attractive to male
> fantasy, that the *Mayor of Casterbridge* begins.

(Cited in Showalter, 1986, p. 129)

Showalter argues that Howe not only ignores the possible responses of female
readers to this scene, but also distorts Hardy's text by imposing on it his own image
of the constricting, suffocating wife who traps and emasculates her husband.

Morris points out that reviews of books by women authors and reviews that are
written by women seldom make the front pages of literary magazines. Literature

anthologies, used in undergraduate teaching and influential in constructing the general public's concept of what counts as literature, are almost all edited by men. Women's writing constitutes less than 9 per cent of the contents of contemporary major British and US literature and poetry anthologies.

Morris suggests that this male dominance of the canon has been recently challenged by feminists in two main ways: first through re-readings (of texts, criticism and history), and secondly by the increasing circulation and promotion of women's writing, past and contemporary, in publishing initiatives and in courses on women's studies in higher education. However, diverting women's writing into women's studies courses or arguing for the inclusion in the canon of women's texts on a case-by-case basis, may leave the essentially masculine bias of criteria of excellence intact. Rather, Morris argues that there should be sufficient numbers of female writers in the mainstream canon to ensure that criteria are developed which encompass women's experience and different writing styles, as well as men's. Further, these criteria should also encompass the varied values and cultural traditions which influence women's (and men's) lives.

Some critics argue that women need to use English in different ways from men and could create new genres, to reflect specifically feminine experience; for instance Virginia Woolf suggested that a 'woman's sentence', glimpsed in occasional fragmentary forms in women's writing, might free women from the dominant male forms of thought.

The possibility of opening up aesthetic criteria to encompass varied cultural as well as different gender experience is a contentious issue, which I explore further in the following sections.

7.4 POSTCOLONIAL WRITERS

Different ways of using English

The literature of American writers has for some time been accepted as part of English literature, but here I want to focus on the challenge presented to the traditional canon from colonial and postcolonial writers – novelists such as R.K. Narayan and Raja Rao in India, Chinua Achebe in Nigeria and V.S. Naipaul in the Caribbean; poets such as Derek Walcott and Edward Kamau Brathwaite in the Caribbean, and dramatists such as Wole Soyinka in Nigeria. These authors are all accepted as great writers across the English-speaking world; they appear on university and school literature syllabuses and carry off prestigious literary awards. Most of them grew up with the traditional English literature canon as part of the education system exported by Britain to its colonies, but in their own writings they have begun to develop new ways of using the English language and literary forms, and they provide alternative perspectives on history and cultural experience in the English-speaking world.

Issues faced by individual writers of literature in English, who come from different language and cultural backgrounds, are explored more thoroughly in Chapter 8.

❖ ❖ ❖ ❖ ❖

Activity 7.4 *(Reading A)*

Read 'English in the Caribbean: notes on nation language and poetry' by Edward Kamau Brathwaite (Reading A).

*   How does Brathwaite describe the differences between the way English is used in Caribbean poetry and in traditional English literature? How is history relevant to this?

*   In what ways would it be difficult for the kind of Caribbean poetry he describes to be part of a Leavisite canon?

Comment

The history which Brathwaite invokes for English in the Caribbean is one of disruption, slavery and an imposed language. This is reflected in the subject matter of Caribbean poetry, the literary forms it is developing and the different ways it uses English syntax. The forms and content of traditional English literature taught in schools in the Caribbean have little to do with Caribbean life, and Brathwaite suggests that the very rhythm and intonation of English poetry, with its persistent use of pentameter (five stressed syllables to a line), is best suited to expressing English, but not Caribbean, experience: it can describe snow falling on fields, but not a hurricane.

In order to express Caribbean experience, to use English in a way that grows out of Caribbean history, Brathwaite describes a variety of English he calls 'nation language'. This draws on African syntax, replaces the rhythm of the pentameter with the dactyls of the calypso and is performed in what he calls 'total expression', in which the music of sound and the involvement of the audience are an intrinsic part of the poem. Interestingly, Brathwaite does not see a poet's use of 'nation language' as mastery of a unique language variety, but still as a form of enslavement, a 'prison language'; there is always a kind of oblique relationship between the poets' true feelings and their use of English, however much they reshape it.

The Caribbean poet, then, is not aiming for the pure 'English' English envisaged by Leavis; language and form are creolized, and the past invoked is not golden but disrupted and brutal. Perhaps the feature of Caribbean poetry which is most at odds with the traditional canon criteria is its orality: Brathwaite is insistent about the importance of sound and noise, its closeness to jazz, and the importance of oral performance and audience involvement. In contrast to this, works included in the traditional Leavisite canon are essentially literary; practical criticism treats meaning and art as embodied in the text, not in an interactive live performance.

> The use of English in song and live performance is explored in Chapter 6, sections 6.2 and 6.3.

❖   ❖   ❖   ❖   ❖

In other parts of the world, writers have consciously drawn on literary, narrative and performance traditions from their other languages when they write in English. This is how Wole Soyinka, the Nigerian playwright, describes his aims when writing plays in English:

> African Drama is sophisticated in idiom. Our forms of theatre are quite different from literary drama. We use spontaneous dialogue, folk music, simple stories, and relevant dances to express what we mean. Our theatre uses stylised forms as its basic accepted disciplines. I am trying to integrate these forms into the drama of the English Language.
>
> (Cited in Nkosi, 1965, p. 108)

You may remember how the South African play *Have You Seen Zandile?*, discussed in Chapter 5, uses songs, dance and stories, and dialogue in Zulu and Xhosa as well as English. Other writers use an English which is close in idiom to their other language; Amos Tutuọla, for instance, wrote first in Yoruba, then translated his material into English. Here is an extract from *The Palm-Wine Drunkard*, first published in 1952:

> When it was early in the morning of the next day I had not palm-wine to drink at all, and throughout that day I felt not so happy as before; I was seriously sat down in my parlour, but when it was the third day that I had no palm-wine at all, all my friends did not come to my house again, they left me there alone, because there was no palm-wine for them to drink.
>
> (Cited in Platt et al., 1984, p. 179)

In the following extract from his novel in English, *Kanthapura*, the Indian writer Raja Rao uses a chain of clauses – something that would be common in narrative in the Kannada language.

> Then the police inspector saunters up to the Skefflington gate, and he opens it and one coolie and two coolies and three coolies come out, their faces dark as mops, and their blue skin black under the clouded heavens, and perspiration flows down their bodies and their eyes seem fixed to the earth ...

(Cited in Platt et al., 1984, p. 181)

In India, despite British rulers' attempts to replace Indian culture and literature with English literature (see below), writers have always drawn on a long and substantial cultural tradition in Indian languages such as Sanskrit, Tamil, Kannada and Hindi, in addition to the English literature they learn at school. In an unpublished paper, 'The Indian novel: a new genre', Ganeswar Mishra suggests that Rao, R.K. Narayan and the nineteenth-century writer Bankim Chandra Chatterjee have all drawn on two Indian narrative forms to blend with the western novel: the Purana (religious verse narrative from the *Ramayana* or *Mahabharata*) and traditional folk tales. The Purana, recited formally by a religious teacher, typically describes a peaceful world which is disturbed (often through the arrival of a stranger), and a subsequent struggle between good and evil. Folk tales include similar stories, but are narrated from memory, embellished and added to by the storyteller in a much more informal setting. Both Purana and folk tales often directly address the audience, with the narrator frequently taking on the part of one of the characters.

Rao's novel *Kanthapura* illustrates how these two traditions are used. It is the story of an Indian village destroyed by the British police for participating in the independence movement, as told by a Kanthapura grandmother who has survived and taken shelter in a neighbouring village. She is asked by the women there to narrate her experiences to them, in the evenings after prayers. In the opening paragraph of the novel the grandmother addresses her listeners (and the reader) directly, describing the stable, peaceful community of Kanthapura:

> Our village – I don't think you have ever heard about it – Kanthapura is its name, and it is in the province of Kara. High on the Ghats is it, high up the steep mountains that face the cool Arabian seas, up the Malabar coast is it, up Mangalore and Puttur and many a centre of cardamon and coffee, rice and sugarcane. Roads, narrow, dusty, rut-covered roads, wind through the forest of teak and of jack, of sandal and of sal, and hanging over bellowing gorges and leaping over elephant-haunted valleys, they turn now to the left and now to the right and bring you through the Alambè and Champa and Mena and Kola passes into the great granaries of trade. There, on the blue waters, they say, our carted cardamons and coffee get into the ships the Red-men bring, and, so they say, they go across the seven oceans into the countries where our rulers live.

(Rao [1938] 1989, p. 1)

The grandmother goes on to describe the arrival of a stranger who is shortly afterwards arrested, and the subsequent conflict between opposing characters and forces as the village is drawn into the freedom struggle. In an unpublished paper, 'The novel as Purana: a study of the form of *The Man-eater of Malgudi* and *Kanthapura*', Mishra suggests that *Kanthapura* is Puranic in its structure and atmosphere – the initial peaceful scene, the disturbance of the equilibrium, the complex and ambivalent conflict between good and evil. But the old woman is not a scholar, and her audience consists only of women, gathered together informally in the evening. The 'Foreword' to the book clearly introduces the story as a folk tale:

> It may have been told of an evening, when as the dusk falls, and through the sudden quiet, lights leap up in house after house, and stretching her bedding on the veranda, a grandmother might have told you, newcomer, the sad tale of her village.
>
> (Rao [1938]1989, p. v)

In developing the theme of the novel, and in using the authorial persona of the grandmother, *Kanthapura* draws on both the Purana and folklore traditions to produce a kind of blended, distinctly Indian genre. However, although Rao and other Indian authors writing in English have established a respected Indian novel tradition, there still remains for many writers the problem of artistic expression in a second language. For instance, how does the following comment by Rao compare with the points made by Brathwaite in Reading A?

> The telling has not been easy. One has to convey in a language that is not one's own the spirit that is one's own. One has to convey the various shades and omissions of a certain thought-movement that looks maltreated in an alien language. I use the word 'alien' yet English is not really an alien language to us. It is the language of our intellectual make-up like Sanskrit or Persian was before – but not of our emotional make-up.
>
> (Rao [1938]1989, p. v)

More recently, in the 1980s a new generation of Indian authors has emerged. In an unpublished paper, 'The charting of cultural territory: post-colonial Indian English fiction' (1995), Nilufer E. Bharucha describes their much more confident use of the English language, and points out that they are writing for a growing indigenous Indian middle-class readership as well as for an international audience. The plaudits earned by writers such as Salman Rushdie and Vikram Seth have established Indian writing at the centre of contemporary literary movements. Indian writing in English is also diversifying as authors use the language to explore a variety of ideological and social issues. It will be interesting to see how far Indian writing will shift perceptions of the English canon, and of English literature.

An alien canon

Brathwaite's dissatisfaction with the forms and styles within the traditional English canon are echoed by African writers. For instance Nkosi, a South African writer and critic, complains that T.S. Eliot's cold, abstract pessimism seems a particularly inappropriate model for the expression of the vigorous optimistic humanism of African experience. He objects to white academics who judge African art and literature by European canons of criticism, and, echoing Brathwaite, describes the experience of living on 'a substitute culture, borrowed from other lands' (Nkosi, 1965, p. 120). Following the rise of black consciousness in the 1970s, there has been a resurgence of black South African poetry and drama in the last 20 years, but this remains outside the mainstream western canon.

The close relationship between the establishment of an English literary canon in other parts of the world and Britain's management of its colonial territories has been documented particularly clearly in the case of India.

In the nineteenth century many British people believed that it was Britain's responsibility to provide education in India, and a fierce debate raged between those who believed this should be based on Indian culture (Orientalists) and those who argued for the European tradition (Anglicists).

The third book in this series *Learning English: development and diversity* (Mercer and Swann (eds) 1996) contains a discussion of English teaching in India.

In India, the 1835 English Education Act, which prescribed the teaching of English literature in India, marked the official victory of the Anglicists, although in practice both traditions, and the ideologies of colonialism they represented, continued to exist side by side (Pennycook, 1994). There was still a dilemma, however, in deciding which works of literature the curriculum should contain.

On the one hand the powerful British missionary societies were pressing for a specifically Christian curriculum; on the other hand Indian people had been resistant to the mission schools' efforts to convert them, and complaints from local rulers had resulted in the official banning of the societies' proselytizing activities. The 1835 Act authorized the teaching of the English literary tradition, but it was feared that exposure to the wrong kind of western literature might encourage thoughts of freedom and independence, which could be particularly disastrous for commercial interests. The answer to these problems was supplied by the colonial administration's selection of a canon for the English literature curriculum which would *implicitly* convey the Christian values that the missionary societies had wanted to teach explicitly, and would, it was hoped, produce docile and obedient subjects (Viswanathan, 1989). British officials scrutinized and promoted particular works of literature for this purpose. Shakespeare was argued to contain 'sound Protestant Bible principles'; Addison's *Spectator* papers included the 'strain of serious piety'; Bacon and Locke displayed a 'scriptural morality' and Adam Smith's work taught 'noble Christian sentiments' (Viswanathan, 1989, pp. 225–6). As in Victorian England, it was believed that English literature in India could 'stand in' for the Christian religion. The British Raj hoped it would shape the character and moral values of Indian students in order to consolidate British colonial rule.

Although the legacy of English literature and its teaching is, for many people, heavily tainted by British colonialism, it has been argued that the English literary icons used in oppression and domination have also provided a language for resistance and opposition. African, Indian and Malaysian intellectuals who received an English literary education were at the forefront of the struggle for independence. English was able to provide a common language for people from different local language backgrounds and it also provided a way of communicating with the outside world. The African novelist Achebe argues that African writing in English represents 'a new voice coming out of Africa, speaking of African experience in a world-wide language' (Achebe, 1965, p. 29).

New readings and writings

Different histories in India, Africa and the Caribbean have produced different readings of the English literature canon and new kinds of writing. These are now developing and diversifying as a second generation of postcolonial writers are increasingly using English as a world, as well as a colonial, language. The experience and work of these new writers challenge the way the traditional canon has been constructed and used, the authority of particular writings and genres within it, and the narrow cultural scope of the stories it contains. To summarize, we can draw out the following points:

*   The purposes for which a canon is constructed influence how its content is selected, and how readers experience the meaning and significance of the literature it contains. In the Caribbean, Africa and India, the authority of the English literature canon was closely tied to the colonial hierarchy.
*   The traditional canon relies exclusively on the printed word and assumes a distance between writer and reader. Postcolonial work often incorporates

oral, performance elements and a more direct dialogic relationship between the author and the audience.

- The moral world invoked by writers in postcolonial countries may draw on moral and religious traditions that are different from those in Britain. And the stories these writers have to tell, of slavery, poverty and exploitation, may undermine cultural and moral assumptions which are deeply embedded in the traditional English canon.

7.5   THEORY AND THE CANON

The questions raised about the canon by feminist and postcolonial writers are part of a more general movement of profound social and intellectual change emerging from the 1960s and 1970s. The acquisition of independence by former British colonies, the civil rights movement in the USA, the rise of feminism, changes in the British class system, and the rapid development of popular commercial art and the mass media all called into question traditional views of the world and traditional cultural authority. Was the canon an important part of cultural and national identity, or an instrument of elitist power? Could English printed canonical texts retain their cultural authority in the face of competition from other media?

At the same time as these radical political developments, new intellectual trends began to change ideas about texts and readers, in a way which seriously disturbed the basic assumptions underlying practical criticism, the literary method so crucial to the Leavisite canon's construction and authority. These new ideas, drawing together Marxism, feminism and psychoanalytic theory, have coalesced within **poststructuralism**. Poststructuralist theorists argue that communication is not just in one direction from speaker to listener, or writer to reader, but that there is constant feedback and negotiation in how meanings are constructed. A particular text will have a different meaning if it is read in the seventeenth century or the twenty-first century, in London or Lagos, by people from different social backgrounds, or at different points in one person's life. The meaning will be affected by previous reading, by films, by conversations with others. Texts address a particular audience or audiences – they encode a particular kind of 'inscribed reader' – but it is always possible for readers to read against this and produce their own alternative readings. Thus the relationship between the signifier (language) and the signified (meaning) is always unstable; meaning is never complete because there can always be new interpretations, and the possible meanings of texts are part of wider discourses about meanings and the relationships between discourses.

As one example, my reading of *Macbeth* is influenced by my changing personal conceptions of tragedy, ambition and betrayal, and also by my interpretation of the readings of influential critics like Wilson Knight and the critical tradition he represents. I was introduced to *Macbeth* at school in Northern Ireland through classroom discourses which positioned it reverentially as a canonical text from a dominant cultural tradition 'across the water'. But as an older student I read it differently after seeing Kurosawa's Japanese film adaptation *Throne of Blood*, which uses the white mask-like faces and stylized gestures of the Noh tradition and transposes the action to feudal Japan. For instance, my perceptions of the character of Lady Macbeth changed dramatically: the vociferous harridan of British productions was very different from the woman in the Japanese version, with her tense brooding silences and rapid shuffling steps. You might like to consider how your own readings of a particular canonical text are related to institutionalized practices (for example, schooling, literary criticism, film tradition), different discourses about the key themes and your own changing life experience.

Poststructuralist theory sees readers as having complex dialogues with texts rather than simply receiving their meanings. Similarly, poststructuralist critics argue that authors write texts in relation to various dialogues, internal or external, which they are having with other texts and speakers, as part of particular institutionalized practices. Within this matrix of dialogic relationships, struggles for power between texts and between speakers take place, in the context of different kinds of institutions and different kinds of economic relationships. Mikhail Bakhtin (1981) describes a constant struggle within language between centripetal and centrifugal forces. Centripetal forces pull inwards towards a standard language, an authoritative canon and political and cultural centralization, while centrifugal forces push outwards towards variation, resistance and disunification.

Conceptions of communication, then, have moved away from the 'transmission model' (see Figure 7.6) which underpins the Leavisite canon, to the poststructuralist, 'dialogic model' (see Figure 7.7).

MEANING IS TRANSMITTED FROM TEXT
TO READER, MEDIATED BY AUTHORITATIVE
TEACHERS AND CRITICS

Figure 7.6
The transmission model

READERS HAVE COMPLEX DIALOGUES WITH TEXTS
INFLUENCED BY THEIR ONGOING DIALOGUES WITH OTHER
PEOPLE AND TEXTS

Figure 7.7
The dialogic model

The focus has shifted from texts to readings. There is no longer one fixed, correct way of interpreting *Macbeth* or *Paradise Lost*. As the American critic Harold Bloom put it: 'I only *know* a text, any text, because I know a reading of it, someone else's reading, my own reading, a composite reading' (Bloom et al., 1979, p. 8). If the entity of the text is questioned, so inevitably is the canon. You may remember Terry Eagleton's position from the beginning of this chapter:

> the so-called 'literary canon', the unquestioned 'great tradition' of the 'national literature', has to be recognized as a *construct*, fashioned by particular people for particular reasons at a certain time. There is no such thing as a literary work or tradition which is valuable *in itself*, regardless of what anyone might have said or come to say about it.
> (Eagleton, 1983, p. 11)

Table 7.2 summarizes the theoretical shift we have been discussing.

Table 7.2   The theoretical shift

Leavisite criticism	Poststructuralist criticism
Text as self-contained artefact	Text as social production
Critical practices focused on writing	Critical practices focused on reading
One unchanging meaning waiting to be discovered by the discerning reader	As many meanings as there are readings
The canon as fixed and unchanging	The canon as an expression of continuing social processes

In the poststructuralist model, texts lose much of their fixity and durability, qualities which have traditionally been an important part of their authority and have distinguished them from transitory, oral forms of language. In addition to poststructuralism's problematizing of the relationship between text and meaning, some British critics have argued that the increasing importance of the spoken word for all social classes in contemporary cultural life – in radio, television, film, popular music – is undermining the authority of printed texts and therefore 'unmaking notions of canonicity on a daily basis' (MacCabe, 1987, p. 6). What we are seeing, Colin MacCabe suggests, is a breakdown of the old dichotomy between speech and writing, and the associations of the former with ephemeral subjective day-to-day experience and the latter with authority, rational argument and truth. The focus of English studies should therefore no longer be a set of canonical texts tied to the printed word, elitist critical practices and a 'mystic national identity', but rather, there should be a new subject, 'cultural studies'. This would focus more broadly on 'a series of questions and problems posed by contemporary culture' (MacCabe, 1987, p. 8), which would then generate a reading list containing traditional classics, a variety of contemporary media and the possibility of local variation. As times changed, so would the questions, and new questions would generate new reading lists.

Activity 7.5   *(Allow 5–10 minutes)*

How feasible do you find MacCabe's suggestion? Would the replacement of the canon by cultural studies provide a satisfactory solution for those criticizing its authority?

Comment

If generic forms emerge from social processes, then we should expect to see new
genres emerging in this current period of rapid cultural change, which might well
include more blending of oral, visual and printed material than is found in the
literate focus of authoritative texts in the first half of the twentieth century. We
have seen that postcolonial writers have found the very literate nature of the
Leavisite canon restrictive and sometimes disabling. MacCabe attempts to capture the changing nature of media and texts through his focus on questions rather
than answers within cultural studies, but there remain the issues of who will
determine the key questions and problems, whose interest and perspectives will
be embodied in the reading list, and which kinds of readings of whatever media
will be authorized. And can a loosely defined and constantly changing collection
of texts provide the cultural cohesion and continuity which seem to be the
function of the canon?

While the traditional canon reflects the centripetal forces in Bakhtin's model,
cultural studies reflects a stronger recognition of centrifugal forces, pushing us
towards diversity and change. For Bakhtin, the relationship between these two
sets of forces is unstable and constantly changing, so that there are historical
swings between one extreme and the other. In the next section, I look at how these
forces have been played out in the development of the literary canon in the USA,
and in recent controversies about alternative canons and cultural literacy.

7.6 CANONS, CULTURAL LITERACY AND POLITICAL CORRECTNESS IN THE USA

Early developments

In the USA, the development of a literary canon has interesting links and parallels
with the British experience. Similar themes emerge, but are expressed somewhat
differently.

First, how did a canon of literature develop in the USA? As in Britain,
literature study originally meant study of the Greek and Roman classics. In the
early part of the nineteenth century, professors of English literature did exist, but
their main job was to train young men from the privileged classes, through the
study of literature and rhetoric, to speak and write in a 'cultured style'. With the
break-up of the powerful rural slave-owning classes after the American Civil War
and the growth of industrial capitalism over the course of the nineteenth century,
an increasing number of lower-class young men began to enter colleges and
universities where learning literature became part of acquiring the culture of the
higher class which they wanted to enter. Matthew Arnold's ideas about literature
ennobling and enlightening the mind had spread rapidly across the Atlantic, but
the emphasis in the USA was on upward mobility through individual merit, rather
than using literature to 'gentle' the lower classes and keep society together, as it
was in Britain, or to control native subjects, as in India.

Well into the twentieth century, the humanities canon included a mixture of
Greek and Roman literature, and English and European classics by authors who
had been dead for at least a century.

A Roosevelt era canon

The following works formed the 1937–8 Freshman Book List, required reading in the humanities at Columbia University:

Homer, *Iliad*
Aeschylus, *Oresteia*
Sophocles, *Oedipus the King*
Sophocles, *Antigone*
Euripides, *Electra*
Euripides, *Iphigenia in Tauris*
Euripides, *Medea*
Aristophanes, *The Frogs*
Plato, *Apology*
Plato, *Symposium*
Plato, *Republic*
Aristotle, *Ethics*
Aristotle, *Poetics*
Lucretius, *De Rerum Natura*
Marcus Aurelius, *Meditations*
Virgil, *Aeneid*
St Augustine, *Confessions*
Dante, *Inferno*
Machiavelli, *The Prince*
Rabelais, *Gargantua and Pantagruel*
Montaigne, *Essays*
Shakespeare, *Henry IV, Parts I and II*
Shakespeare, *Hamlet*
Shakespeare, *King Lear*
Cervantes, *Don Quixote*
Milton, *Paradise Lost*
Spinoza, *Ethics*
Moilère, *Le Tartuffe*
Moilère, *Le Misanthrope*
Moilère, *The Physician in Spite of Himself*
Swift, *Gulliver's Travels*
Fielding, *Tom Jones*
Rousseau, *Confessions*
Voltaire, *Candide*
Goethe, *Faust*

(Cited in *Harpers Magazine*, September 1989, p. 45)

Notice that there are no American authors on this list, no women, and no one outside what might be called the high classical white European tradition.

During the 1930s an influential group of critics began to emerge in the USA who would, like the Leavisites in Britain, establish the study of literature in English as a respectable academic subject. The 'New Critics', as they became known, announced their purpose of combating the vulgar culture of industrial northern America and reinstating the true values of great literature and of the lost golden age of the old American south. Over the next 20 years they developed and established a literature canon through criticism, the publication of anthologies and teaching, which drew heavily on the English literature 'classics' but also included American writers and reflected the strong tradition of European, particularly German, scholarship which early immigrants to the USA brought with them. Marilyn Butler (1990) quotes an intellectual canon developed by academics and critics on the American east coast that includes Kant, Blake,

Wordsworth, Shelley, Hegel, Emerson, Carlyle, Whitman, Nietzsche, Freud and Wallace Stevens (Emerson was a nineteenth-century American essayist and Whitman and Wallace Stevens nineteenth- and twentieth-century American poets, respectively). This retrospective construction of a literary heritage which was American as well as Anglo-European was, like the Leavisite canon, associated with I.A. Richards's practical criticism (Richards, 1929).

The 1960s in the USA, however, as in Europe, brought a period of profound social upheaval. This involved a serious questioning of the traditional canon, the proposing of alternative canons, and the initiation of a series of controversies which are still being fought out today about what counts as great literature or worthwhile knowledge and how these should be passed on to future generations. This is how H. Bruce Franklin, a radical 1960s academic, describes his objections to the traditional canon which structured students' English studies before 1968:

1 This is a means of propagandizing the world view of these works, which tend to be almost entirely the world view of white males from relatively privileged social classes in societies actively engaged in conquering and ruling other peoples.

2 Since the world view within this literature tends to reflect the world view of the social class choosing these canonical works, it reinforces both the authority and the position – ethical, social, and economic – of the professors of literature.

3 Above all, it substitutes a tiny part for the whole, demeaning as subliterary or otherwise unworthy of serious attention almost the entire body of the world's literature, especially popular literature (including science fiction, detective stories, westerns, and tales of adventure and romance), folk literature, oral literature, literature based on the experience of work, especially industrial work and domestic work, and almost all literature by nonwhite peoples.

(Bruce Franklin, 1981, p. 96)

For Bruce Franklin the student revolutions of the 1960s were aimed at producing a new and more just era, but his views were not shared by all other American literary academics. In the best-selling book *The Closing of the American Mind,* the more conservative Allan Bloom (1987) describes the defeat in the 1960s of a small band of committed academics who stood firm by their subject standards, but were betrayed by weak colleagues who gave in to the demands of immature and headstrong students. For Bloom the 1960s ushered in a curriculum of dubious value and negligible content which he fears is leading to the collapse of the entire US educational structure.

Opening up the canon

How much has the traditional US English literary canon changed since the 1960s?

Activity 7.6	*(Allow about 10 minutes)*

The table opposite shows US literature anthologies in use in the late 1980s. How far would you say these reflect a gradual opening up of the literature canon?

Table 7.3   American literature anthologies

Title of text	Total number of contributors	White females	Black males	Black females	American Indians	Chicanos	Puerto Ricans	Asian Americans
Major Writers of America (Harcourt, Brace and World, 1962)	28	1	0	0	0	0	0	0
American Literature (Washington Square, 1966), 3 vols, 18th and 19th centuries only	108	7	0	0	0	0	0	0
American Poetry and Prose (Houghton Mifflin, 1970), 5th ed.	102	8	9	2	0	0	0	0
Anthology of American Literature (Macmillan, 1974), 2 vols	124	10	7	2	0	0	0	0
Literature of America (Wiley, 1978)	127	17	23	3	19a	0	0	0
The Norton Anthology of American Literature (1979), 2 vols	131	25	12	2	0	0	0	0
Major American Short Stories (Oxford, 1980)	34	8	2	0	0	0	0	0
American Literary Survey (Viking, 1980), 3rd expanded ed.	119	15	10	2	0	0	0	0
Magill Surveys in American Literature (Salem, 1980), 4 vols	147	28	9	2	0	0	0	0
The American Tradition in Literature (Random House, 1981)	164	28	8	1	14b	0	0	0

(a) All the contributions are anonymous except for one by N. Scott Momaday and four speeches

(b) All the contributions are anonymous

(Wald, 1989, p. 5)

Comment

I found it interesting to see how there appears to be a gradual broadening in the cultural background of authors selected for anthologies during the 1970s – but that this trend has not continued any further. I was also struck by the fact that native American writing is almost always presented anonymously in the only two anthologies where it appears at all. Like the old ballads and riddles sometimes included in English literature collections, it seems to be classified as 'folklore' rather than as a serious literature tradition. Over 50 per cent of the contributors to all anthologies are white males.

Although the evidence from these anthologies is not particularly encouraging for those wanting radical changes to the traditional canon, since the 1970s there have been a number of curriculum initiatives within higher education aimed at broadening and opening up the canon. For example, in 1988 Stanford University replaced its undergraduate course, or programme, in 'Western culture' with a new programme called 'Cultures, ideas and values'. This programme includes eight tracks (units) and every Stanford undergraduate has to choose one of these to study for a year. As the removal of the term 'western' suggests, tracks in this new curriculum programme include more work by people of non-European ancestry. They also include more work by women. Thirty per cent of the most widely used reading in this curriculum reflects this new diversity (names in italics in Table 7.4 below).

These changes, although modest, were interpreted by conservative US educationalists as a move to dismantle the authority of the traditional canon and replace it with cultural pluralism and 'political correctness'. They objected

Table 7.4 Widely used readings in the new 'Cultures, ideas and values' course, 1990–1

Used in 8 Tracks	Used in 4 Tracks
The Bible	*Chinua Achebe*
Sigmund Freud	*Marie de France*
Karl Marx	*Frederick Douglass*
William Shakespeare	*The Koran*
	Martin Luther
Used in 7 Tracks	*Mary Shelley*
Aristotle	Thomas More
Augustine	*Sappho*
Jean-Jacques Rousseau	Virgil
Virginia Woolf	
	Used in 3 Tracks
Used in 6 tracks	Thomas Aquinas
Plato	Charles Darwin
	Friedrich Engels
Used in 5 Tracks	John Locke
Dante	John Stuart Mill
Christine de Pizan	*Toni Morrison*
René Descartes	Friedrich Nietzsche
Homer	Sophocles
Niccolo Machiavelli	Jonathan Swift
	Voltaire

(Stanford University: Opening up the canon; Wasow, 1995)

(I am grateful to Thomas Wasow for permission to reproduce this information.)

in particular to the multicultural nature of some individual tracks within the new course syllabus. For instance, the 'Europe and the Americas' track includes on its reading list *I, Rigoberto Menchu*, the dictated autobiography of a Guatamalan Indian woman freedom fighter. For conservatives, *I, Rigoberto Menchu* typifies the replacement of traditional literature by subversive political propaganda (this book won the Nobel prize for literature in 1992).

Back to the 'Great Books'?

These complaints about the Stanford curriculum are part of a recent backlash against the multilingual and multicultural policies developed in the wake of the 1960s and 1970s civil rights movements, and against the new poststructuralist theories evolving in Europe around the same time.

Since 1980 in the USA there has been a strong lobby for a return to curricula based on the 'Great Books' and a reaction against multilingual provision for immigrant people, particularly in education. The 'Official English' movement is lobbying for an amendment to the US Constitution which would make English the country's official language, and pressure groups have been working at state level to reduce bilingual support in education and other public services. Arguments for 'Official English' and for a return to the 'Great Books' are closely associated with calls for the reinstatement of the 'traditional American values' of family, nation and Christianity.

Conservative educationalists complain that the new multicultural curricula provide no coherent cultural heritage, no substantial intellectual content to engage students' minds, and no setting up of explicit standards of truth and excellence. Bloom (1987) complains that without the traditional canon students can get no inkling of the great art and literature accumulated over the centuries, which address 'the permanent problems of man', and no common imaginative literary tradition which teaches how one should live. He fears that moral and ethical standards are lost in 'drab diversity' and 'a grey network of critical concepts'.

The argument that Americans need to re-establish a common cultural literary heritage has been taken up by another American literary academic, E.D. Hirsch Jr. Concerned with school students' lack of what he calls 'cultural literacy' – that is, the background knowledge needed to interpret texts which he sees as vital to efficient communication – Hirsch sets out his arguments for the establishment and teaching of a national cultural canon in US schools. In the appendix to his book *Cultural Literacy: what every American needs to know* (1987), he provides a 63-page descriptive list of 'What literate Americans know': dates, sayings, technical terms, place names, historical figures and so on. He claims:

> Literate culture has become the common currency for social and economic exchange in our democracy, and the only available ticket to full citizenship. Getting one's membership card is not tied to class or race. Membership is automatic if one learns the background information and linguistic conventions that are needed to read, write and speak effectively. Although everyone is literate in some local, regional or ethnic culture, the connection between mainstream culture and the national written languages justifies calling mainstream culture *the* basic culture of the nation.
>
> (Hirsch, 1987, p. 22)

Making this information explicit, Hirsch claims, is a democratic move, because it becomes accessible to all Americans. So what does this vital information look like?

Activity 7.7   *(Allow about 15 minutes)*

Reproduced below are the first two pages from the 63-page list given at the end of Hirsch's book. Can a common cultural canon for the USA be distilled in this way? How do the cultural roots of Hirsch's 'cultural literacy' compare with those of other canons discussed above?

The List

1066	adaptation
1492	Addams, Jane
1776	ad hoc
1861–1865	ad hominem
1914–1918	adieu
1939–1945	Adirondack Mountains
abbreviation (written English)	adjective
abolitionism	Adonis
abominable snowman	adrenal gland
abortion	adrenaline (fight or flight)
Abraham and Isaac	Adriatic Sea
Absence makes the heart grow fonder	adultery
absenteeism	adverb
absolute monarchy	AEC (Atomic Energy Commission)
absolute zero	Aegean Sea
abstract expressionism	Aeneas
academic freedom	Aeneid, The (title)
a cappella	aerobic
accelerator, particle	Aeschylus
accounting	Aesop's Fables (title)
AC/DC (alternating current/direct current)	aesthetics
Achilles	affirmative action
Achilles' heel	affluent society
acid	Afghanistan
acid rain	aficionado
acquittal	AFL-CIO
acronym	Africa
acrophobia	Agamemnon
Acropolis	aggression
Actions speak louder than words	Agnew, Spiro
active voice	agnosticism
act of God	agreement (grammar)
actuary	agribusiness
acupuncture	air pollution
A.D. (anno domini)	air quality index
Adam and Eve	Akron, Ohio

Adams, John

Adams, John Quincy

Aladdin and the Wonderful Lamp (title)

Alamo, the

Alaska

Alaska pipeline

Albania

Albany, New York

albatross around one's neck

Alberta

Albuquerque, New Mexico

alchemy

Alcott, Louisa May

Aleutian Islands

Alexander the Great

Alexandria, Egypt

alfresco

algae

Alger, Horatio

Algeria

Algiers

Ali, Muhammad

alias

Alice in Wonderland (title)

Alien and Sedition Acts

alienation

alkaline

Allah

Allegheny Mountains

allegory

allegro

Alliance for Progress

Allies (World War II)

Alabama

à la carte

alliteration

alloy

All roads lead to Rome

All's fair in love and war

All's well that ends well

All that glitters [sic] is not gold

All the world's a stage (text)

allusion

alma mater

alpha and omega

Alps

alter ego

alternator

alto

altruism

Amazonian

Amazon River

ambiguity

American Legion

American Stock Exchange

America the Beautiful (song)

amicus curiae

Am I my brother's keeper?

amino acids

amnesia

amnesty

amniotic sac

amoeba

amortization

amp (ampere)

ampersand (written English)

(Hirsch, 1987, pp. 152–3)

Comment

Although Hirsch's book (like Bloom's *The Closing of the American Mind*) rapidly became a best-seller in the United States, it has also attracted a considerable amount of criticism. It has been argued that the knowledge listed in Hirsch's canon is not neutral, but encodes particular kinds of cultural assumptions and values which reflect racialist and class interests. The very act of setting out 'what every American needs to know' by implication identifies those who don't know as 'not American': membership cards are not, as Hirsch maintains, open to everyone. Far from being a democratic project, Hirsch's proposal can be seen, like Leavis's canon, as strengthening and validating the control exercised by one section of a nation over the others.

We all, of course, use background cultural knowledge in reading and appreciating texts; the question is, rather, which kinds of cultural knowledge are marked as valid and important. Wald (1989) points out that very different kinds of knowledge are required to read poems coming out of the European and the native American cultural traditions. He argues that 'the very terms with which we have been trained to discuss and evaluate Euro-American literature – "Romanticism", "Frontier Epic", "Alienation", "National Consciousness" – are inadequate or must be radically redefined for the non-dominant cultures' (Wald, 1989, p. 11). The intellectual knowledge needed, for example, to appreciate the complexity of Eliot's *The Waste Land* is almost exclusively European-derived. Wald takes the section of the poem beginning 'Unreal city', which describes crowds of commuters coming over London Bridge and down King William Street as the church bell of St Mary Woolnoth strikes nine in the morning. He points out that Eliot's phrase 'Unreal city' is borrowed from the French poet Charles Baudelaire, and Eliot's description of the crowd , 'I had not thought death had undone so many', 'And each man fixed his eyes before his feet', echoes Dante's *Inferno* to suggest that life for these commuters is comparable to a living hell. Geographical knowledge of London is needed to know that St Mary Woolnoth overlooks the financial district of the city, and to appreciate that the crowds here are probably made up of bankers, businesswomen and men, and stockbrokers. There is a special significance in the hour which the clock is striking to mark the beginning of the working day: the ninth hour is when Christ died on the cross, according to St Matthew's Gospel. Thus, Wald argues, Eliot depends on the readers' implicit European cultural knowledge to understand the message in this part of the poem: that when the business day begins, Christianity dies.

Activity 7.8   *(Reading B)*

Read 'Hegemony and literary tradition in the United States' by Alan Wald (Reading B), where Wald discusses 'Plainview: 2' by the native American poet N. Scott Momaday and compares it to Eliot's poem *The Waste Land*. What different kinds of knowledge are needed to interpret this poem, in contrast to those required for *The Waste Land*? Can there ever be culture-free aesthetic criteria?

Comment

I was struck by the extent of specific background cultural knowledge which Wald shows is necessary for the interpretation of both poems. In the case of Eliot, this knowledge is passed on within university departments of literature, together with the application of a particular method of literary criticism. Understanding the Momaday poem, however, requires a different kind of cultural knowledge, unavailable to most non-native Americans. In addition, it cannot be fully understood or appreciated through an analysis of the printed text. An important part of the genre to which this poem belongs is realized through oral performance (like the Caribbean poetry discussed by Brathwaite in Reading A) and the relationship between performer and audience. The words on the page are only a small part of the art form. Genres of language arts in English that invoke oral and performance practice cannot be readily absorbed into the canon of current anthologies and literature departments, which are still strongly focused on printed texts and practical criticism. As Morris (1993) argues in relation to gender, new and different language arts can only be appreciated on their own terms if there are radical changes in ideas about what constitutes literature and different genres within it, and about how these should be 'read'.

7.7   CONCLUSION

In this chapter we have looked at the establishment of English literary canons at particular points of history in Britain, the USA and India. These have incorporated ideas about what counts as great literature, its civilizing effects, and the way it should be read and taught. We have considered the ways in which these canons and their associated practices have been criticized, and looked at attempts to open up the canon or to do away with it altogether.

The current trend in education policy in Britain and the USA towards re-establishing what are seen as more traditional literary canons seems to be part of an attempt to bring people together under a unified cultural identity (whether this is seen as elitist or democratic). Canons are thus an important part of nation and empire building, of trying to weld people together using a common authoritative heritage. But you may want to consider whether canons can ever be a totally unifying force, or whether they will always inevitably represent the interests and power of a particular social group. They seem to be produced by the centripetal forces in language and culture, which are always moving towards a unitary language system and cultural and political centralization (Bakhtin, 1981). These centripetal forces, if you recall, are always pitted against opposing centrifugal forces of inevitable variation, resistance and disunification (represented in efforts to open the canon up or even do away with it altogether). These two sets of opposing forces are always detectable, even though one or other may seem to be in the ascendant. For Bakhtin this perpetual struggle within language is what keeps it alive and functional: total centralization in language standardization and literary canonization would mean an unsustainable rigidity, while too much diversity would mean the loss of shared understanding and the breakdown of communication. From this point of view, canon formation will be particularly important at times when centripetal forces in language and cultural life are dominant, but these canons will inevitably be attacked and at least partly dismantled when the pendulum starts to swing in the opposite direction.

One could argue that canons always contain the seeds of their own destruction, because they are defined by what they exclude as well as by what they include and will therefore always be a site for struggle and contestation. Exclusions – of particular kinds of writers and genres, and of competing representations of cultural experience – have been significant for each of the canons we have discussed in this chapter.

Activity 7.9   *(Allow about 15 minutes)*

Where do you position yourself in relation to the arguments presented in this chapter? How important is it to have an English literary canon as a central part of cultural life and education? Should this be a traditional canon, an updated canon, an open canon … ?

Reading A
ENGLISH IN THE CARIBBEAN:
NOTES ON NATION LANGUAGE AND POETRY

Edward Kamau Brathwaite

This is a written representation of part of an unscripted talk presented at Harvard University in the USA in 1979. The original presentation was accompanied by tape recordings of performances by Caribbean poets.

> You may excel
> in knowledge of their tongue
> and universal ties may bind you close to them;
> but what they say, and how they feel –
> the subtler details of their meaning,
> thinking, feeling, reaching –
> these are closed to you and me …
> as are, indeed, the interleaves of speech
> – our speech – which fall to them …dead leaves …
>
> (G. Adali-Morty,'Belonging' from *Messages*)

> The Negro in the West Indies becomes proportionately whiter – that is, he becomes closer to being a real human being – in direct ratio to his mastery of the language.
>
> (Frantz Fanon, *Peau Noire, Masque Blancs*)

> Yurokon held the twine in his hands as if with a snap, a single fierce pull, he would break it *now* at last. Break the land. Break the sea. Break the savannah. Break the forest. Break the twig. Break the bough.
>
> (Wilson Harris, *Sleepers of Roraima*)

What I am going to talk about this morning is language from the Caribbean, the process of using English in a different way from the 'norm'. English in a sense as I prefer to call it. English in an ancient sense. English in a very traditional sense. And sometimes not English at all, but language …

We in the Caribbean have a plurality of languages. We have English, which is the imposed language on much of the archipelago; it is an imperial language, as are French, Dutch, and Spanish. We also have what we call Creole English, which is a mixture of English and an adaptation that English took in the new environment of the Caribbean when it became mixed with the other imported languages. We have also what is called *nation language*, which is the kind of English spoken by the people who were brought to the Caribbean, not the official English now, but the language of slaves and laborers – the servants who were brought in by the conquistadors. Finally, we have the remnants of ancestral languages still persisting in the Caribbean. There is Amerindian, which is active in certain parts of Central America but not in the Caribbean because the Amerindians are a destroyed people, and their languages were practically destroyed. We have Hindi, spoken by some of the more traditional East Indians who live in the Caribbean, and there are also varieties of Chinese. And, miraculously, there are survivals of African languages still persisting in the Caribbean. So we have that spectrum – that prism – of languages similar to the kind of structure that Dennis [Brutus] described for

South Africa. Now, I have to give you some kind of background to the development of these languages, the historical development of this plurality, because I can't take it for granted that you know and understand the history of the Caribbean.

The Caribbean is a set of islands stretching out from Florida in a mighty curve. You must know of the Caribbean at least from television, at least now with hurricane David coming right into it. The islands stretch out in an arc of some two thousand miles from Florida through the Atlantic to the South American coast, and they were originally inhabited by Amerindian people, Taino, Siboney, Carib, Arawak.

In 1492, Columbus 'discovered' (as it is said) the Caribbean, and with that discovery came the intrusion of European culture and peoples and a fragmentation of the original Amerindian culture. We had Europe 'nationalizing' itself, and there were Spanish, French, English, and Dutch conquerors so that people had to start speaking (and thinking in) four metropolitan languages rather than possibly a single native language. Then with the destruction of the Amerindians, which took place within thirty years of Columbus's discovery (one million dead a year), it was necessary for the Europeans to import new labor bodies into the Caribbean. And the most convenient form of labor was the labor on the very edge of the trade winds – the labor on the edge of the slave trade winds, the labor on the edge of the hurricane, the labor on the edge of West Africa. And so the peoples of Ashanti, Congo, Nigeria, from all that mighty coast of western Africa were imported into the Caribbean. And we had the arrival in that area of a new language structure. It consisted of many languages, but basically they had a common semantic and stylistic form. What these languages had to do, however, was to submerge themselves, because officially the conquering peoples – the Spaniards, the English, the French, and the Dutch – insisted that the language of public discourse and conversation, of obedience, command, and reception, should be English, French, Spanish, or Dutch. They did not wish to hear people speaking Ashanti or any of the Congolese languages. So there was a submergence of this imported language. Its status became one of inferiority. Similarly, its speakers were slaves. They were conceived of as inferiors – nonhuman, in fact. But this very submergence served an interesting intercultural purpose, because although people continued to speak English as it was spoken in Elizabethan times and on through the Romantic and Victorian ages, that English was, nonetheless, still being influenced by the underground language, the submerged language that the slaves had brought. And that underground language was itself constantly transforming itself into new forms. It was moving from a purely African form to a form that was African, but which was adapted to the new environment and adapted to the cultural imperative of the European languages. And it was influencing the way in which the French, Dutch, and Spanish spoke their own languages. So there was a very complex process taking place, which is now beginning to surface in our literature.

In the Caribbean, as in South Africa (and in any area of cultural imperialism for that matter), the educational system did not recognize the presence of these various languages. What our educational system did was to recognize and maintain the language of the conquistador – the language of the planter, the language of the official, the language of the Anglican preacher. It insisted that not only would English be spoken in the Anglophone Caribbean, but that the educational system would carry the contours of an English heritage. Hence Shakespeare, George Eliot, Jane Austen – British literature and literary forms, the models that were intimate to Europe, that were intimate to Great Britain, that had very little to do, really, with the environment and the reality of the Caribbean – were dominant in the Caribbean educational system. It was a very surprising situation. People were forced to learn things that had no relevance to themselves. Paradoxically, in the Caribbean (as in many other 'cultural disaster' areas), the people educated in this system came to know more, even today, about English kings and queens than they do about our own national heroes, our own slave rebels – the people who helped to build and to destroy our society. We are more excited by English literary models, by the concept of, say, Sherwood Forest and Robin Hood, than we are by Nanny of the Maroons, a name some of us didn't even know until a few years ago. And in terms of what we write, our perceptual models, we are more conscious (in terms of sensibility) of the falling of snow for instance – the models are all there for the falling of the snow – than of the force of the hurricanes that take place every year. In other words, we haven't got the syllables, the syllabic intelligence, to describe the hurricane, which is our own experience; whereas we can describe the imported alien experience of the snowfall. It is that kind of situation that we are in.

Now the Creole adaption to that is the little child who, instead of writing in an essay 'The snow was falling on the fields of Shropshire' (which is what our children literally were writing until a few years ago, below drawings they made of white snow fields and the corn-haired people who inhabited such a landscape), wrote 'The snow was falling on the cane fields'. The child had not yet reached the obvious statement that it wasn't snow at all, but rain that was probably falling on the cane fields. She was trying to have both cultures at the same time. But that is creolization.

What is even more important, as we develop this business of emergent language in the Caribbean, is the actual rhythm and the syllables, the very body work, in a way, of the language. What English has given us as a model for poetry, and to a lesser extent, prose (but poetry is the basic tool here), is the pentameter: 'The cúrfew tólls the knéll of párting dáy'. There have, of course, been attempts to break it. And there were other dominant forms like, for example, *Beowulf* (c. 750), *The Seafarer,* and what Langland (1322?–1400?) had produced:

> For trewthe telleth that love. is triacle of hevene;
> May no synne be on him sene. that useth that spise,
> And alle his werkes he wrougte. with love as him liste.

Or, from *Piers the Plowman* (which does not make it into *Palgrave's Golden Treasury,* but which we all had to 'do' at school) the haunting prologue:

> In a somer seson. whan soft was the sonne
> I shope me into shroudes. as I a shepe were

which has recently inspired our own Derek Walcott with his first major nation language effort:

> In idle August, while the sea soft,
> and leaves of brown islands stick to the rim
> of this Caribbean, I blow out the light
> by the dreamless face of Maria Concepcion
> to ship as a seaman on the schooner *Flight.*
> (D. Walcott, 'The Schooner Flight' from *The Star-Apple Kingdom*)

But by the time we reach Chaucer (1345–1400), the pentameter prevails. Over in the New World, the Americans – Walt Whitman – tried to bridge or to break the pentameter through a cosmic movement, a large movement of sound. Cummings tried to fragment it. And Marianne Moore attacked it with syllabics. But basically the pentameter remained, and it carries with it a certain kind of experience, which is not the experience of a hurricane. The hurricane does not roar in pentameter. And that's the problem: how do you get a rhythm that approximates the natural experience, the environmental experience? We have been trying to break out of the entire pentametric model in the Caribbean and to move into a system that more closely and intimately approaches our own experience. So that is what we are talking about now.

It is nation language in the Caribbean that, in fact, largely ignores the pentameter. Nation language is the language that is influenced very strongly by the African model, the African aspect of our New World/Caribbean heritage. English it may be in terms of its lexicon, but it is not English in terms of its syntax. And English it certainly is not in terms of its rhythm and timbre, its own sound explosion. In its contours, it is not English, even though the words, as you hear them, would be English to a greater or lesser degree. And this brings us back to the question that some of you raised yesterday: can English be a revolutionary language? And the lovely answer that came back was: it is not English that is the agent. It is not language, but people, who make revolutions.

I think, however, that language does really have a role to play here, certainly in the Caribbean. But it is an English that is not the standard, imported, educated English, but that of the submerged, surrealist experience and sensibility, which has always been there and which is now increasingly coming to the surface and influencing the perception of contemporary Caribbean people. It is what I call, as I say, *nation language*. I use the term in contrast to *dialect*. The word dialect has been bandied about for a long time, and it carries very pejorative overtones. Dialect is thought of as bad English. Dialect is 'inferior English'. Dialect is the language when you want to make fun of someone. Caricature speaks in dialect. Dialect has a long history coming from the plantation where people's dignity is distorted through their language and the descriptions that the dialect gave to them. Nation language, on the other hand, is the submerged area of that dialect that is much more closely allied to the African aspect of experience in the Caribbean. It may be in English, but often it is in an English which is like a howl, or a shout, or a machine-gun, or the wind, or a wave. It is also like the blues. And sometimes it is English and African at the same time. I am going to give you some examples. But I should tell you that the reason I have to talk so much is that there has been very little written about our nation language. I bring you to the notion of nation language but I can refer you to very little literature, to very few resources. I cannot refer you to what you call an *establishment*. I cannot really refer you to authorities because there aren't any. One of our urgent tasks now is to try to create our own authorities. But I will give you a few ideas of what people have tried to do.

The forerunner of all this was, of course, Dante Alighieri who, at the beginning of the fourteenth century, argued, in *De vulgari eloquentia* (1304), for the recognition of the (his own) Tuscan vernacular as the nation language to replace Latin as the most natural, complete, and accessible means of verbal expression. And the movement was, in fact, successful throughout Europe with the establishment of national languages and literatures. But these very successful national languages then proceeded to ignore local European colonial languages such as Basque and Gaelic, and to suppress overseas colonial languages wherever they were heard. And it was not until the appearance of Burns in the eighteenth century and Rothenberg, Trask, Vansina, Tedlock, Waley, Walton, Whallon, Jahn, Jones, Whitely, Beckwith, Herskovitz, and Ruth Finnegan, among many others in this century, that we have returned, at least to the notion of oral literature, although I don't need to remind you that oral literature is our oldest form of 'auriture' and that it continues richly throughout the world today.

In the Caribbean, our novelists have always been conscious of these native resources, but the critics and academics have, as is often the case, lagged far behind. Indeed, until 1970, there was a positive intellectual, almost social, hostility to the concept of dialect as language. But there were some significant studies in linguistics, such as Beryl Lofton Bailey's *Jamaican Creole Syntax: A Transformational Approach;* also: F.G. Cassidy, *Jamaica Talk;* Cassidy and R.B. LePage, *Dictionary of Jamaican English;* and, still to come, Richard Allsopp's mind-blowing *Dictionary of Caribbean English.* There are three glossaries from Frank Collymore in Barbados and A.J. Seymour and John R. Rickford of Guyana; and studies on the African presence in Caribbean language by Mervyn Alleyne, Beverley Hall, and Maureen Warner Lewis. In addition, there has been work by Douglas Taylor and Cicely John, among others, on aspects of some of the Amerindian languages; and Dennis Craig, Laurence Carrington, Velma Pollard, and several others at the University of the West Indies' School of Education have done some work on the structure of nation language and its psychosomosis in and for the classroom.

Few of the writers mentioned, however, have gone into nation language as it affects literature. They have set out its grammar, syntax, transformation, structure, and all of those things. But they haven't really been able to make any contact between the nation language and its expression in our literature. Recently, a French poet and novelist from Martinique, Edouard Glissant, had a remarkable article in *Alcheringa,* a nation language journal published at Boston University. The article was called 'Free and Forced Poetics', and in it, for the first time, I feel an effort to describe what nation language really means. For the author of the article it is the language of enslaved persons. For him, nation language is a strategy: the slave is forced to use a certain kind of language in order to disguise himself, to disguise his personality, and to retain his culture. And he defines that language as 'forced poetics' because it is a kind of prison language, if you want to call it that.

And then we have another nation language poet, Bruce St. John, from Barbados, who has written some informal introductions to his own work which describe the nature of the experiments that he is conducting and the kind of rules that he begins to perceive in the way that he uses his language.

I myself have an article called 'Jazz and the West Indian novel', which appeared in a journal called *Bim* in the early 1960s, and there I attempt to show that the connection between native musical structures and the native language is very necessary to the understanding of nation language. That music is, in fact, the surest threshold to the language that comes out of it.

So that is all we have to offer as authority, which isn't very much, really. But that is how it is. And in fact, one characteristic of nation language is its orality. It is from 'the oral tradition'. And therefore you wouldn't really expect that large, encyclopedic body of learned comment on it that you would expect for a written language and literature.

Now I'd like to describe for you some of the characteristics of our nation language. First of all it is from, as I've said, an oral tradition. The poetry, the culture itself, exists not in a dictionary but in the tradition of the spoken word. It is based as much on sound as it is on song. That is to say, the noise that it makes is part of the meaning, and if you ignore the noise (or what you would think of as noise, shall I say), then you lose part of the meaning. When it is written, you lose the sound or the noise, and therefore you lose part of the meaning. Which is, again, why I have to have a tape recorder for this presentation. I want you to get the sound of it, rather than the sight of it.

Now in order to break down the pentameter, we discovered an ancient form which was always there, the calypso [or kaiso]. This is a form that I think everyone knows about. It does not employ the iambic pentameter. It employs dactyls. It therefore mandates the use of the tongue in a certain way, the use of sound in a certain way. It is a model that we are moving naturally toward now.

(Iambic   To be or not to be, that is the question
Pentameter)

(Kaiso)   The stone had skidded arc'd and bloomed into islands
               Cuba San Domingo
               Jamaica Puerto Rico

But not only is there a difference in syllabic or stress pattern, there is an important difference in shape of intonation. In the Shakespeare (above), the voice travels in a single forward plane toward the horizon of its end. In the kaiso, after the skimming movement of the first line, we have a distinct variation. The voice dips and deepens to describe an intervallic pattern. And then there are more ritual forms like *kumina*, like *shango*, the religious forms, which I won't have time to go into here, but which begin to disclose the complexity that is possible with nation language. What I am attempting to do this morning is to give you a kind of vocabulary introduction to nation language, rather than an analysis of its more complex forms. But I want to make the point that the forms are capable of remarkable complexity, and if there were time I could take you through some of the more complex musical/literary forms as well.

The other thing about nation language is that it is part of what may be called *total expression*, a notion that is not unfamiliar to you because you are coming back to that kind of thing now. Reading is an isolated, individualistic expression. The oral tradition, on the other hand, makes demands not only on the poet but also on the audience to complete the community: the noise and sounds that the poet makes are responded to by the audience and are returned to him. Hence we have the creation of a continuum where the meaning truly resides. And this total expression comes about because people live in the open air, because people live in conditions of poverty, because people come from a historical experience where they had to rely on their own breath patterns rather than on paraphernalia like books and museums. They had to depend on *immanence*, the power within themselves, rather than the technology outside themselves.

In the remainder of his lecture, Brathwaite introduces the work of a range of Caribbean poets in more detail, using tape readings.

Selected References

[These references are included for the purposes of this chapter.]

ADALI-MORTY, G. (1970) 'Belonging' in KOFI AWOONOR and ADALI-MORTY, G. (eds) *Messages: poems from Ghana*, London, Heinemann

FANON, F. ([1965] 1992) *Peau Noire, Masque Blancs*, Paris, Editions de Seuil.

HARRIS, W. (1970) *The Sleepers of Roraima: a Carib trilogy*, London, Faber.

WALCOTT, D. (1979) *The Star-Apple Kingdom*, London, Cape.

Source: Brathwaite (1981), pp. 15–25

Reading B
HEGEMONY AND LITERARY TRADITION IN THE UNITED STATES

Alan Wald

Let's examine 'Plainview: 2', by N. Scott Momaday :

I saw an old Indian,
at Saddle mountain.
He drank and dreamed of drinking
and a blue-black horse.

Remember my horse running,
Remember my horse

Remember my horse running,
Remember my horse.
Remember my horse wheeling,
Remember my horse.
Remember my horse wheeling,
Remember my horse.
Remember my horse blowing,
Remember my horse.
Remember my horse blowing,
Remember my horse.
Remember my horse standing,
Remember my horse.
Remember my horse standing,
Remember my horse.

Remember my horse hurting,
Remember my horse.
Remember my horse hurting,
Remember my horse.
Remember my horse falling,
Remember my horse.
Remember my horse falling,
Remember my horse.

Remember my horse dying.
Remember my horse.
Remember my horse dying.
Remember my horse.

A horse is one thing.
An Indian is another
An old horse is old
An old Indian is sad.
I saw an old Indian at Saddle Mountain
He drank and dreamed of drinking
And a blue-black horse.

Remember my horse running,
Remember my horse.
Remember my horse wheeling,
Remember my horse.
Remember my horse blowing,
Remember my horse.
Remember my horse falling,
Remember my horse.
Remember my horse dying,
Remember my horse.

Remember my blue-black horse.
Remember my blue-black horse.
Remember my horse.
Remember my horse.
Remember.
Remember.

The central contrast between the Momaday poem and the Eliot poem *The Waste Land* ought to be clear at once. It is as if they came from two different cultures, even though both claim to be poems by Americans. But Momaday's poem has no direct allusions to the Christian Bible, no citations from European history, no references to famous metropolises, no quotations from famous writers – and all the other stuff out of which the dominant Euro-American element in United States culture is comprised. Yet this ... poem is more truly 'American' than the first [*The Waste Land*]: not primarily because of the author's Native American Indian ancestry, but because the setting of and characters in this poem could only be North American. But, ironically, I think that many students and teachers of American literature – trained by our ethnocentric educational system – would have some difficulty coming to grips with Momaday's poem, even though it is written in the English language and even though the events depicted are in certain respects more comprehensible (though not necessarily 'simpler') than those in [the early stanzas of] *The Waste Land*.

The problem for such readers would, I think, be that the aesthetic experience is remarkably different. To begin with, Eliot's poem is intellectual and meant to be read carefully and studied for multiple layers of association, denotation and connotation piled up on each line. But the Momaday poem is really a sort of chant: it is, at least in terms of the tradition from which it derives, a sort of oral poem. A chant, of course, is meant to be sung to a rhythm provided by drums in the background. While Momaday himself is a contemporary writer, a professor of English whose work is not wholly free of Euro-American and possibly other non-native American influences, we must still recognize the centrality of the chant to this piece.

The primary feature of the chant is, of course, repetition. The whole poem is, in fact, a variation of the first stanza, with the extended and repeated description of the horse's death. In the ninth stanza we do have the hint of some sort of philosophic meaning – 'A horse is one thing./An Indian another:/An old horse is old,/An old Indian is sad'. But the meaning here is relatively clear, or at least is not enigmatic, so that one must recognize that the aesthetic dimensions of the poem will have to come from an appreciation of things other than its potential for generating Eliot-like classical allusions and literary puzzles. Probably, if this chant were read effectively or chanted to rhythm or music properly, the repetition would lead to an intensification of the important themes of the poem, which have to do with the role of the horse in Native American culture, the significance of Saddle Mountain, the significance of the aged person as the link to a fading culture, the tragedy of living through memory and so on.

The point is that this poem grows out of a different life experience than the segment of Eliot's poem. It is not derived from the Western cultural tradition that dominates Euro-American literature, and it therefore represents one of the kinds of literature still largely excluded from the canon. Only on rare occasions have I seen a survey course in 'American literature' that included the literature of the first Americans: most purported 'surveys' start in the seventeenth century with the writings of the European invaders.

Source: Wald, 1989, pp. 12–15

8 A TONGUE, FOR SIGHING

Jane Miller

8.1 INTRODUCTION: DILEMMAS FOR WRITERS

In this chapter I shift perspective away from the cultural institutions and historical processes we discussed in Chapter 7 on the English canon, to hear from writers themselves about writing in English. Writers who reflect on the business of writing in English and on their own entry into the activity have a good deal to tell us about language and culture generally. As writers, they have needed to develop knowledge about language and, as a rule, an ear for its meanings that is more acute and subtler than that possessed by the rest of us. Yet theirs is also a heightened version of communal, shared language use; and for the most part their reflections on writing and becoming a writer focus on the complex and changing relations which exist in any society between spoken and written forms of the language, or languages, of that society. The written language is always the product of some form of schooling, and most writers – if very differently – work within the tension produced between the schooled character of writing and the less formal ways in which we first learned to speak and to articulate ourselves within conversations. As this chapter shows, such reflections by writers are often incorporated into their novels and poems, as central preoccupations and as metaphors for the connections that may exist between individual consciousness, and socially and culturally shared assumptions and values. Many writers have also lectured and written extensively about these questions. In this chapter I consider examples of that sort of writing too.

If such reflections by writers are likely to express ambivalence and contradiction about language and, especially, about the complex relations between spoken and written language, we should not be surprised by that. Since ancient times, writing has mimicked and incorporated speech into all its forms: drama, epic poetry, narrative and so on. Yet the role of writer and the activity of writing have also been perceived as specialized, different, in some respects constraining, but in other ways susceptible to new possibilities of form and playfulness. For many writers, there is a complex process of negotiation between the rich resources of memory and childhood, and public expectations of their writing. Writers rarely discuss such issues as if they were primarily academic or abstract ones. Indeed, as we see below, issues of language such as these are lived as aspects of history, politics and social relations; and it is characteristic of such discussion to dwell on division and polarity.

In 'Belfast' the Irish poet Seamus Heaney, for instance, writes of one such division positively, as something at the very heart of his work. History, language, culture and consciousness are implicated in this for him.

> I speak and write in English, but do not altogether share the preoccupations and perspectives of an Englishman. I teach English literature, I publish in London, but the English tradition is not ultimately home. I live off another hump as well …
>
> One half of one's sensibility is in a cast of mind that comes from belonging to a place, an ancestry, a history, a culture, whatever one wants

to call it. But consciousness and quarrels with the self are the result of what [D.H.] Lawrence called 'the voices of my education'.

Those voices pull in two directions, back through the political and cultural traumas of Ireland, and out towards the urgencies and experience of the world beyond it ...

If you like, I began as a poet when my roots were crossed with my reading. I think of the personal and Irish pieties as vowels, and the literary awarenesses nourished on English as consonants. My hope is that the poems will be vocables adequate to my whole experience.

(Heaney, 1980, pp. 34–7)

Yet for Samuel Beckett, another Irish writer, a move from writing in English to writing in French seems to have released something vital in him and to have allowed for the rupture from his childhood, Ireland and even the particular poetic potential of English, which his work required. Writers may come to express proprietorial interests in the language in which they write, but they have usually approached that language with some anxiety about their own rights to it and to the traditions of writing which can seem to haunt the language itself.

In this chapter, I focus first on what have sometimes been called 'the new English literatures', and specifically on a number of writers for whom dilemmas over the language have been particularly pressing ones, since they approached writing and English through schooling within a colonial or ex-colonial society. More than that, the language and culture of their childhood and growing up could never represent a settled and unproblematic world to which they might return at will. The relations between the two or more worlds they inhabit or have inhabited are likely to be even less comfortably allied and even less easily reconciled than the ones Seamus Heaney anticipates for himself. But I also return to Seamus Heaney and to the continuities that exist between writers entering English from the peripheries, as it were, and writers whose relation to what Edward Said has called 'the metropolitan centres' seems less problematic.

In an important sense, I believe, there are tensions and contradictions at the heart of the compulsion to write at all, and their source lies in the divisions and contradictions intrinsic to all language. No speaker is ever, as the Russian literary theorist Mikhail Bakhtin once wrote, 'the first speaker, the one who disturbs the eternal silence of the universe' (Bakhtin, 1986, p. 69). There has always been another speaker, just as any utterance is bound to be followed by another utterance. Every writer is similarly preceded and followed. Thus every writer writes within and against some notion of a tradition, however inhospitable that tradition may be. But every writer also endeavours and needs to contribute something else, something more, something new: to break with tradition as well as to extend and remake it. The tension lies here: in the dialogue a writer engages in with other writers, in the shared, recognizable character of language, *but also* in the equally strong impulse a writer feels to go against what is constraining, determining.

I begin with recent debates among African, West Indian and Indian writers in English. I then hope to link some of the issues arising from these debates with the work of an experimental woman writer from the early part of the twentieth century and with certain postcolonial and feminist approaches to the subject. I end with two contemporary women writers, Maxine Hong Kingston and Eva Hoffman, both of whom write from experiences of exile and dislocation, and from the strengths as well as the drawbacks of becoming a writer in English. These include an acknowledgement that silence and losing your voice may be terrifying; a memory of language learning; and an ability to make use of the additional resources of bilingualism.

Figure 8.1   Ngũgĩ wa Thiong'o

8.2 DECOLONIZING THE MIND

In 1981 Ngũgĩ wa Thiong'o, the Kenyan writer, delivered a paper called 'The language of African literature' at a conference of African writers. It is a piece he has returned to several times and which has been published in a number of forms and places. That paper, now a chapter in a collection of important essays called *Decolonising the Mind* (Ngũgĩ, 1986a), explains the promise he made when his novel *Petals of Blood* was published in 1977, to stop writing in English and to write from that point onwards in either Gĩkũyũ, his first language, or Kiswahili, the Kenyan national language. A statement preceding the essays ends with the words: 'I hope that through the age old medium of translation I shall be able to continue dialogue with all.'

❖   ❖   ❖   ❖   ❖

Activity 8.1   *(Reading A)*

Read the extract from 'The language of African literature' by Ngũgĩ wa Thiong'o (Reading A). How far do you feel Ngũgĩ's decision to stop writing in English is justified?

❖   ❖   ❖   ❖   ❖

A complex history and politics lie behind Ngũgĩ's decision to give up writing in English, and much painful drama and contention have come in its wake. Ngũgĩ was arrested and imprisoned in 1978 as a consequence of some of the anti-government views expressed in his English writing. Other writers all over the world have been moved to explain or justify their own use of English, where it stood for them as the language of imperialism, of racism, of western assertions of cultural superiority, as well as (for some of them) having the status of a second or third language, a language learned in school rather than at home.

In starting from Ngũgĩ and from the specificity of his situation and politics I want to make some preliminary observations about the passage I have chosen from his essay. It is significant that he starts from his first language, from his childhood memories of its music, its meanings, its narrative riches and the linguistic awareness and values he learned as a speaker of it. Any consideration of which language a writer may choose to write in will involve complex questions about power and culture, about the status of the language in the community where it is spoken as well as in the wider world, about traditions of writing and the social relations to which a writer may hope to refer and to contribute. But the choice of language is also an intensely personal issue, a matter of identity and of cultural allegiance. For Ngũgĩ, the language of family, of work, of stories, of literature and of pleasure was also the language in which he and many other children began their schooling. Later, he went to a school where it was banned, literally forbidden. English became, as he puts it, *the* language. Success in English was more important than success in all other areas of the curriculum. It brought with it the potential for 'colonial elitedom' and it also brought knowledge of the work of writers in English – admired writers – many of whom knew nothing of Africa or African life, though they might casually, or deliberately, cast aspersions on its institutions, inhabitants, languages, culture. As Ngũgĩ says, 'Thus language and literature were taking us further and further from ourselves to other selves, from our world to other worlds.'

Writers may be said to write from what they know but to rely on a capacity for recognition in their readers. For Ngũgĩ, his hard-won mastery of an English of great expressiveness and precision remains hopelessly contaminated by the politics of its acquisition, by the history of Kenya's colonial past, by the part played by English in education and other forms of social control, by the fact that the poorest, most oppressed groups and individuals in the country are unable to read English, by the continuing exploitation of Africa by the west and by Africa's need, in his eyes, of its own writers and of their articulation and analysis of people's current experience in the literature they produce. To use English is, for Ngũgĩ, to remain mired in 'colonial alienation' and to refuse the all-important task of enabling the young to transcend the history that produced such alienation. It is to assent to a continuing European theft of African culture, as of its other 'natural' resources.

Ngũgĩ had written four novels in English, as well as essays, plays and short stories, when he decided he would not write in English again, although at first he made a distinction between his creative work and his polemical writing. The language of his early novel, *Weep Not, Child* (first published 1964), for instance, as of his last in English, *Petals of Blood* (first published 1977), is a spare and supple English which is able to stand in for dialogue in other languages and to communicate an elaborate and detailed social world to those who are unfamiliar with it, as well as to those whose life it more closely resembles.

Extract from the opening of *Weep Not, Child*

Nyokabi called him. She was a small, black woman, with a bold but grave face. One could tell by her small eyes full of life and warmth that she had once been beautiful. But time and bad conditions do not favour beauty. All the same, Nyokabi had retained her full smile – a smile that lit up her dark face.

'Would you like to go to school?'

'O, mother!' Njoroge gasped. He half feared that the woman might withdraw her words. There was a little silence till she said,

'We are poor. You know that.'

'Yes, mother.' His heart pounded against his ribs slightly. His voice was shaky.

'So you won't be getting a mid-day meal like other children.'

'I understand.'

'You won't bring shame to me by one day refusing to attend school?'

O mother, I'll never bring shame to you. Just let me get there, just let me. The vision of his childhood again opened before him. For a time he contemplated the vision. He lived in it alone. It was just there, for himself; a bright future … Aloud he said, 'I like school.'

He said this quietly. His mother understood him.

'All right. You'll begin on Monday. As soon as your father gets his pay we'll go to the shops. I'll buy you a shirt and a pair of shorts.'

(Ngũgĩ, 1976, p. 3)

Ngũgĩ does not, as some writers in his position do, mimic the patterns and rhythms of the speech of his characters, or attempt to reproduce their actual language, though in *Petals of Blood* he introduces, without glossary but in helpful context, items of vocabulary from Gĩkũyũ. His novels carry the pain and conflict of the postcolonial experience, and his English smoothly (perhaps too smoothly for Ngũgĩ's own peace of mind) conveys the tensions involved in being schooled out of the culture of childhood and into values and understandings which are explicitly grounded in views of that childhood world as a primitive tribal one, better forgotten and abandoned. Yet the reality of what could be delivered by an

English education was often the kind of empty, rootless, isolated existence lived by Ngũgĩ's central characters, men unnourished by what they have so painfully acquired and cut off from the society they hope to serve.

Such a character is Godfrey Munira in *Petals of Blood*, whose training and experience as a teacher have made him unable to meet the real needs of his pupils. The shoddiness of the educational legacy he has inherited is contrasted with the children's intelligence and curiosity. Here, he has just returned from taking them out on a walk to study nature.

> He was pleased with himself. But then the children started asking him awkward questions. Why did things eat each other? Why can't the eaten eat back? Why did God allow this and that to happen? He had never bothered with those kinds of questions and to silence them he told them that it was simply a law of nature. What was a law? What was nature? Was he a man? Was he God? A law was simply a law and nature was nature. What about men and God? Children, he told them, it's time for a break.
>
> (Ngũgĩ, 1986b, p. 22)

It was not only, of course, that Ngũgĩ's novels in English tackled the effects of colonialism on Kenyan life. He also acknowledges that he learned from western writers (particularly from Joseph Conrad) vital narrative techniques, without

Figure 8.2   Petals of Blood

which he found it hard to imagine writing fiction. When he decided to write in Gĩkũyũ, which had at that time a relatively exiguous and undeveloped literature, he could not at first find traditions of written narrative to help him. Then, as he points out in his essay 'The language of African fiction', which was first published in 1984, he looked elsewhere.

> Now my own observation of how people ordinarily narrated events to one another had also shown me that they quite happily accepted interventions, digressions, narrative within a narrative and dramatic illustrations without losing the main narrative thread. The story-within-a-story was part and parcel of the conversational norms of the peasantry. The linear/biographical unfolding of a story was more removed from actual social practice than the narrative of Conrad and [George] Lamming.
> (Ngũgĩ, 1986a, p. 76)

In the earlier essay, 'The language of African literature' (1986a), Ngũgĩ recalls a conference of African writers at Makerere University in Uganda, which he attended as a young man in 1962. He wanted above all to show *Weep Not, Child* to Chinua Achebe, the somewhat older and already greatly admired Nigerian writer. Much of Ngũgĩ's argumentative writing has taken the form of a dialogue with Achebe. It is helpful, therefore, to consider the older writer's position on the use of English.

8.3   APPROPRIATING ENGLISH

Achebe also remembers the famous Makerere conference in his article 'English and the African writer', which was first published in 1965. In this, he argues strongly for a *national* as opposed to what he calls an *ethnic* literature. He too is arguing from what he sees as the *reality* of an Africa, where alienation has indeed been an inevitable consequence of the kind of education a carefully selected minority of children received. Achebe's 'reality' has also included the dozens of languages spoken in addition to English. For Achebe, though, the imposition of English, however arbitrary, has made it possible for Africans to talk to one another. If, as he puts it, the British failed to give Africans a song, they 'at least gave them a tongue, for sighing'. He acknowledges that English is a 'world language which history has forced down our throats', but is convinced that to insist that 'any true African literature must be written in African languages … would be merely pursuing a dead end, which can only lead to sterility, uncreativity and frustration'. He continues:

> What I do see is a new voice coming out of Africa, speaking of African experience in a world-wide language. So my answer to the question, Can an African ever learn English well enough to be able to use it effectively in creative writing? is certainly yes. If on the other hand you ask: Can he ever learn to use it like a native speaker? I should say, I hope not. It is neither necessary nor desirable for him to be able to do so. The price a world language must be prepared to pay is submission to many different kinds of use. The African writer should aim to use English in a way that brings out his message best without altering the language to the extent that its value as a medium of international exchange will be lost.
> (Achebe, 1965, p. 29)

'For me', he goes on, 'there is no other choice. I have been given this language and I intend to use it'.

Figure 8.3   Chinua Achebe

Activity 8.2   *(Allow about 10 minutes)*

What are the relative advantages and disadvantages of Ngũgĩ's and Achebe's positions, in terms of reaching out to a reading audience?

It is possible to see both Ngũgĩ and Achebe as grappling with versions of the same history, the same dilemma. Both see English as loaded with a past, with traditions of writing and of education which are at once damaging and a challenge to them as African writers. Learning English has usually involved contempt for the languages they grew up with, as well as their banning. A successful education was always meant to separate a child from his or her family, to inculcate other, western values. Both writers know that their entry into English as writers exposes them to criticism on two counts: for betrayal of the people and the values they grew up with and for writing what may then be read as culpably unEnglish English. To write in English is to use the imperialist language to express the experience of people who have been colonized and exploited in a language more accessible to the colonizers than to the colonized. To write in Gĩkũyũ, as Ngũgĩ now does, is to write for a known readership, while leaving a potentially large international audience to encounter his work through translation. For Achebe, his use of English entails 'altering', 'making new' a language which may have been forced on him but which, by now, he has claimed as his own. That appropriation of the oppressor's language constitutes a strength for Achebe. In a later essay, called 'Colonialist criticism', first published in 1975, he writes: 'And let no one be fooled by the fact that we may write in English for we intend to do unheard of things with it' (Achebe, 1988, p. 50).

The English of Achebe's novels is able to represent a subtle range of language: intimate, ritualistic, fiercely resistant to some aspects of English usage, on the one hand; and infected by varieties of English Englishes and African Englishes, on the other.

Extract from *Things Fall Apart* (first published 1958)

That year the harvest was sad, like a funeral, and many farmers wept as they dug up the miserable and rotting yams. One man tied his cloth to a tree branch and hanged himself.

Okonkwo remembered that tragic year with a cold shiver throughout the rest of his life. It always surprised him when he thought of it later that he did not sink under the load of despair. He knew he was a fierce fighter, but that year had been enough to break the heart of a lion.

'Since I survived that year,' he always said, 'I shall survive anything.' He put it down to his inflexible will.

His father, Unoka, who was then an ailing man, had said to him during that terrible harvest month: 'Do not despair. I know you will not despair. You have a manly and a proud heart. A proud heart can survive a general failure because such a failure does not prick its pride. It is more difficult and more bitter when a man fails *alone*.'

Unoka was like that in his last days. His love of talk had grown with age and sickness. It tried Okonkwo's patience beyond words.

(Achebe, 1976, pp. 17–18)

In his essay 'Named for Victoria, Queen of England' Achebe writes of his languages, his bilingualism:

> I don't know for certain but I have probably spoken more words in Igbo than English but I have definitely written more words in English than Igbo. Which I think makes me perfectly bilingual. Some people have suggested that I should be better off writing in Igbo. Sometimes they seek to drive the point home by asking me in which language I dream. When I reply that I dream in both languages they seem not to believe it.
>
> (Achebe, 1988, p. 22)

Achebe sees his contribution to Africa in a different way from Ngũgĩ, for whom, in 'The language of African literature', 'language was the means of the spiritual subjugation', just as 'the bullet was the means of the physical subjugation' (Ngũgĩ, 1986a, p. 9). Achebe writes:

> I would be quite satisfied if my novels (especially the ones set in the past) did no more than teach their readers that their past – with all its imperfections – was not one long night of savagery.
>
> (Cited in Dathorne, 1975, p. 67)

I begin with these two African writers because in arriving at diametrically opposite solutions to questions about using English and other languages in their work as writers they illustrate some central themes about writing. Many monolingual writers have – perhaps surprisingly – expressed very similar kinds of duality in relation to the language of writing, and I return to this later.

8.4   THE POLITICS OF ENTRY INTO ENGLISH

Language is learned in conversations, and conversations are conducted between speakers who are unequal, if only temporarily or shiftingly so. If two speakers were possessed of identical thoughts, knowledge and language there would, after all, be no need for them to communicate at all. So inequalities are built into all language use from the beginning, as intrinsic to dialogue. Children learn from their earliest conversations with adults that they are children, and therefore smaller, younger, less knowledgeable about the world and different from adults in these and other respects. But in their conversations with adults they are also learning about conversations and about how adults behave in them; about difference, inequality and power; and that language enables some manipulation of those relations, some possibilities for change and destabilization of the status quo.

What we may take from the debate between Ngũgĩ and Achebe is that the inevitable inequalities inherent in all language use match larger social and historical inequalities. Where, for instance, English is learned as a second or additional language in parts of the world once colonized by Britain, that language learning has not been neutral, any more than teaching children who speak a London or a Caribbean dialect of English to speak and write in Standard British English is neutral. The languages of schooling will always carry the ambiguities inherent in the reasons there are for learning them. If they are potentially 'empowering' they are also potentially undermining and exposing. There is more to it than that, of course, for Achebe and Ngũgĩ may be thought to have different visions of the future of African countries, and therefore of the role that English and other languages will play in them. For Achebe, the future demands forms of compromise with the rest of the world, in so far as they encourage African unity and productive two-way communication between African and other countries.

For Ngũgĩ, the future must start from revolutionary change within a country like Kenya, and with the recovery and remaking of Kenya's own identity. We are reminded that attitudes to language are always political.

Another Nigerian writer, Buchi Emecheta, says of the heroine of her first novel, *In the Ditch*:

> Trouble with Adah was that she could never speak good London English, or cockney. Her accent and words always betrayed the fact that she had learned her English via *English for Foreign Students*.

(Emecheta, 1979, p. 69)

Emecheta's novels are set sometimes in Nigeria and sometimes in London, where she has spent most of her adult, writing life. All the novels tell stories about the pressures there are in both societies on a woman who manages to snatch her own independence out of the unthinking oppressions meted out to her. English and an education become aspects of such a woman's capacity to resist and make a life for herself. Yet traditional storytelling, as it is performed by women to circles of adults and children, and which Emecheta remembers from her own village childhood, provides her with what she has seen as specifically female narrative vantage points: the storyteller as teacher, explainer, rearer of children. She allows her heroines the specialized role of cultural transmitter, even within cultures which undermine women materially and socially. Like other writers in a similar position, she has used that position's ambivalence and the vulnerability it confers on her as focus, subject matter and narrative approach. Adah's 'good' schooled English can never be an unambiguous good in a world where as a black and single mother on the breadline she must live within as well as against other people's limiting perceptions of her. Yet Adah's sense of the discrepancy between her 'good' English and the worlds she inhabits, whether in Nigeria or in England, is also at the heart of Emecheta's purpose as a writer. Indeed, it is possible to feel that her more recent fiction, often dealing with somewhat undigested autobiographical situations, in which a woman is at last accorded a position of some dignity and even power, lacks the tension and irony of those early evocations of incongruity.

8.5   RECREATING DIALOGUE

The 'good' English of a novel undertakes above all to recreate through fictional narrative the speech and thoughts of its characters. How does English – how, even, do the Englishes of these writers – do that? For in the novels of Ngũgĩ and of Achebe, and in most of Emecheta's, the characters are not – for the most part – having conversations or thinking their thoughts in English. In Achebe's *Arrow of God*, a novel about time and generation and the painful evolution of a tribal community towards a compromise with western values, with Christianity and with English, that process is compressed in the scene in Reading B, as two policemen come to arrest Ezeulu, the chief priest, whose authority is threatened just at the point when he is preparing – disastrously, as it turns out – to make overtures to the local white officials and to the powers they stand for.

Activity 8.3   *(Reading B)*

Read the extract from *Arrow of God* by Chinua Achebe (Reading B). Notice the kind of English he uses to represent the policemen's and villagers' exchanges in Igbo, in contrast to his representation of the policemen's switch to a variety of English when addressing each other.

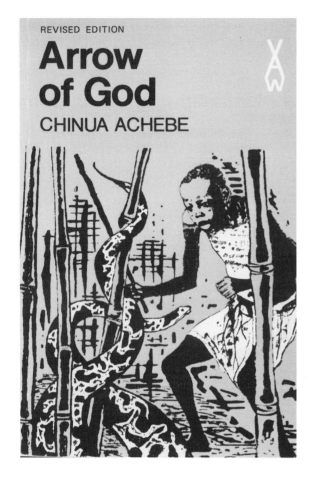

REVISED EDITION

Arrow of God

CHINUA ACHEBE

Figure 8.4   Arrow of God

For the conversation in Igbo, Achebe uses a rather formal Standard English with Igbo idioms (e.g. 'I shall slap okro seeds out of your mouth'). The policemen talking together, however, use a pidgin English and Achebe represents both its simplified grammar ('we no go return back') and pronunciation ('Gi me dat ting') in written form. Here, the language does more than tell us about the penetration of English and of British rule generally into African life. It *enacts* that penetration and the confusions produced by it. What Achebe so ironically achieves here is an impression that the two policemen have literally taken leave of their senses in direct proportion to their reliance on English to disconcert and intimidate their non-English-speaking compatriots. By comparison, the English Achebe uses to represent their speech in Igbo allows them rationality. It is not simply that writers have different histories of writing in English, nor that their reasons for choosing English or another language reflect a different politics or different theories of language. It is also the case that the English they create in their novels enacts quite different kinds of social relations.

Indian writers have also developed a range of techniques for representing dialogue in different languages. In an illuminating essay on the English used by characters in novels by the Indian writers R.K. Narayan and Mulk Raj Anand and by V.S. Naipaul, the Trinidadian East Indian, Ann Lowry (1982) usefully distinguishes between their quite different approaches. Whereas the English of Narayan's novels is in some sense 'transparent', a language for writing about

Figure 8.5   Coolie

Extract from *Coolie* (first published 1936)

Munoo lifted the tray lightly as soon as he heard his mistress answer his question and walked away with a wonderful agility while she abused and warned and threatened with a copious flow of her hard, even chatter.

'Here we are, children!' said Prem, clapping his hands. 'Here is the tea! A bit late, but never mind!'

'The tea! The tea!' exclaimed Sheila, her blue eyes melting, her lips contracting.

'Ooon, aaan! I want the tea, too!' sobbed Lila from where she sat on a table swaying her head to the music, in a ridiculously childish manner, which amused her elder sister, her uncle and her father, when that last worthy was not too embarrassed to come and play with his children.

'Put it down here, you black man!' said Prem, with mock anger in the wrong Hindustani which he sometimes affected, especially in the face of anything so European as a tea tray or when dressed in an English suit, in imitation of the tone in which Englishmen talk to their native servants. 'Put it down on this table, black man, you who relieve yourself on the ground!'

(Anand 1945, pp. 23–4)

people who for the most part speak forms of nonstandard or Standard Tamil, forms which are not represented and are rarely even alluded to by Narayan, the more politically committed Anand assembles an English which acknowledges its complex and everyday proximity to and entanglement with Hindi and the other Indian languages spoken by variously mixed collections of people. For instance, there are in his novels English characters speaking bad Hindi and Indian characters using educated and uneducated varieties of Hindi (see p. 285).

 All this is written in an English made permeable not just to the particular Indian varieties of English spoken in India, but also to the vast range of separate and overlapping languages and dialects which characterize most urban Indian settings. There is clearly a parallel kind of distinction to be found between the relatively 'transparent' English of Ngũgĩ and the English evolved by Achebe to represent the material sounds of language in a postcolonial setting.

Lowry's account of how Naipaul uses English in *A House for Mr Biswas* (first published 1961) suggests yet more possibilities. She points to three principal ways in which English is modified by Naipaul in order to suggest quite different kinds of language spoken by characters in the novel. In the first, Standard (educated) English dialogue stands in for Hindi speech; in the second, English dialect forms are written as they would be spoken; and finally, 'in a few rare cases [Standard] English dialogue is spoken by one of the characters, but the hesitation and care with which he/she speaks is always noted by the narrator' (Lowry, 1982, p. 291). Naipaul marks these shifts across varieties of West Indian speech by modifying the grammar.

❖ ❖ ❖ ❖ ❖

Activity 8.4 *(Allow about 10 minutes)*

In the following extract, can you identify examples of the three ways in which Naipaul represents the different kinds of language spoken by characters in the novel?

This extract comes from the funeral scene at the beginning of the novel, when Mr Biswas's father is about to be buried.

> The photographer, of mixed Chinese, Negro and European blood, did not understand what was being said. In the end he and some of the men took the coffin out to the verandah and stood it against the wall.
>   'Careful! Don't let him fall out.'
>   'Goodness. All the marigolds have dropped out.'
>   'Leave them,' the photographer said in English. 'Is a nice little touch. Flowers on the ground.' He set up his tripod in the yard, just under the ragged eaves of thatch, and put his head under the black cloth.
>   Tara roused Bipti from her grief, arranged Bipti's hair and veil, and dried Bipti's eyes.
>   'Five people all together,' the photographer said to Tara. 'Hard to know just how to arrange them. It look to me that it would have to be two one side and three the other side. You sure you want all five?'
>   Tara was firm.
>   The photographer sucked his teeth, but not at Tara. 'Look, look. Why nobody ain't put anything to chock up the coffin and prevent it from slipping?'
>   Tara had that attended to.
>   The photographer said, 'All right then. Mother and biggest son on either side. Next to mother, young boy and young girl. Next to big son, smaller son.'

There was more advice from the men.

'Make them look at the coffin.'

'At the mother.'

'At the youngest boy.'

The photographer settled the matter by telling Tara, 'Tell them to look at me.'

Tara translated, and the photographer went under his cloth. Almost immediately he came out again. 'How about making the mother and the biggest boy put their hands on the edge of the coffin?'

This was done and the photographer went back under his cloth.

'Wait!' Tara cried, running out from the hut with a fresh garland of marigolds. She hung it around Raghu's neck and said to the photographer in English, 'All right. Draw your photo now.'

(Naipaul, 1992, pp. 33–4)

Comment

In the initial exchange here over the placing of the coffin against the wall, Standard English represents speech in Hindi. The photographer's English dialect, however, is written as it would be spoken (notice the grammatical variation from Standard English). For Tara's final remark, Naipaul has her use a grammatically, but not idiomatically, Standard English.

In such ways Naipaul is able to produce what are in effect new and hybrid forms of language. The social and language situations they evoke are even more complex than the kinds of mimicry to be found in the fiction of monolingual writers working within purely class or regionally differentiated language communities. They also constitute an aspect of the difficulties that many such writers express concerning the relation of what they write to those they write about: difficulties of distance and dissociation. At best, this produces the exquisite ironies of Narayan and Naipaul. Yet that irony is often imbued with pain and ambivalence; and in Naipaul's case the ridicule rarely avoids some element of cruelty. And Narayan, for instance, can seem to be inviting us to laugh at people he understands better than we do, while simultaneously warning us that we mock them at our peril. Yet Narayan gives no sense of having a problem about writing in English and writing novels which are set in a non-English-speaking town in south India. Indeed, he has written:

> English has proved that if a language has flexibility any experience can be communicated through it, even if it has to be paraphrased sometimes rather than conveyed … In order not to lose the excellence of this medium some writers in India took to writing in English, and produced a literature that was perhaps not first-class; often the writing seemed imitative, halting, inapt, or an awkward translation of a vernacular, mode or idiom; but occasionally it was brilliant. We are all experimentalists. I may straightaway explain what we do not attempt to do. We are not attempting to write Anglo-Saxon English.

(Cited in Killam, 1976, p. 131)

Figure 8.6
A House for Mr Biswas

8.6   ENGLISH AND CULTURAL IDENTITY

For many – perhaps most – writers, there is probably no question of having a choice of languages in which to write, as Ngũgĩ and Achebe have. Narayan seems not to have considered writing in Tamil or Kannada, and for Naipaul it appears that Hindi was never a possible language for him to write in. Moreover, slavery, indentured labour and all the other material deprivations of colonialism have often obliterated or at least truncated people's languages; and certainly, for many of those languages, have impeded the development of literacy. In the English-speaking Caribbean, for instance, writers have never had a serious alternative to writing in English. Yet the business of writing at all confronts such writers with parallel issues of identity and of history and power. In the passage from 'Prologue to an autobiography' in Reading C, V.S. Naipaul, whose use of English we have already considered and who grew up in an East Indian, Hindu and rural community in Trinidad, remembers writing the first lines of his first published book, the collection of stories called *Miguel Street*.

❖   ❖   ❖   ❖   ❖

Activity 8.5   *(Reading C)*
Read the extract from *Finding the Centre* by V.S. Naipaul (Reading C). In what ways does he feel ambivalent about writing and about his own cultural identity?

❖   ❖   ❖   ❖   ❖

Figure 8.7   *V.S. Naipaul*

It is a characteristic irony that Naipaul should have produced those first lines in a BBC office at the heart of an empire, whose divisions and depredations underpinned the humorous stories he was writing. These are woven out of his memories of the two years or so when his family moved from the countryside in Trinidad to Port of Spain. Naipaul's emphasis is not on the use of English itself – for, as I've said, despite being brought up in a Hindi-speaking family he seems always to have regarded English as his principal language – but on the crucial nuances of accent and phrasing which characterize the racial and class distinctions that mark out the lives of his characters in *Miguel Street*, and which in their turn reflect a long history of migrations from Africa and India to the Caribbean.

Here the narrator's problems are ones of voice, of point of view, of his own relation to the Trinidad of his childhood and the relation of that experience to the activity of literature, the 'calling' of the writer. That 'calling' – one he has aspired to in emulation of a father who was for a time a journalist as well as a writer of humorous stories about the Indian community in Trinidad, but who seems somehow always to have risked failure and courted ridicule in his son's eyes – occasions for Naipaul the extremes of both ambition and anxiety. For its achievement is understood to be a contradiction in terms within the Trinidadian society he describes. The very notion of 'writer' is felt as foreign, imported from the metropolis, unrealizable. Derek Walcott, the St Lucian poet, has said of his initiation into writing: 'I had entered the house of literature as a houseboy' (Walcott, 1973, p. 77). The purveyors of a culture beamed out from the London headquarters of the BBC to the far-flung Commonwealth, and offered as capaciously inclusive of all those parts of the world once governed from England, can scarcely have dreamed that the worldwide dissemination of the English language might produce not just readers and listeners of English but writers of English too. Was it ever predicted, one wonders, by those who legislated for the teaching of English literature in India in the early nineteenth century that India might one day produce many of the best writers of English in the world?

Naipaul's father 'dangled all his life in a half-dependence and half-esteem between these two powerful families'. Naipaul's rootlessness, his isolation, can seem wilfully dangling at times, even excessive. But for him that 'calling' of writer has entailed a life of restless movement, of needing to recognize and understand what must necessarily be new and strange, to return again and again to the Caribbean and to other parts of the world to which Indians have moved and tried to make lives for themselves. And then, as he puts it:

> A writer after a time carries his world with him, his own burden of experience, human experience and literary experience (one deepening the other); and I do believe – especially after writing 'Prologue to an Autobiography' – that I would have found equivalent connections with my past and myself wherever I had gone.
> (Naipaul, 1984, p. 10)

The exalted and even heroic role of writer accompanies something like a settled pessimism in Naipaul's view of the society he has left and the societies to which he has been – provisionally, as it were – drawn. His additional career as a travel writer confirmed this; for travel, as he has written:

> broadened my world view; it showed me a changing world and took me out of my own colonial shell; it became the substitute for the mature social experience – the deepening knowledge of a society – which my background and the nature of my life denied me. My uncertainty about

my role withered; a role was not necessary. I recognized my own instincts as a traveller, and was content to be myself, to be what I had always been, a looker.

(Naipaul, 1984, p. 11)

The complex world of the Caribbean, in which he grew up, is unable within this view to provide 'mature social experience'. So it is only as a rootless wanderer that Naipaul can find a role for himself as a man and as a writer, or, as he puts it, 'a looker'.

I eased myself into knowledge. To write was to learn. Beginning a book, I always felt I was in possession of all the facts about myself; at the end I was always surprised.

(Naipaul, 1984, pp. 27–8)

His language aspires to become universally communicative, as it were, alluding to the local, the particular, the specialized, but forever determined on keeping its distance from the idiomatic, the oral, the hybrid, the colonial, all that he deemed to be second-rate.

There are useful parallels as well as contrasts here with the work of the Barbadian poet Edward Kamau Brathwaite, for whom the immigrant (indeed the *emigrant*) – a two-way fugitive and an essential figure, actual and metaphoric, of West Indian culture – is quite differently understood. However, in his essay 'Caribbean critics' (first published 1969), an illuminating reading of Naipaul's early novels, Brathwaite writes:

Figure 8.8   Kamau Brathwaite

In the very process of rejecting West Indian society, Naipaul, in *Miguel Street* (1951) and *A House for Mr. Biswas* (1961), embraces and examines it most intimately. This is the real source of Naipaul's irony. It is the literary expression of a deeply rooted cultural dichotomy. The apparently Eurocentric East Indian remains a West Indian.

(Brathwaite, 1993, p. 124)

Brathwaite cannot help admiring the passion of Naipaul's refusal to 'contemplate the acculturation of his people to debased colonial forms, nor yet condone their perpetuation of a false East Indianness' (Brathwaite, 1993, p. 123), yet the trajectory of his own work and politics has taken him in another direction entirely. For Brathwaite, the 'speaking voice', the music, the African inheritance to be found in the West Indies have to be used by writers. The question is how. In an essay he wrote in 1963 entitled 'Roots', Brathwaite was worried by the way in which West Indian writers were using the speech and music of the islands:

very few of our writers are really 'of the people'. They are middle class. The so-called 'folk' rhythms are used, I think, as a sign and symbol of their rejection of society, of their exile. We find the same tendency too in the work of [James] Baldwin, Richard Wright, Peter Abrahams – and of course the Irish exiles. The rhythm becomes a kind of defence mechanism, inhibiting the development of complexity as far as characterization is concerned.

(Brathwaite, 1993, p. 53)

Nearly 20 years later, Brathwaite developed a history of languages and language in the Caribbean in order to arrive at an articulation of what he called 'nation language' (Brathwaite, 1981).

Activity 8.6   *(Allow about 15 minutes)*

Look again at pp. 266–71 in the reading by Brathwaite (Reading A) at the end of Chapter 7. What are the principal issues for Brathwaite in redefining the language of the Caribbean as 'nation language' rather than creole or dialect?

Brathwaite's 'nation language' is not simply dialect by another name. It is, as he puts it, 'the submerged, surrealist experience and sensibility' underlying West Indian English, which may be 'like a howl, or a shout, or a machine-gun, or the wind, or a wave'. For Brathwaite it is the adequacy of language in relation to an actual and peopled landscape that matters, and to those people's sense of their own ancestry and way of life. This sense of the actuality of language, of its capacity to name the hitherto unnamed and so to reinvest its physical character with fresh meanings, he likens to Dante's forging of a poetic Italian to replace Latin in the fourteenth century. It is an analogy we could pursue. How clearly it echoes Chaucer's forging of a poetic language out of several literary and vernacular languages in the fourteenth century, or Gogol's compiling of a Russian dictionary in the nineteenth century, one which would support the transformation of an oral language into a written one.

8.7   MARGINALITY, GENDER AND LANGUAGE

I have already suggested that the tensions to which bilingual writers bear witness have a good deal in common with those described by writers brought up to speak and write Standard English outside Britain, or rather outside its metropolitan fastnesses.

We have seen how the dilemma of writing both within and against the English literary tradition may be articulated by writers coming to English from other languages or from other versions of English. The desire to articulate new ways of life, new truths, can seem to conflict with the learning of rules, with what may even be the subservience required for the learning of another language or a language which is learned as another's. And all language is another's as well as our own. Obedience to rules and conventions is part of how we relate to language, but notions of theft and appropriation have their place too. For we also need to appreciate how writers attempt to 'alter' language, as Achebe puts it, to remake it, in order to say what has not yet been said, to represent or reflect experiences and points of view which have been absent or subsumed within more familiar or vigorous discourses.

'The new English literatures' may be read as by and large a legacy of British colonialism. Their writers have highlighted issues related to the choice of writing in English or in the other languages of a community. But they have done more than that. They have focused on the status of writers and of writing in societies with an oral rather than literate culture, where an emphasis on English is associated with aspirations towards modernity and internationalism, and with education, science and technology. Most of all, writers have demonstrated that confronting these conflicts provides a source of extraordinary vitality in itself.

Many women have written of dilemmas like these as specifically ones of gender. Their need to wrench new or altered meanings out of the language – and their difficulties in doing so – have been experienced by some women writers as comparable to a bilingual's or a colonial's needs and difficulties. Indeed, Gayatri Chakravorty Spivak, the contemporary critic who was born in Calcutta and now teaches in New York, has made a point in her discussion of what she calls 'subaltern' or 'postcolonial' studies of theorizing the situation of women alongside analyses of the effects of colonialism: as both implicated *in* colonialism but also *like* colonialism. Of her own position as a highly esteemed professor in an American university, an Indian woman and an effective Bengali speaker, she is able to say, 'I am bicultural, but my biculturality is that I'm not at home in either of the places' (Spivak, 1990, p. 83): a position that echoes the expressions of dislocation and unease which we have been discussing. Spivak goes further, however, in asserting that 'if there's one thing I totally distrust, in fact, more than distrust, despise and have contempt for, it is people looking for roots' (Spivak, 1990, p. 93). Yet she is also quick to acknowledge that the rejection of any possible singleness of cultural identity and of roots must be understood as a mark of privilege, peculiar to a multilingual cosmopolitan, who is able to sell her skills and knowledge on the international market.

Most women's cultural allegiances are just as ambiguous, and much less likely to provide personal assurances of their own worth. There are certainly women who have expected any 'new meanings' they might bring into being as likely to derive from their own idiosyncratic vision or interpretation rather than from collective insights of some sort. Women have not, after all, written in a male world for nothing. Yet there has also been a gathering sense that something called 'women's meanings' might be either muffled and unheard or even effectively silenced by voices and traditions of writing, which claimed for themselves a general, human – and therefore unsexed – authority. Nor have women felt it easy to model their own sense of marginality on those heroic expressions of the condition which certain male writers (including some of those we have been considering) seemed to offer them.

Dorothy Richardson, who wrote her extraordinary thirteen-volume experimental novel, *Pilgrimage*, between 1913 and 1938, spoke both French and German and had significant experience as a translator. However, she was neither raised as a bilingual nor from a colonial background. Yet her sense of the contradictory forces of language, at once liberating and constraining, chimes in several ways with the kinds of account we have been hearing. To some extent, these contradictory forces are characterized in Richardson's work as male and female, but the novel which her heroine, Miriam Henderson, is preparing to write will emerge from the discovery of some kind of equilibrium between these forces or tendencies, both of which she admits to in herself.

Pilgrimage, like much writing that is self-consciously experimental, is about its own writing. It is also about the life of a woman who is gathering the detailed memories of her past into a kind of narrative which will do justice to their seeming inconsequence. So it is a form of autobiography, but autobiography both fictionalized and commented upon in ways which signal the material as well as imaginative existence of a woman writer. Above all, Richardson and her heroine Miriam wrestle with memory itself, and with its tendency to render itself as history, providing what is recalled with a spurious significance. This Miriam dreads, as her creator does, as subversive of the reality she is after, the reality of the immediate present, of thought and feeling and impression *as* they happen: 'current existence, the ultimate astonisher' (Richardson [1913–38] 1979, vol. 4, p. 611). In such a scenario, plots, endings, opinions develop purposes of their own, which offer somehow to reduce the confusions of life without really explaining them. The struggle is with what is identified as 'man's hilarious expostulating narrative

Figure 8.9
Dorothy Richardson

The front cover of the first volume of *Pilgrimage* is reproduced in Plate 10 of the colour section.

Other aspects of language and gender are discussed in Chapters 1 and 7.

voice' (vol. 1, p. 215), with logic, sequence, monologue, discipline. Something which might approximate to an alternative, even to a 'women's language', would have to embody both thought and impression, and do so within new notions of time and tense.

The language Miriam works for will be neither a purely feminine one, as characterized by a fat woman she sees at a concert, who is 'two-thirds of the way through a life that had been a ceaseless stream of events set in a ceaseless stream of inadequate commentary without and within', but nor will it be a purely male 'talking *about* people and things and never being or knowing anything' (Richardson [1913–38] 1979, vol. 4, p. 305; vol. 2, p. 373).

The language of *Pilgrimage* is at once dense, playful and reflexive, capable of communicating the abbreviations of inner language, of sentences reduced to their predicates because their subjects and even verbs are too obvious to the thinker, or perhaps too painful, to need articulating. It is often difficult language, tumbling over its own potential for glib communication, requiring us to admit ignorance and uncertainty, to reread, doubt, persist. At times, the novel expresses ebullience at its own successes. At others, the struggle with language is seen as sour or even impossible:

> In speech with a man a woman is at a disadvantage – because they speak different languages. She may understand his. Hers he will never speak nor understand. In pity, or from other motives, she must therefore, stammeringly, speak his. He listens and is flattered and thinks he has her mental measure when he has not touched even the fringe of her consciousness.
>
> (Richardson [1913–38] 1979, vol. 2, p. 210)

Here it is masculinity rather than imperialism which, buttressed by the educational and literary institutions from which she and all women were excluded, and by which they have been reductively defined, lures Richardson; just as writers like Ngũgĩ, Achebe and Naipaul, felt themselves lured towards an ambiguous inclusion within precisely those traditions sustained by their exclusion. As a novelist, Dorothy Richardson was always in pursuit of 'what is left out' of even the most marvellous novels by the most imaginative of male writers. And 'what is left out' is, after all, what all writers are after. Language can seem to offer them a way of inserting their own versions of 'what is left out'. It can also work to screen out or inhibit the specificity, the incipient and as yet unformed representation of experience.

Gender – indivisibly implicated in racial and linguistic identity – continues to organize many women's writing. Maxine Hong Kingston, who was brought up in a Chinese community in San Francisco, has written two novels about the history of Chinese emigration to America: a woman's novel and a man's, the two distinguished by their narrative form. *The Woman Warrior* (first published 1977) relies on her mother's stories, on what she calls 'talk-stories', tales and sagas which move between her past in China, a more distant past there, and episodes from the present world of ghosts: white Americans, among whom Chinese people move invisibly and inaudibly.

The history of Chinese emigration to America is of men leaving China for the 'Gold Mountain' to look for work and either returning or sending for their wives and children. So men and women do, quite literally, have different stories to tell. But the story of the exploitation of Chinese men's labour, usually in order to build the railway, is one the men are either too 'frail' or too bludgeoned to tell the girl. In *China Men* (1981a) Maxine Hong Kingston writes a history parallel to the one

Figure 8.10
Maxine Hong Kingston

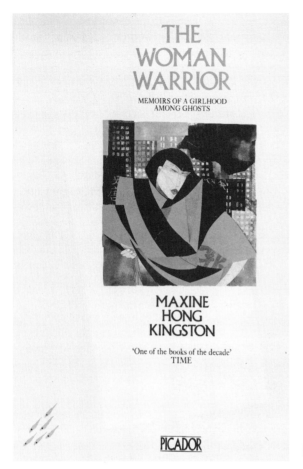

Figure 8.11
The Woman Warrior

she has constructed from her own stories and her mother's. The prose changes. She works in libraries, ferrets out of history books what has usually been ignored by them, fills in the details imaginatively. So little does she hear from men about their feelings and thoughts that she is obliged to invent for them.

Language, speech, writing become mandatory for survival in *The Woman Warrior.* How is the girl at its centre to become visible, audible? In Reading D all the terrors surrounding the voice are rehearsed, as it chants and mimics, vanishes and contorts itself, gives itself away. And then, even in Chinese school, where the children shriek and play freely, she realizes that 'You can't entrust your voice to the Chinese, either; they want to capture your voice for their own use. They want to fix up your tongue to speak for them.'

❖   ❖   ❖   ❖   ❖

Activity 8.7   *(Reading D)*

Read the extract from *The Woman Warrior* by Maxine Hong Kingston (Reading D). How do you interpret the significance of Hong Kingston's initial silence at the American school, and her ambiguous feelings about her own voice?

❖   ❖   ❖   ❖   ❖

It seems to me there are few metaphors more vivid than Hong Kingston's for the compulsion to write, the hazards of doing so and the need to forge a language which will carry what V.S. Naipaul called 'my very particularity' and which Maxine Hong Kingston invokes elsewhere in the novel with the question:

> Chinese-Americans, when you try to understand what things in you are Chinese, how do you separate what is peculiar to childhood, to poverty, insanities, one family, your mother who marked your growing with stories, from what is Chinese? What is Chinese tradition and what is the movies?
>
> (Hong Kingston, 1981b, p. 13)

Through all the whirling and conflicting stories that the novel's nameless heroine hears, tells herself or participates in she is also making herself, and in two languages: 'And all the time I was having to turn myself American-feminine, or no dates' (Hong Kingston, 1981b, p. 49). The pressure is on her to speak and to hear herself speak, for 'insane people were the ones who couldn't explain themselves' (p. 166).

Similar fears and compulsions characterize Eva Hoffman's autobiography, *Lost in Translation* (first published in 1989), which records with great explicitness her simultaneous development as a writer and as a speaker and writer of English.

Figure 8.12
Lost in Translation

In 1959, when she was thirteen, she left Poland with her family to live first in Canada and later in the USA. Her book, and its title, carry the double sense of irrecoverable loss *and* survival once she is translated into a new world, new forms, a new language. While she is still learning English she is already aware that her languages are shifting in their relation to her private thoughts and memories and her public account of them. Questions are also arising about the relation of each language to the past and to the present. To write, let alone to write in English, is for Hoffman a gateway into having opinions and into an authorized and public enunciation of them: and having opinions stands for some kind of maturity in her new world. Yet that achievement is also scored with loss: of feeling, of immediacy, but also of her childhood, of places and people and the taken-for-granted. There is a peculiar tension for her in knowing 'what is correct, fluent, good long before I can execute it'. And how telling that word 'execute' is in this context. How far from the battling, flying Hong Kingston.

Activity 8.8   *(Reading E)*

Read the extract from *Lost in Translation* by Eva Hoffman (Reading E). Why does she see the way she uses language in the diary as so significant?

The move towards learning to write in English entails the assembling of a possible alternative self, one which will occupy the language Hoffman is entering and adapt to its rules and regulations. Once again, we have that sense we have come to expect of division and duality: between past and present, between the private and the public spheres, between feeling and thought. There is the question of whether the same self can inhabit two languages; of which 'I' it is that is voiced in Polish and which in English. Such queries are tied for Hoffman, as for most writers, to her biography, to a desire for continuity between childhood and adulthood and dismay at their separation. The sound of her own voice and the terror at losing control of it echo Maxine Hong Kingston. 'Self-assurance and control' are what she most admires in good speakers of English. Then writing becomes her way of overcoming 'the stigma of my marginality', of acquiring authority: her way of coming home. For, as she puts it, 'we [all] want to be at home in our tongue'.

Figure 8.13   Eva Hoffman

8.8   CONCLUSION: CHANGE AND RENEWAL

I began this chapter with the words of the contemporary Irish poet Seamus Heaney, and with his offer of a poetry which springs from the experience of division and tension between the inherited and the learned. I want to return to Heaney, and to his illuminating engagement with the St Lucian poet Derek Walcott in his essay 'The murmur of Malvern', where he discusses Walcott's collection of poems *The Star-Apple Kingdom*.

Activity 8.9   *(Reading F)*

Read the extract from 'The murmur of Malvern' by Seamus Heaney (Reading F). In what ways does Heaney link Walcott with J.M. Synge, the Irish playwright who used the speech of the west coast peasants in his plays, and with William Langland, the fourteenth-century English poet?

This is Heaney's first characterization of Walcott's achievement:

> I imagine he has done for the Caribbean what Synge did for Ireland, found a language woven out of dialect and literature, neither folksy nor condescending, a singular idiom evolved out of one man's inherited divisions and obsessions, an idiom which allows an older life to exult in itself and yet at the same time keeps the cool of 'the new'.

Heaney insists on Walcott's fine ear for both speech and written language, and on his capacity to make new forms through the exploration and the bridging of these diverse traditions. But he goes further than this, further than a consideration of what Walcott has taken from the speech of the Caribbean and the traditions of English poetry. His comparing of Walcott with J.M. Synge is meant to remind us of the language Synge brought to the plays he wrote about the Irish peasantry, and to reinforce Heaney's elegant formulation that Walcott 'made a theme of the choice and the impossibility of choosing'. The substance of both writers' work emerges from the tensions inherent in attempting to reconcile forms of English which carry the history of colonial hostilities.

Heaney's interest is also in the kind of contribution Walcott makes to poetry written in English. His reading of Walcott's poem 'The Schooner Flight' returns it to what he traces as the poem's 'origins' in *Piers Plowman*, the fourteenth-century poem by William Langland. Heaney makes a bold and resonant move as he argues for Walcott's poetry becoming, as he puts it elsewhere in this piece, 'a common resource', a language deriving its strength and texture from a complex history of struggle and offering quite new connections. It is fitting that two contemporary English poets, one Irish, the other Caribbean, should come together here, as the friends they are, but also as poets who share a sense of difference and a language able to generate forms of literature from what has first been heard as a ringing in their ears.

We have been listening to voices and reading the written language which invokes and comments on those voices. Far from the efficient and transparent tool it is sometimes thought to be, language is the stuff of pain and pleasure, fear and confidence, allegiance and furious rejection. As the Guyanese poet David Dabydeen has put it in his essay 'On not being Milton: nigger talk in England today', 'It's hard to put two words together in creole without swearing. Words are spat out from the mouth like live squibs, not pronounced with elocution' (Dabydeen, 1990, p. 3). Yet languages can seem to stand for authority and regulation while simultaneously inviting us to regard them as malleable, permeable, responsive to our needs.

Towards the end of his book *Culture and Imperialism*, Edward Said, the Palestinian American writer, offers this as a proposal for the future:

> Once we accept the actual configuration of literary experiences overlapping with one another and interdependent, despite national boundaries and coercively legislated national autonomies, history and geography are transfigured in new maps, in new and far less stable entities, in new types of connections ... Newly changed models and types jostle against the older ones. The reader and writer of literature – which itself loses its perdurable forms and accepts the testimonials, revisions, notations of the post-colonial experience, including underground life, slave narratives, women's literature, and prison – no longer need to be tied to an image of the poet or scholar in isolation, secure, stable, national in identity, class, gender, or profession, but can think and experience with [Jean] Genet in Palestine or Algeria, with Tahyib Salih as a Black man in London, with

Jamaica Kincaid in the white world, with [Salman] Rushdie in India and
Britain, and so on ...

Texts ... are tied to circumstances and to politics large and small, and
these require attention and criticism. No one can take stock of everything, of course, just as no one theory can explain or account for the
connections among texts and societies. But reading and writing texts are
never neutral activities: there are interests, powers, passions, pleasures
entailed no matter how aesthetic or entertaining the work. Media, political economy, mass institutions – in fine, the tracings of secular power and
the influence of the state – are part of what we call literature. And just as it
is true that we cannot read literature by men without also reading literature by women – so transfigured has been the shape of literature – it is
also true that we cannot deal with the literature of the peripheries
without also attending to the literature of the metropolitan centres.

(Said, 1993, pp. 384–5)

To many people in the world a lifetime's poverty, disenfranchisement or exile can
make that notion of 'the hybrid' no more than a fashionable and luxurious
imperative, attractive to those who have become bored with the excesses
produced by the barriers of nationalism or sectarianism. Yet ultimately, I think,
Said must be right when he writes:

Exile, far from being the fate of nearly forgotten unfortunates who are
dispossessed and expatriated, becomes something closer to a norm, an
experience of crossing boundaries and charting new territories in defiance of the classic canonic enclosures, however much its loss and sadness
should be acknowledged and registered.

(Said, 1993, p. 384)

It is possible to understand some of the energy of the writers we have been
considering as emerging, nourished, from such a struggle. There is more to it
than that, though. Said directs us not only to the modern world and its characteristic disjunctions and redistributions. He also reminds us of history, of geography and of those patterns of language change and renewal which have so regularly
signalled new vitalities among writers as well as new functions for literature. An
understanding of the geography of language, of its relation to landscape and to
the lives lived within these physical worlds is essential to Said's picture of a culture
in which the metropolitan centres depend on and are revived by the traffic with
the rest of the world that language makes possible.

Reading A
EXTRACT FROM 'THE LANGUAGE OF AFRICAN LITERATURE'

Ngũgĩ wa Thiong'o

I was born into a large peasant family: father, four wives and about twenty-eight children. I also belonged, as we all did in those days, to a wider extended family and to the community as a whole.

We spoke Gĩkũyũ as we worked in the fields. We spoke Gĩkũyũ in and outside the home. I can vividly recall those evenings of story-telling around the fireside. It was mostly the grown-ups telling the children but everybody was interested and involved. We children would re-tell the stories the following day to other children who worked in the fields picking the pyrethrum flowers, tea-leaves or coffee beans of our European and African landlords.

The stories, with mostly animals as the main characters, were all told in Gĩkũyũ. Hare, being small, weak but full of innovative wit and cunning, was our hero. We identified with him as he struggled against the brutes of prey like lion, leopard, hyena. His victories were our victories and we learnt that the apparently weak can outwit the strong. We followed the animals in their struggle against hostile nature – drought, rain, sun, wind – a confrontation often forcing them to search for forms of co-operation. But we were also interested in their struggles amongst themselves, and particularly between the beasts and the victims of prey. These twin struggles, against nature and other animals, reflected real-life struggles in the human world.

Not that we neglected stories with human beings as the main characters. There were two types of characters in such human-centred narratives: the species of truly human beings with qualities of courage, kindness, mercy, hatred of evil, concern for others; and a man-eat-man two-mouthed species with qualities of greed, selfishness, individualism and hatred of what was good for the larger co-operative community. Co-operation as the ultimate good in a community was a constant theme. It could unite human beings with animals against ogres and beasts of prey, as in the story of how dove, after being fed with castor-oil seeds, was sent to fetch a smith working far away from home and whose pregnant wife was being threatened by these man-eating two-mouthed ogres.

There were good and bad story-tellers. A good one could tell the same story over and over again, and it would always be fresh to us, the listeners. He or she could tell a story told by someone else and make it more alive and dramatic. The differences really were in the use of words and images and the inflexion of voices to effect different tones.

We therefore learnt to value words for their meaning and nuances. Language was not a mere string of words. It had a suggestive power well beyond the immediate and lexical meaning. Our appreciation of the suggestive magical power of language was reinforced by the games we played with words through riddles, proverbs, transpositions of syllables, or through nonsensical but musically arranged words. So we learnt the music of our language on top of the content. The language, through images and symbols, gave us a view of the world, but it had a beauty of its own. The home and the field were then our pre-primary school but what is important, for this discussion, is that the language of our evening teach-ins, and the language of our immediate and wider community, and the language of our work in the fields were one.

And then I went to school, a colonial school, and this harmony was broken. The language of my education was no longer the language of my culture. I first went to Kamaandura, missionary run, and then to another called Maanguuū run by nationalists grouped around the Gīkūyū Independent and Karinga Schools Association. Our language of education was still Gīkūyū. The very first time I was ever given an ovation for my writing was over a composition in Gīkūyū. So for my first four years there was still harmony between the language of my formal education and that of the Limuru peasant community.

It was after the declaration of a state of emergency over Kenya in 1952 that all the schools run by patriotic nationalists were taken over by the colonial regime and were placed under District Education Boards chaired by Englishmen. English became the language of my formal education. In Kenya, English became more than a language: it was *the* language, and all the others had to bow before it in deference.

Thus one of the most humiliating experiences was to be caught speaking Gīkūyū in the vicinity of the school. The culprit was given corporal punishment – three to five strokes of the cane on bare buttocks – or was made to carry a metal plate around the neck with inscriptions such as I AM STUPID or I AM A DONKEY. Sometimes the culprits were fined money they could hardly afford. And how did the teachers catch the culprits? A button was initially given to one pupil who was supposed to hand it over to whoever was caught speaking his mother tongue. Whoever had the button at the end of the day would sing who had given it to him and the ensuing process would bring out all the culprits of the day. Thus children were turned into witch-hunters and in the process were being taught the lucrative value of being a traitor to one's immediate community.

The attitude to English was the exact opposite: any achievement in spoken or written English was highly rewarded; prizes, prestige, applause; the ticket to higher realms. English became the measure of intelligence and ability in the arts, the sciences, and all the other branches of learning. English became *the* main determinant of a child's progress up the ladder of formal education.

As you may know, the colonial system of education in addition to its apartheid racial demarcation had the structure of a pyramid: a broad primary base, a narrowing secondary middle, and an even narrower university apex. Selections from primary into secondary were through an examination, in my time called Kenya African Preliminary Examination, in which one had to pass six subjects ranging from Maths to Nature Study and Kiswahili. All the papers were written in English. Nobody could pass the exam who failed the English language paper no matter how brilliantly he had done in the other subjects. I remember one boy in my class of 1954 who had distinctions in all subjects except English, which he had failed. He was made to fail the entire exam. He went on to become a turn boy in a bus company. I who had only passes but a credit in English got a place at the Alliance High School, one of the most elitist institutions for Africans in colonial Kenya. The requirements for a place at the University, Makerere University College, were broadly the same: nobody could go on to wear the undergraduate red gown, no matter how brilliantly they had performed in all the other subjects unless they had a credit – not even a simple pass! – in English. Thus the most coveted place in the pyramid and in the system was only available to the holder of an English language credit card. English was the official vehicle and the magic formula to colonial elitedom.

Literary education was now determined by the dominant language while also reinforcing that dominance. Orature (oral literature) in Kenyan languages stopped. In primary school I now read simplified Dickens and Stevenson along-side Rider Haggard. Jim Hawkins, Oliver Twist, Tom Brown – not Hare, Leopard and Lion – were now my daily companions in the world of imagination. In secondary school, Scott and G.B. Shaw vied with more Rider Haggard, John Buchan, Alan Paton, Captain W.E. Johns. At Makerere I read English: from Chaucer to T.S. Eliot with a touch of Graham Greene.

Thus language and literature were taking us further and further from ourselves to other selves, from our world to other worlds ...

I started writing in Gĩkũyũ language in 1977 after seventeen years of involve-ment in Afro-European literature, in my case Afro-English literature. It was then that I collaborated with Ngũgĩ wa Mĩriĩ in the drafting of the playscript, *Ngaahika Ndeenda* (the English translation was *I Will Marry When I Want*). I have since published a novel in Gĩkũyũ, *Caitaani Mũtharabaini* (English translation: *Devil on the Cross*) and completed a musical drama, *Maitũ Njugũira*, (English translation: *Mother Sing for Me*); three books for children, *Njamba Nene na Mbaathi i Mathagu*, *Bathitoora ya Njamba Nene, Njamba Nene na Cibũ Kĩng'ang'i*, as well as another novel manuscript: *Matigari Ma Njirũũngi*. Wherever I have gone, particularly in Europe, I have been confronted with the question: why are you now writing in Gĩkũyũ? Why do you now write in an African language? In some academic quarters I have been confronted with the rebuke, 'Why have you abandoned us?' It was almost as if, in choosing to write in Gĩkũyũ, I was doing something abnormal. But Gĩkũyũ is my mother tongue! The very fact that what common sense dictates in the literary practice of other cultures is being questioned in an African writer is a measure of how far imperialism has distorted the view of African realities. It has turned reality upside down: the abnormal is viewed as normal and the normal is viewed as abnormal. Africa actually enriches Europe: but Africa is made to believe that it needs Europe to rescue it from poverty. Africa's natural and human resources continue to develop Europe and America: but Africa is made to feel grateful for aid from the same quarters that still sit on the back of the continent. Africa even produces intellectuals who now rationalise this upside-down way of looking at Africa.

I believe that my writing in Gĩkũyũ language, a Kenyan language, an African language, is part and parcel of the anti-imperialist struggles of Kenyan and African peoples. In schools and universities our Kenyan languages – that is the languages of the many nationalities which make up Kenya – were associated with negative qualities of backwardness, underdevelopment, humiliation and punish-ment. We who went through that school system were meant to graduate with a hatred of the people and the culture and the values of the language of our daily humiliation and punishment. I do not want to see Kenyan children growing up in that imperialist-imposed tradition of contempt for the tools of communication developed by their communities and their history. I want them to transcend colonial alienation.

Source: Ngũgĩ, 1986a, pp. 10–12, 27–8

Reading B
EXTRACT FROM *ARROW OF GOD*

Chinua Achebe

Meanwhile the policemen arrived at Ezeulu's hut. They were then no longer in the mood for playing. They spoke sharply, baring all their weapons at once.

'Which one of you is called Ezeulu?' asked the corporal.

'Which Ezeulu?' asked Edogo.

'Don't ask me which Ezeulu again or I shall slap okro seeds out of your mouth. I say who is called Ezeulu here?'

'And I say which Ezeulu? Or don't you know who you are looking for?' The four other men in the hut said nothing. Women and children thronged the door leading from the hut into the inner compound. There was fear and anxiety in the faces.

'All right,' said the corporal in English. 'Jus now you go sabby which Ezeulu. Gi me dat ting.' This last sentence was directed to his companion who immediately produced the handcuffs from his pocket.

In the eyes of the villager handcuffs or *iga* were the most deadly of the white man's weapons. The sight of a fighting man reduced to impotence and helplessness with an iron lock was the final humiliation. It was a treatment given only to violent lunatics.

So when the fierce-looking policeman showed his handcuffs and moved towards Edogo with them Akuebue came forward as the elder in the house and spoke reasonably. He appealed to the policemen not to be angry with Edogo. 'He only spoke as a young man would. As you know, the language of young men is always *pull down and destroy*; but an old man speaks of conciliation.' He told them that Ezeulu and his son had set out for Okperi early in the morning to answer the white man's call. The policemen looked at each other. They had indeed met a man with another who looked like his son. They remembered them because they were the first people they had met going in the opposite direction but also because the man and his son looked very distinguished.

'What does he look like?' asked the corporal.

'He is as tall as an iroko tree and his skin is white like the sun. In his youth he was called Nwa-anyanwu.'

'And his son?'

'Like him. No difference.'

The two policemen conferred in the white man's tongue to the great admiration of the villagers.

'Sometine na dat two porson we cross for road,' said the corporal.

'Sometine na dem,' said his companion. 'But we no go return back jus like dat. All dis waka wey we waka come here no fit go for nating.'

The corporal thought about it. The other continued:

'Sometine na lie dem de lie. I no wan make dem put trouble for we head.'

The corporal still thought about it. He was convinced that the men spoke the truth but it was necessary to frighten them a little, if only to coax a sizeable 'kola' [bribe] out of them. He addressed them in [Igbo]:

'We think that you may be telling us a lie and so we must make quite sure otherwise the white man will punish us. What we shall do then is to take two of you – handcuffed – to Okperi. If we find Ezeulu there we shall set you free; if not …'

He completed with a sideways movement of the head which spoke more clearly than words. 'Which two shall we take?'

Source: Achebe, 1974, pp. 152–4

Reading C
EXTRACT FROM *FINDING THE CENTRE*

V.S. Naipaul

It was in that Victorian-Edwardian gloom, and at one of those typewriters, that late one afternoon, without having any idea where I was going, and not perhaps intending to type to the end of the page, I wrote: *Every morning when he got up Hat would sit on the banister of his back verandah and shout across, 'What happening there, Bogart?'* ...

So I became 'writer'. Though to myself an unassuageable anxiety still attached to the word, and I was still, for its sake, practising magic. I never bought paper to write on. I preferred to use 'borrowed', non-rustle BBC paper; it seemed more casual, less likely to attract failure. I never numbered my pages, for fear of not getting to the end ... And on the finished manuscripts of my first four books – half a million words – I never with my own hand typed or wrote my name. I always asked someone else to do that for me. Such anxiety; such ambition.

The ways of my fantasy, the process of creation, remained mysterious to me. For everything that was false or didn't work and had to be discarded, I felt that I alone was responsible. For everything that seemed right I felt I had only been a vessel. There was the recurring element of luck, or so it seemed to me. True, and saving, knowledge of my subject – beginning with Bogart's street – always seemed to come during the writing.

This element of luck isn't so mysterious to me now. As diarists and letter-writers repeatedly prove, any attempt at narrative can give value to an experience which might otherwise evaporate away. When I began to write about Bogart's street I began to sink into a tract of experience I hadn't before contemplated as a writer. This blindness might seem extraordinary in someone who wanted so much to be a writer. Half a writer's work, though, is the discovery of his subject. And a problem for me was that my life had been varied, full of upheavals and moves: from my grandmother's Hindu house in the country, still close to the rituals and social ways of village India; to Port of Spain, the Negro and G.I. life of its streets, the other, ordered life of my colonial English school, which was called Queen's Royal College; and then Oxford, London and the freelances' room at the BBC. Trying to make a beginning as a writer, I didn't know where to focus.

In England I was also a colonial. Out of the stresses of that, and out of my worship of the name of writer, I had without knowing it fallen into the error of thinking of writing as a kind of display. My very particularity – which was the subject sitting on my shoulder – had been encumbering me.

The English or French writer of my age had grown up in a world that was more or less explained. He wrote against a background of knowledge. I couldn't be a writer in the same way, because to be a colonial, as I was, was to be spared knowledge. It was to live in an intellectually restricted world; it was to accept those restrictions. And the restrictions could become attractive.

Every morning when he got up Hat would sit on the banister of his back verandah and shout across, 'What happening there, Bogart?' That was a good place to begin. But I couldn't stay there. My anxiety constantly to prove myself as a writer, the need to write another book and then another, led me away.

There was much in that call of 'Bogart!' that had to be examined. It was spoken by a Port of Spain Indian, a descendant of nineteenth-century indentured immigrants from South India; and Bogart was linked in a special Hindu way with my mother's family. So there was a migration from India to be considered, a migration within the British Empire. There was my Hindu family, with its fading memories of India; there was India itself. And there was Trinidad, with its past of slavery, its mixed population, its racial antagonisms and its changing political life; once part of Venezuela and the Spanish Empire, now English-speaking, with the American base and an open-air cinema at the end of Bogart's street. And just across the Gulf of Paria was Venezuela, the sixteenth-century land of El Dorado, now a country of dictators, but drawing Bogart out of his servant room with its promise of Spanish sexual adventure and the promise of a job in its oilfields.

And there was my own presence in England, writing: the career wasn't possible in Trinidad, a small, mainly agricultural colony: my vision of the world couldn't exclude that important fact.

So step by step, book by book, though seeking each time only to write another book, I eased myself into knowledge. To write was to learn. Beginning a book, I always felt I was in possession of all the facts about myself; at the end I was always surprised. The book before always turned out to have been written by a man with incomplete knowledge. And the very first, the one begun in the freelances' room, seemed to have been written by an innocent, a man at the beginning of knowledge both about himself and the writing career that had been his ambition from childhood.

The ambition to be a writer was given me by my father. He was a journalist for much of his working life. This was an unusual occupation for a Trinidad Indian of his generation. My father was born in 1906. At that time the Indians of Trinidad were a separate community, mainly rural and Hindi-speaking, attached to the sugar estates of central and southern Trinidad. Many of the Indians of 1906 had been born in India and had come out to Trinidad as indentured labourers on five-year contracts. This form of Indian contract labour within the British Empire ended, as a result of nationalist agitation in India, only in 1917.

In 1929 my father began contributing occasional articles on Indian topics to the *Trinidad Guardian*. In 1932, when I was born, he had become the *Guardian* staff correspondent in the little market town of Chaguanas. Chaguanas was in the heart of the sugar area and the Indian area of Trinidad. It was where my mother's family was established. Contract labour was far behind them; they were big landowners.

Two years or so after I was born my father left the *Guardian*, for reasons that were never clear to me. For some years he did odd jobs here and there, now attached to my mother's family, now going back to the protection of an uncle by marriage, a rich man, founder and part owner of the biggest bus company in the island. Poor himself, with close relations who were still agricultural labourers, my father dangled all his life in a half-dependence and half-esteem between these two powerful families.

Source: Naipaul, 1984, pp. 16, 26–9

Reading D
EXTRACT FROM *THE WOMAN WARRIOR*

Maxine Hong Kingston

During the first silent year I spoke to no one at school, did not ask before going to the lavatory, and flunked kindergarten. My sister also said nothing for three years, silent in the playground and silent at lunch. There were other quiet Chinese girls not of our family, but most of them got over it sooner than we did. I enjoyed the silence. At first it did not occur to me I was supposed to talk or to pass kindergarten. I talked at home and to one or two of the Chinese kids in class. I made motions and even made some jokes. I drank out of a toy saucer when the water spilled out of the cup, and everybody laughed, pointing at me, so I did it some more. I didn't know that Americans don't drink out of saucers.

I liked the Negro students (Black Ghosts) best because they laughed the loudest and talked to me as if I were a daring talker too. One of the Negro girls had her mother coil braids over her ears Shanghai-style like mine; we were Shanghai twins except that she was covered with black like my paintings. Two Negro kids enrolled in Chinese school, and the teachers gave them Chinese names. Some Negro kids walked me to school and home, protecting me from the Japanese kids, who hit me and chased me and stuck gum in my ears. The Japanese kids were noisy and tough. They appeared one day in kindergarten, released from concentration camp which was a tic-tac-toe mark, like barbed wire, on the map.

It was when I found out I had to talk that school became a misery, that the silence became a misery. I did not speak and felt bad each time that I did not speak. I read aloud in first grade, though, and heard the barest whisper with little squeaks come out of my throat. 'Louder,' said the teacher, who scared the voice away again. The other Chinese girls did not talk either, so I knew the silence had to do with being a Chinese girl.

Reading out loud was easier than speaking because we did not have to make up what to say, but I stopped often, and the teacher would think I'd gone quiet again. I could not understand 'I'. The Chinese 'I' has seven strokes, intricacies. How could the American 'I', assuredly wearing a hat like the Chinese, have only three strokes, the middle so straight? Was it out of politeness that this writer left off strokes the way a Chinese has to write her own name small and crooked? No, it was not politeness; 'I' is a capital and 'you' is a lower-case. I stared at that middle line and waited so long for its black centre to resolve into tight strokes and dots that I forgot to pronounce it. The other troublesome word was 'here', no strong consonant to hang on to, and so flat, when 'here' is two mountainous ideographs. The teacher, who had already told me every day how to read 'I' and 'here', put me in the low corner under the stairs again, where the noisy boys usually sat.

When my second grade class did a play, the whole class went to the auditorium except the Chinese girls. The teacher, lovely and Hawaiian, should have understood about us, but instead left us behind in the classroom. Our voices were too soft or nonexistent, and our parents never signed the permission slips anyway. They never signed anything unnecessary. We opened the door a crack and peeked out, but closed it again quickly. One of us (not me) won every spelling bee, though.

I remember telling the Hawaiian teacher, 'We Chinese can't sing "land where our fathers died".' She argued with me about politics, while I meant because of curses. But how can I have that memory when I couldn't talk? My mother says that we, like the ghosts, have no memories.

After American school, we picked up our cigar boxes, in which we had arranged books, brushes and an inkbox neatly, and went to Chinese school, from five to seven thirty p.m. There we chanted together, voices rising and falling, loud and soft, some boys shouting, everybody reading together, reciting together and not alone with one voice. When we had a memorization test, the teacher let each of us come to his desk and say the lesson to him privately, while the rest of the class practised copying or tracing. Most of the teachers were men. The boys who were so well behaved in the American school played tricks on them and talked back to them. The girls were not mute. They screamed and yelled during recess, when there were no rules; they had fistfights. Nobody was afraid of children hurting themselves or of children hurting school property. The glass doors to the red and green balconies with the gold joy symbols were left wide open so that we could run out and climb the fire escapes. We played capture-the-flag in the auditorium, where Sun Yat-sen's and Chiang Kai-shek's pictures hung at the back of the stage, the Chinese flag on their left and the American flag on their right. We climbed the teak ceremonial chairs and made flying leaps off the stage. One flag headquarters was behind the glass door and the other on stage right. Our feet drummed on the hollow stage. During recess the teachers locked themselves up in their office with the shelves of books, copy-books, inks from China. They drank tea and warmed their hands at a stove. There was no play supervision. At recess we had the school to ourselves, and also we could roam as far as we could go – downtown, Chinatown stores, home – as long as we returned before the bell rang.

At exactly seven thirty the teacher again picked up the brass bell that sat on his desk and swung it over our heads, while we charged down the stairs, our cheering magnified in the stairwell. Nobody had to line up.

Not all of the children who were silent at American school found voice at Chinese school. One new teacher said each of us had to get up and recite in front of the class, who were to listen. My sister and I had memorized the lesson perfectly. We said it to each other at home, one chanting, one listening. The teacher called on my sister to recite first. It was the first time a teacher had called on the second-born to go first. My sister was scared. She glanced at me and looked away; I looked down at my desk. I hoped that she could do it because if she could, then I would have to. She opened her mouth and a voice came out that wasn't a whisper, but it wasn't a proper voice either. I hoped that she would not cry, fear breaking up her voice like twigs underfoot. She sounded as if she were trying to sing through weeping and strangling. She did not pause or stop to end the embarrassment. She kept going until she said the last word, and then she sat down. When it was my turn, the same voice came out, a crippled animal running on broken legs. You could hear splinters in my voice, bones rubbing jagged against one another. I was loud, though. I was glad I didn't whisper. There was one little girl who whispered.

You can't entrust your voice to the Chinese, either; they want to capture your voice for their own use. They want to fix up your tongue to speak for them. 'How much less can you sell it for?' we have to say. Talk the Sales Ghosts down. Make them take a loss.

Source: Hong Kingston, 1981b, pp. 149–52

Reading E
EXTRACT FROM *LOST IN TRANSLATION*

Eva Hoffman

For my birthday, Penny gives me a diary, complete with a little lock and key to keep what I write from the eyes of all intruders. It is that little lock – the visible symbol of the privacy in which the diary is meant to exist – that creates my dilemma. If I am indeed to write something entirely for myself, in what language do I write? Several times, I open the diary and close it again. I can't decide. Writing in Polish at this point would be a little like resorting to Latin or ancient Greek – an eccentric thing to do in a diary, in which you're supposed to set down your most immediate experiences and unpremeditated thoughts in the most unmediated language. Polish is becoming a dead language, the language of the untranslatable past. But writing for nobody's eyes in English? That's like doing a school exercise, or performing in front of yourself, a slightly perverse act of self-voyeurism.

Because I have to choose something, I finally choose English. If I'm to write about the present, I have to write in the language of the present, even if it's not the language of the self. As a result, the diary becomes surely one of the more impersonal exercises of that sort produced by an adolescent girl. These are no sentimental effusions of rejected love, eruptions of familial anger, or consoling broodings about death. English is not the language of such emotions. Instead, I set down my reflections on the ugliness of wrestling; on the elegance of Mozart, and on how Dostoyevsky puts me in mind of El Greco. I write down Thoughts. I Write.

There is a certain pathos to this naive snobbery, for the diary is an earnest attempt to create a part of my persona that I imagine I would have grown into in Polish. In the solitude of this most private act, I write, in my public language, in order to update what might have been my other self. The diary is about me and not about me at all. But on one level, it allows me to make the first jump. I learn English through writing, and, in turn, writing gives me a written self. Refracted through the double distance of English and writing, this self – my English self – becomes oddly objective; more than anything, it perceives. It exists more easily in the abstract sphere of thoughts and observations than in the world. For a while, this impersonal self, this cultural negative capability, becomes the truest thing about me. When I write, I have a real existence that is proper to the activity of writing – an existence that takes place midway between me and the sphere of artifice, art, pure language. This language is beginning to invent another me. However, I discover something odd. It seems that when I write (or, for that matter, think) in English, I am unable to use the word 'I'. I do not go as far as the schizophrenic 'she' – but I am driven, as by a compulsion, to the double, the Siamese-twin 'you' …

It's as important to me to speak well as to play a piece of music without mistakes. Hearing English distorted grates on me like chalk screeching on a blackboard, like all things botched and badly done, like all forms of gracelessness. The odd thing is that I know what is correct, fluent, good, long before I can execute it. The English spoken by our Polish acquaintances strikes me as jagged and thick, and I know that I shouldn't imitate it. I'm turned off by the intonations I hear on the TV sitcoms – by the expectation of laughter, like a dog's tail wagging in supplication, built into the actors' pauses, and by the curtailed, cutoff rhythms. I like the way Penny speaks, with an easy flow and a pleasure in giving words a fleshy fullness; I like what I hear in some movies; and once the Old Vic comes to Vancouver to perform *Macbeth*, and though I can hardly understand the particular words, I am riveted by the tones of sureness and command that mold the actors' speech into such majestic periods.

Sociolinguists might say that I receive these language messages as class signals, that I associate the sounds of correctness with the social status of the speaker. In part, this is undoubtedly true. The class-linked notion that I transfer wholesale from Poland is that belonging to a 'better' class of people is absolutely dependent on speaking a 'better' language. And in my situation especially, I know that language will be a crucial instrument, that I can overcome the stigma of my marginality, the weight of presumption against me, only if the reassuringly right sounds come out of my mouth.

Yes, speech is a class signifier. But I think that in hearing these varieties of speech around me, I'm sensitized to something else as well – something that is a matter of aesthetics, and even of psychological health. Apparently, skilled chefs can tell whether a dish from some foreign cuisine is well cooked even if they have never tasted it and don't know the genre of cooking it belongs to. There seem to be some deep-structure qualities – consistency, proportions of ingredients, smoothness of blending – that indicate culinary achievement to these educated eaters' taste buds. So each language has its own distinctive music, and even if one doesn't know its separate components, one can pretty quickly recognize the propriety of the patterns in which the components are put together, their harmonies and discords. Perhaps the crucial element that strikes the ear in listening to living speech is the degree of the speaker's self-assurance and control.

As I listen to people speaking that foreign tongue, English, I can hear when they stumble or repeat the same phrases too many times, when their sentences trail off aimlessly – or, on the contrary, when their phrases have vigor and roundness, when they have the space and the breath to give a flourish at the end of a sentence, or make just the right pause before coming to a dramatic point. I can tell, in other words, the degree of their ease or disease, the extent of authority that shapes the rhythms of their speech. That authority – in whatever dialect, in whatever variant of the mainstream language – seems to me to be something we all desire. It's not that we all want to speak the King's English, but whether we speak Appalachian or Harlem English, or Cockney, or Jamaican Creole, we want to be at home in our tongue. We want to be able to give voice accurately and fully to ourselves and our sense of the world.

Source: Hoffman, 1991, pp. 120–4

Reading F
EXTRACT FROM 'THE MURMUR OF MALVERN'

Seamus Heaney

'The Schooner Flight', the long poem at the start of the book [*The Star-Apple Kingdom*], is epoch-making. All that Walcott knew in his bones and plied in his thought before this moves like a swell of energy under verse which sails, well rigged and richly cargoed, into the needy future. I imagine he has done for the

Caribbean what Synge did for Ireland, found a language woven out of dialect and literature, neither folksy nor condescending, a singular idiom evolved out of one man's inherited divisions and obsessions, an idiom which allows an older life to exult in itself and yet at the same time keeps the cool of 'the new'. A few years ago, in the turbulent and beautiful essay which prefaced his collection of plays, *Dream on Monkey Mountain,* Walcott wrote out of and about the hunger for a proper form, an instrument to bleed off the accumulated humours of his peculiar colonial ague. He has now found that instrument and wields it with rare confidence:

> You ever look up from some lonely beach
> and see a far schooner? Well, when I write
> this poem, each phrase go be soaked in salt;
> I go draw and knot every line as tight
> as ropes in this rigging; in simple speech
> my common language go be the wind,
> my pages the sails of the schooner *Flight.*

The speaker fixes his language in terms that recall Walcott's description of an ideal troupe of actors, 'sinewy, tuned, elated', and the language works for him as a well-disciplined troupe works for the dramatist ...

For those awakening to the nightmare of history, revenge – Walcott had conceded – can be a kind of vision, yet he himself is not vengeful. Nor is he simply a patient singer of the tears of things. His intelligence is fierce but it is literary. He assumes that art is a power and to be visited by it is to be endangered, but he also knows that works of art endanger nobody else, that they are benign. From the beginning he has never simplified or sold short. Africa and England are in him. The humanist voices of his education and the voices from his home ground keep insisting on their full claims, pulling him in two different directions. He always had the capacity to write with the elegance of a [Philip] Larkin and make himself a ventriloquist's doll to the English tradition which he inherited, though that of course would have been an attenuation of his gifts, for he also has the capacity to write with the murky voluptuousness of a [Pablo] Neruda and make himself a romantic tongue, indigenous and awash in the prophetic. He did neither, but made a theme of the choice and the impossibility of choosing. And now he has embodied the theme in the person of Shabine, the poor mulatto sailor of the *Flight*, a kind of democratic West Indian Ulysses, his mind full of wind and poetry and women. Indeed, when Walcott lets the sea-breeze freshen in his imagination, the result is a poetry as spacious and heart-lifting as the sea-weather at the opening of Joyce's *Ulysses*, a poetry that comes from no easy evocation of mood but from stored sensations of the actual:

> In idle August, while the sea soft,
> and leaves of brown islands stick to the rim
> of this Caribbean, I blow out the light
> by the dreamless face of Maria Concepcion
> to ship as a seaman on the schooner *Flight.*
> Out in the yard turning gray in the dawn,
> I stood like a stone and nothing else move
> but the cold sea rippling like galvanize
> and the nail holes of stars in the sky roof,
> till a wind start to interfere with the trees.

It is a sign of Walcott's mastery that his fidelity to West Indian speech now leads him not away from but right into the genius of English. When he wrote these opening lines, how conscious was he of another morning departure, another allegorical early-riser? The murmur of Malvern is under that writing, for surely it returns to an origin in *Piers Plowman*:

> In summer season, when soft was the sun,
> I rigged myself up in a long robe, rough like a sheep's,
> With skirts hanging like a hermit's, unholy of works,
> Went wide in this world, wonders to hear.
> But on a May morning, on Malvern Hills,
> A marvel befell me – magic it seemed.
> I was weary of wandering and went for a rest
> Under a broad bank, by a brook's side;
> And as I lay lolling, looking at the water,
> I slid into a sleep...

The whole passage could stand as an epigraph to Walcott's book in so far as it is at once speech and melody, amorous of the landscape, matter-of-fact but capable of modulation to the visionary. Walcott's glamorous, voluble Caribbean harbours recall Langland's field full of folk. Love and anger inspire both writers, and both manage – in [T.S.] Eliot's phrase – to fuse the most ancient and most civilized mentality.

Reference

WALCOTT, D. (1979) *The Star-Apple Kingdom*, New York, Farrar, Straus & Giroux.

Source: Heaney, 1988, pp. 23–5

REFERENCES

ACHEBE, C. (1958) *Things Fall Apart*, London, Heinemann Education.

ACHEBE, C. (1965) 'English and the African writer', *Transition: a journal of the arts, culture and society*, vol. 4, no. 18.

ACHEBE, C. (1974) *Arrow of God*, 2nd edn, London, Heinemann.

ACHEBE, C. (1976) *Things Fall Apart*, London, Heinemann.

ACHEBE, C. (1988) *Hopes and Impediments: selected essays 1965–1987*, London, Heinemann.

AHL, F. (1988) 'Ars est celare artem (art in puns and anagrams engraved)' in CULLER, J. (ed.) *On Puns: the foundation of letters*, Oxford, Blackwell.

ANAND, M.R. ([1936] 1945) *Coolie*, Harmondsworth, Penguin.

ARNOLD, M. (1880) 'General introduction: the study of poetry' in WARD, T.H. (ed.) *The English Poets*, London, Macmillan.

ATKINSON, J.M. (1984a) *Our Master's Voices: the language and body language of politics*, London, Methuen.

ATKINSON, J.M. (1984b) 'Public speaking and audience responses: some techniques for inviting applause' in ATKINSON, J.M. and HERITAGE, J. (eds) *Structures of Social Action: studies in conversation analysis*, Cambridge, Cambridge University Press.

ATKINSON, J.M. and HERITAGE, J. (eds) (1984) *Structures of Social Action: studies in conversation analysis*, Cambridge, Cambridge University Press.

AUDEN, W.H. (1969) *Collected Shorter Poems 1927–1957*, London, Faber & Faber.

BAKHTIN, M.M. (1981) *The Dialogic Imagination*, Austin, State University of Texas Press.

BAKHTIN, M.M. (1986) *Speech Genres and Other Late Essays*, trans. V.W. McGee, edited C. Emerson and M. Holquist, Austin, University of Texas Press.

BARKER, H. (1994) *Minna*, Leeds, Alumnus.

BARTON, D. (1994) *Literacy: an introduction to the ecology of written language*, Oxford, Blackwell.

BARTON, D. and PADMORE, S. (1991) 'Roles, networks and values in everyday writing' in BARTON, D. and IVANIČ, R. (eds) *Writing in the Community*, London, Sage.

BAYNHAM, M. (1995) *Literacy Practices*, Harlow, Longman.

BEATTIE, G. (1983) *Talk: an analysis of speech and non-verbal behaviour in conversation*, Buckingham, Open University Press.

BECKETT, S. (1984) *Collected Shorter Plays*, London, Faber & Faber.

BESNIER, N. (1993) 'Literacy and feelings: the encoding of affect in Nukulaelae letters' in STREET, B. (ed.) *Cross-cultural Approaches to Literacy*, Cambridge, Cambridge University Press.

BHATT, S. (1991) *Monkey Shadows*, Manchester, Carcanet.

BIERCE, A. (1970) *The Complete Short Stories of Ambrose Bierce*, New York, Doubleday.

BIRCH, D. (1992) 'Gender and genre' in BONNER, F., GOOKMAN, L., ALLEN, R., JANES, L. and KING, C. (eds) *Imagining Women,* Cambridge, Polity in association with Blackwell/The Open University.

BLOOM, A. (1987) *The Closing of the American Mind,* New York, Simon & Schuster.

BLOOM, H., DeMAN, P., DERRIDA, J., HARTMAN, G. and MILLER, J.H. (eds) (1979) *Deconstruction and Criticism,* London, Routledge & Kegan Paul.

BLUME, R. (1985) 'Graffiti' in VAN DIJK, T. (ed.) *Discourse and Literature,* Amsterdam, Benjamins.

BOWANS, G. (ed.) (1964) *Penguin Book of Japanese Verse,* trans. G. Bowans and A. Thwaite, Harmondsworth, Penguin.

BRATHWAITE, K. (1981) 'English in the Caribbean: notes on nation language and poetry, an electronic culture' in FIEDLER, L.A. and BAKER, J.R. (eds) *English Literature: opening up the canon,* Baltimore, Md. and London, Johns Hopkins University Press.

BRATHWAITE, K. (1993) *Roots,* Ann Arbor, University of Michigan Press.

BRICE HEATH, S. (1983) *Ways with Words: language, life, and work in communities and classrooms,* Cambridge, Cambridge University Press.

BRINK, A. (1982) *A Chain of Voices,* London, Faber & Faber.

BRONTË, E. ([1847] 1985) *Wuthering Heights,* Penguin Classics.

BROWN, D.E. (1991) *Human Universals,* New York, McGraw-Hill.

BROWN, P. and LEVINSON, S. (1987) *Politeness: some universals in language usage,* Cambridge, Cambridge University Press.

BRUCE FRANKLIN, H. (1981) 'English as an institution: the role of class' in FIEDLER, L.A. and BAKER, J.R. (eds), *English Literature: opening up the canon,* Baltimore, Md. and London, Johns Hopkins University Press.

BRUNER, J. (1986) *Actual Minds, Possible Worlds,* Cambridge, Mass., Harvard University Press.

BURNETT, P. (ed.) (1986) *Penguin Book of Caribbean Verse in English,* Harmondsworth, Penguin.

BURROWS, J. (1987) *Computation into Criticism,* Oxford, Clarendon.

BUTLER, M. (1990) 'Repossessing the past: the case for an open literary history' in WALDER, D. (ed.) *Literature in the Modern World,* Oxford, Oxford University Press.

CARTER, R. and NASH, W. (1990) *Seeing Through Language: a guide to styles of English writing,* Oxford, Blackwell.

CHEEPEN, C. and MONAGHAN, J. (1990) *Spoken English: a practical guide,* London, Pinter.

COATES, J. (1993) 'No gap, lots of overlap' in GRADDOL, D., MAYBIN, J. and STIERER, B. (eds) *Researching Language and Literacy in Social Context,* Clevedon, Multilingual Matters.

COATES, J. (1994) 'Discourse and career' in EVETTS, J. (ed.) *Women and Career: themes and issues,* Harlow, Longman.

COOK, G. (1992) *The Discourse of Advertising,* London, Routledge.

COOK, G. (1994) *Discourse and Literature,* Oxford, Oxford University Press.

CREMER, R.D. and WILLES, M.J. (1991) 'Stock in trade: the role of English in international trade proceedings', *CERC Discussion Paper 91/1,* Macau, University of East Asia, China Economic Research Centre.

CREMER, R.D. and WILLES, M.J. (1994) 'Overcoming language barriers of international trade: a text-based study of the language of deals', *Journal of Asian Pacific Communication*, vol. 15, no. 3.

CRYSTAL, D. (1987) *Cambridge Encyclopaedia of Language*, Cambridge, Cambridge University Press.

cummings, e.e. (1969) *selected poems 1923–1958*, London, Faber & Faber.

CUTTS, M. (1995) 'Writing on the wall for law language', *English Today*, vol. 11, no. 3, July, pp. 45–53.

DABYDEEN, D. (1990) *The State of the Language*, London, Faber & Faber.

DATHORNE, O.R. (1975) *African Literature in the Twentieth Century*, London, Heinemann.

DICKENS, C. ([1853] 1907) *Bleak House*, London, Dent.

DRABBLE, M. (1987) *The Radiant Way*, Harmondsworth, Penguin.

DUFFY, C.A. (1993) *Mean Time*, London, Anvil.

DURANT, A. and FABB. N. (1990) *Literary Studies in Action*, London, Routledge.

EADES, D. (1991) 'Communicative strategies in Aboriginal English' in ROMAINE, S. (ed.) *Language in Australia*, Cambridge, Cambridge University Press.

EAGLETON, T. (1983) *Literary Theory: an introduction*, Oxford, Blackwell.

ELIOT, T.S. (1932) *Selected Essays*, London, Faber.

EMECHETA, B. (1979) *In the Ditch*, London, Allison & Busby.

ERVIN-TRIPP, S.M. (1969) 'Sociolinguistics' in BERKOWITZ, L. (ed.) *Advances in Experimental Social Psychology*, New York, Academic Press.

ESNOL, A., LEES, G. and POTE, M. (1985) *English for Business Purposes: teacher's handbook*, Oxford, Oxford University Press.

FAULKNER, W. ([1929] 1989) *The Sound and the Fury*, London, Picador.

FIRMAGE, G. (ed.) (1973) *e.e. cummings: the complete poems 1910–1962*, London, Granada.

FISHMAN, J. (1971) 'The sociology of language' in FISHMAN, J. (ed.) *Advances in the Sociology of Language*, vol. 1, The Hague, Mouton.

FOWLER, R.G. and KRESS, G. (1979) 'Critical linguistics' in FOWLER, R.G. et al. (eds) *Language and Control*, London, Routledge & Kegan Paul.

FOWLER, R. (1991) *The Language of the News*, London, Routledge.

FRANCE, L. (1993) *Sixty Women Poets*, Newcastle upon Tyne, Bloodaxe.

FREUD, S. ([1905] 1952) *The Complete Psychological Works*, London, Hogarth/ Institute of Psychoanalysis.

FUGARD, A. (1990) *My Children! My Africa!*, London, Faber & Faber.

GOFFMAN, E. (1967) *Interaction Ritual*, Harmondsworth, Penguin.

GOODMAN, S. and GRADDOL, D. (eds) (1996) *Redesigning English: new texts, new identities*, London, Routledge/The Open University.

GOODWIN, M.H. (1990) 'Tactical use of stories: participation frameworks within girls' and boys' disputes', *Discourse Processes*, vol. 13, no. 1, pp. 33–71.

GRADDOL, D., CHESHIRE, J. and SWANN, J. (1994) *Describing Language*, 2nd edn, Buckingham, Open University Press.

GRADDOL, D., LEITH, D. and SWANN, J. (eds) (1996) *English: history, diversity and change*, London, Routledge/The Open University.

HALLIDAY, M.A.K. (1973) *Explorations in the Function of Language*, London, Arnold.

HALLIDAY, M.A.K. (1978) *Language as Social Semiotic: the social interpretation of language and meaning*, London, Edward Arnold.

HALLIDAY, M.A.K. (1985) *Spoken and Written Language*, Deakin, Victoria, Deakin University Press.

HALLIDAY, M.A.K. (1987) 'Spoken and written modes of meaning' in HOROWITZ, R. and SAMUELS, S.J. (eds) *Comprehending Oral and Written Language*, Orlando, Fla., Academic Press.

HANKS, P. (ed.) (1993) *Collins Dictionary of the English Language*, London, Collins.

HARRISON, T. (1987) *Selected Poems*, 2nd edn, Harmondsworth, Penguin.

HASAN, R. (1989) *Linguistics, Language, and Verbal Art*, Oxford, Oxford University Press.

HEANEY, S. (1980) *Preoccupations: selected prose, 1968–1978*, London, Faber & Faber.

HEANEY, S. (1988) *The Government of the Tongue: the 1986 T.S. Eliot memorial lectures and other criticial writings*, London, Faber & Faber.

HEARST, D. (1994) 'It loses something in the translation', 'Moscow Diary', *Guardian*, 25 July.

HERITAGE, J. and GREATBATCH, D. (1986) 'Generating applause: a study of rhetoric and response at party political conferences', *American Journal of Sociology*, vol. 92, part 1.

HEWITT, R. (1982) 'White adolescent creole users and the politics of friendship' in MAYOR, B. and PUGH, A.K. (eds) *Language, Communication and Education*, London, Croom Helm.

HIRSCH, E.D. Jr (1987) *Cultural Literacy: what every American needs to know*, Boston, Mass., Houghton Mifflin.

HODGENS, J. (1994) 'How adult literacy became a public issue in Australia', *Open Letter*, vol. 2, no. 2.

HOFFMAN, E. (1991) *Lost in Translation: a life in a new language*, London, Minerva.

HOLMES, J. (1994) 'Case study 1: the role of compliments in female–male interaction' in SUNDERLAND, J. (ed.) *Exploring Gender: questions and implications for English language education*, London, Prentice Hall.

HONG KINGSTON, M. (1981a) *China Men*, London, Picador.

HONG KINGSTON, M. (1981b) *The Woman Warrior: memoirs of a girlhood among ghosts*, London, Picador.

IVANIČ, R. (1993) 'I is for interpersonal: the discourse construction of writer identities and the teaching of writing', *Working Paper Series no. 42*, Lancaster, Centre for Language in Social Life, University of Lancaster.

JEFFERSON, G. (1984) '"At first I thought": a normalising device for extraordinary events', unpublished manuscript, Tilburg, Katholieke Hogeschool.

JEFFERSON, G. (1991) 'List construction as a task and resource' in PSATHAS, G. (ed.) *Interaction Competence*, Washington, University Press of America.

JEFFRIES, L. (1993) *The Language of Twentieth Century Poetry*, Basingstoke, Macmillan.

JOHNSON, L.K. (1975) *Dread Beat and Blood*, London, Bogle L'Ouverture.

KEITH, W.M. and WHITTENBERGER-KEITH, K. (1988/9) 'The conversational call: an analysis of conversational aspects of public oratory', *Research on Language and Social Interaction*, vol. 22.

KELL, C. (1994) 'An analysis of literacy practices in an informal settlement in the Cape Peninsula', MPhil dissertation, Cape Town, Faculty of Education, University of Cape Town.

KERMODE, F. (1988) *History and Value*, Oxford, Clarendon.

KILLAM, D. (1976) 'Notes on adaptation and variation in the use of English in writing by Haliburton, Furphy, Achebe, Narayan and Naipaul' in NIVEN, A. (ed.) *Commonwealth Writer Overseas*, Paris, Didier.

LABOV, W. (1972) *Language in the Inner City*, Philadephia, University of Pennsylvania Press.

LAKOFF, R. (1975) *Language and Women's Place*, New York, Harper & Row.

LARKIN, P. (1964) *The Whitsun Weddings*, London, Faber & Faber.

LEAVIS, F.R. (1943) *Education and the University*, London, Chatto & Windus.

LEAVIS, F.R. (1948) *The Great Tradition: George Eliot, Henry James, Joseph Conrad*, London, Chatto & Windus.

LEECH, G. and SHORT, M. (1981) *Style in Fiction*, Harlow, Longman.

LOUW, B. (1993) 'Irony in the text or insincerity in the writer? The diagnostic potential of semantic prosodies' in BAKER, M., FRANCIS, G. and TOGNINI-BONELLI, E. (eds) *Text and Technology: in honour of John Sinclair*, Philadelphia, John Benjamins.

LOWRY, A. (1982) 'Style range in new English literatures' in KACHRU, B.B. (ed.) *The Other Tongue: English across cultures*, Urbana, University of Illinois Press.

MacCABE, C. (1987) 'The state of the subject English', *Critical Quarterly*, vol. 29, no. 4, winter.

MAGARSHACK, D. (1967) *Pushkin*, London, Chapman & Hall.

MALCOLM X (1991) *Malcolm X Talks to Young People: speeches in the US, Britain and Africa*, edited S. Clark, New York, Pathfinder.

MALINOWSKI, B. (1923) 'The problem of meaning in primitive languages' in OGDEN, C.K. and RICHARDS, I.M. (eds) *The Meaning of Meaning*, London, Routledge & Kegan Paul.

MALTZ, D.N. and BORKER, R.A. (1982) 'A cultural approach to male–female communication' in GUMPERZ, J.J. (ed.) *Language and Social Identity*, Cambridge, Cambridge University Press.

MARENBON, J. (1987) *English our English: the new orthodoxy examined*, London, Centre for Policy Studies.

MARRIOTT, H. (1995) 'Deviations in an intercultural business negotiation' in FIRTH, A. (ed.) *The Discourse of Negotiation: studies of language in the workplace*, London, Pergamon.

MAYBIN, J. (1993) 'Children's voices: talk, knowledge and identity' in GRADDOL, D.J., MAYBIN, J. and STIERER, B. (eds) *Researching Language and Literacy in Social Context*, Clevedon, Multilingual Matters.

MAYNARD, D. (1992) 'On clinicians co-implicating recipients' perspective in the delivery of diagnostic news' in DREW, P. and HERITAGE, J. (eds) *Talk at Work: interaction in institutional settings*, Cambridge, Cambridge University Press.

MERCER, N. and SWANN, J. (eds) (1996) *Learning English: development and diversity*, London, Routledge/The Open University.

MORRIS, P. (1993) *Literature and Feminism*, Oxford, Blackwell.

MORRISON, T. (1992) *Jazz*, London, Chatto & Windus.

NAIPAUL, V.S. (1984) *Finding the Centre: two narratives*, Harmondsworth, Penguin.

NAIPAUL, V.S. (1992) *A House for Mr Biswas*, Harmondsworth, Penguin.

NASH, W. (1993) *Jargon: its uses and abuses*, Oxford, Blackwell.

NGŨGĨ WA THIONG'O (1976) *Weep Not, Child*, London, Heinemann.

NGŨGĨ WA THIONG'O (1986a) *Decolonising the Mind: the politics of language in African literature*, London, James Currey.

NGŨGĨ WA THIONG'O (1986b) *Petals of Blood*, London, Heinemann.

NKOSI, L. (1965) *Home and Exile*, London, Longman.

NWOYE, O.G. (1993) 'Social issues on walls: graffiti in university lavatories', *Discourse and Society*, vol. 4, no. 4, pp. 419–42.

O'BARR, W.M. and ATKINS, B.K. (1980) '"Women's language" or "powerless language"?' in McCONNELL-GINET, S., BORKER, R. and FURMAN, N. (eds) *Woman and Language in Literature and Society*, New York, Praeger.

ODEAN, K. (1990) 'Bear hugs and Bo Dereks on Wall Street' in RICKS, C. and MICHAELS, L. (eds) *The State of the Language*, London, Faber & Faber.

OPEN UNIVERSITY (1980) PE232 *I'll Tell You What Price I Charge*, TV 4, *Language Development*, Milton Keynes, BBC Open University Productions.

OPEN UNIVERSITY (1991) A319 *Literature in the Modern World*, Radio Programme 1, *The Problem of the Canon*, Milton Keynes, BBC Open University Productions.

PADEL, R. (1993) *Angel*, Newcastle upon Tyne, Bloodaxe.

PANDHARIPANDE, R. (1992) 'Defining politeness in Indian English', *World Englishes*, vol. 11, nos. 2/3, pp. 241–50.

PENNYCOOK, A. (1994) *The Cultural Politics of English as an International Language*, Harlow, Longman.

PINCH, T.J. and CLARK, C. (1986) 'The hard sell: "patter merchanting" and the strategic (re)production and local management of economic reasoning in the sales routines of market pitchers', *Sociology*, vol. 20, part 2.

PINTER, H. (1979) *Plays Two*, London, Methuen.

PLAIN ENGLISH CAMPAIGN (1992) *Plain English Campaign: information and publications brochure*, Stockport, Plain English Campaign.

PLATT, J., WEBBER, H. and HO, M. L. (1984) *The New Englishes*, London, Routledge & Kegan Paul.

POTTER, J. and WETHERELL, M. (1987) *Discourse and Social Psychology*, London, Sage.

POUND, E. (1961) *ABC of Reading*, London, Faber.

PURVIS, J. (1987) 'Social class, education and ideals of femininity in the nineteenth century' in ARNOT, M. and WEINER, G. (eds) *Gender and the Politics of Schooling*, London, Hutchinson.

RAO, R. ([1938] 1989) *Kanthapura*, 2nd edn, New Delhi, Oxford University Press.

REDFERN, W. (1984) *Puns*, Oxford, Blackwell.

REES, N. (1980) *Graffiti 2*, London, Unwin.

REES, N. (1981) *Graffiti 3*, London, Unwin.

RICHARDS, I.A. (1929) *Practical Criticism: a study of literary judgement*, London, Routledge & Kegan Paul.

RICHARDSON, D. ([1913–38] 1979) *Pilgrimage*, 4 vols, London, Virago.

ROBERTS, C. and SAYERS. P. (1988) 'Keeping the gate: how judgements are made in interethnic interviews' in KNAPP, K. et al. (eds) *Analysing Intercultural Conversation,* The Hague, Mouton.

ROMAINE, S. (1990) 'Pidgin English advertising' in RICKS, C. and MICHAELS, L. (eds) *The State of the Language,* London, Faber & Faber.

RUSHDIE, S. (1982) *Midnight's Children,* London, Pan.

SACKS, H., SCHEGLOFF, E. and JEFFERSON, G. (1974) 'A simplest systematics for the organization of turn-taking in conversation', *Language,* vol. 50, no. 4, pp. 696–735.

SACKS, H. (1984) 'On doing "being ordinary"' in ATKINSON, J.M. and HERITAGE, J. (eds.) *Structures of Social Action: studies in conversation analysis,* Cambridge, Cambridge University Press.

SAID, E.W. (1993) *Culture and Imperialism,* London, Chatto & Windus.

SAUSSURE, F. de ([1916] 1960) *Course in General Linguistics,* trans. W. Baskin, London, Fontana.

SAXENA, M. (1994) 'Literacies among the Panjabis in Southall' in HAMILTON, M., BARTON, D. and IVANIČ, R. (eds) *Worlds of Literacy,* Clevedon, Multilingual Matters.

SEBBA, M. (1993) *London Jamaican: language systems in interaction,* London, Longman.

SHOWALTER, E. (1982) *A Literature of their Own: British women novelists from Brontë to Lessing,* rev. edn, London, Virago.

SHOWALTER, E.. (1986) *The New Feminist Criticism: essays on women, literature and theory,* London, Virago.

SHUMAN, A. (1993) 'Collaborative writing: appropriating power or reproducing authority?' in STREET, B. (ed) *Cross-cultural Approaches to Literacy,* Cambridge, Cambridge University Press.

SHUY, R. (1993) *Language Crimes: the use and abuse of language evidence in the courtroom,* London, Blackwell.

SINCLAIR, J. (ed.) (1987) *Collins Cobuild English Language Dictionary,* London, Collins.

SMITHERMAN, G. (1986) *Talkin and Testifyin,* Detroit, Mich., Wayne State University Press.

SPIVAK, G.C. (1990) *The Post-Colonial Critic: interviews, strategies, dialogues,* edited S. Harasym, London, Routledge.

STREET, B. (ed) (1993) *Cross-cultural Approaches to Literacy,* Cambridge, Cambridge University Press.

SUTCLIFFE, D. and TOMLIN, C. (1986) 'The black churches' in SUTCLIFFE, D. and WONG, A. (eds) *The Language of the Black Experience,* Oxford, Blackwell.

SWALES, J. (1990) *Genre Analysis: English in academic and research settings,* Cambridge, Cambridge University Press.

TANNEN, D. (1984) *Conversational Style: analyzing talk among friends,* Norwood, N.J., Ablex.

TANNEN, D. (1989) *Talking Voices: repetition, dialogue and imagery in conversational discourse,* Cambridge, Cambridge University Press.

TODD, L. (1979) *Some Day Been Dey: West African pidgin folktales,* London, Routledge & Kegan Paul.

TODD, L. (1989) *The Language of Irish Literature,* Basingstoke, Macmillan.

ULMER, G. (1988) 'The puncept in grammatology' in CULLER, J. (ed.) *On Puns: the foundation of letters*, Oxford, Blackwell.

VISWANATHAN, G. (1989) *Masks of Conquest*, London, Faber & Faber.

VOLOSINOV, V.N. (1973) *Marxism and the Philosophy of Language*, New York, Seminar.

VYGOTSKY, L.S. (1978) *Mind in Society: the development of higher psychological processes*, London, Harvard University Press.

WALCOTT, D. (1973) *Another Life*, London, Cape.

WALD, A. (1989) 'Hegemony and literary tradition in the United States' in DE CASTELL, S., LUKE, A. and LUKE, C. (eds) *Language, Authority and Criticism: readings on the school textbook*, London, Falmer.

WALDER, D. (1987) *Literature and the Modern World*, Oxford, Oxford University Press.

WALES, K. (1989) *A Dictionary of Stylistics*, London, Longman.

WEST, C. (1990) 'Not just "doctors' orders": directive-response sequences in patients' visits to women and men physicians', *Discourse and Society*, vol. 1, no. 1.

WILLIAMS, R. (1976) *Key Words: a vocabulary of culture and society*, London, Fontana.

WILSON, J. (1989) *On the Boundaries of Conversation*, Oxford, Pergamon.

WILSON KNIGHT, G. (1949) *The Wheel of Fire*, London, Methuen.

WOLFSON, N. (1982) *CHP: the conversational historical present in American English narrative*, Cinnaminson, USA, Foris.

WOODS, N. (1988) 'Talking shop: sex and status as determinants of floor apportionment in a work setting' in COATES, J. and CAMERON, D. (eds) *Women in their Speech Communities: new perspectives on language and sex*, Harlow, Longman.

WOOFFITT, R. (1992) *Telling Tales of the Unexpected: the organisation of factual discourse*, Hemel Hempstead, Harvester Wheatsheaf.

WOOLF, V. ([1927] 1977) *To the Lighthouse*, London, Grafton.

WOOLF, V. ([1929] 1992) *A Room of One's Own*, New York, Peter Smith.

WORDSWORTH, W. ([1850] 1991) *The Thirteen Book Prelude*, edited M. Reed, vol. 2, Ithaca, N.Y., Cornell University Press.

YATES, S. (1993) 'The textuality of computer-mediated communication: speech, writing and genre in CMC discourse', PhD thesis, Milton Keynes, The Open University.

ZIMMERMAN, D.H. and WEST, C. (1975) 'Sex roles, interruptions and silences in conversation' in THORNE, B. and HENLEY, N. (eds) *Language and Sex: difference and dominance*, Rowley, Mass., Newbury House.

ACKNOWLEDGEMENTS

Grateful acknowledgement is made to the following sources for permission to reproduce material in this book:

Colour plates

Plate 1: © POPPERFOTO; *Plate 2:* John Yuen; *Plates 3 and 4:* Literacy Research Group, Lancaster University; *Plate 5:* Donald Mackinnon; *Plate 6:* John Yuen; *Plate 7:* Reproduced by permission of Warner Music Singapore; *Plate 8:* Literacy Research Group, Lancaster University; *Plate 9:* Photo supplied by BBH. Reproduced by permission of the Select Model Agency; *Plate 10:* P&O Scottish Ferries advertisement, P&O Scottish Ferries Ltd; *Plate 11:* Detail from *The Convalescent* by Gwen John, The Fitzwilliam Museum, Cambridge. Reproduced by kind permission of Ben and Sara John.

Text

Page 22: Wolfson, N. 1982, 'Internal analysis', *The Conversational Historical Present in American English Narrative*, pp. 25–6, Mouton de Gruyter. A Division of Walter Gruyter & Co.; *pages 28-32:* Eades, D. 1991, 'Communicative Strategies in Aboriginal English' in Romaine, S. (ed.) *Language in Australia*, pp. 84–93, Cambridge University Press; *pages 32-6:* Holmes, J. 1994, 'Case Study 1: The Role of Compliments in Female–Male Interaction' in Sunderland, J. (ed.) *Exploring Gender: questions and implications for English language education*, Phoenix ELT incorporating Prentice Hall Macmillan; *pages 64-7:* Saxena, M. 1993, 'Multi-literacy Practices and Values: An ethnographic account of a Panjabi family in Britain', in Hamilton, M., Barton, D. and Ivanič, R. (eds), *Worlds of Literacy*, Multilingual Matters Ltd; *pages 84 and 85:* Shuy, R.W. 1993, *Language Crimes*, p. 24, Blackwell Publishers Ltd; *pages 112–16:* Christopher Ricks, Leonard Michaels, *State of the Language*, 1990 edn. Copyright © 1989 The Regents of the University of California, University of California Press, reproduced by permission; *pages 125, 126, 128, 131 and 145–9:* Atkinson, M. 1984, *Our Masters' Voices*, pp. 63–71, Methuen & Co.; *page 170:* 'Days' from *Collected Poems* by Philip Larkin. Copyright © 1988, 1989 by the Estate of Philip Larkin. Reprinted by permission of Farrar, Straus & Giroux, Inc.; *page 170:* Louw, B. 1993, 'Irony in the Text or Insincerity in the Writer', in Baker, M. et al. 1993, *Text and Technology*, John Benjamins Publishing Company, Amsterdam/Philadelphia; *page 182:* Breeze, J.B. 1992, An excerpt from 'Spring cleaning' from *Spring cleaning: A collection of poems*, Virago Press; *page 192:* Mhlophe, G. et al. 1988, *Have you seen Zandile?*, Heinemann Publishers (Oxford) Limited; *pages 199–200:* Wood, V., Transcript of a television sketch, BBC, by permission of Victoria Wood; *pages 201–2:* Johnson, L.K. 191975, 'Time Come', *Dread Beat and Blood*, Bogle-L'Ouverture Publications Ltd, by permission of LKJ Music Publishers Ltd; *page 202:* cummings, e. e. 1923, 'I l(a leaf falls) oneliness', The Complete Works of e. e. cummings, W.W. Norton & Co. Inc.; *page 206:* Berry, C. 1958, 'Round and Round', © 1958 Arc Music Corp. Jewel Music Publishing Company Limited, by permission of Mautoglade Music Ltd; *pages 215-6:* The Sun, 26 October 1993, 26 March 1994 and 21 March 1994, Rex Features Ltd; *page 219:* The Sun, 18 February 1994 and 20 October 1993, Rex Features Ltd; *page 225:* P&O Scottish Ferries advertisement, P&O Scottish Ferries Ltd; *pages 228-30:* Tan, M. 1993, 'Language play in Dick Lee's songs – the Singapore element', BA Thesis submitted to the National University of Singapore; *page 230-4:* Nwoye, O.G. 1993, 'Social issues on walls: graffiti in university lavatories', *Discourse and Society*, Sage Publications Ltd.; *page 235:* Copyright © 1992 Kingsley Amis, first published in *The Times Higher Supplement*, 24 January 1992. Reprinted by kind permission of Jonathan Clowes Ltd, London on behalf of Kingsley Amis; *pages 235-6:* Bragg, M. 1992, first published in *The Times Higher Supplement*, 18 September 1992. Reprinted by permission of Melvyn Bragg; *page 257:* Copyright © 1989 by *Harper's Magazine*. All rights reserved. Reproduced from the September issue by special permission; *pages 262-3:* Excerpt from *Cultural Literacy* by E. D. Hirsch. Copyright © 1987 by Houghton Mifflin Co. Reprinted by permission of Houghton Mifflin Co. All rights reserved; *pages*

266–71: Brathwaite, E.K. 1981, 'English in the Caribbean', in Fiedler, L.A. and Baker Jr, H.A. 1981, *English Literature: Opening up the canon,* pp. 15–25. Reprinted by permission of John Hopkins University Press; *page 268:* Excerpt from 'The Schooner Flight' from *The Star-Apple Kingdom* by Derek Walcott. Copyright © 1979 by Derek Walcott. Reprinted by permission of Farrar, Straus and Giroux, Inc.; *pages 272–4:* Wald, A. 1989, 'Hegemony and Literary Tradition in the United Kingdom States' in de Castell, S., Luke, A. and Luke, C. 1989, *Language, authority and criticism: readings on the school textbook,* pp. 12–15, Taylor & Francis Group Ltd; *pages 23–4:* From *Culture and Imperialism* by Edward W. Said. Copyright © 1993 by Edward W. Said. Reprinted by permission of Alfred A. Knopf Inc.; *pages 299-301:* Thiong'o, N.W. 1986, *Decolonising the Mind: The politics of language in African literature,* James Curry Ltd; *pages 302-3:* Excerpt from *Arrow of God* by Chinua Achebe. Copyright © 1964 by Chinua Achebe. Reprinted by permission of HarperCollins Publishers, Inc. and William Heinemann Ltd; *pages 303-4:* From *Finding the Center: Two Narratives* by V. S. Naipaul. Copyright © 1984 by V.S. Naipaul. Reprinted by permission of Alfred A. Knopf Inc.; *pages 305-6:* Kingston, M. H. 1981, *The Woman Warrior,* pp. 149–52, Picador Books and Random House Inc., © Maxine Hong Kingston 1975, 1977; *pages 307-8:* From *Lost in Translation* by Eva Hoffman. Copyright © 1989 by Eva Hoffman. Used by permission of Dutton Signet, a division of Penguin Books USA Inc. and by permission of William Heinemann Ltd; *pages 308-10:* Heaney, S. 1988, 'The Murmer of Malvern', *The Government of the Tongue: The 1986 Memorial Lectures and Other Critical Writings,* pp. 23–25, Faber & Faber and from *The Government of the Tongue: Selected Prose 1978–1987* by Seamus Heaney. Copyright © 1989 by Seamus Heaney. Reprinted by permission of Farrar, Straus & Giroux, Inc. and Walcott, D. 1979, *The Star-Apple Kingdom,* Jonathan Cape and reprinted by permission of Farrar, Straus & Giroux, Inc.

Figures

Figure 2.2 (top left, middle left and centre): John Yuen*; Figure 2.2 (top right and bottom right):* Literary Research Group, Lancaster University; *Figure 2.2 (middle right and bottom left):* Joan Swann; *Figure 2.3, (middle left):* John Yuen; *Figure 2.4:* © Northamptonshire Record Office, Ref: SSF/A/70; *Figure 2.5:* By kind permission of Linnells; *Figures 1 and 2 (pages 69 and 70):* Catherine Kell; *Figure 3.2:* Courtesy of Comat Distributions (S) PTE Ltd; *Figure 3.4:* Reproduced by kind permission of the Harris Museum and Art Gallery; *Figure 4.2:* © POPPERFOTO; *Figure 4.3:* This Was Your Life! Chino, California, Chick Publications. Reproduced by permission of Jack T. Chick; *Figure 1 (page 146) and Figure 4 (page 148):* by permission of the BBC; *Figure 2 (page 147) and Figure 1 (page 150):* © POPPERFOTO; *Figure 5.1:* Carter, R. and Nash, W. 1990, *Seeing through language,* Basil Blackwell Ltd*; Figure 1 (page 189):* Hoban, R. 1980, *Riddley Walker,* Jonathan Cape Ltd, © 1980 by Russell Hoban; *Figure 2 (page 190):* Twain, M. 1976, *Huckleberry Finn,* Purnell Books, pages reprinted by permission of Macdonald Young Books; *Figure 1 (page 192):* Cover © Eric L. Smith, 1990. Reproduced by permission of Heinemann Educational Ltd; *Figure 2 (page 194):* Brian Tarr; *Figure 3 (page 196):* Janet Hand and Anna O. *Figure 6.1:* © POPPERFOTO; *Figure 6.2 (page 211):* © Stan Winer; *Figure 7.1:* Master and Fellows, Magdalene College, Cambridge; *Figure 7.2:* By permission of the Folger Shakespeare Library; *Figure 7.3:* The Bodleian Library, Oxford. Shelfmark = Douce. MM.459; *Figure 8.1:* Ngũgĩ Wa Thiong'o, photo by Carrie Craig; *Figure 8.2:* Cover of *Petals of Blood* by Ngũgĩ Wa Thiong'o, reproduced by permission of Heinemann; *Figure 8.3:* Chinua Achebe, photo by Paul Freestone; *Figure 8.4:* Cover of *Arrow of God* by Chinua Achebe, reproduced by permission of Heinemann; *Figure 8.5:* Cover reproduced by permission of Penguin Books. Cover photograph reproduced by permission of The Council for World Mission; *Figure 8.6:* Cover reproduced by permission of Penguin Books. Detail from *Deyahs at Dusk* by Karen Hammond; *Figure 8.7:* V.S. Naipaul © Jerry Bauer; *Figure 8.8:* Kamau Brathwaite, photo by Julian Stapleton; *Figure 8.9:* Dorothy Richardson, reproduced by permission of Virago; *Figure 8.10:* Maxine Hong Kingston, © Jerry Bauer; *Figure 8.11: The Woman Warrior* by Maxine Hong Kingston, Picador 1981. Cover reproduced by permission of Picador; *Figure 8.12:* Cover *Lost in Translation* by Eva Hoffman, reproduced by permission of Minerva and Eva Hoffman; *Figure 8.13:* Eva Hoffman, © Jerry Bauer.

Tables

Table 5.1: Burrows, J.F. 1987, *Computation into Criticism*, p. 3, Oxford University Press, by permission of Oxford University Press; *Table 7.3:* Wald, A. 1989, 'Hegemony and Literary Tradition in the United Kingdom States' in de Castell, S., Luke, A. and Luke, C. 1989, *Language, authority and criticism: readings on the school textbook*, table 1, Taylor & Francis Group Ltd.

Other illustrations

Page 29: A.I.A.T.S.I.S.; *page 214:* Jill Posener.

INDEX